# *The* New Crowd

# The New Crowd

## The Changing of the Jewish Guard on Wall Street

## Judith Ramsey Ehrlich & Barry J. Rehfeld

**HarperPerennial**
*A Division of HarperCollinsPublishers*

A hardcover edition of this book was published in 1989 by Little, Brown and Company. It is here reprinted by arrangement with Little, Brown and Company.

THE NEW CROWD. Copyright © 1989 by Judith Ramsey Ehrlich and Barry J. Rehfield. All rights reserved. Printed in the United States of America. No part of this book may be used or reproduced in any manner whatsoever without written permission except in the case of brief quotations embodied in critical articles and reviews. For information address HarperCollins Publishers, 10 East 53rd Street, New York, NY 10022.

First HarperPerennial edition published 1990.

LIBRARY OF CONGRESS CATALOG CARD NUMBER 90-55195

ISBN 0-06-097352-8

90 91 92 93 94 FG 10 9 8 7 6 5 4 3 2 1

For Harold Ehrlich, who bore the brunt and made this book possible. J.R.E.

To the memory of my father, Daniel Rehfeld. B.J.R.

# Acknowledgments

This book depends immeasurably on the more than three hundred interviews with Wall Street entrepreneurs, executives, and employees, and their families, who gave so generously of their time and knowledge. Of the major figures in the book, only John Gutfreund and Michael Milken declined to participate. To write the chapters about Gutfreund, we spoke with more than forty people who have known him over the years. For the chapters about Milken, we talked with the top Drexel executives, some of the firm's clients, and others. The occasional dialogue of Gutfreund and Milken is reconstructed from recollections of those who knew and spoke with them. We obtained what we believe is the first inside account of the annual Drexel bond conference formerly presided over by Milken, which Barry Rehfeld attended in 1986. The quotations in this chapter are taken from his recordings of the event.

A few of the many people who helped us deserve special mention. We owe a very large debt to our agent, Wendy Lipkind, who shepherded us from start to finish with unfailing assistance, grace, and humor. Special thanks are due to our editor, Fredrica S. Friedman, for her insightful suggestions in revising the manuscript. We are most grateful to Professor Samuel Hayes III of the Harvard Business School, who reviewed key sections of the manuscript, to Mark Kaplan, a partner of Skadden, Arps, Slate, Meagher & Flom, who read all of it, to photojournalist Jill Krementz for her generous help, and particularly to Harold Ehrlich, a former chairman of Bernstein-Macaulay, Inc., whose comprehensive knowledge of the financial world proved invaluable throughout this project.

Each of us has our own personal debt of gratitude to acknowledge:

No words of thanks could ever repay my husband, Harold Ehrlich, without whose intelligence, insights, and unending support the book would never have been published. Special thanks are also due to my friend Berenice Hoffman for her thoughtful reading of the manuscript and extremely helpful suggestions. Among the other people to whom I am indebted are Terry Brykczynski, who provided a consistently high level of editorial assistance in various aspects of printing the drafts of the book; Andrea Miller for her careful transcribing of many of our tapes; and my stepdaughter Pamela Ehrlich, who gave me a crash course on how to use a PC word processor and who did some research for us at the Columbia Business School Library.

J.R.E.

My family has always stood by me and for that I am extremely grateful. I would especially like to thank my wife, Elizabeth, for her patience and understanding throughout the writing of this book.

B.J.R.

# Contents

# *The* New Crowd

# CHAPTER ONE

# The End of an Era

On a cold, gray December day in 1979, a chauffeur-driven Cadillac inched its way through the lunchtime traffic and pulled up in front of the Harmonie Club, on Sixtieth Street near Fifth Avenue. Emerging from the limousine, John Langeloth Loeb entered the club's hushed lobby.

The tuxedo-clad desk attendant, the polished marble columns, the brass rosters of members — all were familiar sights to the seventy-seven-year-old Loeb, founder of the noble Wall Street investment banking and brokerage firm, Loeb Rhoades, Hornblower & Co. He had been to the Harmonie Club often but had never bothered to join. It wasn't the same as when only his kind of people belonged. Since the end of World War II, the historic 127-year-old club had admitted "the other kind of people," Jews who weren't associated with New York's German-Jewish dynasties — the powerful and privileged society known to those who were part of it as "Our Crowd."

Today Loeb hadn't come to the club for his usual reasons — an occasional business meal or drinks with old friends or acquaintances, in his accustomed role of peer among equals. He was there to fulfill an obligation to attend a combined reception and board of directors meeting that represented the most decisive defeat of his career. The brash, self-made man who was hosting the reception was definitely not John Loeb's kind of people.

Loeb was as close to an aristocrat as America could claim. In the world in which he dwelt, a world of awesome wealth, considerable power, and quiet luxury, his status was unassailable. Though he hadn't been born into an Our Crowd family, his marriage to a Lehman would have ensured his acceptance. But he also brought with him his own aura of dignity and command, superb manners, and compelling fine looks. He had been raised in his parents' town house, in the eighties off Central Park West, one of the preferred neighborhoods for wealthy families of German-Jewish extraction. A staff of five kept the household running smoothly. Young Loeb was expected to progress steadily upward. He had exceeded expectations.

In startling contrast, the man who had succeeded him and had taken over control of Loeb Rhoades — Sanford I. Weill — was a blunt-spoken, cigar-smoking stockbroker, who had grown up in Flatbush, Brooklyn, the son of immigrant Polish Jews. Starting as a lowly Wall Street messenger, he had gone on to become head of his own hugely successful brokerage firm, now called Shearson Hayden Stone Inc., which he and a few partners had formed with modest expectations nineteen years before.

The contrast between the two men was more than one of style. They represented the obverse and reverse sides of Wall Street — the old-guard grandees and the brassy new men who were recasting the Street in their own image.

At the heart of the old guard were the gilded nineteenth-century investment bankers who bore the revered names of the Protestant Establishment. Alongside them stood the group of German-Jewish banking families who made up Our Crowd — the Seligmans, Lehmans, Goldmans, Sachses, Warburgs, Schiffs, and Loebs of the Solomon Loebs, who made vast fortunes and were celebrated for their philanthropy, public service, and patronage of the arts. These families were linked by business interests and inbreeding. For three-quarters of a century, either you belonged to Our Crowd or you didn't.

It was a society defined by common rituals and values. Dancing classes and tea dances set the tone for the younger set, along with coming-out parties and formal weddings. The families made annual migrations to vast "camps" — rustic but grand retreats — in the Adirondacks and to Jewish resorts like Elberon on the Jersey shore. They deplored trendiness and flashiness, but they enjoyed all the possessions and privileges of wealth.

Before the 1920s, when high-rise apartment buildings began to fill New York's blocks of prime real estate, the prominent Our Crowd families occupied splendid Fifth Avenue mansions or stately town houses on the Upper West Side that were equipped with private elevators, ornate marble fireplaces, and servants' quarters. For three generations, the group flourished, inbred and self-contained. To the city at large, Our Crowd seemed almost impenetrable behind its imposing walls of estimable and powerful Wall Street firms. All of that was to change. The walled citadel couldn't survive in the post–World War II economic environment and self-made men like Sanford Weill were there to pick up the pieces.

By 1979, Loeb Rhoades stood alone, the last surviving firm run by the founding family in the tradition of Our Crowd. Goldman Sachs, Lehman Brothers, and Seligman still existed, but the families that generated and ruled them had lost control. Now John Loeb joined the others who had bowed to the forces of change. Loeb Rhoades had been sold to the aggressive Shearson Hayden Stone, and in time the Loeb Rhoades name would be dropped from the merged firm, as would the equally ill-fated Hayden Stone.

\* \* \*

John Loeb may have been a latecomer to Our Crowd — he wasn't related to Solomon Loeb of Kuhn Loeb or to any of the older German-Jewish investment banking clans — but he cherished its traditions and had hoped to preserve them. Unlike the challengers who were now outdistancing him and his peers, he had never intended to remold the world that represented Our Crowd, but rather to assimilate into it. It was a perfect fit. His own upbringing had prepared the way.

His father, Carl Loeb, had emigrated to the United States from Germany as a teenager to work for the trading subsidiary of the American Metal Company. Despite his youth, he moved up rapidly, through a combination of acumen, drive, and a judicious marriage — his wife, Adele, was the daughter of Alfred Huger Moses, head of one of the most prominent Jewish families in the South. Though Carl Loeb became rich, his family was still known as "the other Loebs." It was his eldest son, John, who gained acceptance in the elite Our Crowd through his accomplishments, his marriage within the Crowd, and his commitment to family and community.

John Loeb married Frances ("Peter") Lehman, the beautiful, gracious granddaughter of Mayer Lehman, a founder of Lehman Brothers, on one side of the family, and the granddaughter of copper-mining magnate Adolph Lewisohn on the other. Their wedding ceremony, at which there were seventeen attendants, was performed by a rabbi from Temple Emanu-El in the opulent ballroom of grandfather Lewisohn's Fifth Avenue mansion — reputedly the largest private ballroom in New York City at the time. They returned from a leisurely honeymoon in England and France, where the young couple enjoyed the finest of everything, to settle in New York.

In January 1931, a new firm, run by father and son, opened its doors. Later it acquired Rhoades & Co., an old Wasp brokerage that had been ravaged by the Depression. Carl M. Loeb, Rhoades & Co. grew into a major Wall Street house.

On his father's death in 1955, John Loeb was the sole head of Loeb Rhoades and one of the senior statesmen in the world of finance. His style became a benchmark for the Street. Although he was a demanding, hard-headed businessman who could be ruthless in negotiating a deal, his word had the force of a legal contract.

By then, Loeb had become a consummate member of Society and in the process had given up many Jewish customs. He continued to contribute regularly to several German-Jewish charities, but the family never attended synagogue, nor were his two sons Bar Mitzvahed. (At his wife's insistence, a tutor briefly instructed all five children about their Jewish heritage at home.) He hobnobbed with America's top Wasp tier in philanthropy, business, and politics. He was known for having given millions away to his alma mater, Harvard, to New York University, and to other institutions, and for having been a confidant of President Lyndon Johnson and a frequent visitor at the White House.

Loeb and his wife lived gracefully in the elegant, understated style of "old money." Nothing was ostentatious but everything they owned was of the finest quality. Their fifteen-room Park Avenue apartment, in which they had raised their family, was adorned with English antiques and master paintings, including works by Manet, Degas, Cézanne, van Gogh, and Renoir. Their large country home in Purchase, New York, was conveniently located near their club, Century Country — which had eclipsed the Harmonie since the 1920s as the most exclusive club for Jews in the United States. A third home was in the Bahamas, in the selective Nassau Wasp enclave called Lyford Cay. They also owned a fourteen-acre "camp" that included a main house and a guest house on waterfront property in the Adirondacks. The Loebs had a full complement of household staff. During the golden years of Loeb Rhoades, they employed a cook, butler, kitchenmaid, waitress, chambermaid, personal maid, and John Loeb's chauffeur in New York City. They had additional help at their other residences.

As resourceful as he had been for decades, Loeb, like the leaders of other Our Crowd firms, was unprepared for the currents that were transforming Wall Street. From the sixties onward, the house of Loeb Rhoades had expanded aggressively, paying scant attention to costs. In 1978, it acquired Hornblower, Weeks, Noyes & Trask, Inc., an old-line but hobbled Wasp firm. That acquisition proved to be Loeb Rhoades's last fling. The enlarged house's downhill course was so precipitous that there seemed to be no alternative other than to sell the firm. Weill was waiting eagerly for the opportunity to buy it. In late 1979, after nine months of often-bitter negotiations, the deal was done.

\* \* \*

Had Weill even been able to gain entry into the ranks of Loeb Rhoades when he was starting out, it's unlikely he would have gotten very far in a firm where, generally speaking, old school ties, style, and family connections exceeded the premium put on raw talent, drive, and performance. His early years were spent as part of a closely knit extended Jewish family, an arrangement that was still commonplace in the 1930s. He lived in Brooklyn with his parents, his younger sister, his maternal grandparents, an aunt and uncle and their two children in an ordinary but comfortable three-story house owned by his father. His immediate family occupied the second floor; his relatives the floor below. The top floor was rented out. Weill's father had been a dress manufacturer and later a steel importer. His mother was a housewife who kept a kosher home. To have a son in college was a milestone achievement for the Weill family. In June of his senior year at Cornell University, with no job prospects in sight, Weill married Joan Mosher, a stunning Brooklyn College education major whom he had met on a blind date. The money Joan's parents gave them in lieu of a large wedding — $3,500 — was all they had. For the Conservative Jewish ceremony and small reception at Essex House in Manhattan, Joan Weill borrowed her best friend's wedding gown. The couple spent the first week of their honeymoon at the Concord Hotel in the Catskill Mountains, a middle-class Jewish resort area in upstate New York and home of the "borscht belt," where so many famous Jewish entertainers made their first professional splashes. Joan had won a free week there on a quiz show. When the $3,500 wedding money was used up, Weill cleaned out his Bar Mitzvah account. "In the first few years of our marriage," Joan Weill recalls, "there were times when we couldn't pay the milk bills."

By the time of the meeting with John Loeb at the Harmonie Club, Weill was a multimillionaire. He and Joan lived in a three-bedroom Upper East Side co-op in New York City. Their son and daughter were in college. They also owned a thirteen-room Normandy-style house on an eight-acre estate in Greenwich, Connecticut, complete with swimming pool and tennis court. Unlike Loeb, who immersed himself in public issues and the world outside Wall Street, Weill at that time focused on his business. Even his social life revolved around Shearson. When the Weills entertained, generally at their Greenwich home, the guests were mostly Shearson personnel, some of whom were among their closest friends. Weill's other activities were confined to tennis and golf, a seat on the board of a real estate company, and gardening. He remained a shirt-sleeve manager at heart, never happier than when he was about to clinch a deal. The deal that brought him Loeb Rhoades was the biggest one of his career, and it was particularly sweet because, when his firm was just starting out and vulnerable, he and his young partners felt that John Loeb had snubbed them.

\* \* \*

Taking the elevator to the Harmonie Club's fourth floor, Loeb headed for a private banquet room, where the small reception for the Shearson board of directors was under way. Inside, little knots of men were drinking and talking animatedly. Most were much younger than Loeb, and of that group none were related to Our Crowd. Several dozen Shearson men exuberantly chomped on their cigars, downed drinks, munched on hot and cold hors d'oeuvres. The Shearson team were clearly enjoying their triumph, none more so than Sandy Weill. He rushed over to greet Loeb.

The two men grasped hands. There was still great strength in the old banker's grip. Loeb, the tall, slim patrician, some thirty years older than Weill, conveyed a sense of immense pride and authority. With his erect bearing, high-cheekboned visage, and gray-streaked black hair, he evoked the image of an Old Testament king. Courtly and well spoken, he was sensitive to the subtleties of tone, right down to his impeccably tailored Savile Row suit.

Weill was his evident opposite. A heavy-set man of less than average height, he had sparkling hazel eyes, unruly dark hair, and an effervescent, unbridled manner. He could be easily angered when he didn't get his way, but on the whole he struck people as a genial person who wanted desperately to be liked. The spectacular growth of his fledgling four-man partnership into the formidable corporation of Shearson Hayden Stone (Shearson Loeb Rhoades after the meeting) earned him the respect and affection of many of his associates; they enjoyed his rough-edged way and found in it a reflection of their own style and origins. He also had an engaging grin, and he was smiling broadly that day, but in truth he wasn't relaxed. He toyed nervously with his cigar, even though he knew Loeb hated smoking. He would never think of brandishing a cigar at Loeb's office or home, but this was his club and he wasn't about to give up his Te-Amo. It was an effort for him to make small talk with Loeb: Weill lacked the social graces that Loeb displayed so effortlessly.

The two men met this afternoon at the Harmonie Club, the site

Weill had chosen, because Weill and his kind were now calling the tune. They were the sons and grandsons of immigrant Jews who had begun pouring into America after the 1880s and had broken into the mainstream of American life. Some had turned to Wall Street in the hope of finding success, and a few scrambled to the top. Weill, who had learned how to scramble with the best of them, could hardly contain his delight. "John," he said to Loeb with unrestrained enthusiasm, "this is going to be one helluva company."

Loeb replied stiffly, "The combination of Loeb Rhoades and Shearson makes a lot of sense, Sandy." His smile was polite but strained. He had lost his firm. And he had lost it to a tough, street-smart aggrandizer from Brooklyn, for whom Loeb Rhoades was the brightest bead on a string of once-great firms with resonant names like Hayden Stone, Shearson Hammill, and H. Hentz.

Publicly, Loeb was always careful to praise Weill ("I have the greatest respect for Sandy and for his abilities"). Only those close to him, especially his wife, Peter, knew how much his decision to sell Loeb Rhoades had hurt him personally.

Loeb's gnawing sense of loss had little to do with money. After the deal was completed, he remained an exceedingly wealthy man, with a personal fortune then reckoned to be $100 million. What mattered was that he and his crowd had been overtaken as Wall Street leaders. Afterward, and to this day, no member of an Our Crowd family has been in a position of great power or prominence on the Street. An era had come to an end.

Loeb and Weill separated. Loeb, who was to be named honorary chairman of the merged firm, didn't stay for the scheduled board meeting of what was now the second-largest brokerage house in the country. He greeted several Shearson executives who came over to him to pay their respects, and then departed.

Weill was swept away in the hubbub of the reception. Though outwardly brimming with confidence, he was still somewhat nervous about acquiring a firm as large as Loeb Rhoades. He recalled a conversation he had had with his lieutenant, Peter Cohen, two weeks earlier, during a weekend lunch at the Carlyle Hotel.

"We still have to make this deal work," Weill had told him apprehensively.

"Sandy, it's really going to go from the sound of the bell," Cohen had replied. "I've never felt more confident about a transaction."

Now, buoyed by the recollection, Weill located Cohen in the mingling crowd and said, "Let's get this meeting started."

\* \* \*

In supplanting Loeb, Weill joined the ranks of the enterprising Jewish financial luminaries who prospered in the post–World War II world of finance. Taken as a whole, they form the New Crowd — self-made, talented, and highly competitive men willing to assume almost any challenge on Wall Street. Their success — played out against the turbulent events of the past four decades — is part of the social history of Jews in America and their enactment of the American dream of wealth and power.

# CHAPTER TWO

# The New Crowd

W ho are the New Crowd? Innovative empire builders. Merger masters. High-powered traders. Takeover lawyers. Feared corporate raiders. High-risk venturers. Celebrated dealmakers. Eminent investment bankers. All of these and more.

In the forty-odd-year sweep covered by this book — from the late 1940s through 1989 — these self-made Jewish entrepreneurs worked at the forefront of the new financial era that followed World War II. They were outsiders who made their way, in tune with their times, through imagination and forcefulness and by seizing their opportunities where they found them. For some, that path led beyond wealth to respect and esteem as statesmen of the financial world. Others became notable for their excesses. All of them stood among the richest and most influential men on Wall Street.

The men who made it to the summit did so by testing the limits or, in the language of test pilots, "pushing the outside of the envelope" in their professional lives. Through their risk taking and daring, they participated in making Wall Street perhaps the most dynamic industry in America and the most competitive U.S. industry in the world economy. These qualities and their shared character traits, their style and vision of financial enterprise, are what connects the New Crowd, what draws them together even as competitors.

Their stories begin with an independent spirit bred into them from an early age.

Usually only children or the first-born sons of middle-income or working-class families headed by a self-employed father, they were expected to do far better than their parents, most of whom were immigrants or the children of immigrants — many from Eastern Europe. Their parents understood that education was crucial, and often these young men were the first in their families to attend college. They studied for careers in medicine, law, science, and teaching.

Jews found career choices limited in the world of finance and in corporate America at the end of World War II. They were held back by deep-rooted prejudices against them. And when the earliest members of the New Crowd began to make their way in business, as outsiders — men who weren't part of any Establishment, Wasp or Jewish — they had other strikes against them. They lacked the credentials and contacts required to reach the highest levels of corporate management. Even in the New York City area, where the centers of three of the nation's largest industries were located — insurance, oil, and commercial banking — Jews had (and to a large extent still have) only token representation in the executive suites, even though they accounted for a highly significant number of the city's college graduates.

But New York is also home to another vital industry, Wall Street, where every major American investment banking and brokerage firm has been based. The grand Our Crowd investment banking and brokerage houses represented an important minority tradition of Jews prospering on Wall Street. Yet even here these new Jews faced discrimination. They were shut out of Wasp firms for being Jews and denied admission to the Our Crowd firms for being the "wrong" Jews. The older German-Jewish bankers actually had more in common with Wasp Establishment financiers than with these young Jewish hopefuls. Like their Wasp counterparts, the Jewish Brahmins were wedded to the time-honored role of being gentlemanly custodians of their clients' capital. They were proud of being traditional. Having the proper background and breeding was paramount. But the times favored the outsiders. If the door to the top suite wasn't exactly wide open for the new Jews, it was at least ajar. The very success of the old-line bankers obscured a fundamental change that was overtaking their business.

Economic power in America and on Wall Street was shifting. Suddenly, new opportunities, like shards of light, pierced Wall Street's gray canyons. It was a wide-open game where performance, instead of old money and connections, closed the deal or made the sale. Fresh faces, not seen in a generation, came forward as if answering a call. They were the children and grandchildren of Italians, Irish, Poles, and other Europeans who were not of Anglo-Saxon ancestry. But most of all they were Jews, "the black-shoe, white-stocking Jews from Brooklyn," as the Establishment derisively called them. The New Wall Street would suit their temperaments and would provide unparalleled opportunity.

Soon after World War II, the nation entered one of the longest cycles of sustained growth in its history. In 1949 the stock market took off on a virtually unbroken seventeen-year climb. Shortly, and in increasing numbers, young Jewish upstarts appeared on the Street. Since they were outsiders, lacking the background and connections to move into the inner sanctums, they had nothing to lose in taking risks. They were quick to adapt to the market-responsive climate and eager to take advantage of new resources and strategies open to them to make their fortunes. Having no other way to enter, they would go where the opportunities were.

As the 1950s gave way to the 1960s, on Wall Street performance and results came to matter more than breeding, background, and long-term client relationships. The New Crowd, unhampered by preconceived notions or protocol, brought a shirt-sleeve style to the financial district — a style so informal that they were on a first-name basis with virtually everyone. If they were brash, they were also energetic and sharp, in the manner of the Yankee traders of old and the venturesome Rockefellers and Carnegies — the mighty industrial pioneers.

They gravitated to small up-and-coming Jewish firms, where they made their initial impact in brokerage, dealmaking, and trading; they could make their mark in these areas while they were still in their twenties or thirties. In these firms and fields they didn't have to buck the closed bureaucracies of large corporations or the tradition-bound ways of old-line bankers. They sought financial winners. If a bet didn't pay off, they were quick to pursue another idea. Some of them eventually moved up and out of the fields they had started in to become heads of the most powerful and successful Wall Street houses or to lead corporations that would have been out of reach for them as Jews in earlier periods. In the dizzying pace of the postwar years, the best and the luckiest of them became rich in a relatively short time. Some of them became rich *and* famous, and a few of them became infamous.

Several of the New Crowd emerge as the most influential — and those are the ones, out of other possibilities, who are highlighted in this book.

Perhaps no one exemplifies the New Crowd's thrust to the top better than Sanford I. Weill, who, after beginning his career as a messenger on Wall Street, amassed a brokerage empire and eventually became president of American Express. Then he became chairman, chief executive officer, and president of Primerica — a giant diversified financial services company — and was recognized as one of the most powerful Jewish businessmen in the nation.

Equally prominent, John Gutfreund helped transform a small, scrappy bond trading house into the most powerful securities firm in the Western world, before runaway expenses in 1986 led to questions about its continuing leadership. As chairman of Salomon Inc, he personified the consummate Wall Street player and boss, whose strength in trading and dealmaking spanned the globe. His success led to a new wife, an extravagant life-style, and a conspicuous place in New York Society.

If Gutfreund represented the New Crowd's triumph over the Old Establishment, Felix Rohatyn was its impresario. In an age of business celebrities, only the name of Rohatyn among New Crowd leaders attained the widespread fame of names like Lee Iacocca, Armand Hammer, Ted Turner, and Donald Trump. His name, perhaps more than any other, was linked with the flood of massive corporate combinations that reshaped American business for much of the past three decades. As the man who helped save New York City during its mid-seventies fiscal crisis, he gained a national reputation and emerged as a social lion. Yet it was for his skills as a merger guru that he was known on Wall Street and in corporate America.

*   *   *

These men are among the most important members of the New Crowd. Dozens of others also left their impressions. For four decades, Alan ("Ace") Greenberg, the hard-boiled chief of the brokerage firm of Bear Stearns, played the stock market like a high-stakes poker game. Under his guidance, the firm became an awesome money machine for the profit of its partners.

In the booming field of takeovers, the New Crowd dealmakers often outdistanced the competition. Besides Rohatyn, Ira Harris of Salomon (and, later, Lazard Frères), Stephen Friedman of Goldman Sachs, Bruce Wasserstein — formerly of First Boston, who later went out on his own with Joe Perella — and Jerome Kohlberg and his born-to-wealth partner Henry Kravis of Kohlberg Kravis Roberts became stars of the continuing merger mania that struck in the late seventies. Peter Cohen, Sandy Weill's protégé, engineered two landmark deals of his own after he succeeded Weill as chief executive of Shearson. The dealmakers boosted the careers of lawyers who could master the tricky shoals of takeover contests. Two New Crowd legal strategists won quick recognition: Joseph Flom, senior partner at Skadden, Arps, Slate, Meagher & Flom, and Martin Lipton, senior partner at Wachtell, Lipton, Rosen & Katz.

Colorful new words or old words with new meanings made their way into the financial lexicon — *greenmail, poison pill, white knight, Pac-Man defense, junk bonds, LBO* (leveraged buyout), *arbitrage,* among others — most of them associated with *M&A,* the abbreviation for mergers and acquisitions.

By the eighties, along with T. Boone Pickens and a few others of like strength and power, the New Crowd were at the very center of the mergers and acquisitions field. The high stakes appealed to risk takers. In months or even weeks, they could reap vast fortunes — or lose them. Innovative strategies and daring, rather than superior resources, often meant victory in takeover contests. Within a half-dozen years, Carl Icahn rose from obscurity to become one of the most feared corporate raiders in the country, chairman of TWA, the largest shareholder in Texaco and USX (formerly U.S. Steel), and a billionaire. Henry Kravis, in making some of the most audacious and successful leveraged buyouts of the era, including the megadeal for RJR Nabisco — $25 billion — took LBOs past the financial pages and onto the editorial and front pages of the press. He and his wife, socialite designer Carolyne Roehm, were invited everywhere and written about everywhere. Saul Steinberg, using as his base a staid insurance company, fought pitched battles with the corporate Establishment, survived political and personal scandal, and enjoyed a life-style of baronial splendor enhanced by his famed collection of valuable art.

A mysterious and controversial figure who earned over a billion dollars in a few years, young Michael Milken of Drexel Burnham Lambert took part of Wall Street west, in effect. Operating from Los Angeles, he seemed to have built a better mousetrap that led financiers and heads of corporations to beat a path to his door in the 1980s. His dazzling wealth and power rose from the marketing of once-obscure securities commonly known as "junk bonds," which quickly became a major source of financing for hostile takeovers. Despite his deliberately unimpressive style — he wore an obvious toupee and spoke in a low-keyed manner — many considered him the most formidable American financier since J. P. Morgan.

Whatever enterprise they pursued, the most successful demonstrated a fierce persistence — whether landing a major client or making the largest trade or doing the most lucrative merger deal. Trader Lewis Glucksman spent his entire career locked in a bitter personal struggle with the Establishment. Against all reasonable expectations, he forged his way to the helm of the prestigious investment banking house of Lehman Brothers, only to precipitate its disintegration and with it his reputation as one of the modern stars of Wall Street. In 1988, he returned to the Street as head of trading at Smith Barney, owned by Primerica.

Pressure to excel spilled over into the New Crowd's personal lives. The social newcomers emulated the ways of the old guard, the German-Jewish and Wasp bankers and financiers they replaced. They collected the predictable trappings of wealth, while pursuing acceptance, culture, and the social graces. They bought luxurious homes, expensive art, high-priced foreign cars, designer clothes, and jewelry; they hosted or appeared at the right parties and in the right places. Many shed long-term marriages for new wives and women friends. Some became part of what one fashion tabloid dubbed "Nouvelle Society," a catchall phrase for the celebrated, the rich, and the hangers-on who replaced High Society as the center of media attention and who set the tone for what was "in" and what was not. The New Society was open to almost all comers, regardless of religious, ethnic, or social background — anyone with enough money, power, or fame could find social standing.

The New Crowd arrived at the right moment. There were fewer barriers to social prominence because of the turmoil of the times. Conspicuous materialism was respectable — even coveted. In the second half of the seventies, the prediction made by Andy Warhol in the late sixties that everyone would be famous for fifteen minutes didn't sound like hype any more. The success of *People* magazine — which made celebrities out of complete unknowns almost overnight — spawned a raft of imitators. Profiles became a staple of the news. Even the formerly impersonal financial press sought to spotlight business leaders. *Fortune, Business Week,* and *Forbes* led the way for features on business personalities in such general-interest publications as *Time, Newsweek,* and the *New York Times.*

The upheaval of the eighties — from the takeover waves and leveraged buyouts and the resulting restructuring of American business that made job security more questionable even for executives at the top of the heap — all helped to create an uncertain climate, in which the need to accumulate more and more money was one measure of certainty. At such times, according to historian Maury Klein, "money becomes a way of defining who you are and what you have."

More often than not, the New Crowd gained a social foothold by becoming philanthropic luminaries — donating and helping to raise huge sums of money for hospitals and universities, social service organizations, art museums, dance companies, and orchestras. The old Wasp Establishment — which had run the large philanthropies for decades — had seen its wealth eroded by changing tax laws and inflation; it now needed an infusion of new money and connections to support its causes. In time, arriviste Jews began to appear on the boards of such time-honored Wasp institutions as the Metropolitan Museum of Art, the Metropolitan Opera, and the New York Public Library.

However awesome their net worth, however dazzling their possessions, the New Crowd had no wish to be remembered simply as very rich. Saul Steinberg estimates that he gave $90 million away to cultural and charitable endeavors, including $25 million to his alma mater, the University of Pennsylvania, in early 1989; Sandy Weill donated $2.5 million to rebuild Carnegie Hall and a recital hall that was named in his and his wife's honor; John Gutfreund, a vice chairman of the New York Public Library and a director of Montefiore Medical Center, rolled up his sleeves and washed dishes at the hospital during a strike; Felix Rohatyn and his wife — as did several other millionaire businessmen — adopted a high-school class, committing themselves to pay the four-year tuition of every student who was admitted to college.

Many of the New Crowd also became generous patrons of Jewish charities. As Jews, they fulfilled a long tradition of *tzedakah,* an obligation to help others inherent in one's membership in the community. As outsiders, most of them found ways to achieve status on their own terms.

* * *

The very personality traits and business conditions that enabled so many other Wall Street Jews to succeed through risk taking became transmuted in a few individuals who pushed beyond the boundaries of securities law. In May 1986, Dennis Levine, a dealmaker at Drexel Burnham Lambert, pleaded guilty to charges of "insider trading" (profiting from the use of material confidential information), which led investigators to uncover one of the most hotly publicized and still-unfolding scandals in Wall Street history. At the time, the two men implicated were among the most powerful warriors in the takeover field: arbitrageur Ivan Boesky and dealmaker Martin Siegel. A number of other Jews were caught among the more than twenty men named in the story of the insider trading cases. (Two years after the scandal began, information obtained from Boesky had further consequences. Drexel was indicted, as was the biggest target of them all, Michael Milken.) *

The scandal caused grave concern within the Jewish community

---

* Drexel agreed to plead guilty for its role in the insider trading scandal, but Milken maintained his innocence. His trial was expected to begin in federal court by early 1990.

at large, and among Wall Street professionals in particular who were in no way identified with the excesses of a few of their peers. Ludwig Bravmann, an old Wall Street hand and longtime leader of the Wall Street division of United Jewish Appeal-Federation of Jewish Philanthropies, quickly pointed out: "They [the Jews caught in the insider trading net] comprise a tiny fraction of the Jews on Wall Street who conduct themselves with honesty and integrity. Judaism condemns the sort of unethical, uncompetitive, and illegal acts of which they have been accused."

Explanations for the behavior of Boesky and the others were sought and debated. A constellation of factors seem to have played a part. The implicated Jews were involved in corporate takeovers, either as professional investors or as merger makers putting together deals. Since millions can be made faster in the mergers and acquisitions area than in any other Wall Street business, the greater the temptation and the higher the payoff for cheating by using insider information. Given the fact that Jews were among the biggest M&A players, the probability increased that some of them would flout the securities regulations. When similar scandals were exposed in financial markets outside of Wall Street, at home and abroad, where Jews were fewer in number, predictably they weren't seen as the central figures in the crimes.

But the personal failings of the implicated Wall Street men couldn't be discounted. Their seemingly insatiable need to make more and more money led them to act as though they were above the law and brought about their own downfall. "It was a sickness," Boesky acknowledged after being exposed.

Still, the premium put on money and the sanction for "get-rich-quick" wheeling and dealing contributed to the underpinnings of the trading scandal. Ways and means change with the times, but the dream of becoming rich remains deeply rooted in our culture. In a fast-dollar, short-term-gains, quick-turnover economic climate that crested in the 1980s, money became an end in itself in a way this country hadn't seen since the heyday of the robber barons and the 1920s revelry before the first Great Crash. Even the staid *Wall Street Journal* began to proclaim in its media ads that it represented "The daily diary of the American dream."

* * *

Wall Street is, and always has been, a center of power that is little understood by outsiders. That power takes many forms, but it finally comes down to the ability to raise gigantic sums of money and to provide opportunities for investors. In the postwar years, the funds available and the competition for them grew unimaginably.

At stake in the United States, by the end of 1988, was some twelve *trillion* dollars in the stock and bond markets and in all kinds of debt instruments. That sum was equal to more than twice the value of all the goods and services produced in America that year — some six times the combined assets of the Fortune 500 companies. Where the money went and what happened to it were greatly influenced by Wall Street power brokers.

The New Crowd are part of the continuing cycles of concentration and dispersal that characterize financial power in America. The great cycle that came in the decades after the Civil War, led by such Wasp financiers as J. Pierpont Morgan, coincided with the impact made by the German-Jewish investment bankers in the New York financial world. Together, they helped raise the capital that transformed America from an agricultural to an industrial society.

A half century later another of these profound economic shifts toward concentration got under way. The postindustrial society, as it was called for its service-oriented, high-tech and leisure-time business activities that emerged in the late fifties, has continued to evolve. For forty-odd years, from shortly after the end of World War II to the end of the 1980s, in spite of several recessions, some sharp drops in the stock market, the crash of 1987, and other warning signals, the market maintained its pursuit of ever higher levels. But even as the decade of the eighties was coming to a close, there were predictions that the pursuit would run out of momentum, that the weight of corporate debt levels it had helped to create would crush junk bond financing, that some financial empires would have trouble absorbing and integrating their newer acquisitions, and that some of the biggest players on Wall Street would be dealt out of the game, while others would rely on their own resourcefulness to withstand change and turn the market conditions of the emerging decade to their advantage.

Whatever their individual fates in the future, the outsiders who make up the New Crowd became very rich and prominent over the course of the four decades chronicled in this book. They were able to do so because they propelled their own destinies forward in step with the times. This, then, is their story.

# CHAPTER THREE

# First Stirrings

*A*t the end of World War II, America emerged from years of hardship with a dual personality. Flushed with victory, the country was optimistic. Clothing, car, home, and appliance sales pumped life into the economy. After years of fashion dictated by government fabric restrictions, the New Look with its long, swirling skirts was delighting women. For one breathtaking year, the country went on a buying spree. America was becoming a nation of unabashed consumers. Unemployment stood at 2.3 million, the lowest peacetime level since 1929.

But there was an underside as well to the American consciousness. The nation was on edge over the developing Cold War. The balance of the world economy was precarious and worldwide recovery uncertain. Wall Street, one of the principal barometers of the economy, reflected that unease. After its initial buoyancy at the end of the war, the stock market fell sharply in 1946. Wall Street, it seemed, was unable to step out of the long shadow of the Great Crash.

The mighty mandarins who headed the old-line investment banking firms had no reason to feel threatened. They were still fabulously wealthy and still running Wall Street their way. Little new business was coming along. But the relationships built by their fathers and grandfathers with the railroads, utilities, and industrial heartland held fast and kept them safe from competition.

The partners of a few family-run German-Jewish firms were included in this exclusive group, but the majority of its members were blue-blooded Wasps from the Northeast. Within this influential core, there was one conspicuous exception: Sidney James Weinberg, senior partner of the German-Jewish Our Crowd investment banking firm of Goldman Sachs & Co., who came early to Wall Street, in 1907, and was there long enough to see it change from a stable community of upper-crust investment bankers to a volatile hub of all comers.

The son of a struggling wholesale liquor dealer from Brooklyn, Weinberg — fresh out of elementary school — started out at Goldman Sachs as an assistant porter. He was to be phenomenally successful in Wall Street's premier business, investment banking, at a time when most Jews without the right background had trouble even finding work in the great Wall Street firms. Through his example, he made it easier for the new breed of self-made Jewish entrepreneurs to follow in his path on Wall Street — a path that led right into the first circle of power.

In January of 1947, the fifty-five-year-old Weinberg traveled to Washington, D.C., to attend a meeting of the Business Advisory Council hosted by the Department of Commerce. The organization, which Weinberg had helped found in the late thirties, was made up of America's leading corporate figures to provide financial advice to government leaders, including the president. At this particular session, Weinberg was introduced to a new Council member, Henry Ford II, the young president of the Ford Motor Company.

Two decades earlier, Ford's grandfather, Henry Ford, the founder of the auto company, had been one of the most vociferous anti-Semites in America. In his newspaper, the *Dearborn Independent,* the same theme was hammered at every week: Jews were a corrupting influence on American politics, public life, finance, living habits, and morality in general. No attack against American Jews had ever been so vicious, sustained, or backed by such a prominent citizen. In response, many Jews, and even some non-Jews, refused to buy Ford automobiles. The American Jewish Congress went so far as to urge newspapers not to publish Ford advertisements. In 1956, Weinberg would handle one of the biggest deals in business history, the initial public sale of Ford Motors' common stock.

A study that ran in *Fortune* magazine in 1946 analyzed the extent of anti-Semitism in this country. It found that anti-Semitism was widespread among the rich in large northeastern and midwestern cities. That evidently held as true for the partners at the staid, traditional Wasp investment banking houses that then dominated Wall Street as it did in the corporate boardrooms of America. Weinberg was one of the handful of Jews — apart from Our Crowd — who broke through class and religious barriers. In this unreceptive climate, he rose spectacularly through a combination of hard work and talent and by beating the Establishment at its own game.

He also joined Our Crowd's Century Country Club in Westchester, where he mingled with elite German Jews; made new friends among non-Jews by becoming a Mason; created his own network of allies in the Business Advisory Council; and acted as a director of more big corporations over the years than any other American had before him. At one time, he sat on thirty-one corporate boards and invitations to join other boards kept coming in at the rate of at least one a month. All of this helped to fuel his reputation in the postwar era as "Mr. Wall Street."

His advice on everything from personal investments to politics was avidly sought by heads of industry and government. For a generation, he was the leading financial guru to whom high government officials and three presidents — Roosevelt, Truman, and Eisenhower — listened.

Most of the Wasp leaders of Wall Street treated Weinberg as their professional equal. "My father had the greatest respect for Sidney Weinberg and did business with him regularly," said Alexander White, the grandson of one of the founders of the venerable Wasp banking house of White, Weld & Co.

But in Weinberg's time, Jews and Gentiles rarely socialized. Alexander White's father may have associated with a very small number of Jews, but they — unlike Weinberg — had largely been assimilated into Wasp society. There were other Wasp bankers who had no social contact whatsoever with Jews and some who were openly anti-Semitic. (As an indication of how times have changed, Alexander White has worked for a small American investment banking firm run by an Australian Jew and is married to a Jew.)

* * *

Sidney Weinberg looked less like a senior statesman of finance than a beaming elf with glasses, who by mere happenstance wore a three-piece business suit. A pudgy five feet four, with legs so short that his clothes had to be custom-made, he seemed dwarfed by the oversized furniture that was standard issue in corporate boardrooms. His own office was decidedly functional, with a low-backed swivel chair, a blotter-covered desk strewn with reports and papers, and a standard black phone at his elbow. Despite his diminutive size, no chairman dared ignore him.

A vintage story about Weinberg reveals the cutting edge of his style. On one occasion, or so the story goes, one of his most important clients, Thomas McInnerney (then chairman of National Dairy, makers of Kraft cheese among other well-known products), called Weinberg and advised him to get over to his office immediately; otherwise, he warned, Weinberg, who was a director of National Dairy, was going to lose the account to Morgan Stanley. Henry Morgan, one of the firm's founders, had brought along his father, the banking icon J. P. Morgan, Jr., and they were making a play for National Dairy's business.

Arriving at McInnerney's office, Weinberg, a contemporary of the younger Morgan, announced, "I'm sorry, gentlemen. My father is dead. But I have an uncle over in Brooklyn who is a tailor and looks like him, and if that would mean anything to you, I'd be glad to bring him over."

Weinberg's opening gambit allegedly broke up the meeting, and with it Morgan Stanley's chance of landing the account. The anecdote had all the earmarks of a legend, as it made the rounds of Wall Street for years, though no one would acknowledge openly that competition was frowned on. In reality, no leading investment banker would have tried surreptitiously to woo away another banker's client. To those who understood the inner workings of the Street, it was clear that there existed within — and outside — its "clubby" atmosphere a caste system as structured as that of any royal court.

That a self-educated Jew from Brooklyn named Sidney Weinberg had become the most influential figure in this principality — when Jews were still being denied access to the corporate suite, Gentile business and social clubs, residential neighborhoods, and private schools — made his odyssey to the apex of financial power a uniquely American kind of success story.

* * *

When Weinberg arrived on Wall Street in 1907 at sixteen, the world of finance revolved around a single axis. At one pole was the mighty J. Pierpont Morgan of J. P. Morgan & Co., and at the other was the august Jacob Schiff of the German-Jewish Kuhn Loeb & Co. More than any other individuals, these two bankers financed the building of America's railroads, the creation of mammoth industrial corporations, and the arming of world powers.

In time, the rivalry between Morgan and Schiff came to symbolize the split among the rich in America that had existed ever since the Civil War. It was the split between the dominant Wasp Establishment and the German-Jewish Our Crowd, which had at its roots a pronounced, although not always acknowledged, anti-Semitism. On Wall Street, the capital wielded by Our Crowd enabled the Jewish bankers to invest the firm's money or their own in industry and to participate in the important underwriting syndicates,* but they weren't made partners at the Gentile banking firms or, in most cases, even hired by them. Nor were they accepted socially by the Morgans and Astors and other reigning dynasties of New York City.

In response, they formed their own society, their own elite German-Jewish private clubs (Harmonie in New York and Century Country in Westchester), their own synagogue (Temple Emanu-El), their own communities and schools. Over time, many strove to assimilate. Some anglicized their names; others married Gentiles; and a few even converted to Christianity. The fathers of some of them had started out as peddlers, buying and selling everything from dry goods to slaves; eventually they became financiers, handling speculative businesses such as commodities (trading cotton, coffee, and sugar), commercial paper, and financing new ventures from textile mills to ironworks — all undertakings that the non-Jewish bankers tended to avoid because of the higher risks involved. They established firms that evolved into the great Our Crowd investment banking houses, with partnerships descending largely to sons, sons-in-law, and nephews.

It was the massive wave of new immigrant Jews, primarily from Russia and Eastern Europe, fleeing the pogroms and other forms of persecution, who incurred the greatest outpouring of anti-Semitism in America and the test of Our Crowd's Jewish faith. Between 1880 and the mid-1920s, more than two-and-a-half million poured into the United States. They settled mainly in the urban areas of the East, especially in New York City. In comparison to the German Jews, who had preceded them by some thirty years, they had a far more difficult time fitting in because they were so poor, uneducated, and numerous as a group.

The dilemma the immigrants posed for the German-Jewish financiers was painful; such an association could be harmful socially and economically. While they didn't want to fraternize with the immigrants, many of the Our Crowd leaders did set up a vast network of philanthropic agencies and a wide range of services designed to aid them in finding jobs and homes and adjusting to their new surroundings.

Despite their charitable spirit the German-Jewish financiers con-

---

* The bankers' primary function was to help raise capital for both industry and government. However, a single venture often required more money than any one source had to invest or was willing to commit. Only by organizing a syndicate, or a group of bankers, could an investment banking firm guarantee, or underwrite, the sale of stocks and bonds.

tinued to look down on the Jewish newcomers as aliens. This view of their "difference" persisted even after the immigrants began to make their own way. As Stephen Birmingham wrote in *Our Crowd,* the difference was between the "quiet, cultivated Wall Street type" and the "noisy, pushy, Seventh Avenue type."

In the financial community, few of the immigrant Jews were hired by the Our Crowd banking houses. When the first nonfamily partners were finally taken in, they were more likely to be Gentiles with established reputations than Jews who were not of their kind. In those days, it was only a rare maverick on Wall Street who charted his own course to the top. One of the most prominent was Bernard Baruch, a Jew with aristocratic bloodlines, who developed into a lone-wolf speculator. In that sense, he was a forerunner of the kind of Jewish entrepreneur who would rise to power in the second half of the century.

\* \* \*

Weinberg's background was actually no more acceptable to Our Crowd than was that of the new immigrants. His father, Pincus, struggled to support a family of thirteen.

Before he was ten (in 1901), Weinberg was hawking newspapers. Later, he held a variety of after-school jobs, from shucking oysters for a neighborhood fish vendor to carrying feathers for a milliner. At fourteen, he landed a summer job as a runner for a brokerage firm. Finding one source of income inadequate, he also carried stocks and bonds for two other brokerage houses, in direct violation of an old custom that runners worked for just one employer. His multiple jobs were soon uncovered, and he was fired by all three houses.

He held a couple of odd jobs before embarking on a singularly ambitious project. Starting at the top of 43 Exchange Place, then one of the tallest skyscrapers in the financial district (a twenty-five story building), he made his way down floor by floor, looking for work. On the second floor, he reached the offices of Goldman Sachs, which hired him in November 1907 for all of three dollars a week. He cleaned spittoons in the basement and brushed the partners' silk hats. When he could get away with it, he played practical jokes. Once he secretly placed a want ad in a local newspaper, announcing that Samuel Sachs, the aging senior partner, was about to assemble a chorus line for a Broadway show. For a week or so, a parade of lovely candidates showed up at Sachs's office.

Weinberg's progress in the firm was slow — as was typical for the "wrong" kind of Jew on Wall Street. Eight years later, while World War I raged throughout Europe, he was still just another employee.

Nonetheless, despite his marginal career, Weinberg's random choice of employers would soon turn out to have been an inspired one. Begun in 1869, Goldman Sachs had grown into a thriving business, largely by buying commercial paper (IOUs a company issues and promises to redeem in a matter of weeks or months) and selling it to banks at a profit. By the turn of the century, Goldman Sachs — the house of Marcus Goldman and his son-in-law, Samuel Sachs — was one of the premier banking firms on Wall Street — Gentile or Jewish. Only two other German-Jewish firms could make that claim: Kuhn Loeb, established in 1850, and Lehman Brothers, founded in 1848.

With the outbreak of World War I, the Goldman and Sachs families' participation in the partnership was destroyed when Henry Goldman, the only son of the late Marcus Goldman, became a vocal supporter of Germany. His resignation and the damage done to the firm's reputation and capital took their toll on Samuel Sachs, who withdrew from an active role.

As a result of the shakeup, Weinberg, who had spent the war years in the Navy, emerged from obscurity. Waddill Catchings — a former personal assistant to J. P. Morgan and one of the first nonfamily and non-Jewish senior partners — chose him as his assistant. Before long, he was doing the spadework on one corporate financing after another. He formed syndicates, determined the pricing of new corporate stocks and bonds, and supervised trading. He developed a keen understanding of stocks and bought a seat on the New York Stock Exchange for $104,000 in 1925. The financial community at large was beginning to take notice of him. It referred to the thirty-five-year-old financier as "the boy wonder of Wall Street."

Weinberg was unaffected by the praise. He kept things in perspective. When he went home at the end of the day, he left Wall Street politics behind him for his wife, the former Helen Livingston, and his two young sons, Sidney, Jr., and John. The daughter of a dress manufacturer, Helen Weinberg was an intelligent, unpretentious woman and a talented pianist, who fit the expectations of her time as a mother and suburban homemaker. Shortly before Weinberg took his seat on the Stock Exchange, the family moved into a twelve-room English-style house with creamy stucco walls and dark-brown beams in Scarsdale, New York, which would always be Sidney and Helen Weinberg's home.

In 1927, he was made a partner. He didn't have to wait much longer for an opportunity to move up again. Late in 1928, Catchings unveiled his "masterpiece," the Goldman Sachs Trading Corporation, an investment trust (i.e., a separate company that, unlike the parent company, which was a private partnership, sold its shares to the public and traded securities with the proceeds).

Like so many of the other investment trusts of the period, it was built on a shaky foundation. Caught up in the sweep of speculative fever and in expectation of miraculous returns on their money, gullible investors were pushing the price of trust shares to fanciful heights. After the Great Crash of October 29, 1929, the trusts collapsed. Investors lost millions, and brokerage firms failed in record numbers. From this wreckage, Goldman Sachs emerged as a symbol of everything that was bad and ill-fated about Wall Street. Among those burned was comedian Eddie Cantor, who turned Goldman Sachs into a national joke by making the firm the hapless target of his comic routines.

Less humorous were the suits brought by outraged investors. Cantor himself filed one against management for a hundred million dollars. Little came of these actions, but the trust disaster spelled the end of Catchings's career at Goldman Sachs. In 1930, Weinberg led the other partners in ousting him. As the new senior partner, Weinberg took over many of Catchings's seats on corporate boards and set about persuading companies across America that Goldman Sachs was still solid and trustworthy.

Through his corporate and political network, he knew more important people than anyone else on Wall Street — a priceless asset in an industry where relationships were what mattered most. And Weinberg carefully nurtured them. A self-described "practical liberal," he was one of the few people in the financial community to support Franklin D. Roosevelt from the beginning and later served as a close adviser to the president. Weinberg was also offered numerous ambassadorships, including one to the Soviet Union, but, unwilling to uproot his family, he decided not to accept any of them. Unlike many directors, he was an active member of every board on which he sat. Every weekend, he would spend at least eight hours in his Scarsdale home boning up on the workings of all the companies. He was also fiercely loyal to their products. He drove a Studebaker, wore Munsingwear briefs, and stocked his kitchen with Campbell soups, Heinz ketchup, Pet milk, Pillsbury flour, and Kraft cheese.

*   *   *

In spite of his nineteenth-century view of business, Weinberg was developing a firm that was to become a prototype of the thoroughly modern investment bank. Shortly before his resignation, Catchings had begun a policy of hiring MBA graduates from his alma mater, Harvard. At first Weinberg opposed it. He was skeptical about fancy sheepskin collectors and handed out to the arrogant "college boys" Phi Beta Kappa keys he had picked up in pawn shops. But he would soon change his mind and become a firm supporter of the MBA policy, when he saw that it produced a solid cadre of smart team players.

None of the leading Wall Street houses, including the other Our Crowd firms, followed him. They were a contented lot. But if they were satisfied with the status quo, the federal government was not. As a result of the uncontrolled speculation and spurious practices that had led to the 1929 crash and the Depression, the government initiated much-needed banking laws and regulations.

The Banking Act of 1933 (commonly known as the Glass-Steagall Act) split banking into two parts: investment and commercial. Banking in the traditional sense — accepting deposits and making loans — was ruled off-limits for investment banks. Moreover, few bankers risked their own or their firm's capital in investments, as had been done by Schiff and Morgan. Instead, investment bankers had been basically "agents" or middlemen, marketers of new securities and advisers on financial strategy. When companies needed money, the investment bankers would underwrite the stock or bond issues — purchase them from the company and resell them to institutions or to wealthy investors — for a handsome commission at little risk to the firm.

The new legislation effectively made corporate America more dependent on Wall Street's most important investment banking houses for marketing stocks or bonds. It left the top rungs of the hierarchy on Wall Street more entrenched than ever, safe and profitable even in the depth of the Depression.

\*   \*   \*

Weinberg was so much a part of the business Establishment by 1947 that when the U.S. government accused leading financiers of violating federal antitrust laws, his name and that of Goldman Sachs were highlighted in the case. The trial would turn out to be one of the longest and most virulent assaults on Wall Street in its history.

In October of 1947, the Justice Department sued all the partners at Goldman Sachs, along with sixteen other leading banking firms, for conspiring to restrain trade. By making such charges, the Truman administration was challenging the very way the investment banking Establishment did business.

The government contended that the seventeen defendant firms constituted a monopoly. Inundating U.S. Circuit Judge Harold Medina with reams of data, the prosecution showed that the seventeen defendants, out of two hundred or so investment banking houses, had, indeed, captured the bulk of the investment banking business. In the previous dozen years, they had underwritten about two-thirds of the deals — worth more than $14 billion — whereas the other two hundred investment banking firms had handled the remaining one-third, or only $6 billion.

The fact that they were singled out for notice was in and of itself an indication of the rank and status of these firms, which were perceived as the elite group of investment banking. They were labeled by the press and thereafter became known as Club 17.*

As the case dragged on for years, forcing the accused to spend millions in legal fees, Club 17 attained unprecedented celebrity. That was an identification Weinberg loathed. What he wanted people to remember was the Goldman Sachs team that was ready to take on any opportunity. Under Weinberg's leadership, the firm became a major player in a field where few of the great investment bankers cared to venture — trading.

At the time trading was virtually the only ticket to Wall Street for many young Jews without the right background. The province of the traders — and the legions of stockbrokers, bond salesmen, and statisticians (later securities analysts) who supported them — was the other side of Wall Street. They kept the engines of finance humming by buying and selling blocks of stock and providing the market with a flow of money, or "liquidity."

For small investors and the general public, the stockbrokers were their primary link to and way of identifying Wall Street. Brokerage firms such as Merrill Lynch and Bache were far bigger, did more business, and were better known than even the regal banking houses like Morgan Stanley.

Their shirt-sleeved brothers, the traders, were a faceless mass

---

* In addition to Sidney Weinberg, the "Club" included the most powerful and prestigious mandarins of Wall Street: Henry Morgan of Morgan Stanley & Co., John Schiff of Kuhn Loeb & Co., Harry Addinsell of The First Boston Corporation, Robert Lehman of Lehman Brothers, Clarence Dillon of Dillon, Read & Co., Inc., J. Ford Johnson of Smith, Barney & Co., Joseph Ripley of Harriman Ripley & Co., Inc., and Charles Mitchell of Blyth & Co., Inc. The other eight firms indicted, which the prosecution maintained were less important, were White, Weld & Co., Kidder, Peabody & Co., Glore, Forgan & Co., Stone & Webster Securities Corporation, Union Securities Corporation, Harris Hall & Co., Inc., Eastman, Dillon & Co., and Drexel & Co. Also named in the suit was the Investment Bankers Association of America.

of pennypushers, who were obliged to make countless trades before they earned what many bankers did over lunch. They worked long, grueling hours in drafty, noisy, crowded trading rooms that resembled warehouses for storing paper.*

Sidney Weinberg might have gone along with the views of the typical investment bankers, who looked down on trading, but once committed, he never wavered in his support. It hardly hurt his commitment that by then a man named Gustave ("Gus") Levy handled the trading operations.

As a result of the Great Depression, Gus Levy could have become just another "jobless" statistic if it hadn't been for a chance recommendation from a friend, which led to his working at Goldman Sachs for $27.50 a week.

The son of a manufacturer of wooden crates, Levy was uprooted at the age of sixteen when, following his father's death, his mother moved with Levy and his two sisters to Paris. He was unsupervised and undisciplined. His favorite pastime was skipping off to the racetrack instead of attending school. Once the family was back in the United States, he didn't change his habits much. During his short stay at Tulane University in New Orleans he substituted football and parties for betting on horses. After the insurance money from his father's policy ran out and he had to leave Tulane, he joined his mother, who was then living in New York City.

The harsh realities of poverty forced him to mature quickly. The eighteen-year-old headed for Wall Street and was grateful to find a job as a runner at a small brokerage, hauling bundles of securities from one Wall Street house to another. A promotion to assistant in the trading department improved his prospects, but he lost his job when the firm went under during the Depression. He was so broke that he had to take the cheapest room at the Ninety-second Street Young Men's Hebrew Association, run by the Federation of Jewish Philanthropies.

Finding employment at Goldman Sachs and earning a quick promotion at least made him optimistic enough to marry within his first year on the job. His bride, Janet Wolf, a trim, petite commercial artist, came from a well-to-do Jewish family.

---

* In describing the non–investment banking side of Wall Street, most people generally think of trading, but the firms the traders work for are usually called brokerages. Although Goldman Sachs and Merrill Lynch, for instance, often did the same kind of work, each was known by its mainstay business, respectively, investment banking and brokerage.

By the late forties, Levy had made the quantum leap that was to change forever the nature of trading. Instead of dealing basically with the customers' securities for a commission, he would risk Goldman Sachs's money on a trade if he thought it would reap a sufficient profit. Not surprisingly, that strategy won him few converts at the time. The guiding principle was that you stood no chance of losing your firm's capital if you gambled only with other people's money.

That lack of recognition didn't faze Levy. That good ole' boy with a deceptively lazy Southern drawl, who had a taste for a martini or two after work, was a dynamo during market hours. From his open-door glass-enclosed office in the trading area, the broad-shouldered, five-foot-eleven former college football player barked out orders over the din of the ticker tape. He wanted every trade for himself and was fearless in going after them. The trades that made the adrenaline flow quickest involved risk arbitrage.

Arbitrage as a form of trading had a long history dating back to medieval times, when Venetian merchants traded interchangeable currencies to profit from price differentials. In the middle of the twentieth century, Levy led the way from traditional to risk arbitrage.* The strategy was artfully simple. Risk arbitrageurs (or "arbs," as they are now called) bought shares in companies being reorganized or merged into other companies, based on the premise that if the transaction was completed, they would be holding new stock worth considerably more than their investment. It was not a game for the timid, but the payoffs could be huge.

At the time, virtually the only Wall Street players, other than Goldman Sachs, who ventured into this uncharted territory were a handful of small Jewish firms often at odds with the consensus mentality of the Street. The old nineteenth-century refrain — "Let the Jews have that one" — seemed to apply increasingly as the risks of trading grew. Excluded from the inner circles of the underwriting franchise, these Jews explored the uncrowded arbitrage field.

Though Levy and others like him were riding the postwar economic market upward, the Wall Street Establishment continued to feel securely entrenched. In 1953 the bankers won a major victory over the only apparent threat to their supremacy: six years after it had begun,

---

* Traditional arbitrage is the relatively risk-free trading that takes advantage of small price differences for securities, currencies, or commodities that exist between one market, city, or country, and another. From here on, all references to arbitrage in this book refer to risk arbitrage.

the case brought by the Justice Department against Club 17 was thrown out of court for lack of evidence. Judge Harold Medina concluded that no conspiracy existed among the elite banking houses — they were acting solely as independent agents. (By the 1980s, the Medina opinion would prove as misguided as it was decisive.)

Even as the court blessed the status quo, a new force exerted pressure on the financial world. Control of the money was moving away from America's wealthiest families into the hands of a burgeoning cadre of professional investors who oversaw the holdings of banks' trust departments, insurance companies, corporate pension funds, college endowments, and mutual funds — all of which were growing phenomenally in the fifties. Practically unheard-of before the war, mutual funds ballooned an astonishing 700 percent — to $11.5 billion by the end of the decade. With so much money at stake, trading firms and market professionals did all that they could to win business from the mutual funds and other institutional investors. New people were hired to handle the expanding trading volume.

Those who signed on for these jobs got in on the proverbial ground floor of one of the most spectacular booms in Wall Street's history. Some came because they couldn't find jobs elsewhere. As the market zigzagged upward in the next decade, those who were already there seemed like prophets.

* * *

Gus Levy had been in the vanguard of the trading explosion for some time. He had been building a market in block trades — 10,000 or more shares — since the early fifties, when blocks evolved from his huge plays in arbitrage. By the midsixties, Levy had eased into his role of Wall Street power broker. In part, his success derived from his phenomenal ability to get things done. Every morning at the office he would jot down on a yellow legal pad a list of everything he planned to do that day. No matter how long the list grew, he would not rest until every item was crossed off. The standing joke at Goldman Sachs was that he was called "Gus" by everyone because in the time it took to say "Mr. Levy" he was on to something else.

His black hair was now peppered with gray, and he had developed a slight paunch, a visible sign of the nearly nightly business and testimonial dinners he attended from September through May. (He sometimes went to as many as three events in one evening.) In keeping with his elevated status and his constant battle with his weight, he favored dark-blue custom-made suits with baggy pleated pants. He usually looked sloppy. In one pants pocket he stuffed a change purse filled with good-luck coins and in a jacket pocket a wallet bulging with mementos.

Levy and his wife, Janet (who had given up commercial art in favor of portraits and collages she made for her own pleasure), occupied an attractive duplex apartment on Manhattan's elegant Sutton Place. Their co-op — containing a mixture of modern and antique furniture — was considered innovative for its time. In its white-walled living room, white damask-covered sofas were set off by teak floors and a Wolf Kahn painting.

His most relaxed moments were spent at Apple Hill Farm, the Levys' colonial home on four acres in Armonk, New York. On weekends he and his cronies played golf at the Century Country Club in nearby Purchase. For Levy, business and friendship were inseparably intertwined. His closest friends were his Wall Street colleagues and competitors and their wives. He didn't socialize much with his own boss, the aging Sidney Weinberg, who was of a different generation.

For all of his toughness and worldly experience, Levy had a soft caring side. His office was open to any Goldman Sachs employee who wanted to see him. Though he had joined Temple Emanu-El in the sixties, he never went to synagogue, but in his own way he was religious. On weekdays, after arising at 5:30 A.M. and jogging on a treadmill, he read prayers from a pamphlet entitled *The Daily Word*.

Apart from the trading-room pressures and his commitments to thirteen corporate boards, he spent countless hours working on behalf of various Jewish philanthropies and civic groups — an outpouring of energy and time the likes of which the Wall Street Jewish community had not seen since the days of Jacob Schiff. He also became a director of Lincoln Center for the Performing Arts (and then its treasurer), served on a committee that helped reorganize the American Stock Exchange after it had run afoul of the Securities and Exchange Commission, was elected president of the Board of Trustees of the Mount Sinai Hospital, and became chairman of the New York Stock Exchange. That last honor was unique. It had never gone to a trader, and one who was a power broker in his own right. It was a measure of how far he had come.

\* \* \*

With the inauguration of President John F. Kennedy in 1961, the mood of the country had turned euphoric. Kennedy and his administration came to symbolize a new style of leadership. When John Glenn orbited the earth, the future seemed limitless. Less than two years later, Kennedy was assassinated. Still, one promise of the Kennedy years would be fulfilled — that the times, they were "a-changing," as the (Bob Dylan) song would proclaim. In November 1964, President Lyndon B. Johnson, fresh from his landslide victory, embarked on his Great Society and the Vietnam War. Martin Luther King, Jr., stamped the civil rights movement on the American consciousness. Kaleidoscopic images — the antiwar movement, Bob Dylan singing folk songs, the Beatles, Timothy Leary getting high on hallucinogenic drugs, R. D. Laing expounding on the sanity of madness, Ralph Nader battling General Motors, and Andy Warhol making pop icons of Campbell soup cans — reflected the profound, helter-skelter dislocations affecting Americans.

Wall Street also mirrored the upheaval. By the midsixties, Levy's spiritual disciples were found all over the Street, and more were on their way. Some of the most powerful members of today's New Crowd stumbled into trading and brokerage and into newer forms of Wall Street business during the early years of the boom. In the midsixties, the Go-Go Years had arrived, a label that seemed to express the nation's surging unrest. (The term was probably imported from the Parisian disco named Whiskey A Go Go, which had gained international notoriety earlier in the decade.) It came to symbolize the special excitement in the market during those years, characterized by huge investments, increased trading volume, quick large profits, and trendy investment gimmicks such as warrants — the rights to buy a stock at a certain price — and advertising the stocks of small companies as the next Polaroid and Xerox investment opportunities. Jumping into the market faster than at any time since the twenties, the small investor became a potent force, while financial institutions expanded to the point of doing almost half the trading. A constellation of market-wise fund operators and money management stars, mostly self-made men, rose swiftly and cast a dazzling light.

The times were also bringing other changes to the forefront: raiders, conglomerateurs, and empire builders became the most visible players of the era. Whatever their labels, all catered to corporations' new and voracious appetite for consuming one another.

Despite some dramatic successes, prior to the mergers and acquisitions wave in the late sixties, the field had been largely ignored by the Wall Street elite. They failed to see that the latest merger wave was bigger, more widespread, and wilder than anything that had preceded it. To them, the conglomerateurs were outsiders and interlopers who dispensed with all that was sacred in corporate practice.

The term *conglomerateurs* — from the Latin *conglomerare* meaning "to roll together" — came into widespread usage in the late sixties. The conglomerates expanded their businesses not by selling more of whatever they were marketing but by acquiring other companies in other businesses.* An added attraction was that in bypassing the previous concentration of power in one industry, these conglomerates neatly sidestepped sticky antitrust problems. Thus, acquisition-minded companies could continue to swallow other companies without restraint. They often had little concern with how the acquisition meshed with their present or future holdings. Their emphasis was on empire building.

As the size and the number of acquisitions grew, so did the rewards. Watching from the sidelines, the investment bankers could only look on with envy as the business skyline changed.

Meshulam Riklis, the son of Russian Jews, was among the first of the free-swinging group of conglomerateurs to make a splash.† Riklis, who was born in Istanbul and raised in Palestine, had emigrated in 1947 to the United States. By the midsixties, he had already built a conglomerate and seen it virtually collapse. Now he was constructing a second one out of the ruins. By 1969 the pixieish yet sly financier had picked up B.V.D., Playtex, RKO-Stanley Warner, and Schenley to re-create his ragtag retail sales empire called Rapid-American. This odd-lot collection of underwear manufacturers, movie theaters, and a liquor company had all been run by other Jews. It was no coincidence. Riklis, who at one time taught in Hebrew school, believed he was better off going after businesses where he would be accepted, which, not surprisingly, were mostly led by Jews. And he had picked his targets carefully to avoid getting hurt — unlike Louis Wolfson,

---

* The conglomerateurs' underlying philosophy was that if the purchase price of any company was reasonable and made the sales, earnings, or stock price of the corporation go up, buy it. This was based on a fashionable concept in American business during the sixties — synergy — which meant, as it was used, that the whole was far greater than the sum of its parts: two plus two equals five.

† Some of the early conglomerateurs were neither Jewish nor immigrants. In the fifties, it was the rare takeover artists with "the right credentials" — such as Harvard-bred Royal Little of Textron and former top Ford executive Charles "Tex" Thornton of Litton Industries — who did manage to win support of the Wall Street Establishment, although not without difficulty. James Ling built a thriving contracting business in Dallas, then assembled the high-tech business known as LTV, Ling-Temco-Vought, Inc., the fastest-growing company in America between 1955 and 1965.

another Russian Jew, who had advised Riklis when he was just starting out.

By then, Wolfson had taken a small family business and built
it through acquisitions into a huge construction company, Merritt-
Chapman. In his first — and only — bid as a conglomerateur, he had
reached too far into the Establishment and become the victim of a bitter
anti-Semitic assault. A cause célèbre in the business world of 1955, he
tried to take over Montgomery Ward, the mail-order company, by
ousting its octogenarian chairman, Sewell Avery. The Montgomery
Ward forces counterattacked with every weapon in their arsenal. According to Wolfson, they labeled him a raider, made disparaging references to his immigrant heritage, and worse. At the height of the
battle, he received an anonymous phone call one evening. "Listen, you
Jewish son-of-a-bitch," the voice on the other end warned, "you lay
off Avery or you won't wake up to see your family again." Wolfson
was unnerved. The intensity and viciousness of the campaign cost him
his victory.

Racing just a step behind Riklis and Wolfson was Charles
Bluhdorn, a Viennese refugee known as "the Mad Austrian" for his
explosive temper. Within fifteen years of having fled the Nazis and
arriving in America alone and penniless at sixteen, he was a millionaire
cotton broker. In 1957, Bluhdorn bought control of an auto parts manufacturing company and then started gobbling up other companies.
Nine years and many corporate deals later, the firm, now known as
Gulf & Western, snapped up Paramount Pictures. Gulf & Western's
glitzy new image helped the stock more than triple in less than one
year.

\* \* \*

The empire builders were joined in the late sixties by a new
breed of investment bankers, who stood out from the old-boy underwriting network and put their own stamp on American business. The
first of these banker dealmakers — adroit, skillful, open to new ways
of thinking and fresh challenges — was coming to the forefront.

# CHAPTER FOUR

# Deal Architect

U rbane, imperturbable under fire, acknowledged for the intelligence and intensity he brought to the art of negotiation, Felix Rohatyn was to emerge as the quintessential dealmaker, the new era's most important mergers and acquisitions specialist, an architect of giant corporate consolidations and, consequently, the most visible investment banker of the late sixties.

In a relatively short time, this Jewish refugee who narrowly escaped becoming a victim of the Holocaust had gone from glorified bookkeeper to numbers-crunching analyst to established dealmaker at the small but respected investment banking house of Lazard Frères. The journey hadn't been an easy one. He could take in stride the many meetings, the long hours, the endless reports, the frequent trips — which were all part of the job — but it wasn't as simple to adjust to the tension of meeting new people constantly, of having his performance scrutinized during every deal, and having to prove himself again and again. He was essentially a private person. He was also a very ambitious man.

Felix George Rohatyn (pronounced *Row*-a-tin) learned in his thirties to play the roles of muse, negotiator, and mediator successfully. His strength came from seeming to remain detached and calm no matter how great the pressure. That was something he didn't have to learn: he disliked revealing his feelings. His conversational skill helped him control most situations. Words and ideas came easily, and few could tell on meeting him that English wasn't his native tongue.

He was confident — some would say arrogant — enough about his abilities to believe that he needed little else to succeed. He didn't belong to business, political, fraternal, or social clubs, or other formal organizations, but managed, through years of business networking, to meet and get to know on his own terms the people who mattered.

His small, unadorned office at Lazard reflected a messy functionalism. The old wooden desk was crammed with copies of company prospectuses, annual reports, memos, magazines, telephone message slips, and coffee cups. The yield from this clutter was impressive. Prosperous and well respected in the financial community, he enjoyed the prestige from sitting on two corporate boards, and in late 1967 was about to sit on a third that would give him access to undreamed-of influence.

He had achieved all this under the controlling eye of André Meyer, the undisputed senior partner of Lazard Frères, who had made Rohatyn, thirty years his junior, his protégé after ignoring him for years. Under ordinary circumstances, Meyer (pronounced My-air) was formidable. When roused, he was one of the most feared and hated men on Wall Street, a reputation he had carried with him almost from the day he arrived in New York City in 1940 at the age of forty-two. A French Jew, the short-tempered Lazard partner had already made a name for himself in the firm's Paris office before he was forced, like Rohatyn, to flee the Nazi occupation of France. Three years later, Meyer seized control of the New York office by ousting its managing director, Frank Altschul.

Ironically, it was Altschul — an Our Crowd banker whose social status was further enhanced by his marriage to a Lehman — who had conferred on Lazard a respectability it had not previously known. Until he took over, the investment banking house had been considered the longest-running collection of upstarts on Wall Street. Begun in 1848 by three Lazard brothers who had emigrated from France to New Orleans before opening an office in New York, the firm had never been accepted by the German-Jewish bankers through three generations of family control.*

Meyer cared less about fitting in than about making money. Under Altschul's leadership during the war years, the firm had been largely committed to underwriting, which had been in a deep slump. The situation was ripe for Meyer. He saw the postwar boom coming, and he wanted to be a part of it — just as in their heyday the original German-Jewish bankers had been involved as principals and not simply as underwriters and financial advisers. Getting in early and making a quick but handsome profit was the Meyer trademark, a talent that

---

* Pierre David-Weill, a descendant of the founding family, ran the Paris office and dominated the firm until Altschul took over the New York branch. He supported Meyer's move to dump Altschul.

would earn him a fortune estimated in excess of $100 million. In the fifties, Meyer ranged far afield, with investments in a huge Texas cattle ranch, Parke-Bernet Gallery, Loews Theatres, and a then virtually unknown hotel chain called Holiday Inns. He had a particular affinity for mergers, counting among his successes the forging of the giant pharmaceutical company, Warner-Lambert.

The rich and powerful gravitated toward this stout, owlish-looking Frenchman with thick horn-rimmed glasses. He lived like a potentate, surrounded by the works of Monet, Chagall, and Picasso, which covered the walls of his suite at the Carlyle Hotel.

If he had one nagging regret, it was that his only son, Philippe, had not followed him into banking. Rohatyn — three years younger than Philippe, fluent in French, and a refugee European Jew — was treated like a surrogate son whose duty it was to remain at his father's side. The pugnacious Meyer might scream and wheedle and, an adversary to be reckoned with, might threaten other people till he got what he wanted, but not Rohatyn, who controlled his temper and played the perfect wise counsel from the sidelines. By 1967 Rohatyn enjoyed the kind of power — without the ultimate accountability — that gave him access in Meyer to a man on whom he could exercise his influence. He amply demonstrated a talent for doing that.

Meeting him for the first time after knowing him by reputation, many people were surprised by Rohatyn's youthful appearance. A compactly built man with cropped dark hair, crinkly blue eyes, a pug nose, full lips, and prominent teeth, at thirty-nine he still had the eager, smiling face of a student. He spoke rapidly in a soft, high-pitched voice, and his manner was enthusiastic and self-effacing. But there was no mistaking his tenacity when he was convinced the prize was worth the effort. Confrontations were a last resort for him, and even then most of his real feelings would be hidden behind a mask of inscrutability. If he had learned one lesson in life, it was to travel light.

*   *   *

By the time Rohatyn arrived in New York City in 1942 at the age of fourteen, he had already lived in seven countries and on three continents. His family originally came from Galicia — in an area that once was part of Poland but now belongs to the Soviet Union. (According to family legend, his great-grandfather had been the grand rabbi of the region.) At the turn of the century, the family moved to Vienna, where Rohatyn's grandfather, Arturo, joined the city's Stock Exchange, founded a small bank, Rohatyn & Company, and started several breweries. Rohatyn's father, Alexander, worked in the breweries and eventually managed some of them. In 1927, Alexander Rohatyn married Edith Knoll, who came from a family of wealthy Viennese merchants. Neither of them was particularly religious. The following year she gave birth to her only child, a son named Felix.

As a small boy Rohatyn never knew the comfort and security his parents had known as children. During the Depression, the Rohatyn bank failed. His family moved to Romania for several years, where his father managed one of the few remaining family breweries, then back to Vienna briefly before emigrating to France to escape the growing anti-Semitism in Austria.

For Rohatyn, the sadness of leaving his native country was followed by another trauma — his parents were divorced soon after the family settled in Orléans. At the age of eight, he was sent off to a French-speaking boarding school in Switzerland. Always an ungainly child, he became so unathletic and overweight that he even had difficulty tying his shoelaces. "It took me so long to get dressed in the morning that I would go to bed with my pajamas over most of my clothes in order to save time," he said later. Within a year, he left the boarding school to join his mother, who had remarried and moved to Paris.

The peripatetic Rohatyn would not stay settled for long. The most harrowing phase of his nomadic existence was about to begin. The Nazis were closing in on France, and Rohatyn's family was in extreme danger of being hunted down. Not only was the family Jewish; Rohatyn's stepfather, Henry Plessner, who worked in his family's precious-metal-refining business, was a Polish citizen and a committed Zionist. In the spring of 1940, Plessner was placed in an internment camp by the French.

Early in June — just before the fall of France — mother and son fled south together. (At one point during their escape, Rohatyn was nearly caught distributing anti-Nazi pamphlets. And for a time, he said, he had to wear a Star of David armband.) In Biarritz they found Plessner, who had escaped from the internment camp, and Plessner's mother. The four of them, soon forced to flee again, could take only a few belongings. In two empty toothpaste tubes, Rohatyn hid some gold coins and his mother's jewelry — the only objects of value they dared carry with them to meet unforeseen expenses. (That experience left him with a refugee's theory of wealth: "The only things that count, basically, are things you can put in a toothpaste tube or carry in your head, and I have never changed that view at all.")

At the next point in their journey, they appeared to have reached the end of the line.

As they were driving toward Cannes, they encountered a German roadblock. Looking around, Rohatyn saw that they were trapped inside a lineup of cars. His stepfather Plessner was on various gestapo wanted lists, and the two soldiers guarding the checkpoint were checking for proper identification papers. Rohatyn's family had no such documents. But as the car in front of them pulled up beside the soldiers, one of the Germans paused to smoke a cigarette. When the driver waved some piece of paper, the other soldier allowed him to pass. Rohatyn's mother did the same thing with her driver's license, and the soldier waved her by too.

His mother's quick gesture saved them. They remained in Cannes for almost a year, living in a *pension de famille*. In at least one respect, it was a particularly happy time for Felix. His father had also managed to reach Cannes, and Rohatyn saw him frequently.

But they were all painfully aware that they could not remain in Cannes much longer. In early 1941, Rohatyn, his mother, stepfather, and stepgrandmother managed to reach Lisbon. (Rohatyn's father was hidden by the French underground for the remainder of the war.) From there, it was on to Casablanca and then to Rio de Janeiro and, finally, in June of the following year, they reached New York.

With help from relatives already living in the city and with some money Plessner had transferred before the war, the family managed to live comfortably. They occupied a small Park Avenue apartment, and Rohatyn was enrolled at the McBurney School, a relatively modest private school for boys. He adjusted well to life in America, mainly because of his complete ease with languages. Starting with a smattering of English, he mastered the language, as he had already mastered French and Portuguese.

Middlebury College in Vermont was attractive to Rohatyn because it had a good physics program — he planned to pursue a career in either physics or engineering — and because he liked to ski. In his junior year, he and a black student achieved notoriety on campus when they were invited to join the Alpha Sigma Phi fraternity. The Middlebury chapter, faced with expulsion from the national fraternity, refused to bow to prejudice. The episode was an ugly reminder of the past.

College physics proved more difficult than high school math and science. Reluctantly, Rohatyn concluded that his studies in pursuit of "what serious people did" would take him no farther than a bachelor of science degree.

His stepfather, who had worked with André Meyer in Paris before the war, suggested that Felix try business after graduation. With only mildly disguised disdain for the "money shufflers," as he called them, Rohatyn started full-time employment at Lazard — he had worked there summers as a clerk during college — for a salary of $37.50 a week. His job involved doing the bookkeeping for the securities accounts of individual customers, which required no greater skill than the ability to add and subtract columns of figures.

At first his career seemed to be going nowhere, but he did get to return to Europe. He was sent to Paris in 1950 to be trained at the Lazard office there and then to London for a brief stint with Samuel Montagu & Company, a banking firm that had close ties to Lazard. To Meyer, New York was the center of financial power. Working abroad wasn't as promising as it sounded.

Soon he was in the army — during the Korean War — where he eventually reached the rank of sergeant in the intelligence section of an infantry unit, while stationed in Germany.

He was back at Lazard in 1953. Meyer, in true form, stuck him in a small banking house in Zurich jointly owned by Lazard and Samuel Montagu. It was a great time for young Rohatyn, not because of his work, which consisted mostly of repetitive financial transactions, but because of his life in Zurich. The fun began innocently enough when he looked for living quarters.

"I went to a pension in the old part of town," he recalled, "which was actually a well-known brothel, but being Switzerland, it was also a neat, clean place. The only thing unusual about it was that there were a lot more attractive women living there than at most pensions. A large lady in a kimono carrying a tea service met me at the door, and I told her I wanted a room, maybe with a kitchenette and a little dining room. She asked me how long I was planning to stay and I said a year or so. She dropped the tray.

"I was pretty innocent. It wasn't until I had been there a while that I noticed that the place seemed to operate on a different time schedule from mine. I obviously got to know some of the women. When the Swiss businessmen I met at parties after work learned where I lived, they'd push their wives aside and ask me to tell them about the pension. I felt a little like Toulouse-Lautrec."

Rohatyn was now getting paid to bounce around Europe. Unaware of how far away he was from the dealmaking pulse of Lazard, he was a happy-go-lucky young man, pleased enough with his life to let events take their own course.

\* \* \*

He might have stayed an ocean away from the heart of Lazard's business had not one of Meyer's European connections offered him a competing job, which made Rohatyn suddenly seem more attractive to the French banker. By 1955 he was assigned to the foreign exchange department at Lazard's New York office. The pay was $21,000, a generous income at that time for Rohatyn, who lived in a two-bedroom apartment on Manhattan's Upper East Side, a half-hour subway ride from Lazard's Wall Street office.

Through a diverse collection of refugees, Rohatyn was invited to a weekend gathering at the estate of Seagram founder Samuel Bronfman. The liquor company chief, who knew Meyer well, told Rohatyn, "André Meyer is interested only in mergers and corporate finance. If you want to get anywhere with him, I'd advise you to get into that end of the business." That this came as a revelation to Rohatyn, who worked for one of the premier financiers on Wall Street, said something about his complacency and naïveté then.

Although Rohatyn remarked to Bronfman that he had never taken an economics course in his life and could not even read a balance sheet, he immediately took Bronfman's advice straight to Meyer. Meyer, in characteristic fashion, agreed to the transfer, but exacted his price. Rohatyn would have to take a salary cut of $7,000 and also learn accounting and securities analysis. He felt he could manage the pay cut, even though he would soon be married. His bride-to-be, Jeannette Streit, of mixed American-Protestant, French-Catholic background, worked as a simultaneous interpreter of French and Spanish into English at the United Nations. (Her father, Clarence, was a leading *New York Times* correspondent, whose book, *Union Now,* and whose dedication helped spawn an international movement for a federation of Western democracies.) She was an independent woman who wasn't concerned with getting rich.

Rohatyn soon was spending time with Meyer, brought along to meetings at first because he knew how to use a slide rule. There he learned the fundamentals of how deals were structured. The two men could talk easily about a broad range of subjects and often spoke in a patois that even those who knew French had trouble following. For one so young, Rohatyn had an instinctive talent for coping with Meyer's high-strung, ego-centered personality. In his own quiet, diplomatic way he stood up to Meyer by never allowing himself to become dependent on either his boss or the firm. That didn't exempt him totally from the explosive outbursts everyone else at Lazard was subjected to. "I almost quit a couple of times," Rohatyn has admitted.

It wasn't unusual for Meyer to turn up for dinner at the Rohatyns' small, modestly furnished apartment on Manhattan's East Ninety-second Street, don an apron, and help Jeannette Rohatyn cook

the meal. The Rohatyns were occasionally invited to drop in and see
Meyer and his wife at the Carlyle over the weekend. Partners were
rarely treated that way, let alone a young associate. Rohatyn welcomed
the attention.

At the office and in the more relaxed atmosphere of the Carlyle,
he met some of the powerful and important people who came regularly,
not for socializing but to imbibe Meyer's financial wisdom or to be
part of his ventures. They included RCA chairman David Sarnoff, CBS
chief William Paley, banker David Rockefeller, Fiat boss Gianni Agnelli, industrialist Charles Engelhard, Bell & Howell chairman Charles
Percy and his lieutenant Pete Peterson. This circle of influential people — and their deals and connections — made Rohatyn more eager to
establish himself. Though no one could have predicted it at the time,
Harold Geneen, the head of ITT, would be the vehicle for his ascent.

*　*　*

Rohatyn could at least claim to have met Geneen without an
introduction from Meyer. He was Rohatyn's first important independent contact. Even as a young banker, Rohatyn attracted people
who might some day advance his career, and he was quite capable of
charming and impressing them. Through a casual conversation, not
long after Geneen first took control of ITT in 1959, Rohatyn was to
be introduced to him.

Rohatyn ran into Albert Hettinger, a senior Lazard partner, one
afternoon as he was waiting for the elevator. Hearing that Hettinger
was having lunch with Geneen, Rohatyn quickly got himself invited
to go along. The meeting was uneventful, but the contact was made.
Early in 1961, when Lazard was given its first chance to handle an
acquisition for ITT — a small electronics firm in California called Jennings Radio — Rohatyn was assigned by Meyer to help Geneen negotiate and structure the acquisition. The $20 million takeover was
Rohatyn's first deal, and afterward he kept in touch with the ITT
executives. On occasion he would stop off at ITT's midtown Park
Avenue headquarters on his way home. He came to know the company
well, what its needs were and who counted, especially among the young
comers. But most important were his talks with Geneen. To some
observers Geneen seemed almost inhuman — "the automated executive," as one former ITT employee called him — but to Rohatyn he
was accessible. The ITT chief enjoyed ranging across the business landscape for hours at the end of the day over tea and cookies, a Geneen
passion. What made Rohatyn's relationship with Geneen so special was

how naturally the two men conversed. From just such informal get-togethers sprang the idea of ITT's buying Avis and other, bigger, moves.

* * *

The rent-a-car company proved a unique showcase for Rohatyn's talents. When Avis put itself on the selling block in 1961, he immediately voiced his support for acquiring it for Lazard instead of finding some other purchaser, which would bring the firm only an advisory or finder's fee. It was a risky move on his part: he had been made partner only the previous year. More than the purchase price was at stake. Avis was losing money, and given its number-two status in car rentals, behind Hertz, Meyer's reputation as a financial guru could suffer if he didn't turn the company around.

Rohatyn's first assignment was to find someone with considerable managerial experience to run Avis. The quest led to Robert Townsend, who had just left American Express, where his iconoclastic, freethinking ways had probably derailed his promotion to chairman. He was knowledgeable, driven, and now, understandably, restless. With Townsend aboard, Meyer rounded up some of his closest friends as coinvestors, including David Rockefeller and David Sarnoff, and formed a holding company to buy Avis for $5.5 million. The new Townsend management team was installed, and Rohatyn was given a board seat.

The next concern was an aggressive marketing strategy. Hertz was far out in the lead. It had a much larger advertising budget and the catchy slogan about Hertz putting you "in the driver's seat." William Bernbach, the head of Doyle, Dane, Bernbach, took on the Avis advertising with a budget of only $1 million (one-fifth of the Hertz budget) on the condition that no revisions be made in the ad copy. After three months of studying Avis, the only thing he could offer was that the car-rental company was the second largest and that its employees were really trying. From that came the classic advertising line: "We're number two. We try harder."

With America's love of the underdog, Avis's revenues started picking up, though not fast enough to reassure Rohatyn. Throughout the entire first year under Lazard's aegis, Avis lost money. In October of 1962 alone, the company was $400,000 in the red. When that happened, Rohatyn panicked. The risks Lazard was taking became too much for him. A very frightened young dealmaker, he went to see Meyer at the Carlyle one Saturday morning.

"We've got to get some help," Rohatyn told the banker. "I think we should bring in some outside consultants."

Meyer was, surprisingly, unruffled. The old banker replied, "Let's wait a little longer before we do anything." His resolve gave Rohatyn the reassurance he needed and hardened him for future crises.

The following month Avis reversed its decline, and soon turned a profit. Even so, Meyer kept Rohatyn there as his watchdog. He was thorough but unobtrusive and was able to function without antagonizing the Townsend team. He worked late and often missed dinner with Jeannette and his three sons. More and more his work was absorbing his time and taking him away from his family — which would have serious consequences for all of them. He now traveled about the country with Townsend, accompanying him to sales meetings sporting the red Avis blazer and button that everyone — including the executives — was required to wear.

Rohatyn handled giant egos with calculated aplomb and had a remarkable gift for soothing frayed tempers. He was often on the phone with Townsend or Meyer, acting as a buffer and patching up their rifts. "Townsend delighted in driving André crazy," Rohatyn recalls. Townsend was cocky and uncommunicative and annoyingly out of the office when Meyer wanted to speak with him. Rohatyn became convinced that Townsend was growing bored with his job. When it was clear in September 1964 that he intended to leave, Meyer felt it was an appropriate moment to put up the For Sale sign.

It fell to Rohatyn to find a buyer. His first attempt proved a disaster. Mobil was seriously interested in acquiring Avis until Townsend — who felt Avis would get lost in the oil giant's bureaucracy — did all he could to scotch the deal, including telling the Mobil executives that he advised Avis's customers to buy the cheapest gas available. Geneen indicated that ITT would be interested. Once again, Rohatyn was pressed into service as a negotiator. In January 1965, when Lazard sold Avis to ITT for stock worth $52 million, Townsend was incensed, maintaining that Meyer "sold it cheap to get a seat on ITT's board." Rohatyn found the insinuation absurd, but immediately after the sale, Meyer did suggest that Geneen appoint a Lazard partner as a director — a suggestion Geneen angrily rejected.

The following year Rohatyn found Geneen a companion piece for Avis — the Airport Parking Company — which he had discovered in 1962, while researching the purchase of Avis for Lazard. Deals like this led Geneen to offer Rohatyn a seat on the ITT board, but opposition came from an unlikely quarter, Meyer.

After months of a stalemate, Meyer — who had someone else in mind for the ITT board — finally caved in and agreed that Rohatyn could accept the seat. At heart, Meyer was a practical man, and, like it or not, Rohatyn had become the bridge between Lazard and ITT. He attended his first board meeting on January 1, 1968. That may have been an unusual way to celebrate New Year's Day, but Rohatyn was pleased nonetheless: "As an immigrant, someone who clearly was not part of the Establishment, I was now on the board of this big Establishment company."

For Rohatyn, "It was the first breaking out of the little cocoon I had been living in, and it meant a great deal to my career. It meant being recognized professionally." It also meant an even closer business relationship with Geneen.

* * *

Although a latecomer to the conglomerate scene, Geneen more than made up for his slow start. Rohatyn had never known anyone else who worked as hard and as competitively. He had no family or social life. Work was his obsession. He found in Rohatyn a listener and a learner, someone whose career he could bring forward. Rohatyn rewarded him with unfailing loyalty. He also found in Rohatyn someone who in turn could bring him along farther toward his goal of building an ever-expanding and richer global empire. That distinction went to him, in no small part, through having Lazard as his investment banker and Felix Rohatyn as his Richelieu.

Geneen was deceptive. With his pinched face, clear eyeglass frames, and basic-blue corporate suits, he appeared to have led a life of narrow conformity. Yet his early years, like Rohatyn's, were neither easy nor comfortable. Secretive about his background, Geneen made the trail into his past difficult to follow. He was British by birth, the product of a marriage troubled from the start, when his Russian-Jewish father and his Italian-Catholic mother married over the religious objections of their families. While he was an infant, his parents fled that hostile environment in London for a new life in New York, where soon afterward the father deserted mother and son. At seven, Geneen was packed off to a Baptist boarding school in Connecticut, while his mother pursued a modestly successful career in the theater. Small, unathletic, and introverted, he spent those academic years isolated and lonely.

Following college, he became an accountant, then leapfrogged upward through the managerial ranks from camera maker Bell & Howell to steel producer Jones & Loughlin to electronics manufacturer Raytheon. Finally, in 1959, he was made president of ITT, a then somewhat disjointed communications network. His dry, colorless personality belied the fact that the blunt-spoken former accountant would set about building the most aggressive industrial company in the world.

During his first six years at ITT's helm, he was relatively cautious, as he began implementing his vision of ever-increasing growth and profits. He wanted to be welcomed by any firm he was interested in acquiring. At the same time, his bid for the American Broadcasting Company in 1966 was a telling example of the extremes to which he was willing to go to get his way. When the Justice Department sued to stop the merger, Geneen's minions tried to build a dossier on the personal life of the *New York Times* reporter covering the case, in a futile attempt to discredit her.

Rohatyn played only a minor role in the abortive ABC venture, and had nothing at all to do with ITT's dirty little campaign to control the press coverage of the case. Yet his loyalty to Geneen made him blind to any serious criticism of the ITT chief — a loyalty that would eventually drag Rohatyn before a Senate investigating committee and, for a time, blemish his reputation. But, until then, together Rohatyn and Geneen were to become virtually unstoppable on the merger landscape.

# CHAPTER FIVE

# A House Divided

S anford ("Sandy") Weill lacked the credentials to qualify for a career in the old-line Wall Street. He also lacked the style of the cosmopolitan Felix Rohatyn. But, like many others, he arrived at the right time — which gave him the chance to overcome a whole set of seeming "disabilities" for success. Desperately insecure, unwilling to take a position of leadership, all of his life he had felt like an outsider in any crowd. Aside from his colleagues and his clients, he rarely spoke easily to anyone, out of shyness bordering on fear. He would spend hours sitting at his desk with his eyes glued to the stock quotation computer terminal, watching hundreds of stocks flutter by, letting his associates handle the day-to-day management of Carter, Berlind & Weill.

The up-and-coming brokerage firm was analogous to what Lehman Brothers and Kuhn Loeb had been a century earlier: a hot new house trying to build a name for itself. In the late sixties, the young executives at Carter, Berlind & Weill took in any business that came their way — meaning whatever they could sell to their collection of individual and institutional customers. By the summer of 1968, their eight-year-old company was taking off — profits from fiscal year July 1967 to June 1968 had practically quadrupled to $1.3 million — and among the more than 600 members of the New York Stock Exchange, it ranked in the top quarter in capital. Still, Weill leaned heavily for reassurance on Arthur Carter, the firm's president and guiding force. If not rich men, the senior officers were at least prospering.

Buoyed by their bright earnings and their rosy outlook for the future, they were expanding their operations. New employees were being hired, and they had just made plans for their fourth move, this time to posh, spacious offices in the prestigious new General Motors building on Fifth Avenue. Though he would eventually move into the upper reaches of the corporate executive suite, Sandy Weill felt he had already made a great leap forward by 1968. He took great pride in being part of his young group's achievements, and he longed for recognition.

* * *

Despite a tendency later on to portray his life as a rags-to-riches story, Weill had grown up in the moderately comfortable middle class. His early childhood in his father's three-story house in Brooklyn among close relatives was uneventful, unmarked by any special accomplishments or trauma. It was only when his family moved to Miami Beach in 1945 — his father having decided that his small garment-manufacturing business would do better in Florida — that the twelve-year-old Weill felt uprooted; he didn't adjust well to his new school and his grades suffered. The family's return to Brooklyn two years later and young Weill's stint at the Peekskill Military Academy provided him with the goal he needed. In the military school's regimented environment, "I tried harder because of the discipline and competition," he recalled.

At Peekskill he also began playing tennis. The more popular sport of basketball had proved difficult for him — he had a tendency to jump off the wrong foot. When he returned home to Brooklyn on vacations and showed up at the local playground's basketball courts dressed in white shorts, the young players made fun of him. Tennis wasn't a neighborhood sport, but Weill stuck with the game.

Graduating third in his class, he was accepted by Harvard and by Cornell. He chose Cornell. Initially, he planned to study metallurgical engineering and later go into business with his father, who by then had turned from manufacturing clothing to importing steel. But his first semester he did so poorly, particularly in physics, that he would have flunked out had there not been a special program that gave students like him a second chance in another department. Weill selected government, which he considered "a good bullshit major." And again his life turned around. His grades improved.

In his junior year he fell in love with a girl he met on a blind date, Joan Mosher, a Brooklyn College student with a willowy figure and a wry wit who was planning to become an elementary school-teacher. The couple made plans to get married the June of his senior year. Weill expected to serve two years in the Air Force before joining his father in business.

In February, his dreams were shattered when his father deserted his mother for a younger woman. The elder Weill went out for ice cream one evening and never returned. Young Weill rushed home from college in a futile attempt to find his father and change his mind. His father's defection was his first major betrayal and — though he denied it later — he seemed a little more wary and afraid of the world than was good for him as a consequence. "It was a turning point in my life," he admitted. "I felt I had to stand up on my own from then on." Badly shaken, he failed to complete a required course at college and couldn't graduate with his class. As a result, Joan Mosher's parents tried to persuade their daughter not to marry him; they didn't want a son-in-law without a diploma. And in light of the elder Weill's actions, Joan's father cautioned her, "The apple doesn't fall far from the tree." Forced to accept the inevitable as Joan Mosher went ahead with the wedding plans, her parents made the couple a peace offering: a large wedding or money. They took the cash.

Weill's prospects were dim. He took a job delivering commercial directories. Joan, who was completing her senior year at Brooklyn College, worked as a substitute teacher and earned more money than he did. The newlyweds avoided paying rent by shuttling back and forth between their families' homes.

Frightened and unsure of himself, Weill sometimes went to play amusement arcade games in Times Square and phoned Joan at her parents' home.

"What should I do now?"

Joan's father, still worried about his daughter's future, strained to follow her end of the conversation.

"What's Sandy up to?" he would ask later.

And Joan would reply, "He's out looking for a job, Dad."

The healthy economy of the midfifties didn't bring Weill any better career opportunities. He came to Wall Street almost by accident. Attracted by the activity he saw at a branch office of Bache, he tried to enter broker training programs there and also at Merrill Lynch and Harris Upham, but all three houses rejected him. As he saw it, he had no money or connections to get ahead on Wall Street. Finally, Bear Stearns hired him as a $35-a-week runner, which meant, in effect, he was still a "delivery boy," or messenger, only now, instead of lugging directories, he was delivering bundles of securities around the financial district.

In the fall, he completed his degree and with that confidence builder, he demanded a shot at becoming a broker; if his request was denied, he would enlist in the Air Force. Bear Stearns agreed to let him try. "They realized that I had a college degree, while all the other runners were over sixty-five and on Social Security," he said later. Tapping his Brooklyn roots for customers, he soon was making enough money to move with his pregnant wife into their own apartment, a modest one-bedroom unit that backed on the railroad tracks, in East Rockaway, New York. Soon after their son, Marc, was born, Joan recalled, "Sandy changed one diaper, gave Marc one bottle, and took him to the supermarket once. Sandy was trying to establish himself." Joan gave up teaching to take care of the baby.

Just as chance had led Weill to Wall Street, it also led him to the next juncture in his life. Living across the hall from the Weills was another Wall Street hopeful, named Arthur Carter, who had only recently gone to work for Lehman Brothers. A sharp, humorless young man, the son of an Internal Revenue agent, Carter had not planned to enter the securities industry. A French literature major at Brown University, he dreamed of becoming a concert pianist. But after serving in the U.S. Coast Guard at a New York harbor base, he caught the same Wall Street fever Weill had and returned to school for an MBA.

The two found they had much in common. Both were Jewish, married and the fathers of baby boys, and were living modestly. Their wives soon became close friends and the two families shared a beach cabana in the summer. As Weill and Carter became more experienced Wall Street hands, their talk frequently turned to the hope of starting their own securities firm.

At first, Weill found the idea overly ambitious. He did have a desire to succeed, but his goals in those days were simple and short-range. He was pleased when his family moved into a two-bedroom apartment in the same building in East Rockaway so that Marc could have his own room. A deep-fryer, which he bought as soon as he had the money, was, for him, a "significant acquisition." His specialty became fried shrimp. He now yearned for a slide projector to display pictures of his family. "My dream then was to be able to afford a Kodak Carousel," he said, remembering those years. "When I bought one, I thought it was fantastic."

He soon got a taste of what it would be like to run his own company when he took a job in 1957 at a small brokerage house for a chance to share in the profits. His timing was off. In a recession year, the market slumped, and he was forced to find work elsewhere. He wound up at Burnham, a Jewish brokerage house run by I. W. ("Tubby") Burnham, the grandson of the original distiller of I. W. Harper bourbon.

When Weill came to Burnham he couldn't afford new clothes.

He wore his old suits, ties, and shirts from his college days, as well as his ROTC raincoat. Former Burnham partner Dan Cowin recalls, "He had such terrible clothes that we were worried he couldn't make a good impression on potential clients. So a few of us got together a few hundred dollars to buy him a couple of suits and some shirts."

Weill's appearance improved, and so did his earnings. When the bull market resumed its climb in 1958, he not only did well for the firm but also made $7,500 trading for his own account. The following year he made $25,000. Six months after their daughter, Jessica, was born, the Weills moved to an attached house in Baldwin, Long Island. They had enough money by then to join the nearby Shelter Rock Tennis Club. No longer was the prospect of starting his own firm so intimidating. He was ready to break out on his own now with Carter if they could find someone else with whom to share the risk.

Carter already had that someone in mind. He invited his old high school friend Roger Berlind to join them. A Princeton English major, Berlind had fancied himself a songwriter, but since none of his tunes sold, he was forced to find more stable employment. He had picked Wall Street. He was interviewed and rejected by some thirty firms before Eastman Dillon hired him as a broker. He agreed to join Carter and Weill only after they also accepted his friend Peter Potoma. (Berlind had already committed himself to forming a partnership with Potoma, with whom he worked at Eastman Dillon.)

The cushion of two extra partners comforted Weill, who wanted to do everything possible to minimize his own risk. His mother was taking an even bigger chance than he was; she had lent him half of the $60,000 required for his share of the partnership. With more than $200,000 raised (only Carter's share hadn't come in part from relatives), they had just enough to buy a seat for $160,000 on the New York Stock Exchange, hire a secretary, and provide the barest of office essentials. Weill held on to $1,000 for emergencies and prayed that the $12,000 salary the partners were going to pay themselves would meet his family's needs. He persuaded Tubby Burnham to rent the newly formed firm temporary office space in his trading room. In May of 1960, Carter, Berlind, Potoma & Weill announced that they were opening their own office at 37 Wall Street.

For all the preparation and expense, Weill was still the same retail broker who slept badly at night before making a presentation to a client the next day. Peter Potoma, a savvy stockbroker, took it on himself to teach Weill the finer points of the business. The son of an immigrant Italian steelworker, Potoma had earned his way into Harvard

Law School, then quit after two years and married a wealthy woman. Like Weill's former associates at Bear Stearns, Potoma wasn't pleased with Weill's appearance, so he persuaded Weill to buy a three-piece suit and gave him a hat and a black umbrella to make him seem older than twenty-seven.

The new Weill look was out of character. But his more prosperous appearance had, at least, some basis in reality. His deepest fear — that of losing money — was partly allayed the first year, when the firm racked up sales of $225,000. The partners had cause for celebration and soon raised their salaries to $18,000. The bull market had helped, as it helped many of the new firms that were springing up in the soaring market of the late fifties and early sixties.

Making the biggest splash was Donaldson, Lufkin & Jenrette (DLJ), which had opened its doors only six months earlier and sold Wall Street on the notion of the "research boutique." Their main claim was that a stock's future could be predicted through securities analysis, a far more glamorous term than the traditional one, "statistics." It was a brilliant sales tool that spread quickly through the financial community, helping other small firms like Weill's attract the attention of institutional investors such as pension funds and insurance companies.

In the winter of 1962, Weill was ready to buy his first home, when word came from the surveillance office of the New York Stock Exchange that Potoma faced suspension for "free riding." Through his wife's and his own personal account, Potoma had been buying stock on its way up without paying for it. That is, he sold the shares before he had paid for them.

The news was a devastating blow for the partnership, both professionally and personally. In a business where everyone's name hung on the door, disciplinary action by the Big Board would not be easily overcome. To make matters worse, the firm's Stock Exchange seat was registered under Potoma's name. Carter had felt that as a non-Jew, Potoma would be more accepted on the Exchange floor. Though the partners had known for some time that Potoma had problems — he drank and disappeared mysteriously for days at a time — they hadn't thought he would go so far as to violate the Big Board's rules. They had to act quickly. Taking over his Stock Exchange seat, they forced Potoma's resignation and dropped his name — months before the Exchange gave him a year's suspension. By the time the announcement hit the Dow Jones news ticker, the firm had become Carter, Berlind & Weill.

Throughout this period, Weill was worried that the taint of

Potoma's transgression would hurt business. There were violations even at the most prominent old-line houses, but their prestige could survive the misdeeds of one man. For a firm such as Weill's, the experience could be far more negative and longer-lasting.

Putting aside his anxiety long enough to sign for a loan, Weill went ahead with the purchase of his new $60,000 colonial home in the middle-class suburban community of Brookville, Long Island. He and his family joined a synagogue in nearby Jericho, where their children went to school. Belonging to a synagogue was important to him. Though the Weills observed only Passover, Rosh Hashanah, Yom Kippur, and Chanukah, he believed in "God and in the moral tenets of religion." Weill and his family moved in on a warm spring day. Soon after, on May 28, 1962, Blue Monday struck.

It was a case of a disaster on top of a calamity. Stocks plummeted 35 points on sales of over 9.3 million shares, a one-day collapse at that time second only to the drop during the Great Crash of 1929. In the days that followed, Weill — who had acquired his wife's enthusiasm for gardening and needed to vent his frustration — found himself spending much of his time when he was at home fiercely altering the landscape by planting pine trees and rose bushes. Joan did her best to be supportive, to the point of joining in the hard physical labor of uprooting and planting. On one occasion they bought so many trees and shrubs from a discount store called Cheap Sam's that they planted well into the night, using the car lights to guide them.

*  *  *

In midsummer the market began to recover and went on a persistent uptrend. Throughout Weill's career the market had experienced brief slumps followed by long rallies. Overall, it had kept climbing in the postwar period. The Dow Jones average hit 450 in 1955, when Weill had first started out, and by 1965 had passed 900.* Trading volume was also up, more than double what it had been a decade before. Brains, as the old Wall Street adage goes, are no substitute for luck, and Weill's firm was very lucky to be in business during the early sixties.

When the two rooms Weill and his partners occupied were

---

* The general measure used throughout the book is the Dow Jones Industrial Average, a composite of thirty blue-chip corporations listed on the New York Stock Exchange — the major American market for stocks and bonds.

crammed to capacity, they moved to larger offices at 60 Broad Street, and in 1967 they moved across the street, taking the entire top floor and half of the one below in a new building at 55 Broad Street. They also had made their first acquisition, the money management firm Bernstein-Macaulay, which at the time managed assets of about $60 million.

That year the Weills bought a larger colonial home, this time on the sound in Great Neck, Long Island, closer to New York City. (The commute from Brookville to Wall Street had proved too time-wasting.) Their new house had plenty of space for a family to roam around in: four bedrooms, a living room, dining room, den, and finished playroom, which Joan Weill decorated in her favorite colors: yellow, red, and black. Many affluent Jewish professionals and their families were attracted to Great Neck because of its fine public schools, recreational facilities, and synagogues. This description applied to the Weills, but they soon found the community too homogeneous. They yearned for greater diversity.

At work, Weill did find diversity — and change. Of the dozens of ambitious young men who had been accepted into the Carter, Berlind & Weill fold in the previous five years, two joined the three founders as members of the governing executive committee.

Arthur Levitt, Jr., a glib, lanky young man, who had come aboard in 1963, was the first to be promoted. The Levitt name was well known. Arthur Levitt, Sr., had been elected comptroller of New York State over and over again. After earning a degree in English from Williams College, young Levitt worked as a critic for the *Berkshire Eagle,* did promotional work for *Time,* and sold tax shelters (in his case, investments in cattle) before heading for Wall Street. After numerous rejections elsewhere, he accepted an offer from Arthur Carter.

Marshall Cogan, a plump, bespectacled Bostonian several years younger than the others, became the fifth member of the executive committee in the midsixties. He was the only one in the group who had always wanted a career on Wall Street, by then a popular alternative to medicine, law, or science for an ambitious young Jewish man. Cogan's academic credentials were impeccable: a bachelor's degree from Harvard and an MBA from its graduate business school. Yet he, too, had initially run into difficulty getting a job on Wall Street, having been rejected by the Our Crowd firms Goldman Sachs and Lehman Brothers. "I was too brash and too fat," he said later.

In this newly formed quintet, Weill's doubts about making it on Wall Street found company. Still, they all tried not to appear vulnerable. Cogan was loud, headstrong, and excitable, the unpredictable element in the group. Levitt, the politician's son, kept his own counsel, so much so that he sometimes seemed aloof and distracted. Berlind was well-mannered, gentle, and passive. Carter, meanwhile, had begun to lead the firm with the self-assured hand of a maestro.

Every week, the group would get together for dinner at Christ Cella, an expensive East Side steak house. On the surface, at least, the conversation revolved around business. But these evenings were closer to an exercise in sibling rivalry. Pressured by Carter, who played the role of the eldest brother, each partner maintained a separate account of his output in the office. Carter's leading question often was, "How much business did you do today?" when it was well known that the one being asked had done the least. Another typical parry began: "If you had any brains, you'd be dangerous."

In this fraternitylike atmosphere, Weill was lampooned as the partnership's proletarian Brooklynite who couldn't make a good impression on the firm's clients; Berlind was ribbed because he had gone to the whitest of "white shoe" colleges and had almost forgotten how to be Jewish; Levitt was derided for coattailing the success of his famous father; and Cogan was put down as a hysterical mass of tics, wild gestures, and loud outbursts. Carter, who typically escaped criticism, orchestrated the high-volume banter. Weill often wished his friend weren't quite so domineering.

Sometimes Weill gave as good as he got at these gatherings. But by the middle of 1968 responding to Carter's all-important question was becoming harder. Unlike the others, Weill, ever the retail broker (that is, one who sells shares to individuals rather than institutions), and Berlind, the thoughtful securities analyst, were not firebreathers. Carter stood out as the firm's budding presence on corporate boards, with four seats, including one at Studebaker. Levitt got the credit for putting together the Bernstein-Macaulay deal and for organizing the firm's syndicate department in the midsixties. And Marshall Cogan, through his connections to the conglomerateurs, was the partners' coming-attraction, Go-Go brokerage star.

Cogan soon made contact with Gulf & Western chief Charles Bluhdorn, who was just building his conglomerate. Bluhdorn conjured up deals, while Cogan traded securities for Gulf & Western and acted as a financial adviser to Bluhdorn. The relationship proved to be a boon for the partners' trading department and created a mergers and acquisitions department where none had existed before.

With these flashy connections, the young firm was winning

the reluctant respect of the financial community in a business where most thirty-one-year-olds like Cogan had rarely been taken seriously. New brokerages like Carter, Berlind & Weill were forcing the Street to accept the youth movement that was sweeping the nation. For the first time, it was all right to be under forty, brash, and Jewish.

\* \* \*

Cogan and Carter had just hooked one of the biggest deals of 1968, which would bear heavily on the turmoil that was going to rock the young house. Insurance companies hardly seemed like the kind of business to excite investors during the Go-Go Years, until a report came out of Carter, Berlind & Weill's research department in 1967 concluding that fire and casualty companies held vast untapped financial resources: the insurers, in many cases, had cash-heavy reserves from paid premiums, which were far in excess of those required by law to cover policy risks. The untried idea of acquiring such companies for their rich assets needed a little push. The budding dealmakers sounded out potential institutional investors and told them if they bought stock in an asset-rich insurance company and it was taken over, as share-holders they most likely would make a substantial profit.

Reliance, a stodgy old Philadelphia insurance company, was selected by Cogan and Carter as their target. Even as they made their pitch to institutional investors to buy Reliance stock, they were on the prowl for a predator. They located Saul Steinberg, a twenty-nine-year-old financial whiz from Brooklyn, who was then running a computer leasing operation, Leasco Data Processing Equipment Company. He agreed to pay them a finder's fee of $750,000 for pointing him toward Reliance. The next step was for Cogan quietly to buy the Reliance stock for Steinberg on the open market, so as not to drive up the price of the stock. To preserve secrecy when referring to the insurer, Steinberg's staff began using the code name Raquel, after Raquel Welch, because, like the actress, the company was big, beautiful, and desirable.

When Steinberg eventually walked away with this financial prize, Carter made up his mind that he was ready to move on to bigger things — either by starting a new company of his own or by restruc-turing Carter, Berlind & Weill. He set in motion events that would lead to the shakeup within the firm and to his firing.

\* \* \*

Weill was so content with the firm's progress and had so in-sulated himself from the rest of Wall Street that he had no idea that anything was wrong. He was stunned when Arthur Levitt, Jr., and

Marshall Cogan told him in confidence that Carter had been making plans to reshape the company to his own design. Carter, apparently tired of the brokerage business, wanted to turn the firm into a merchant bank, providing advice and its own capital to companies in exchange for a share of the ownership. Worse still, in an obvious attempt to advance that aim, he had complained to Levitt that Weill, whose strength was as a stockbroker, and Roger Berlind, the firm's chief securities analyst, weren't pulling their weight. His plan was to cut the profit participation of these two to the humiliatingly low level of perhaps one percent.

When the shock wore off, Weill felt betrayed. He had considered Carter, whom he had known for a dozen years since their earliest days on Wall Street, among his closest friends. He had an inkling that Carter had turned against Berlind, but didn't think Carter would turn on him as well. "We'd been through so much together," Weill recalled. "The Carters were almost like family to Joan and me. And he and I had shared the same dream of building our own brokerage firm." When Levitt pressed the others to unite against Carter, since all of them would be vulnerable if Carter succeeded in reducing any officer's share, Weill was torn. It was hard for him to act quickly. He liked to sift his options. Here was an apparent broadside attack on his own role and standing in the firm, yet all he could think of now was whether he could manage without Carter. Instinctively, he was against change. But he also recognized that they had to do something to block Carter. They prepared to act.

On the morning of September 10, 1968, the firm of Carter, Berlind & Weill held a board meeting. In an atmosphere filled with tension, Carter announced that he wanted the title and authority of chief executive officer, and that he wanted to reshuffle the stock ownership percentages, elevating Cogan and Levitt and reducing Weill and Berlind. Calling for a recess, Levitt, Weill, Cogan, and Berlind huddled together. Weill learned that Carter had actually filed the papers to set up a holding company without the knowledge and consent of all of the officers. That revelation left him devastated.

"I've known about this for some time, but I couldn't tell you before," admitted Levitt. "We've got a guy in there — if we confront him and allow him to stay at the firm — he'll act like a wounded animal who'll come back to kill us. I'm not going to stick around if we let him stay."

"Forget it," said Weill quickly. "He's left us no choice. But let's give him some time, a few months' grace."

Levitt remained adamant. "He has to be out by today." When

the meeting was reconvened, Carter, asked to resign on the spot, refused, saying he wanted to consult an attorney.

Either resign today, the others replied, or we'll fire you.

Carter looked at his colleagues long and hard. "I'll resign," they recall him saying, before he walked out.

Afterward, they and their attorney, Kenneth Bialkin, regrouped at the law offices of Willkie Farr & Gallagher and talked until two o'clock in the morning, ironing out all the details of Carter's departure. Weill left the meeting feeling drained and saddened, more beaten than victorious. "We did what we had to do, but something was lost," he said in retrospect. The next day, the *Wall Street Journal* described Carter's exit as a "friendly" parting.

Weill appeared to be in a state of shock, unable to concentrate on his work. He had a wife and two children to support, all of his assets were in the company, and he still wasn't at all sure that the firm would succeed without Carter. His deep sense of insecurity had led him, in his thirty-five years, to realize the truth of the cliché that the distance between success and failure is a thin line.

*   *   *

One evening, a few days after Carter was ousted, Weill, Levitt, and their wives went out to have a lobster dinner on City Island in the Bronx. (The two couples were very friendly. Though the Weills lived in Great Neck and the Levitts in Manhattan, they often got together, sometimes with their children, and the two families had taken vacations in Florida and Puerto Rico.) Now they tried talking about the food, the weather, anything, but their conversation always came back to the same questions. Was this the end of the firm? Was there any way they could hold it together? Their families depended on its future. Joan Weill joked with Marilyn Levitt, both of whose sons would have their Bar Mitzvahs soon, that they could save money by buying only one pair of dress shoes for the celebrations.

Weill knew that he had to come to a decision. Before they left City Island, he agreed to back Levitt in his resolve to hold the company together. The next person to be won over was Marshall Cogan, who hadn't made up his mind yet whether to join with Carter in a new venture. If he went, the firm would be painfully shorthanded. More to the point, the others needed Cogan, the firm's star commission producer.

Later that evening, at Cogan's East End Avenue apartment, Levitt told Maureen Cogan, "You'll undoubtedly have more money if

Marshall goes with Arthur. But he'll always play second fiddle to him. If he stays with us he'll be part of something where he'll be much more important, where he'll have greater control, and he'll be able to sleep easily at night."

Cogan agreed to stay only if his name replaced Carter's up front, and he got his wish. Levitt's name was added to the roster of partners. The firm was now known as Cogan, Berlind, Weill & Levitt.

Once out of Carter's shadow, Weill would become more assertive. That was the beginning of major changes in his aspirations that would move him to the forefront of the financial world.

# CHAPTER SIX

# The House of Salomon

$F$ all of 1969. The malaise that gripped the nation seemed interminable. The Vietnam War dragged on, sapping the country of confidence in its leadership. Wall Street didn't know what to fear more: the inflation brought on by a guns and butter pumped-up economy or a recession resulting from the government's efforts to control rising prices. Only one thing was certain. The Go-Go Years were over, the market was shaky, having lost nearly 150 points, or some 15 percent, since the spring, and commission volume and underwriting both plummeted. The financial community was stuck with the expensive legacy of the Go-Go Years: the thousands of employees hired, the rash of computers purchased, the spate of new offices opened, and, of course, the millions of disillusioned investors.

The Street was abuzz with rumors about which firms were in the most serious trouble. One that was the subject of heated speculation was the institutional brokerage house of Salomon Brothers & Hutzler. So wild, in fact, were the reports of its losses that the firm felt compelled, for the first time, to release its earnings figures.* The news could not have been more startling. Far from losing money, Salomon had in 1969 produced a record profit of $14.7 million in pretax earnings.

To a large extent, the explanation for its success as well as for the mean-spirited rumors could be traced back to the same source: its lowly origins. Salomon Brothers & Hutzler was the very symbol of a raffish, aggressive outsider, and it had spent much of its fifty-nine-year existence accumulating slights. The firm still bore the stigma of being left out of Our Crowd.

---

* Unlike most other industries, few Wall Street firms were publicly held companies, which are required to report their income. No member firm of the New York Stock Exchange was a publicly held company at the time.

* * *

Salomon Brothers & Hutzler first opened its doors for business in 1910 at 80 Broadway, when three young brothers, Arthur, Herbert, and Percy Salomon, went into partnership with a businessman named Morton Hutzler. By that time, the Salomon brothers had learned the ways of the Street from their father, Ferdinand, in his money brokerage firm, where they had worked since they were teenagers. But they were motivated to strike out on their own, less because of youthful ambition than because of the widening rift with the senior Salomon.

In the 1850s Ferdinand Salomon was a toddler when his parents came to the United States from Alsace, a region with a long German history and tradition, then part of France. His upbringing in a strict, religious household not only set him apart from the Our Crowd leaders, it was also at the heart of his subsequent problems with his sons. As an orthodox Jew, he refused to do business on Saturdays, the Jewish Sabbath, then one of the busiest working days of the week. Staying closed cost him business, but he would not bow to financial pressures, no matter what the consequences, and he insisted that his unreligious sons carry on the tradition.

The strain was made worse for the sons by unpleasant tensions in the Salomon household between their father and their mother, Sophia, an immigrant English Jew who was a skilled concert pianist. Rebellious and unhappy, the young men would sneak off to work on Saturdays. When their father learned of their disobedience, the relationship between them deteriorated rapidly. The final break came when Ferdinand and Sophia divorced and Ferdinand remarried. The sons sided with their mother and went into business on their own.

Arthur, a tough, humorless young man with a bushy mustache, was the eldest and the unquestioned leader. His contact with the Hutzler family, owners of a large department store in Baltimore, led to a meeting with Morton Hutzler, who had a seat on the New York Stock Exchange, and to the formation of the partnership, with each brother and Hutzler chipping in $1,250 apiece.* (A fourth Salomon brother, Leo, the second-oldest, who had quit Ferdinand's firm several years

---

* The firm advertised itself as the Discount House of Salomon Brothers and Hutzler. Hutzler never took an active role. In 1929, he became a limited partner. He died in 1945. His name was dropped in 1970, when the firm became Salomon Brothers.

earlier to start an insurance company that exists to this day, helped out by lending his brothers the money to pay the first three months' office rent.)

The Hutzler connection proved largely window dressing. Little of the business the new firm conducted had to do with stocks. In the beginning, the sons competed with their father in the money brokerage business and also traded bonds. Following the nation's entry into World War I in 1917, they settled on the specialty that would be their primary source of income over the next half-century: trading U.S. government securities. It was a safe, dependable business. Their customers, mostly banks and insurance companies, were reliable and prosperous. No securities offered lower risks than did government bonds.

In 1922, the firm moved to the second and third floors at 60 Wall Street, where it would spend nearly fifty years. To reach the offices, one either climbed the marble staircase or rode up in the creaky elevator. On the second floor the lowly clerks and messengers worked in a crowded "cage." Here, securities were sorted and stored for delivery, and bookkeepers slaved over their ledgers. From time to time, Arthur, impeccably dressed in a white starched collar, silk tie, and double-breasted suit, paraded through with an entourage in tow.

But the real action took place on the third floor inside "the Room," as the trading area was dubbed. It was the size of a basketball court, with desks positioned in rows just inches apart. On one wall a ticker tape display moved along steadily when the market volume was heavy. During the trading day, the Room was a cacophony of commotion. The brown linoleum floor reflected an unhealthy sheen. Harried traders spat frequently — chewing tobacco was popular then — and under pressure, often missed the spittoons.

Outside the trading area were a dining room and offices for the partners. The three brothers shared a corner room. Each had a clearly defined role: Arthur concentrated on administration; Percy, the next in seniority, handled sales; and Herbert, the youngest, traded securities. The arrangement seemed destined for a long, bright future until Arthur went into the hospital for what today would be considered a routine gall bladder operation. In July 1928, he died at age forty-eight from complications sustained during surgery.

With Arthur gone, the leadership passed on to Herbert, though he was younger than Percy. Percy, a dapper little man, wasn't seriously interested in the business and suffered a variety of minor ailments (which some people thought were imagined) that kept him out of the office much of the time. By contrast, Herbert was a keen trader, bright and knowledgeable with a gambler's instinct.

His authority was offset by the presence of other partners with growing influence, most importantly, Rudolph Smutny and the highly popular Benjamin Levy, the firm's first employee. Herbert also never earned the respect Arthur had had, partly because of his rather cruel sense of humor. He delighted in practical jokes and once dragged a dead rat tied to a string past the desks of unsuspecting secretaries. Occasionally, he telephoned young traders with phony bond orders.

Herbert's shrewdness, combined with his juvenile black humor, was to set the character of the firm for all time. It was a place where only the strongest survived and the ethos was every man for himself. The squabbling, the internal competition, the buccaneering spirit — all became part of the Salomon culture. Some notable events in the thirties helped cast its identity in stone.

Salomon Brothers captured the attention of all Wall Street in 1935 by a daring move into underwriting, only to lose its foothold almost immediately. Angered by a slew of New Deal regulations, the Wall Street investment banking community had staged a protest by agreeing not to underwrite any new corporate issues. Salomon Brothers quickly invaded the bankers' playground. It brought out a bond issue from Swift, the Chicago-based meatpacker, using the fresh and very profitable approach to selling the new securities called the "agency" method. Instead of underwriting or purchasing and then reselling the issue, Salomon acted only as the meatpacker's sales agent and sold the securities to the institutional investors for Swift. Although it earned a much lower commission on the transaction than it would have from a normal underwriting, Salomon Brothers didn't have to share the income with a syndicate.

The coup broke the back of the so-called underwriters' strike. But the members of the banking Establishment viewed the Swift deal as a threat to their customary way of doing business, and brought Salomon Brothers before the National Association of Securities Dealers, the industry policy body, on charges of unfair trade practices. The trumped-up charges were soon dropped, when Salomon Brothers agreed under pressure to give up the agency method. By then, the Brahmins had picked up where they had left off before the boycott, and Salomon became just another anonymous Wall Street house fighting for scraps from the syndicate table. A grateful Swift virtually remained for decades Salomon's only prestigious corporate investment banking account.

There the episode might have rested if the Establishment had at least slowly relinquished its monopoly. But it did not. The government's antitrust suit, brought against the seventeen investment banking firms in 1947, stirred up all the bitter memories when the prosecution presented Salomon Brothers' experience with the syndicate hierarchy as evidence of a conspiracy among the banking powerhouses.* Salomon learned to live with and in some ways nurtured its image as a trouble-maker.

*  *  *

Salomon Brothers knew the sting of anti-Semitism even though throughout much of its history it boasted a mix of ethnic backgrounds — with a strong Irish representation. To compound its insecurity, while many of the partners were college graduates — several had Ivy League degrees — none of the Salomon brothers or such key partners as Benjamin Levy and Rudolph Smutny had gone beyond high school.

Salomon's low status and poor self-image worsened in the disarray that followed the death in 1951 of Herbert Salomon at the height of the antitrust suit. Each department — government bonds, syndicate, sales — more or less ran itself. Percy was still around, but he had virtually withdrawn from the activities of the firm to tend his various ailments. Arthur's marriage had produced no children, and Herbert had sired two daughters. Percy's older son, Robert, had been given his independence when Percy bought him a seat on the New York Stock Exchange. But Percy did have one son, William R. ("Billy") Salomon, in the firm. For the family, Billy was a beacon of hope of Salomon succession: he was the only Salomon left in the business.

Billy, as he was called by everyone from Percy on down to the shoeshine boy, was then simply another partner in the small brokerage firm founded by his father and his uncles. He had little in common with them other than his name and his lack of a college education. He had come to the firm in 1933 fresh out of the King School, a small Connecticut prep school. He had no interest in college, only in marrying his teenage sweetheart Virginia, a petite brunette. He was eighteen, and his father had told him, "If you want to settle down, you'd better earn yourself a few dollars." Since he was a Salomon, the family firm hired him despite his lack of experience and put him to work as a runner.

---

* The choice of seventeen defendants was ludicrous. Wall Street was actually dominated by eight houses. Had it been twenty-five, Salomon undoubtedly would have gotten the same free boost to its image as the other nine non-dominant defendants did.

Eleven years later, in 1944, he was made a partner, a relatively quick promotion for one so young on Wall Street in the forties. Of course, the family name was an important plus. Like his father, Billy wasn't overly ambitious, a serious problem if he was ever going to advance, let alone be a contender for the firm's leadership. At the time of his uncle Herbert's death, he was thirty-seven, still an indifferent salesman who preferred playing golf to selling bonds to institutional clients. And when he did make an appearance in the office, it wasn't to study the financial minutiae and customer needs that were the lifelines of any trading concern. Partners called him "the floor walker" because of his natty clothes, the carnation in his lapel, and his penchant for meandering around the trading floor to pass the time with whomever he could engage in conversation.

\* \* \*

With no one in the Salomon family strong enough to stop him, Rudolph Smutny began assuming more and more power, and as the market came out of a brief tailspin in 1953, he took control, though a number of partners didn't want him at the helm. Their concerns were intensified by the direction in which he was taking the firm.

Smutny evidently knew that Wall Street was changing in response to the postwar economic expansion and was determined to lead Salomon Brothers into the new era and into a variety of businesses. Stocks in particular interested him, despite how risky they were compared to the safety of trading government bonds.

Sometimes he made investments without consulting his partners. Early one morning, he confided to a young Salomon trader his enthusiastic purchase of a large stake in a small company, explaining that it had developed an entirely new way of photocopying pages. The company was called Haloid. "You wait and see," he said. "Everybody is going to be buying their product."

He had purchased a piece of the American dream and had only to hold on to the Salomon shares of Haloid a few more years to realize it. In 1960, Haloid became Xerox and, soon after, the darling of investors everywhere. But Smutny's Salomon Brothers would not be among them.

Smutny's stock purchases rankled the partners. For all his boldness, he had not done much to improve the firm's standing on Wall Street. In a market that turned sluggish in February of 1956, his expansion plans were not working out as he had promised.

A cocky, balding, short man with a mean, narrow face, he was rough, loud, and arrogant. He would summon a partner to his office and then ignore him while he conversed with someone else on the phone. More and more, the partners wanted to dump him, as much for his despotic rule as for the risks he was taking with the firm's capital. However, in the forty years he had been with Salomon Brothers, since his discharge from the Navy following World War I, he had accumulated a large stake in the firm and had also won the support of another powerful partner, Ned Holsten. Any group trying to oust Smutny would be taking a sizable risk.

Jonas Ottens and Ted Von Glahn, two strong senior partners, led the uprising against Smutny. Yet were it not for Billy Salomon, the revolt might never have succeeded. Billy had what no one else could offer: the right name. He understood that as well as anyone. The old Jewish firm had started at the wrong time, in the wrong business, and seemed locked in an eternal struggle to win the respect of Our Crowd. The struggle had lost none of its intensity now that it was neither a family firm nor, in terms of its leadership, even a Jewish one. Those in power — Smutny and Holsten — and those leading the fight against them — Ottens and Von Glahn — were not Jewish.*

Once Billy Salomon committed himself, he joined the conspirators with a determination that surprised everyone. Though the youngest among them, he was no longer acting like a dilettante, and it showed in his more mature appearance and assured manner. The modest impression he had made within the firm — up until then — and his seemingly easygoing manner had worked in his favor. In a house known for its tough, independent partners and warring factions, no one had any serious reason to dislike him. That he had more guts than experience hardly seemed to matter. At forty-three, he had an aura of success. His face was the kind that belonged on a gold coin, with its granite jaw, aquiline nose, sparkling bright eyes, and thick wavy hair. When he smiled, as he often did, he radiated charm. His voice was rich and strong, and he carried himself with a self-confidence that bordered on conceit. It was as though he expected to come out ahead — no matter how great the odds.

By the start of 1957, the dissident group felt they would have to move decisively and swiftly. In April, when Smutny was out of

---

* Holsten and Ottens were born Jewish but had converted to the religions of their wives, becoming Episcopalian and Catholic, respectively.

town, the partners held a general meeting in their dining room, one of the few spaces large enough to accommodate everyone. In an emotional and hotly debated session they voted Smutny out. Given the opportunity to resign, he chose to go quietly rather than be fired.

In May, the new leadership took over. Because of the losses incurred in the last year of Smutny's reign and the capital he had taken out of the partnership, Billy Salomon made his first important executive decision. In 1958 he pushed through rules making it exceedingly difficult for the partners to withdraw their capital while they were still members of the firm. Exceptions were made for purchasing homes, paying medical expenses, or for charitable contributions. Furthermore, after a partner retired or died, the firm could take up to five years to pay out the money.

It was an unusual move for a time when, at the end of every fiscal year, the most successful Wall Street houses doled out partnership profit percentages like bounty. The rules were designed for the long term, to provide Salomon Brothers with financial stability, and began paying dividends almost immediately.

The recession of 1957–58 was quickly forgotten as another herd of bulls stampeded through Wall Street. The number of U.S. shareholders grew by some half-million a year. Playing the market became a national pastime through investment clubs, which pooled the interests of every kind of nonprofessional investor, from dentists to firemen to teachers. In this partylike atmosphere, Salomon's capital rebounded from a low of $7 million in Smutny's last year to $10 million in 1959.

Still marked as an outsider, Billy Salomon was sensitive about the firm's lower-class business image. Intent on reversing the Establishment's view of Salomon Brothers as "tradespeople," he set out to build a house that, by the strength of its performance, could compete with any other in the securities business.

To the Wall Street cognoscenti and to many of his own partners, Billy Salomon hardly seemed like the right man for the job — now that the revolt was over and the hard work was at hand. He was neither dynamic nor, many said, the intellectual equal of the heads of most other Wall Street houses. Whatever the merits of that assessment, he did possess a number of the very qualities needed to make his firm a success. He was, instinctively, a strong manager with an unshakable vision; he was determined to push the firm to the apex of the industry.

Not long after he had in effect become managing partner of Salomon Brothers, he hired the firm's first publicity man to pump up Salomon Brothers' image as a "financial supermarket" capable of meeting all the needs of investors, and he paid a visit to Harold Stuart, the head of Halsey Stuart. The octogenarian had seen almost everything in something like seven decades on Wall Street. Stuart's firm was one of the leading underwriters of such securities as public utilities, which were subject by law to competitive bids. Competitive underwriting provided a means to establish a presence in investment banking, and Salomon was eager to have his house known as more than a government bond trading house.

To that end, his hat literally in his hand — as was the custom of the day — he approached Stuart and proposed that Halsey Stuart share its lead manager's role in its underwriting syndicates with Salomon Brothers. The meeting was brief. When Salomon departed, Stuart, who had spent most of his days of late nodding off, came out of his office and gathered around him whoever was in the vicinity. Smiling broadly, he told everyone why Salomon had come and, with a satisfied chuckle, told them he had said no.

Salomon's disappointment turned into a stroke of good luck. About the time of his meeting with Stuart, Merrill Lynch was starting a syndicate that would unite several adversaries fighting to grab a major chunk of the competitive issues monopolized by Halsey Stuart and its arch rival, First Boston. Salomon Brothers was asked to join, as were Lehman and Blyth. The quartet would be labeled the Fearsome Foursome by the financial press, and Salomon Brothers was taking a giant step toward fulfilling Billy Salomon's dream.

# CHAPTER SEVEN

# Moving Up

T he job of strengthening Salomon's position in underwriting fell to thirty-three-year-old John Gutfreund, whose booming presence and dynamic ability to take control would shortly be felt throughout the house of Salomon — and beyond it. He was perfectly adapted for the Salomon atmosphere — tough, combative, and unafraid to stare down a challenge. He would say about himself, "I wanted us to be the best. I was a fierce competitor in my way."

He had recently been elevated to the post of Salomon's syndicate chief, a post that was central in the firm at that time. When an offering came up, Gutfreund and his team had to bound into place immediately so that they could move stocks or bonds quickly. To do that, he had to juggle a lot of different responsibilities at once: alert his sales force and persuade institutional customers to buy the securities; oversee the traders; and decide whether to hold on to part of the shares for the firm — while keeping track of prices, volume, and the bottom line. A partner traditionally held that job, and the following year, in 1963, Gutfreund was made one, when Billy Salomon was officially installed as the firm's managing, or senior, partner. The two events were a mere coincidence, according to Salomon.

The opportunity to compete on an equal footing with Halsey Stuart, and the high stakes and rewards involved, fueled Gutfreund's ambition. With Gutfreund as syndicate chief, Salomon Brothers began making a name on the Street. Now, when it joined a Halsey Stuart syndicate, it wouldn't come with hat in hand, but as a syndicate manager in its own right.

Gutfreund sauntered in late to one Halsey Stuart meeting in the midsixties and took his place alongside William Hager (head of Halsey Stuart's New York office and its syndicate chief), who was barking out orders with impunity to a roomful of investment bankers. For a few minutes Gutfreund sat quietly, puffing on his huge cigar, and then bellowed, "Hager, you're full of shit."

The tension in the room was almost palpable. All eyes shifted to Gutfreund, who clamped down hard on his cigar. The message was clear; Gutfreund was certainly a man to watch.

\* \* \*

As a boy, John Gutfreund seemed to have no unfulfilled needs or longings. There were no major obstacles to overcome, no dark patches in his family life. His father was a model of upward mobility. Manuel ("Buddy") Gutfreund was in the meat business when he married Mary Halle, a member of a socially prominent Jewish family from Cleveland. Over the years, he built up his trade into a successful wholesale meat and trucking business. The family moved from an apartment in Manhattan, where John Gutfreund was born, to a house on Long Island, and later, in 1940, when he was eleven, settled into a comfortable stucco home in affluent Scarsdale, in Westchester County, New York.

The family leaped several rungs up the social ladder when Gutfreund's parents joined the most prestigious Jewish country club in the nation, the Century Country Club in Purchase, New York, a cornerstone of Our Crowd's culture. Founded in 1898, Century offered a rambling stone clubhouse, manicured lawns, gracious dining, fine golf, swimming, and tennis facilities.

By the 1940s, the club had lost some of its exclusivity because many of the scions of the reigning families had joined the gentile landed gentry known as New York Society. By then a few non-Our Crowd Jews were being cautiously admitted to Century. Still, Century maintained its standards. The social standing of a nominee — and how well liked and known he was to the members — remained the most important qualifications for admission. Manuel Gutfreund slipped in only because of the prominence of his wife's family.

"When the Gutfreunds were admitted," recalls one club member, "it created a big to-do. Some members were furious; they felt Buddy Gutfreund wasn't classy enough for Century."

The Gutfreunds were even more ambitious for their son. They encouraged his friendship with a classmate, Bobby Bernhard, whose family was Our Crowd on both sides (his mother being a Lehman). Gutfreund did his part at Scarsdale High School by getting good grades, participating in the right extracurricular activities, and making honor society. He was an excellent student: bright, ambitious, and competitive. Yet he was not so accomplished that he didn't need a little something extra to push him into the upper reaches of a society his parents so obviously coveted. And so he transferred to Lawrenceville, an exclusive prep school in New Jersey, which sent many of its students to the Ivy League. The Gutfreunds' aim — which their son shared — was the top: admission to Harvard, grandfather Halle's alma mater.

Young John did so well at Lawrenceville that the school reportedly advised him to apply only to Harvard. However, he was rejected. He seemed devastated and had to scramble around for a college that would accept him. He never openly said so, but his failure to get into Harvard seemed to intensify his feelings of resentment against certain Our Crowd families. "Some of them snubbed him when he was growing up," recalled an old friend. "They didn't appreciate his taking out their daughters. John acted as if he had to show the Lehmans and Loebs that he was going to be as good as they were."

He withdrew from his parents: their goals for him were no longer his goals. "My parents and I lost intimacy," he said stiffly to a reporter years later.

He settled for the artsy Oberlin College in Ohio, which was also known for its liberal tradition. There he earned a bachelor's degree in English literature, won a letter in soccer, and worked as the business manager for a musical comedy group called the Mummers Guild. His ambition was to teach English literature at the college level. But he didn't pursue that plan after graduation. He entered the Army and was sent to South Korea while the war was being fought there, serving as a private in the military police. After his discharge, he returned home with no clear idea of what he was going to do with his life. He was, in his own words, "a typical, ambivalent, young Jewish man." He didn't remain adrift for long. Opportunity, in the guise of Billy Salomon, came to him and changed his life forever.

As it happened, Salomon had known Gutfreund for years through Gutfreund's father, with whom he had played golf at Century. When Billy Salomon asked Gutfreund's mother what kind of work her ex-GI son was planning to do, she told him that she had no idea, and when he asked, "Do you think he would be interested in Wall Street?" she replied, "That's the last thing he would be interested in."

Winning over a recalcitrant young man like Gutfreund didn't seem much of a challenge. Salomon pressed ahead by inviting Gutfreund to lunch in the partners' dining room and stressed the opportunities that awaited a bright fellow. Gutfreund wasn't entirely persuaded. Salomon's offer of $42 a week as a clerk hardly sounded promising, but with the same noncommittal attitude with which he had seemed to make most decisions in his young life, he agreed to try the job for a few months. That was in 1953.

The timing worked in his favor. The market began one of its strongest surges. In the fast-paced Salomon environment, Gutfreund quickly exhibited an icy concentration that made him unlike anyone else in the trading room, where emotions ran high. Even in his mid-twenties he displayed the somber, steadfast, and distant manner that made him so unflappable and that would work to his advantage as he moved from clerk to higher clerk to trader in the municipal bond department to number-two man in that department to head of the syndicate department.

Success and habit soon began to make Gutfreund a willing prisoner of Wall Street. He anchored second base on the Salomon Brothers softball team and became a well-known figure in the trading world. In 1958, he married Joyce Low, an intelligent, plain-mannered young woman who devoted herself to liberal social and political causes. Like his father before him, Gutfreund made a good match. Joyce Low was the daughter of Theodore Low, a senior partner at Bear Stearns. The newlyweds moved into a two-bedroom apartment on the Upper East Side, and a year later, the first of three sons was born.

In many ways, Gutfreund had become a model employee, the kind who would make the new guidelines — such as locking up the partners' capital — work. Billy Salomon admired Gutfreund's modest way of life. His own attempts at setting an example for his employees were at best an uneasy compromise. The two-bedroom Park Avenue apartment in which he lived with his wife, Virginia, and their two children wasn't luxurious by Wall Street standards, but Virginia bought expensive clothes and entertained lavishly. Salomon discounted these extravagances, maintaining that they were good for business. If anything, he wished that Gutfreund would show some interest in business entertaining that was part of the ritual of wooing clients.

After he was made a partner in 1963, though he was only thirty-four, Gutfreund became a force to be reckoned with. His knowledge of the firm's affairs was vast. Through his own efforts as head of the syndicate department — with its great contacts among institutional investors — he was transforming Salomon into one of the Street's leading underwriters, and the Establishment began to take notice but still didn't welcome the firm into the fold. It remained, in the eyes of the Street, a rough-riding securities dealer, neither as big as Merrill Lynch nor as respected as Goldman Sachs. Gutfreund seemed determined to change all that.

In the next few years, the Gutfreund-run syndicate carried Salomon Brothers to first place in competitive offerings and fifth place overall among underwriting managers, up from fourteenth the year he took over the syndicate. (At the end of the decade the Fearsome Four-some persuaded First Boston to join the group instead of competing with it.)

By now, despite how junior Gutfreund was among the firm's partners, a number of them saw him as Billy Salomon's heir apparent. He was already putting his personal stamp on everything. New traders got to know him immediately because he did much of the hiring. In the same spirit in which he bid for securities, he offered prospective candidates salaries among the lowest on the Street. One bright young candidate was offered $6,500, well below what he had been promised by Goldman Sachs. Clearly uncomfortable, he said he would like to work for Salomon Brothers but needed $2,500 more.

"You've got it," Gutfreund responded, rising from the table, the interview evidently over. "We'll lend it to you."

Before the young man could reply, Gutfreund had left the room. The future trader realized that he had just agreed to work for Salomon Brothers, but on Gutfreund's terms.

At the end of 1966, Gutfreund joined the Salomon executive committee. He represented the first new blood on the committee since the revolt against Smutny a decade earlier. But he didn't have time to enjoy his new status; he was too busy.

John Gutfreund had become the trader's trader. Part analyst, part manager, part actor, part gambler, he possessed both the mannerisms and judgment of a much older man, a man long accustomed to power. He was there to do business and nothing else mattered. And he looked the part: sparse graying hair, heavy eyebrows, plain black eyeglasses, a tight-lipped and unsmiling mouth — the effect was a perpetual scowl that created deep creases of flesh, like jowls, along the sides of his mouth. He wore conservative dark suits bought off the rack at Brooks Brothers, and he wore them until the pants turned shiny.

His methods were his own — not standard executive issue — and were designed to let people know that they had someone to answer to. And he was always there to enforce them. Gutfreund arrived at Salomon's 60 Wall Street headquarters for breakfast at 7:30 along with the other early arrivals, and he remained straight through the closing bell at 3:30 and often into the evening for meetings. He gave his traders freedom to maneuver, and encouraged them to take risks. He eased their burdens with fatherly strength and provided keen insights into their problems. Traders sought him out for advice even about marital difficulties. That was the good cop in him. But the bad one was never far away.

He managed people through a combination of fear and respect.

He was capable of launching savage attacks, prickly with obscenities, cruel wit, or sarcasm, against almost anyone when his volatile temper was unleashed. Often they came like a single jolt of lightning.

"Get off your ass," he would bellow at a trader or salesman who was not moving stocks or bonds as fast as Gutfreund wanted him to. He was the prototype pit boss — hard-bitten and shrewd — who did whatever it took to get the job done amid the din of the trading room. In a sense, he was the actor turned director. It was a game he had played for years, one in which his talents were honed with experience.

With Gutfreund steering the traders, Salomon Brothers won one scarring battle after another. He took advantage of the firm's underdog image and urged the traders on to outdo everyone. "I've tried to use our inferiority complex," was the way he saw it.

Although the two men weren't close professionally or personally, Gutfreund and Salomon enjoyed a symbiotic relationship. If Gutfreund was driven to gain complete control and power, the zealous Salomon was a man with a mission. What he dreamed of doing for Salomon Brothers was what Sidney Weinberg and Gus Levy had done for Goldman Sachs years earlier. He wanted to build a powerful investment bank that would provide a full range of financial services.

By this time, he was growing more and more dependent on Gutfreund. As the de facto number-two man, Gutfreund managed the firm's day-to-day business, with all departments reporting to him. In a profound sense, Salomon didn't understand the business. John Gutfreund did. Several bright, able senior partners — who now were all over fifty — had too much respect for the Club to bang heads with it. Increasingly, Gutfreund was the only one capable of realizing Billy Salomon's dream.

* * *

By the late sixties, Salomon Brothers was expanding rapidly, hiring new people. College graduates, even MBAs, were no longer a rarity on the trading floor. Yet the lack of a formal education didn't stand in the way. Anyone who thrived in a competitive culture had an excellent chance of winning Gutfreund's approval. One of them was Jay Perry, an English major and college graduate who had bounced around Wall Street and at Salomon before landing in the trading department in 1968. He would change a department that had failed to make an impact in the block trading market to one that was responsive to the trading revolution ignited by the spark of a small group of mutual fund operators in the Go-Go Years who stamped that era, namely:

Howard Stein, who joined Dreyfus in 1956 when it was a relatively small brokerage and investment management business and helped turn it into a company boasting $3 billion in assets a decade later;

Gerald Tsai, Jr., a native of Shanghai, who worked his trading magic first for the Boston-based Fidelity Capital Fund in the early sixties with such stocks as Xerox, Polaroid, Chrysler, and Litton, then launched his own mutual fund, the Manhattan Fund, in 1966, with a record start-up of $270 million; and

Bernie Cornfeld, who built a mutual fund empire, Investors Overseas Services, with investors from one hundred countries and who, by living on the edge of legality and manipulating his company's $2.5 billion in assets, came to symbolize all the greed and excess of the Go-Go Years.

By 1968, block trading was becoming a big business, with larger and larger sizes and numbers of blocks continually being moved on the New York Stock Exchange. The mutual fund operators — trading everything from blue-chip stocks to speculative warrants — led a powerful wave of new, bigger, and rangier institutional investors. These institutional investors, in turn, put tremendous pressure on firms like Salomon to deliver. Moving huge blocks sometimes resulted in financial firestorms for the big traders. The only way they could keep the price of the stock at market levels was to buy large chunks of the blocks themselves.

The game required steely nerves and sure instincts, with dozens of decisions involving millions of dollars needed in a matter of minutes. Jay Perry, who earned such nicknames around Salomon Brothers as Prince of Peace and Prince of Darkness, had it all.

Uncharacteristically for a Jewish newcomer, Perry was from a small town in Arkansas. An intense man with hooded eyes and flaring nostrils, he was determined to succeed and he did — in a big way, but at an extremely high cost to his career and health. Smoking three Lucky Strikes at a time — one each in his mouth, his hand, and ash tray — and drinking up to thirty cups of coffee a day, he gave Salomon another push into the future. Within months after he had taken over the trading department, Salomon became the dominant force in the field, supplanting Goldman Sachs and Bear Stearns.

At 9:30 one summer morning in 1968, Perry got a call from Tsai, who told him, "I stayed awake all last night trying to decide who I should call this morning. I thought of calling Gus Levy and Cy Lewis." But in the end, Tsai wanted Perry to take on a block of 374,000 shares of Control Data.

Hanging up, Perry turned to Billy Salomon, who sat six feet

away, and told him what Tsai had just said. Most of Perry's trades were completed before anyone knew about them, but on ones this size he consulted with Salomon. Salomon summoned Gutfreund, who was also close by. The three men then went into a small conference room to weigh their options. In a rare display of caution, Billy Salomon admitted that he was fearful of doing the trade: "We'd have a lot of capital at stake. This could be more than we can handle."

Gutfreund spoke forcefully in its favor. His main reason was, "Let's get our name on the tape."

The opportunity to be listed on Wall Street's marquee next to a record trade, whatever the risks, proved a persuasive argument. Within minutes, Salomon told Perry to go to work.

Plugging into the 120-key telephone console that with the flick of a few buttons connected him directly to major institutional investors across the country, he began hawking the stock, now pushing, cajoling, and screaming at traders and salesmen all over the trading room to find buyers, while Salomon and Gutfreund provided advice and egged him on. When he couldn't sell Control Data shares outright, he swapped shares for some other stock of equal value.

In forty-five minutes, it was all over. Salomon Brothers had traded stock worth $52 million dollars. Once again, Gutfreund's judgment had proved correct. Once again, the Street took notice. It was the largest block in the history of trading at that time.

\*     \*     \*

Salomon Brothers flaunted its new-found block trading clout with all the cockiness of the newly arrived, but it was still hampered by its shortcomings. If his father had had to woo the Establishment, to John Gutfreund it might have seemed that the polished world of the investment banker was suspect, as were the host of new products like equity (stock) research that were inundating Wall Street. It was clear by the late sixties that Salomon had to keep pace and expand into new areas like investment banking and equity research.

Except for the young Bronx-born J. Ira Harris (né Horowitz), who built a mergers and acquisitions outpost for Salomon Brothers in Chicago, the firm wasn't doing well in M&A work. But Gutfreund made no effort to push the company into building an effective M&A operation in New York. The Room — the name always used for the Salomon trading room — was his working life. By 1969, for the first time, Gutfreund had serious competition for control of it and the future leadership of the firm.

* * *

William E. Simon — the most feared man at Salomon Brothers — was Gutfreund's rival. The future Secretary of the Treasury was a powerhouse from the day he arrived, in 1964, in the municipal bond department, where Gutfreund had started eleven years earlier. Before the year was over, Simon was elevated to partner. Five years later, the forty-one-year-old New Jersey native of French-Catholic descent joined Gutfreund on the executive committee as head of all government bond trading. His ability to attract new business dazzled even his detractors. Simon would set his mind on something and get it done, or more than likely, would have his subordinates do it for him. He led his troops through intimidation and astute delegation of authority. And when the job was completed, Simon usually took all the credit.

He had a distinctive edge over Gutfreund in one area, as far as Salomon was concerned. Simon enjoyed making important contacts and championed public-spirited causes. He counted among his friends many powerful people in Washington and on Wall Street and was heavily involved with the Boy Scouts and Republican politics. To the partners, Simon was the only threat to Gutfreund for the top spot in the firm. Billy Salomon, who loved encouraging competition, made no secret of the fact that one of them would succeed him as managing partner some day.

Rarely, though, was the rivalry between Gutfreund and Simon played out at close range. They remained wary and distant — respectful of each other's strengths. Both were mercurial men whose explosive tempers often flared up at anyone who happened to be nearby. One morning in 1968, Gutfreund, in a rage, hurled a trash can at Jonathan Bigel, whose father, a leader in the sanitation workers union, was then in the midst of conducting a garbage strike in New York City. "Here," Gutfreund shouted, "You clean it up. It's your father's strike."

But even Gutfreund's temper paled before Simon's legendary fury. No one else in the firm yelled so loudly or bellowed profanities so venomously. Partners and employees also learned to dread his insulting sense of humor and his pranks. Everyone at Salomon had his own Simon story.

From time to time, Simon's and Gutfreund's whims would work in tandem, as they did in the case of Robert Dall, a raw recruit who worked for Simon. Simon told Dall one day that he wanted to begin his own syndicate and dispatched Dall to learn the business from Gutfreund. A conscientious employee, he hurried over to Gutfreund's syndicate department. "Get the fuck outa here," Gutfreund snarled when Dall told him why he was there.

Dall then scurried back to Simon's side of the room and attempted to hide, but when his superior spotted him, he shouted, "Get the fuck back up there."

After a week of shuttling back and forth, it finally dawned on poor Dall that he was the butt of a practical joke.

What led Bigel, Dall, and all the others to take such abuse was the potential of partnership at Salomon Brothers, which would make them instant millionaires even if the capital rules virtually made it impossible for them to take their money out while they were at the firm. The competitively charged atmosphere and the concern over what percentage of the profits each partner would get kept everyone chained, scrapping to increase his share.

Gutfreund never let his edge in seniority over Simon be taken for granted. Occasionally, he seemed to exercise it deliberately. He would casually walk into meetings that Simon was holding. Simon couldn't do the reverse to Gutfreund. Only Gutfreund could claim that all the departments at Salomon Brothers were his territory.

* * *

Such clashes were part of the way of life at Salomon. A trader overcame obstacles, one by one, on a minute-by-minute basis. Little long-range planning was practiced, and when it was, the firm's heavy reliance on trading muscle could be counterproductive. No institutional clients wanted to anger Salomon; Salomon could sell their securities faster than any other house. At the same time, the institutions were reluctant to give their other business to a firm so wedded to trading. It was Catch-22.

Still, as the seventies opened out, Salomon Brothers was really moving, in every sense of the word. After nearly fifty years in the same dusty, noisy, dingy trading room, Billy Salomon had invested $8 million of the firm's precious capital to move to larger headquarters, high up in a huge new skyscraper, overlooking New York harbor. In July of 1970, it took possession of another Room — this one one hundred feet long and two stories high, with double-height windows — twice the size of the old trading area. It was loaded with state-of-the-art computers and a massive electronic price quote board.

Gutfreund wargamed with his troops at one end of the vast Room, while Simon and his troops were stationed at the opposite end. There was no escaping the competition and ambition that drove these two men. But few objected. They were all part of the unfolding success story that was Salomon Brothers.

The first day at the new headquarters, a sentimental Billy Salomon gathered several people around him on the trading floor and gazed out the window at the Statue of Liberty. "Remember where you came from," he said. It had been a long journey. But the window that looked back at the past also spanned out toward the future. That was the direction that beckoned Gutfreund.

# CHAPTER EIGHT

# Enormous Changes

The former and future leaders of Wall Street were passing one another in opposite directions in the last few years of the sixties. That pattern, set in motion in the postwar years, accelerated. It defined who was who on Wall Street and who would have the power for the next two decades.

The death of Sidney Weinberg, in July 1969 at the age of seventy-seven, was in many ways the symbol of the end of an epoch. He had been with Goldman Sachs for sixty-two of its one hundred years, the last thirty-nine as its senior partner. In that time Weinberg had transformed a troubled Our Crowd investment banking house; he had turned it into a highly professional and profitable firm on sheer energy, vision, intelligence, and skill, and a talent for being liked and accepted in business, if not socially, by the "right" people. At his memorial service the leaders of the financial community turned out to pay their last respects to the little man from Brooklyn who was known as "Mr. Wall Street." Among those at the ceremony held at Temple Emanu-El was Henry Ford II, who had cut short a vacation in the Greek islands to be there. Vigorous almost to the end, Weinberg, a widower, had married the year before and left a widow thirty years his junior.

He was the great crossover figure, the Jew without the right credentials or education who had risen to the top echelons of Wall Street. The venerable house he left behind would fare well under the leadership of his chosen successor, the astute Gus Levy, who straddled the past and the future and was ready to take huge financial risks and compete in any market.

Other houses with gilt-edged Our Crowd names didn't do as well in the transition period that sealed the end of established ways of doing business.

Few were willing to admit it, but after 102 years as one of Wall

Street's great banking houses, Kuhn Loeb was pervaded by decay. Fourth-generation John Schiff, aged sixty-four in 1969, who shared control with his seventy-one-year-old cousin, Frederick Warburg, kept the firm deeply rooted in the past. Although the partners were all wealthy men, they had seen the power of Kuhn Loeb fade, as it fell to eleventh place in the pecking order of underwriters by 1967. Schiff had withdrawn from daily management, and spent most of his time at his estate in Oyster Bay, Long Island. Having married into an old Wasp family, the Bakers, he emulated the life of a country squire. His children, the descendants of Our Crowd's great Jewish philanthropist Jacob Schiff, attended St. James Episcopal Church in New York City.

Harold Bache, by contrast, was a busy man in his corner of Our Crowd. A latecomer, Bache & Co., founded in 1879, was the only large German-Jewish firm that had been run as a retail brokerage house virtually from its earliest days. It had been looked down on for accepting business from anyone, and for being receptive in its indiscriminate network of branch offices to small-time investors, including Eastern European Jews working in the garment industry. The sixties had been the company's greatest period of expansion and exposed it to its greatest danger. Harold Bache's weakness was adding new offices, too rapidly. At the time of his death, in March 1968, he left the firm a bloated, aimless giant — perhaps in worse shape than at any time in its history.

The great 118-year-old Our Crowd firm of Lehman Brothers was also in disarray. For several years Bobbie Lehman had been absent much of the time because of failing health. No Lehmans were ready to succeed him, and he hadn't prepared for the next generation. He died in August 1969, a month after his closest competitor, Sidney Weinberg, and like him, at the age of seventy-seven. But the ailing Bobbie Lehman had lived long enough to see himself and his partners censured by the New York Stock Exchange for negligent and incompetent management.

The troubles that afflicted the Our Crowd houses were shared by the Wasp Establishment firms. Francis I. du Pont, Goodbody, and Hayden Stone sustained losses in 1968 and were doing even worse in 1969. What had set these tribulations in motion was in part a failure to anticipate the demands of the market and to catch up with modern technology for tracking and moving the unprecedentedly heavy transactions on Wall Street.

Investors traded in and out of the market on whim, rocketing volume in 1968 to levels (20 million shares a day) past the record set during the Crash of 1929. Stock prices pushed toward the 1,000 mark again. The combination of a rally in the face of an uncertain economic future and huge trading volume should have made investors more cautious — in the past such conditions had often been followed by a market slump. But the urge to take in as much money as possible kept most Wall Street players from pausing to consider the consequences of such a speculative atmosphere.

Throughout much of 1968, conservatism was on the run. The new players were ready to service the freewheeling mutual fund operators and empire builders of the Go-Go Years. Speculative fever was rampant. It was Wall Street's show of madness as other forms engulfed the world. The Vietnam War raged out of control. In January, the Viet Cong had launched its Tet offensive, which contributed to President Johnson's decision in March not to seek reelection. In April, the Reverend Martin Luther King, Jr., was murdered. In June, Robert Kennedy was assassinated. That spring there were riots throughout Western Europe, rebellion in France, and a loss of confidence in the Bank of England. In August, the Soviets invaded Czechoslovakia at the same time that the Democratic National Convention in Chicago was punctuated by the crack of nightsticks on the heads of protestors.

Wall Street was bullish on peace. The cost of the Vietnam War and Lyndon B. Johnson's Great Society was pushing inflation out of control. The stock market stuttered, leaped, declined — in reaction to signals of hope and despair. Either way, the descent of sheer paperwork on Wall Street was reaching the proportions of an avalanche that would crush or bury some houses under its weight.

As the year wore on, a paperwork crisis was bearing down on the Street. The heart of the problem was the back offices of the brokerage firms — the otherwise mundane world that tracked the comings and goings of securities and money. Bookkeeping on Wall Street, with its bundles of stocks, runners, and still some handwritten ledgers, had more in common with the nineteenth than the twentieth century. In June, the New York Stock Exchange began closing on Wednesdays so that brokerage firms could spend one day a week catching up on what was actually an essential part of the securities business. The Street on the whole hadn't paid enough attention to the back offices and their needs because they were an expense, not a profit center.

Thousands of employees worked in these offices — the paper-handling departments of the brokerage firms — at tasks that were detailed and demanded meticulousness. The back offices transferred securities from one owner to another and kept records of ownership — tasks essential to protecting the integrity of the firms and safeguarding their clients' being credited with proper ownership. The Street had experienced back office problems before. Securities were misplaced, lost, or stolen. But by December of 1968 "fails to deliver" — securities transactions that were not completed for one reason or another in the required time — rose to a record $4 billion. It was as though the equivalent of approximately one out of every three dollars' worth of securities traded that month had disappeared without a trace.

Theories pointed the finger of blame at everything from Mafia involvement to drugs. Studies were made and recommendations proposed, but nothing seemed to relieve the chaos. As a result, Wall Street was faced with a bizarre situation. The more revenues many firms reaped, the more money they actually lost. The cost of running the business was simply outstripping its income. Moreover, negligence and incompetence in keeping track of investments endangered the interests of clients.

And if all that wasn't enough to shake up Wall Street, the government exploded a bombshell that was tantamount to the opening volley of a revolution. In the summer of 1968, in a flurry of antitrust activity, it began a campaign to eliminate the system of fixed commission rates on securities purchases and sales, a system that had been sacred since trading in stocks had first started on Wall Street in 1792, under a buttonwood tree. Wall Street was the only industry that openly had a policy among its members preventing its better customers (investors who bought and sold in volume) from enjoying lower prices (reduced commissions). The Justice Department had a word for it: price-fixing. The system of fixed commission rates, which guaranteed the traders a specific percentage on each transaction, was an antitrust violation and went to the very core of how commissions were set and to Wall Street's clubby way of doing business.

Wall Street came alive and tried to rise majestically to its own defense, but by September the Stock Exchange yielded and found a way to grant discounts on trades involving 1,000 or more shares.*

The "solution" struck some observers as a stopgap measure

---

* Actually the Street had already devised a method to provide its best customers with preferential treatment through "give-ups," permitting commission splitting between two or more member firms. Most smaller Exchange firms didn't handle their own transactions, enlisting another member firm to do the work for them. In return, a small or out-of-town firm "gave up," or paid its trading partner a small portion of the commission it received from a customer. The government saw no difference between that and kickbacks and forced the Street to abandon the practice.

that would lead to the doom of the Establishment. (Others wryly suggested that it had died the previous year when Muriel Siebert, a young broker who was New Crowd in every way except for her sex, became the first woman to buy a seat on the Stock Exchange.)

Wall Street was also shaken — in a very different way — by the bid of a relative newcomer, twenty-nine-year-old Saul Steinberg, to buy Chemical Bank of New York, the sixth-largest bank in the country, with assets of $9 billion. What happened next would show that although the new Jews had become a presence in finance and part of Wall Street's daily life and rhythms, they hadn't won acceptance from the Street's most important client and customer — the American business community.

Nothing had prepared Steinberg for the outpouring of loathing and fury and the blatant anti-Semitism that followed his move on Chemical, suggesting that more was involved than mere objections to the bid or Steinberg's outsider status. Most of Wall Street and a significant part of corporate America seemed to gang up on him. Steinberg said he received more than fifty hate calls from corporate executives, many of which were openly anti-Semitic. One such call came from a vice president of U.S. Steel, who said flat out to Steinberg: "We don't think you should buy the Chemical Bank because you're too young and you're Jewish. Don't you think the Jews in America have gone too far?"

Some banks informed Steinberg that they would pull their credit lines from his parent firm, Leasco, while Leasco customers made noises about taking their business elsewhere. Leasco's own investment bankers at Lehman Brothers and White Weld informed him that they would not support a hostile bid. According to Steinberg, Lehman Brothers succumbed to pressure from certain Establishment bankers, alleging that Lehman had been told that if it continued to support Steinberg, it would lose its commercial paper and bank credit lines and it would be known as an investment bank run for, and by, Jews only.

The chairman of Chemical Bank, William Renchard, pulled out every weapon at his disposal to defeat the raid. Amid what passed for friendly banter over lunch, he warned Steinberg that if there were any chance of a hostile takeover, he, Renchard, was "a pretty good gutter fighter."

Chemical had the strong support of Governor Nelson A. Rockefeller, who urged the state legislature of New York to enact a law enabling the state to stop the takeover of a bank by a nonbank if the bank's ability to do business effectively was jeopardized (such an act was passed into law later that spring). Opposition also came from Washington, as Steinberg learned when he met with influential senators and members of the Federal Reserve Board. In addition, large blocks of Leasco stock, presumably held by institutions, were dumped, driving down the price.

Within a few weeks after he had opened his bid for Chemical Bank in February 1969, Steinberg — who had assumed that he had new status after his acquisition of Reliance Insurance — was forced to admit defeat. "I always knew there was an Establishment," he exclaimed ruefully. "But I used to think I was part of it."

Steinberg may have been beaten, as least temporarily, but the Establishment was losing the war for its own survival. On May 21, 1969, three Harvard MBAs forced the financial community to face the most radical restructuring of its business since the government had separated commercial from investment banking in the 1930s. They announced that they had filed a prospectus with the Securities and Exchange Commission to float a public issue of stock for their then-private firm, Donaldson, Lufkin & Jenrette, Inc. Their goal was to raise $24 million. Howls of protest could be heard all over the Street. What was being proposed — taking a private firm public — was nothing less than the clear destruction of the Club.

If William Donaldson, Daniel Lufkin, and Richard Jenrette succeeded, then any number of investors with enough money could buy up all the stock in a brokerage or banking house and become members of the New York Stock Exchange. When the market was flush, they could go to the public for additional capital. In bad times their losses would be limited only to what they had invested, not to every asset they held, in contrast to the typical Wall Street partnership.

Outside the Establishment, the idea was an immediate hit. Some fifteen firms prepared to go public — Cogan, Berlind, Weill & Levitt among them.

Sandy Weill was ecstatic over the prospect. During the paper-work crises, the four young executives at CBWL had been forced to study ways of developing a computer system. Most small companies like theirs didn't have a back office of their own, but "cleared," or recorded, securities transactions through another brokerage house which, for a fee, processed the purchases and sales. But when the management of its clearing house, Burnham (run by Weill's old boss, Tubby Burnham), decided that they didn't want CBWL to use so much of their back-office space, the four men at CBWL were forced to look elsewhere.

At Loeb Rhoades, which cleared for many other firms, John Loeb turned them down. New accounts would cause a greater strain on his back office system, which was stumbling badly under Loeb Rhoades's own dramatic expansion in retail trading during the sixties. Taking on more clearing accounts, as John Loeb knew, would risk throwing the whole company into the red. Nevertheless, his turndown was perceived by the four men as one more slight from the Wall Street Establishment, since Loeb was known for clearing only for the most prestigious houses. They wouldn't forget.

With no alternative, Roger Berlind and Sandy Weill got stuck with the assignment nobody wanted: learning about the back office — under fire. If they had to set up their own computer system, they also had to find a way to expand their operations to make good use of it. Becoming a public corporation would give them access to the capital they needed. It would also give Sandy Weill the means to keep in step with the traders and dealmakers of the future, including the well-positioned Felix Rohatyn and the up-and-coming John Gutfreund of Salomon Brothers.

# CHAPTER NINE

# Crisis

The winter of 1969–70 was the cruelest season on Wall Street since the Depression. After more than a year of falling prices and shrinking trading volume, what everyone hoped wouldn't happen, did. On March 13, a Friday, McDonnell & Co. announced it was going out of business. The sixty-five-year-old brokerage and investment banking house, whose partners had prospered by virtue of their marital unions with the Fords and other important families, wasn't able to survive the paperwork crunch and the collapse of the stock market. That such a well-connected old firm could actually fail sent shock waves through the financial Establishment. Though smaller firms had been going under without causing much of a ripple, now, for the first time, it was clear that it wasn't only marginal houses that were in deep trouble.

Before the tribulations were over, many houses, large and small, went under; others were yoked together in mergers; and still others, strapped to the tracks of financial disaster, were hoping to be salvaged. Felix Rohatyn would be pressed into service as a leader of the rescue operation, and Sandy Weill, one of the participants in the drama, would find himself richer and more powerful.

In May, the governors of the Exchange finally took decisive action and formed a committee to maintain surveillance over the member firms' finances. Their mandate was to prevent further failures by whatever means necessary. The Crisis Committee, as it was known, was a desperate effort to save the old Wall Street, and the man picked by crusty Bernard ("Bunny") Lasker, the Exchange's current chairman and a close friend of President Richard Nixon's, to run the committee was Felix Rohatyn.

Given his talents and reputation, it wasn't surprising that the upstart Rohatyn was chosen. *Corporate Finance* magazine had already called him "possibly the best in the business." That business was deal-making, which was, in effect, the committee's function. Lasker wanted

Rohatyn to represent the Exchange and use his considerable skills to bail out a lineup of dying firms.

The prospect of serving as chairman of the Stock Exchange's Crisis Committee appealed to Rohatyn's taste for challenge and to his business sense. He felt that he could make a worthwhile contribution, and he knew it would put him in touch with a new circle of Wall Street people. The only problem Rohatyn saw was persuading André Meyer to let him do it. Lazard would not profit from his work on the committee, and it would keep him away from the firm much of the time. Moreover, public service invited press coverage, and Meyer was a very secretive man, who went to great lengths to conceal many aspects of his business activities. With some trepidation Rohatyn went to see his boss, expecting the Lazard chief to try to talk him out of taking the job. Meyer evidently valued Rohatyn too highly to force him to make the choice. For Rohatyn, it was another step out from under Meyer's dominance.

By the time Rohatyn joined the committee, things had gone from bad to worse. Firms were crumbling from one end of Wall Street to the other. Rohatyn was appalled. Brokerage houses that the Exchange had believed were in good shape were shown to be carrying assets on their books that had never existed.

"It was a nightmare," Rohatyn said later. "You probed here, you probed there, and wherever you probed, you found softness."

In July, the committee was faced with the impending collapse of Hayden Stone and Company. The seventy-eight-year-old house, where Joseph P. Kennedy had made much of his fortune, was the largest of the firms in danger of going under at the time. Although it still had a solid investment banking business, it was in worse shape than any of the others, largely because of severe losses the previous two years and an overambitious brokerage expansion policy pursued in the sixties. When its record keeping had become entirely unmanageable, Hayden Stone had hired Coast Guardsmen to moonlight in the back office. But nothing worked.

Desperately in need of funds to stay above the capital requirements as an Exchange member, let alone remain in business, the beleaguered Hayden Stone borrowed $12.4 million from a consortium of Oklahoma businessmen — investment banking clients of the Wall Street house — who pledged stock in their own companies as collateral for the loan. It was further evidence of how bad things were that Hayden Stone could no longer count on New York financial sources, and even the distant Oklahomans refused to put up hard cash. To make matters worse, in the next two months, the value of the collateral stocks sank like a rock, and one of the companies whose shares had been pledged to Hayden Stone went bankrupt. The Oklahoma investors were outraged to learn that, in all probability, their entire investment was lost. Suddenly, the brokerage house was in even greater danger of going out of business — fast.

In any other industry the company would have been allowed to die quietly. But, unlike any other industry, Wall Street had an obligation to try to protect its members, and, by extension, its members' clients. The Stock Exchange had established a special trust fund, financed by its members, to help investors hurt by the failure of a member firm. But by then the fund had been severely taxed by the rash of Wall Street failures.

The demise of Hayden Stone, many thought, might set off widescale panic selling. Through a broad and rather complicated interpretation of the fund's application, the Crisis Committee was able to provide Hayden Stone with a $5 million loan, enough to meet the Exchange's capital requirements and to allow the firm to stay in business while it continued to shop around for a buyer. Of all the firms Hayden Stone approached, only Walston, a retail brokerage house, seemed to be a serious suitor. But the prospect wasn't satisfactory to the only people whose vote mattered at the time: the Oklahomans, who had veto power over any proposed merger and who believed Walston's own finances were suspect. Larry Hartzog, the lawyer and negotiator for the Oklahomans, searched frantically for another candidate. Eventually his quest led to the small firm of Cogan, Berlind, Weill & Levitt (CBWL), whose name most people could remember only if they thought of Corned Beef With Lettuce.

* * *

The troubles that tumbled down Wall Street like boulders down a canyon raised Sandy Weill's normally high levels of anxiety. The spine-chilling events left him alarmed about the fate of a small house like his. He had watched in horror as CBWL's earnings fell from a high of $2.7 million in 1969 to a half-million dollars in 1970.

But opportunity followed Weill and his cohorts like a faithful dog. A mutual friend introduced Don Stroben, the new chief executive of Hayden Stone, to Roger Berlind in late spring. Berlind was the chief executive of CBWL — a compromise candidate — elected by Weill, Levitt, and Cogan at the beginning of the year. He and Stroben had begun talking about the possibility of merging their firms. Stroben, who had barely heard of CBWL, would have preferred a more prestigious house, but he was determined to avoid a shotgun marriage with Walston at all costs. And there were plusses, too. CBWL was actually in better financial shape than Walston.

Berlind saw in Hayden Stone an instant expansion into the ranks of sizable retail brokers. Cogan was iffy. He favored the institutional over the retail business, but he also saw in Hayden Stone an opportunity not unlike Reliance: a wealth of poorly utilized resources. Levitt was opposed, and Weill was too concerned about Hayden Stone's problems to vote for acquisition. Lacking a consensus, Berlind had to tell Stroben that CBWL wasn't interested.

As spring turned into summer, Hartzog was still arguing before the Crisis Committee as well as to some leading power brokers on the Street that if the Walston merger went through, his Oklahoma clients would assuredly lose every cent of their investment. But everyone treated him like a country lawyer who didn't understand the business. Except Rohatyn.

After one particularly heated argument between Hartzog and a Crisis Committee member, Rohatyn told the disheartened lawyer: "I guess in your part of the country they call this nut cracking time." This familiar reference to neutering bulls got a laugh out of Hartzog and made him realize that he had at least one sympathetic ear on the Crisis Committee.

The name of Cogan, Berlind, Weill & Levitt came up again. Hartzog got in touch with the principals. This time, with the Stock Exchange offering $7.6 million as an inducement, all the CBWL officers listened. Weill was the final piece to fall into place. He had studied all of the details of the merger, and some of his earlier concerns about the risks involved had been effectively resolved — now that it was clear that the Exchange would throw in a handsome capital contribution, and that CBWL would be able to choose which Hayden Stone offices it wanted to keep open.

Weill was tapped by his firm to negotiate with Hartzog, and talks began in earnest at CBWL's offices. The two men met regularly for long sessions, sometimes breaking for a quick lunch, which was often a hot dog from one of the vendors near Central Park. It was the first time Weill had represented the firm in anything of consequence. He brought a new determination to the negotiating table. "I was afraid the smallest mistake would lead to a catastrophe, so I took nothing for granted," he recalled. He even got the Exchange to sweeten the financial terms of the deal by agreeing to acquire more Hayden Stone offices.

For the merger to go through, the individual Oklahomans and

other subordinated lenders had to be won over. It wouldn't be easy. Virtually all of them thought they had been misled and lied to by a bunch of incompetents. Moreover, time was critical: on September 2, the Chicago Board of Trade, the nation's largest commodity exchange, announced unexpectedly that it was going to suspend Hayden Stone for insolvency — which would have obliged the New York Stock Exchange to follow suit the next day. Then the Securities and Exchange Commission demanded a resolution of Hayden Stone's fate. A worried Rohatyn, Bunny Lasker, and Exchange President Robert Haack, who had pleaded with the Chicago Board well into the night before winning a delay, set a hard deadline: the agreement of all 108 lenders was needed by noon, September 10, to ensure that none of them would sue CBWL after the acquisition.

By the end of the first week in September, thanks to the persuasive tactics of the Crisis Committee, all but three lenders had signed.

That wasn't good enough for Rohatyn. He believed in resolving the hard issues in any negotiation as early as possible rather than leaving them for the end, because hard issues are even harder under pressure. With only a few days left before the deadline, he demanded, and got, complete authority to use all the powers of the Exchange as well as the Special Trust Fund, if needed. With the help of Haack and a member of the Crisis Committee, Rohatyn induced two more lenders to fall into line. On the morning of September 10, the cutoff date, only Jack Golsen, one of the original Oklahoma businessmen, had not signed.

Tensions were running high as the principals of CBWL, Hayden Stone, and the members of the Crisis Committee waited nervously at the Exchange to learn if Golsen would make the deadline. Around 11:00 A.M. Golsen's lawyer, Michael Yamin, phoned. He informed the Exchange that his client wasn't going to sign and wasn't even available to discuss the matter — Golsen was away on a business trip in Texas and wouldn't be back in Oklahoma until the following day. But Rohatyn wasn't finished. He extended the deadline to the opening bell at 10:00 A.M. the next day. He then called Golsen's lawyer to admonish him that the only way Golsen could get any of his money back was to keep Hayden Stone alive, and if Golsen didn't sign before the deadline, he alone would be responsible for putting Hayden Stone out of business. Its 90,000 customers would lose everything, confidence in Wall Street would be shattered, and the securities industry would be placed in jeopardy. It was uncharacteristic of Rohatyn to make such an impassioned speech, but he was genuinely fearful that the market faced a serious crisis.

Golsen actually surfaced that afternoon, but gave no cause for celebration. His lawyer reported Golsen's answer: "No. I'm interested in justice being done. I want an example made. The only way to make it is to go into liquidation and let the Exchange lose twenty-five million or so."

The group assembled at the New York Stock Exchange that afternoon wasn't ready to admit defeat. The CBWL principals chose Cogan and Berlind to confront Golsen directly. A chartered Learjet was waiting at Teterboro Airport in New Jersey. Cogan was disturbed that the only one standing in the way of an agreement was another Jew. He was keyed up to do everything to change Golsen's mind. If he doesn't sign, Cogan thought, the anti-Semites would have a field day.

Weill, who was uncomfortable with ethnic references, focused on the deal. He was not going on the trip and could only hope that Berlind could persuade Golsen strictly on a business level. Meanwhile, Weill would stay overnight in a room at the Plaza Hotel to make the technical changes needed to turn the Hayden Stone accounts over to the merged CBWL-Hayden Stone if Golsen came around.

Early that evening Cogan, Berlind, Larry Hartzog, and David Stone, grandson of one of Hayden Stone's two founding partners, arrived at Teterboro, but because of fog and rain, the plane didn't leave until after midnight. At 4:00 A.M. Central time they finally reached Oklahoma City. For the next few hours, Cogan and Berlind, but mostly Cogan, cajoled, argued, harangued, and pleaded with Golsen to change his mind. At one point, Golsen decided that Cogan was covertly threatening to drive him out of business if he didn't go along. Angrily he got up to leave the room, while Cogan continued to yell at him. Eventually the two men calmed down.

Around dawn, an exhausted Golsen was told that someone was calling him from the White House. "No," said the Oklahoman, "I won't take the call." He didn't want to know who was on the phone. He had already been told by President Nixon's good friend Bunny Lasker that the president was deeply concerned about Wall Street's problems. If Golsen had taken the call and it had been Nixon, it would have been almost impossible not to have gone along with the president's request.

As the deadline approached, Cogan tried one more tactic. Drawing Golsen aside, he said: "If Hayden Stone goes under, there's something like $500 million to $750 million of stocks that won't clear, and there's a possibility of an enormous panic. You're a Jew. I'm a Jew. You'll do more harm than Eichmann has done to Jews in this culture. Jack, you sign the document and I'll see that you're okay."

That was Cogan's last word, but not the last argument tried on Golsen. Rohatyn and Lasker called him from Lasker's wood-paneled office at the New York Stock Exchange, while the Crisis Committee waited anxiously in the outer office. Rohatyn spoke first, laying out again in cold, calm, objective language what was at stake. There would be no more postponements; either the merger with CBWL would take place or Hayden Stone would be suspended. Golsen was still angry. He didn't care what happened to Hayden Stone. Rohatyn absorbed the outburst, sensing that there was a chance that Golsen might change his mind. He signaled to Lasker to get on the extension.

Lasker, a very conservative man who had made a fortune on Wall Street and who was in agony over the prospect of a Wall Street calamity, made a heartfelt appeal to Golsen, urging him to sign as a service to his country. When he was done, Lasker turned the phone back to Rohatyn. Now it was closing time, the merger maker's last shot to clinch a deal. Rohatyn's gift was his ability to cut through the essence of an argument, to disentangle complexities, to come to what seemed to be the inescapable conclusion. Yet when Rohatyn had finished, he still had nothing to show for it. Golsen said he would call back in five minutes. The tension was unbearable. Alex Chapro, CBWL's floorwalker, paced anxiously as he waited to hear whether Hayden Stone's orders, reprinted in anticipation on CBWL's stationery, could be brought onto the floor of the Stock Exchange.

Five minutes later, there was still no call from Golsen. He was hearing one last argument, this one from a fellow Oklahoma investor who told Golsen that, in the end, he still had to live with the other lenders. Golsen walked away from the crowd assembled in his office, then turned to Hartzog, nodded, and said: "All right, but you make the call."

At 9:50 A.M., ten minutes before the deadline, the phone rang in Lasker's office. Rohatyn picked it up.

"Okay, Felix," Hartzog said. "You've got a deal."

In preparation for this moment, the Stock Exchange had readied two news releases, one noting Hayden Stone's suspension and the other its merger into CBWL. As the name CBWL-Hayden Stone flashed across the ticker, the people on the floor gave forth a collective cheer that built into a roar. Hayden Stone was saved.

Few had more reason to shout than Weill and his cronies, although they were too tired at the moment to rejoice. Through luck and astute bargaining, this group of upstarts had amazingly been given a big boost by the Establishment. What made their triumph even more unusual was that the man who served the Establishment was another upstart, Rohatyn. He had taken no sides but had merely focused on the merger, arranging the terms so adroitly and smoothly that Wall Street hardly knew what it had given up. For nothing more than a few weeks of negotiation and a token payment of one dollar, the firm of Cogan, Berlind, Weill & Levitt — which few seemed to recall had suffered its own financial difficulties — had walked away with an enormous prize.

The bonanza included not only Hayden Stone's offices, furniture, customers, and other assets, plus $31 million in capital from Golsen and the other lenders, but also $7.6 million contributed by the Exchange's special trust fund. Equally important, the trust fund also assumed all of Hayden Stone's liabilities, which eventually amounted to another $9.8 million. The Establishment was, in effect, paying the New Crowd to compete with it.

In November 1970, when a firm with a venerable Establishment name and dominated by one of America's richest and most powerful families, Francis I. du Pont, Glore Forgan, the second-largest house on Wall Street, was driven to the edge of bankruptcy, it turned to a self-made computer software mogul from Dallas, H. Ross Perot, founder of Electronic Data Systems. The imperial du Pont people were unwilling to risk their family's personal wealth to rescue the firm and, as much as they needed him, couldn't disguise their condescension toward the nouveau riche Perot. One of the partners went so far as to call the prospect of Perot's taking over du Pont "the sacking of Rome by the vandals." From Perot's viewpoint, the du Pont partners were a bunch of arrogant, rich snobs, who treated him like a homespun country boy lacking brains and breeding.

After months of broken agreements and uneasy truces, everything would have fallen apart totally if the Crisis Committee hadn't continued to act as mediator. Perot saw Rohatyn as the only friendly face in a crowd that was after his money. Rohatyn liked Perot and sympathized with him over the snobbish disdain of the du Ponts and their counterparts on Wall Street.

The day was saved at least temporarily. But the scepter of power was passing from one Wall Street group to another. And the new group was ready to come into its own.

# CHAPTER TEN

# On the Firing Line

The demands of his work on the Crisis Committee and the personal and professional attention paid to Felix Rohatyn took their toll. They also further strained the Rohatyns' already weakened marriage. "Jeannette was very intelligent, genteel, and decent," remembers a friend, "but she was also very introverted." Neither Jeannette nor Felix Rohatyn will discuss those years, but he does echo the first part of his friend's observation. "She was an extraordinarily bright, intelligent, very high-quality person." Another friend who visited them during that period remembers that the conversation at the Rohatyns' dinners was always intense, focused on serious underlying political and social issues, rarely lighthearted or gossipy. Their country home in Mt. Kisco wasn't elaborate — if anything, it was characterized by an "intellectual disarray," full of books and consistent with the Rohatyns' values that spurned lavish display and frivolity in taste. Their house was situated on four or five hilly, wooded acres touching on a lake that would freeze up in winter, where Felix and his sons played ice hockey. Jeannette Rohatyn seemed devoted to her husband and their three sons. Their close circle of friends came primarily from her world, people at the UN (her fellow interpreters). But he was out too often, pursuing a life that was separate, among people who weren't part of their social circle.

One of them was a French divorcée, Hélène Gaillet de Barcza, whom he had met at a dinner party. She was a vivacious, independent woman in her early thirties, who had her own public relations company. Born in France, Hélène had come to the United States as a young girl. Her formal education ended at eighteen. By the time she met Rohatyn, she was separated from her husband, Count Charles de Barcza of Hungary, who had custody of their two daughters. She appealed to a more spontaneous, playful side of Rohatyn. He found himself drawn deeper and deeper into his relationship with her.

Rohatyn now seemed to have as many lives as a cat, moving from one world to another with remarkable agility. During this time, he and Lazard managed to wrap up a merger for ITT and Geneen that was one of the most intricately orchestrated deals in American history.

To think of Harold Geneen's intense pursuit of the old-line, Connecticut-based Hartford Fire Insurance Company simply as the story of another merger is analogous to calling *Moby Dick* simply the story of a whale. The events that followed in its wake would reverberate throughout Felix Rohatyn's life for years and would bring him an unwanted sobriquet, bestowed by a journalist: Felix the Fixer.

The story started in the summer of 1968, when Geneen began stalking Hartford at the suggestion of Rohatyn, who saw in Saul Steinberg's takeover of Reliance Insurance and its assets an example of how to fuel ITT's growth. Founded in 1810, Hartford — which could list both Abraham Lincoln and Robert E. Lee among its customers and Morgan Stanley as its banker — at first wanted nothing to do with Geneen and ITT and mounted a defense against a takeover. Incensed, Geneen bought more Hartford shares in addition to the large block he had already purchased. In a matter of weeks, Hartford dropped its resistance. By June 1970, Rohatyn had arranged the acquisition for a record $1.5 billion. But reaching an accord with Hartford was only the first way station.

Formidable obstacles loomed; the antitrust division of the Justice Department, consumer activist Ralph Nader, and the Internal Revenue Service opposed the merger. (ITT had planned to pay for Hartford with newly issued ITT stock in a tax-free exchange for Hartford shares. Before the IRS would permit this tax-free incentive, it ruled that ITT must first sell all its Hartford shares acquired prior to the deal. They were disposed of in Europe quickly through Meyer's long-standing connections with an Italian bank at a much higher price than they would have brought on the open market. The sales raised questions and resulted in an IRS investigation that would last for years. But apparently nobody involved raised questions at the time, certainly not Rohatyn, who felt he had no reason to.)

The government, which hadn't acted to prevent ITT from acquiring Hartford, subsequently tried to undo the merger, to the amazement of observers in and out of the Nixon administration. Richard McLaren, the feisty new antitrust chief appointed (in early 1969) by the president, was an apostle of the "big is bad" philosophy. He led an attack against the conglomerates. His number-one target was ITT.

Geneen and ITT launched an all-out campaign in Washington,

trying to enlist the help of anyone who mattered, to persuade McLaren to drop the case. It took them almost a year but they finally gained access to the Justice Department. John Ryan, an ITT executive based in Washington, found a sympathetic listener in his neighbor, Richard Kleindienst, who was then deputy attorney general.

On Geneen's instructions, Rohatyn went over the head of McLaren to his immediate superior, and made an appointment with Kleindienst — which would be labeled a covert attempt on the part of a powerful corporation to obtain special treatment from the Justice Department.

Rohatyn had no way of knowing then that someone else was interested in allowing the ITT/Hartford merger, someone in the highest office of government. The day before his meeting with Rohatyn, Kleindienst received a call from Richard Nixon.

The president would no longer tolerate any antitrust action against ITT: "If (that's) not understood, McLaren's ass is to be out of there in one hour. The ITT thing — stay the hell out of it. Is that clear? That's an order."

Kleindienst tried to stall. He told the president how difficult it would be to interfere so late in the game.

The president became enraged. "The order is to leave the god-damned thing alone. . . . I do not want McLaren to run around prosecuting people, raising hell about conglomerates, stirring things up at this point. . . ."

Kleindienst tried again to explain how difficult it was to stifle such an appeal now.

"You son of a bitch," Nixon barked. "Don't you understand the English language? Drop the goddamned thing. Is that clear?"

Kleindienst had his orders. He authorized the solicitor general to request another extension. A day later, April 20, 1971, Rohatyn walked into Kleindienst's office, unaware that the president of the United States supported his bid for a special favor. Rohatyn maintained he was merely "making an economic case of hardship" rather than negotiating a settlement with McLaren's boss.

The meeting was brief, no longer than about twenty minutes. Rohatyn disarmed Kleindienst immediately by saying that he "was not a lawyer" and that "this was not political." He even volunteered that he was a Democrat. He then summed up for Kleindienst the issues he said were relevant — the extreme hardship that divesting Hartford would cause ITT, the stock market, and America's balance of payments.

He scheduled two further meetings at the Justice Department —

both for April 29 — one with Kleindienst and one with Attorney General John Mitchell to discuss the legal aspects of Perot's involvement in the brokerage business.

Earlier in April, the deal Perot and the du Ponts had knitted together a month before had threatened to unravel. "I want out!" Perot screamed into the telephone when he got the message in Dallas that the du Ponts' losses were higher than all previous estimates. But the Crisis Committee wouldn't let him out. Rohatyn managed to calm him down, and an agreement was reached, which this time held. A few days later, Rohatyn and Perot flew to Washington to keep their appointment with Mitchell. (Presidential adviser Peter Flanigan was also present.)

That day was rife with unbelievable coincidences, ironies, Machiavellian plots, and subplots, and Rohatyn was at the center of the drama. As it happened, he didn't travel to Washington with the Perot/du Pont group, but instead flew there in an ITT plane, along with a support group from ITT. They were to see Kleindienst after the Perot meeting with Mitchell and Flanigan.

When they arrived at the Justice Department, Rohatyn went first to Mitchell's office, while Kleindienst, who would soon be attorney general, and McLaren, head of the antitrust division, and the ITT consultants were forced to wait for him for an hour. Rohatyn had always assumed that his work on the Crisis Committee would be good for Lazard's business, but he couldn't have known that it would pay such unexpected dividends in the perception of his importance in high places.

When Rohatyn joined the group in Kleindienst's office, he launched into his case, needing little help from the legal and business experts he had brought along. As he talked, Kleindienst took notes. Rohatyn's pitch was similar to the one he had made to Kleindienst earlier. If ITT were forced to divest itself of Hartford, Rohatyn argued, ITT's stock would drop, and its fall would have a "ripple" effect on other stocks, which would be calamitous for the nation. Later, it would be pointed out by some observers that the first argument was irrelevant and the second implausible: the Justice Department's role wasn't to protect stockholders from the consequences of merger activities or to protect ITT from allegedly crippling cash flow problems it might suffer through divestiture of Hartford. As for the so-called ripple effect, stocks of other big companies like IBM fluctuated in total value more than a billion dollars a day with no real damage to the economy.

Yet it was all the ammunition Kleindienst needed to justify dropping the case. Rohatyn, unaware of the president's intervention and not knowing that he had in reality already won, kept pressuring Kleindienst. On May 10, he again met with the deputy attorney general. Two days later, Geneen apparently attempted to influence the administration by pledging $400,000 to have the 1972 Republican presidential convention held in San Diego. It was good for business, according to ITT spokesmen, since the company had a Sheraton Hotel in that city, but subsequent events would point to a different reason.

On the morning of June 17, McLaren called Rohatyn from Kleindienst's office. With his boss participating in the conversation, the tough antitrust chief, who for almost two years had tried to fight it, told Rohatyn he would no longer oppose the ITT/Hartford merger, but the Justice Department did have its stipulations and conditions: ITT would have to divest itself of several companies, including Avis, Levitt (the homebuilder of "Levittown" fame), Canteen, and part of Grinnell in order to keep Hartford. Moreover, ITT would be prohibited from acquiring any corporation with assets of $100 million or more without getting government approval. On July 31, 1971, the settlement was announced.

After three years of struggle — from the time Rohatyn first suggested Hartford to Geneen to the day of the Justice Department's accommodation — the battle was won. To the world of finance, it seemed that Rohatyn's star had never shone brighter. He was the agent of powerful forces, and he had served them well.

The truth behind ITT's victory in the Hartford merger wasn't known outside a relatively small circle. And even within that circle, few — including Rohatyn — knew or ever would know all the facts. But enough would be revealed in the coming years so that afterward no one would call Hartford Rohatyn's finest hour.

*   *   *

Rohatyn found his growing prestige as a Wall Street guru conferred too narrow an identification, one that didn't encompass his personal liberal values. As a boy he had admired Franklin Delano Roosevelt, and as an adult had supported Adlai Stevenson and John F. Kennedy. But aside from voting Democratic, he had never actively participated in any political campaign.

In early 1971 he was given an opportunity to change that. Edmund Muskie, a liberal Democrat, was just getting his presidential campaign under way. Meyer's office was a standard stop for any Democrat looking for campaign funds. Meyer told the Senator that if he needed any advice on economic matters he should talk to Rohatyn, who was brought in to meet Muskie. Taking Meyer's offhand suggestion seriously, Muskie asked Rohatyn if he would work with him as an economic adviser.

Rohatyn hesitated. He wasn't sure that he was ready to make the commitment of time and energy, and working for Muskie — perhaps the least popular potential nominee among businessmen — would win him few friends in the business community. But Rohatyn, like other liberals, wanted a new president, and Muskie was the Democratic frontrunner. Within a matter of months he became Muskie's chief economic adviser. Rohatyn was far more pessimistic than Muskie about the nation's future. Without appropriate government intervention, he felt, the gap between the rich and poor would only widen. To that end, he proposed a revival of the Reconstruction Finance Corporation, the Depression era federal agency that had acted like a bank for public works. The potential he saw in federal financing, as well as other economic proposals he had in mind for Muskie, led him to think of arenas larger than investment banking.

In his heart, Rohatyn had a secret wish. He confided to Hélène Gaillet de Barcza that he dreamed of becoming Secretary of the Treasury. It was not outside the realm of possibility: Muskie saw him as possessing the talent and stature worthy of a cabinet post.

In December, Rohatyn took the unusual step, for him, of organizing a fund-raiser luncheon to align businessmen behind Muskie. The event showed all the earmarks of a well-orchestrated Rohatyn venture. Among the chief drawing cards was Harold Geneen. But one morning before the luncheon, an Associated Press story ran in the *New York Times* and elsewhere: the Democratic National Chairman, Lawrence O'Brien, challenged the Nixon administration to explain the connection between ITT's Sheraton subsidiary's pledge of $400,000 to the Republican national convention and the Justice Department's ITT/Hartford settlement.

Rohatyn appeared embarrassed by the news. It was the first he had heard about the contribution. The conversation at the luncheon revolved, diplomatically, around the economy and the campaign. Later he asked Geneen why ITT would make such a commitment and if the pledge had anything to do with the Justice Department's decision to drop its suit against the ITT/Hartford merger. Geneen told him that the contribution hadn't been linked to the Hartford settlement and that the Sheraton Hotel in San Diego had not pledged $400,000 but had contributed $100,000, plus a matching gift of another $100,000 — merely a "normal substitute" for advertising the hotel.

To this day, Rohatyn insists that he believes Geneen's explanation. He has never publicly questioned Geneen's word. But if Rohatyn was satisfied, he was very much in the minority. Chief among those who thought there was more to the story was Ralph Nader. The consumer activist turned to muckraking syndicated columnist Jack Anderson to investigate. In February 1972, a document that proved to be a bombshell arrived at Anderson's office in Washington.

The memo was from the ITT Washington lobbyist Dita Beard to William Merriam, ITT's vice president in charge of the company's office in the nation's capital. It seemed to document a direct link between the ITT commitment of $400,000 to the Republican convention and the Hartford settlement. Written on June 25, 1971 (nine months before it reached Anderson) — when the bid to hold the convention in San Diego was being organized and just before the final ITT settlement was made — the memo also connected the president, the attorney general, Harold Geneen, and several White House aides to a sinister network designed to obstruct the Justice Department's antitrust proceedings against ITT.

The gist of the memo was that the source of the $400,000 pledge must be kept confidential. Only Nixon, John Mitchell, San Diego Mayor Bob Wilson, and White House chief of staff H. R. Haldeman, the memo stated, knew the money had come from ITT. Revelation of the ITT pledge would create publicity that could shoot down the antitrust settlement. In the same memo, Beard also wrote that she was convinced that ITT's commitment to San Diego had gone a long way toward helping the negotiations come out "as Hal [Geneen] wants them." The memo went on to say that Nixon told Attorney General Mitchell "to see that things are worked out fairly" and that Mitchell "is definitely helping us, but cannot let it be known."

Anderson knew he was sitting on a story so hot that it implicated the president of the United States. He dispatched his assistant Brit Hume to talk to Dita Beard at ITT's Washington office. At first, she admitted that she had written the memo, but denied that ITT or she had anything to do with any settlement. The next day, however, when Hume went to see her at her Virginia home, she broke down and admitted that there had been a settlement, which she now claimed she had negotiated herself with Attorney General Mitchell the previous May, when they were both guests at a Derby week buffet luncheon given by Kentucky governor Louie Nunn. But she insisted that Geneen knew nothing about this agreement, and, in spite of what the memo said, that there was no connection between the settlement and the convention pledge.

Anderson's March 1 column (prepared by Hume) began with these explosive words: "We now have evidence that the settlement of the Nixon administration's biggest antitrust case was privately arranged between Attorney General John Mitchell and the top lobbyist for the company involved."

No one knew then how close Dita Beard had come, in a much milder and more sanitized form, to fingering the president's role in the ITT case. The pieces hadn't all fallen into place yet.

Dita Beard's memo raised questions that couldn't be answered without further probing. If, indeed, ITT had bought off the government, how had the deal to keep Hartford been engineered and by whom? A clue came from an unnamed former ITT director, who told Anderson that Geneen would never rely on just one person for such an important assignment and pointed Anderson in the direction of a key figure in the antitrust negotiations: Felix Rohatyn.

Rohatyn was at Kennedy Airport on that March 1, talking on the phone with his children while waiting for an outgoing flight, when an urgent message was delivered to his home to call Hume in Washington. He didn't know who Hume was, but he returned his call immediately. Hume identified himself as an Anderson associate and began reading Rohatyn the Beard memo.

"That's absolute bullshit," Rohatyn interrupted angrily. He was in a position to know, he continued, because he had been assigned by Geneen to make the ITT case to the government on the basis of economic hardship. He told the reporter that he had met with Kleindienst about six times during the same period that the ITT lawyers had been meeting with McLaren.

That was all Hume needed. Why else would Rohatyn and Deputy Attorney General Kleindienst, McLaren's boss, have met behind closed doors other than to circumvent McLaren? Anderson's next column, on March 2, charged that the Nixon administration was hiding the truth about the ITT settlement and the $400,000 convention pledge, when it led the nation to believe that the case was settled on legal grounds alone.

Some seven hundred newspapers throughout the country reported the news in Anderson's columns. The repercussions were immediate and far-reaching.

The appearance of the columns couldn't have been more timely. Kleindienst was scheduled to become attorney general on March 1, taking over from John Mitchell, who was leaving to run Nixon's re-election campaign. Kleindienst had undergone his first round of Senate confirmation hearings just the previous week. Now he moved to reopen the hearings to dispute Anderson's charges. He was confident he would prevail. His nomination had sailed through the Judiciary Committee the first time around. Its chairman, Senator James Eastland, was an old friend, and most of its members were conservative. Kleindienst did, however, take some precautions. He knew he would come under fire from the liberals, who had questioned him closely during the first round of hearings. So he decided he would not go it alone in fending off the ITT questions. He hadn't seen or spoken to Rohatyn since a brief social visit in his office the previous September, but he called Rohatyn now and told him he would appreciate his testimony at the hearings. Rohatyn said he would be pleased to help.

Rohatyn thought then — and still does — that there wasn't the slightest fix in the Hartford case. "There was some kind of clumsy attempt to be on good terms with the Republicans through a promotional contribution by the hotel chain. Dita Beard, whoever she is, wrote these memos as a way of self-aggrandizement. She had never met Mitchell; she was an utter nothing and wrote these memos in order to make herself important and get a raise or something. And it was all baloney."

Dita Beard vanished mysteriously just before the start of the hearings. She was traced by the FBI to a hospital in Denver, where she was being treated, allegedly for cardiovascular disease. Here, she languished until the hearings were almost over.*

When Rohatyn stepped into Room 2228 of the New Senate Office Building on the morning of March 2, the chamber was packed with reporters. Dozens of witnesses, among them John Mitchell, Harold Geneen, and Jack Anderson, were scheduled to appear before the Senate Judiciary Committee's reopened hearings on the Kleindienst nomination. Rohatyn had given little thought, perhaps naively, to the

---

* Finally, three weeks after the start of the hearings, a few senators were allowed to take Beard's testimony at her hospital bedside. She denied again that she had written the memo, but under questioning admitted that many bits of the memo seemed familiar. Before the senators were finished, Beard began to suffer chest pains. Her doctor stopped the questioning — for six months. However, a week after meeting with the senators, she made a remarkable recovery and was well enough to leave the hospital and appear on TV with interviewer Mike Wallace. The media was having a field day with Dita Beard.

hearings' impact on him. This was his first appearance before Congress. He saw his own role as simply providing information; that it could be interpreted as something very different came as a complete shock to him.

* * *

The meeting opened at 10:40 A.M. Rohatyn joined Kleindienst at a table facing Eastland and the other members of the Judiciary Committee. Kleindienst was also flanked by McLaren, now no longer the antitrust chief. He had been recently appointed a federal judge in his native Chicago. The prestige of the judgeship and the timing of the appointment made it seem to many like a reward for his sudden decision to settle the ITT divestiture.

The Democrats on the committee hammered away at the witnesses. Very quickly, Senator Philip Hart, a liberal Democrat from Michigan, focused on Rohatyn's meetings with Kleindienst and the role the Lazard banker had played in ITT's fight to keep Hartford.

> Hart: . . . You thought you were negotiating a settlement; did you not?

> Rohatyn: I did not think I was negotiating a settlement, sir.

> Hart: What did you think you were doing, giving an economics course?

> Rohatyn: I was trying to, sir.

Hart then asked Rohatyn what role Kleindienst had played in influencing McLaren to allow ITT to keep Hartford. He continued to hammer at Kleindienst's participation, and Rohatyn continued to insist that though Kleindienst was present at the discussions, he had been a passive nonparticipant.

> Rohatyn: The meetings were exactly as I have described them.

> Hart: The tragedy of this is that ninety percent of the people that read the papers and listen to this story, no matter what we do, are just going to not believe it. That is the hell of it.

Being virtually called a liar by a U.S. senator was only the first assault on Rohatyn's credibility. Time and time again, the senators on the committee, mainly the three liberal Democrats (Hart, Birch Bayh of Indiana, and Edward Kennedy of Massachusetts) who asked many of the questions, found it impossible to believe that he had had only a small role as an "educator" trying to prevent a settlement that to him seemed "so harsh and smacking of dismemberment of ITT." But under questioning from Senator Bayh, he conceded that his efforts to influence the outcome had not been "wasted."

The most damaging blow to Rohatyn's credibility came quite by accident, as a result of an exchange between Senator Kennedy and Kleindienst. The Massachusetts Democrat had asked the acting attorney general about his initial contact with Rohatyn.

Kleindienst replied that Rohatyn had called him out of the blue and asked to see him. As Kennedy moved on to McLaren for questioning, Kleindienst was seen quietly huddling with Rohatyn. Afterward Kleindienst testified that he had just had his "recollection refreshed" by Rohatyn. In reality, John Ryan, a neighbor of his in Washington who worked for ITT's Washington office, had told him that Rohatyn would be calling him soon regarding Hartford. Kleindienst now recalled having agreed to talk to Rohatyn.

The *New York Times* ran a front-page photograph that showed Kleindienst and Rohatyn conferring together. The picture, along with the continuing coverage of the hearings, gave symbolic, if not literal, credence to the collusion charges. The incident inspired an ongoing attack on Rohatyn by liberal *Washington Post* columnist Nicholas Von Hoffman, who bestowed the label that would stick to Rohatyn for years afterward: Felix the Fixer.

Rohatyn was devastated. His career had been built on the solidness of his reputation, and now people were implying that he was a back-room manipulator who influenced highly placed federal officials. The public criticism even filtered down to his family. One of his son's teachers brought up the "Felix the Fixer" epithet at school, and his three sons were teased by their classmates. "I felt this was outrageous," Rohatyn recalled. "My kids were very young and impressionable. I tried to explain to them what had really happened. And I even went to the school and complained about the teacher — to no avail."

To add to the damage, an editorial in solidly probusiness *Fortune* magazine severely reprimanded "Geneen and ITT director Felix Rohatyn for roaming all over" Washington arguing for a favorable settlement: "ITT's arrogant use of its corporate wealth and power has done a profound disservice to the whole business community."

Rohatyn felt the charges against him were groundless, but he could do nothing to stop the swelling tide of criticism. Working against him was the image he had conveyed at the hearings. The soft voice, the even temper, the precise language — the "trademark" qualities that served him so well as a dealmaker — made him seem devious and inscrutable when he fended off questions. To a degree, he was a victim of his own negotiating style.

Among the dozens of witnesses to parade before the committee, Rohatyn was the only significant unknown. Well into the questioning, Senator Bayh had to ask him how he pronounced his name. Yet, virtually overnight, he was transformed into a notorious figure of national proportions.

* * *

That spring, various strands of Rohatyn's life seemed to be unraveling. He was incensed and hurt by his treatment in the press; in April, Muskie dropped out of the presidential race and whatever hopes Rohatyn may have harbored for public office were dashed. (But as a dealmaker, he was as strong as ever: in the business community, having clout in Washington was seen as an asset.)

Rohatyn's personal life had also been shaken up a few months before the hearings. According to Hélène Gaillet de Barcza, Rohatyn kept his interest in her a secret because of his concern about hurting his family, especially his sons, Pierre, Nicholas, and Michael, all bright, appealing boys. Winter was their time together, attending the New York Rangers hockey games and going on ski trips to Vermont. But after sixteen years, his marriage to Jeannette was exhausted. "These things happen without being anybody's fault," he would explain. But he was determined to reorder his life and moved out of their Park Avenue apartment.

Taking with him only his clothes, some books, and a few prints, Rohatyn rented a small suite at the Alrae, a faded old residential hotel on Sixty-fourth Street between Madison and Park avenues. Unquestionably, he could have afforded a much better place, but the Alrae seemed in harmony with his lack of interest in possessions. A relatively wealthy man, he needed very little; he attributed his simple surroundings to what he called his "refugee mentality." All he really missed were his children, to whom he was devoted. The hotel was a short walk from his former apartment and he could see them frequently.

Rohatyn finally introduced Hélène to André Meyer, who charmed her (he was attentive to attractive women). They visited Meyer at the Carlyle almost every weekend. In the summer Rohatyn and

Hélène rented a house in Ridgefield, Connecticut, so that his sons could spend time with them in the country.

* * *

Throughout much of 1972, while Hélène Gaillet de Barcza and Felix Rohatyn were building their life together, the Watergate break-in was exposed. The scandal preempted all previous Nixon administration scandals in national attention, and the ITT affair was largely forgotten by the public and the press. A year to the day after the *New York Times* ran the front-page story on his appearance with Kleindienst, *Business Week* ran a flattering cover story entitled "The Remarkable Felix Rohatyn." In it, he was described as "the man most responsible for the renown of Lazard Frères." It was the first step in the remaking of Rohatyn's public image. Although his troubles with Hartford would rear up again, Rohatyn would return to the public arena and win the greatest acclaim of any one member of the New Crowd as the Man Who Saved New York City.

# CHAPTER ELEVEN

# Unbridled Ambition

The change over time in background and style among those who reigned on Wall Street could be measured in part by the differences in two men closely identified with Lehman Brothers, the estimable investment banking house. A leading member of Our Crowd, Bobbie Lehman, who by the late sixties had run the family firm as his personal fiefdom for the better part of four decades, had always enjoyed all the privileges and social acceptability that his glittering name bestowed. Lewis Glucksman, thirty-five years his junior, was an oddity in an Our Crowd firm, the antithesis of the Lehman bankers' idea of a partner. His style was so out of harmony with the style of Lehman Brothers in the late sixties that it seemed like a deliberate form of rebellion.

Bobbie Lehman was not much of a banker; it was said he didn't know one stock from another, but that didn't matter. He was born to his position. His wealth was dazzling. His art collection, consisting of paintings by El Greco, Renoir, Rembrandt, and other masters, was worth some $100 million. Many of his paintings hung in the Lehman headquarters, a constant reminder to his partners of just how rich and powerful their senior partner was. He also had incredible business and political contacts — at a time when that was virtually all it took to be a baron of finance — through the Whitneys, Harrimans, and, of course, his own family.

At Lehman Brothers, Glucksman wasn't a banker. He belonged to the hurly-burly world of traders, and he was a master in his field. A short, puffy man with a face reminiscent of a thirties union leader and dark hair that sprouted up in matted tufts, he eyeballed people with the unyielding stare of a bulldog. When angered, he cursed so forcefully that his face reddened and his pale-blue eyes narrowed into tiny slits. When he smiled, his plump cheeks expanded like a chipmunk's. He smoked foul-smelling cigars and wore ill-fitting suits, garish ties, and wrinkled white shirts. Most of the Lehman bankers looked down on trading as beneath them; they also found Glucksman personally "crude." But his subordinates appreciated his generous, spontaneous acknowledgment of good work; he was known to engulf them in bear hugs to express his pleasure in their accomplishments.

Glucksman had little to do with his partners; he didn't even work where most of the bankers did. His commercial paper division* was housed in a typical noisy, open trading room in an anonymous lower-Manhattan office building. The bankers held sway in one of New York's most noted architectural landmarks.

The imposing headquarters at One William Street — built originally in eighteenth-century French style — was remodeled for Lehman Brothers to resemble an Italian palazzo. The entrance was adorned with polished marble. In the travertine-walled lobby, the square-coffered ceiling contained murals of ancient coins. The doorway leading to the anteroom off the lobby was framed by carved stone columns and lintel, capped by Wall Street symbols of bears, bulls, and lambs.

Working there was the equivalent of belonging to one of the most exclusive and elegant men's clubs in the country. The boardroom had a carved limestone fireplace and hearth and leaded glass casement windows embellished with Wall Street motifs. Over the fireplace was a wood carving in the style of Grinling Gibbons. Partners sat in the grand partners' room that was paneled in dark, rich English oak; antique silver chandeliers hung from its ceiling. The Georgian-style partners' dining room, the creation of noted society designer Sister Parish, boasted another antique silver chandelier and a Sheraton table that seated ten. The kitchen, managed by the former chef of the famed Pavillon restaurant, was celebrated for its fine food. The wine list was extensive. In the morning, waiters in beige linen jackets served coffee, tea, and pastries from "our kitchen," as the partners referred to it. They also enjoyed the privileges of a private gymnasium, a masseur, and a plentiful supply of Havana cigars.

Glucksman cared for none of this, including the expensive cigars. His work was his life. In the office at 6:30 A.M., he was usually

---

* Commercial paper is a corporate IOU that is traded much like a stock or bond. Instead of borrowing from a bank, a company can issue debt certificates repayable in a set period of time, typically less than a year. (They can be cheaper than a bank loan.) Acting as agents, firms like Lehman and Goldman Sachs collect a fee for placing these IOUs with large investors. They sometimes take such paper in their own accounts to help provide funds sought by clients.

there until after dark. He preferred eating lunch out of a brown paper bag to the endless rounds of business luncheons, dinners, and social functions attended by the bankers.

The separation between Glucksman and his partners was virtually total. As long as he stayed out of trouble and made money, they left him alone, an arrangement that suited him just fine. He didn't like to be managed, and his independence served him well. He had made the firm a pile of money with both commercial paper and government securities. His commercial paper division may have been the only one at Lehman that enjoyed a corporate sense of teamwork. Glucksman was effective in motivating and managing his employees. He got the best out of "my team," as he called them. While he had no tolerance for fools, he rewarded performance. And there was nothing meager about the results. His team had become one of Lehman's most profitable, handling billions of dollars of securities annually.

After Bobbie Lehman's death in 1969, Lehman Brothers became a private corporation (in 1970). Glucksman's partners (officially now known as managing directors) could no longer completely ignore him. As head of one of the biggest divisions, he was automatically appointed to the Lehman board of directors, its policy-making body. Two years later, he ascended to a truly rarified atmosphere when he was named executive managing director and joined the four-man executive committee, which ran the company on a daily basis. Chairman Frederick Ehrman and president Warren Hellman, who was Ehrman's nephew, were the very soul of Our Crowd's Jewish banking aristocracy. The Hellmans had built the Wells Fargo bank in San Francisco into one of the most powerful financial institutions in the country. They were related by marriage to the Seligmans, the most important Our Crowd family in New York during the nineteenth century. Vice chairman Andrew Sage II, who ranked second to Ehrman, came from a very rich and old New York Wasp family.

The reception Ehrman gave Glucksman was the coldest yet. A gruff but talented banker, Ehrman had never wanted Lehman Brothers to be in trading, and he didn't like Glucksman. According to one partner, he had once said to Glucksman: "We made you a partner, but you'll never be a member of the Century Country Club."

But Glucksman, who would apply to the New York Athletic Club and receive more blackballs (seventeen) than anyone else in the club's history — which he attributed to anti-Semitism and snobbery — now had a special place at the dining room table with the lords of Lehman.

Lewis Glucksman had grown up on Manhattan's West End

Avenue, the son of second-generation Hungarian Jews. His father made enough money from a factory that assembled table lamps to enable his wife and three children to live comfortably.

A precocious student, he graduated from DeWitt Clinton High School in the Bronx at the age of fifteen, and then spent a year at the University of Indiana before he transferred to the College of William and Mary in Virginia. A year later — on his seventeenth birthday — he lied about his age and enlisted in the Navy to serve during World War II on a submarine-chaser in the Atlantic; he rose to the rank of lieutenant. In 1946, after his discharge, he returned to William and Mary, where he switched from pre-med to accounting, abandoning his parents' dream of his becoming a doctor. He had been captivated by his first corporate finance text. "I read it as if it were a novel," he recalled years later.

In 1947, with a bachelor's degree in hand, he headed for Wall Street, setting his sights on the Our Crowd firm of Lehman Brothers. "Lehman Brothers was a name that had special magic to people in the Jewish community," Glucksman said. "The family had produced a great financial firm and a Jewish governor of New York." He strode boldly into the firm's headquarters seeking a job. He never got past the receptionist, who showed him the door.

The experience stayed with him. For years he resented the Our Crowd investment bankers, whom he associated in his mind with the Lehman family. He thought of them not as fellow Jews but as Wasps who had held back him and others like him, Jew and non-Jew, in the financial world. Over the next few years, the embittered Glucksman bounced around the financial community. He picked up an MBA at NYU and did a brief stint in women's wear retail merchandising and assorted other jobs before becoming comanager of A. G. Becker's commercial paper division in 1958. Goldman Sachs was then the only firm of consequence in the commercial paper business. Becker was so determined to catch up that it offered Glucksman a percentage of the profits. He proved such an exceptionally gifted trader that within five years, according to Glucksman, he had built a $1 billion business for Becker and was earning up to $2 million for himself annually.

Along the way, he married Inez Salinger, an editor at a publishing company, and became the father of two girls. Despite the money he made, the Glucksmans lived relatively modestly. What began as random job-hopping became a classic model of the driven, upwardly mobile Wall Street professional. Glucksman was typical of the outsiders who first made their mark during the postwar bull market. As the sixties unfurled, there seemed to be no limit to how high he could go.

In the summer of 1963, the gates of heaven miraculously flew open when Bobbie Lehman invited him to join Lehman Brothers. His being hired was, as he described it, almost a "fluke."

For some time, Bobbie Lehman had coveted the success of Goldman Sachs and Gus Levy's commercial paper operations. He wanted to build a commercial paper division of his own, and he wanted to do it fast. So he raided Becker — an unsportsmanlike move coming from one of the last Our Crowd princes, but, nevertheless, a successful one.* It netted Lehman Brothers James Friedlich, the head of Becker's commercial paper operation in its Chicago headquarters. More defections, including Glucksman's, followed.

Friedlich soon left Lehman. Glucksman stayed. He was the one who had actually been responsible for making Becker's commercial paper operation so competitive, and he quickly built Lehman's commercial paper business into the industry's third largest. Three years later, in 1966, his reward was what he had coveted so long: a Lehman partnership.

But his promotion was scarcely noticed. He was, after all, a relative nobody in a house where the only standards that mattered were Bobbie Lehman's own, and Lehman brought all of his weight to bear in the way he handled his partners. They were the recipients not only of his largesse but of his willful autocracy.

For all the years that he ran Lehman Brothers, he encouraged partners to pursue their own enterprises. He fostered little sense of camaraderie or team spirit. Indeed, he liked pitting the partners against each other, watching them squabble over bonuses or over credit for having delivered a piece of business. As long as Bobbie Lehman was there to govern his competitive partners, the firm flourished. His death in 1969 left it in chaos.

When Fred Ehrman finally took over, his harsh, disciplinary rule quickly antagonized most of the partners. A few left, and before long others began seeking an opportunity to knock him out of the chairmanship. No one would have more to gain or be more pleased by Ehrman's removal than Glucksman. The third spot in the firm, president, that was held by Warren Hellman, was practically in his grasp. Hellman was moving up because Andrew Sage, who had been with the banking house for two decades, didn't have the taste for

---

* Becker cried foul and the New York Stock Exchange launched an investigation, but the case was dropped for lack of evidence.

management. He let it be known that he would resign as vice chairman to take on a limited role. Glucksman's new role as number three seemed set. That is, until Ehrman threw a boulder in the path of the Glucksman Express.

Ehrman wanted the vice chairmanship to go to Pete Peterson, former secretary of commerce in the Nixon administration. Glucksman was furious. He felt that Peterson was an interloper and had no qualifications for the number-two slot. Nothing ever made Glucksman change his mind about Peterson. Unlike the three men with whom he would share management responsibilities, Peterson had no interest in grappling for power. In Glucksman's view, Peterson's primary goal was to become very wealthy — very quickly.

Peterson was even farther removed from the Lehman origins than Glucksman. His father, George Petropoulos (the name was changed to Peterson) came to America as a teenager and worked on a freight train as a dishwasher. As a boy, Peterson waited on tables after school in the small twenty-four-hour-a-day restaurant owned and operated by his immigrant parents in Kearney, Nebraska. By the time Peterson was thirty-four, he had ascended to the presidency of the giant camera company Bell & Howell. Eleven years later, in 1971, the small-town boy reached one of the highest levels in American society, when President Nixon appointed him secretary of commerce.*

He was an immediate hit in Washington social circles. He and his lively wife, Sally, entertained — and were entertained by — the "in" political and publishing notables. But some of his friends — who included *Washington Post* publisher Katharine Graham and columnist Art Buchwald — were on the White House "enemies" list. That cost him dearly. He was locked into a territorial struggle with Secretary of the Treasury John Connolly. Peterson was viewed as the expendable one. Six months into Nixon's second term, he found himself without a job until he accepted Ehrman's offer.

No sooner had Peterson joined Lehman Brothers than its business started to slip. After years of being counted among the top three underwriters, the Our Crowd firm had dropped to sixth place in 1972. As business soured, Lehman's capital shrank, demoting it from eighth in capital ranking in 1966 to twenty-fifth in 1973, two slots lower in

---

* Felix Rohatyn, whose firm was Bell & Howell's investment banker, managed the blind trust Peterson had while he was in office. Also, Peterson was one of the high government officials Geneen talked to when the government was trying to take Hartford away from ITT.

ranking than Sandy Weill's aggressive Hayden Stone. The timing was bad. The heyday of Our Crowd was over and the major firms — which now had trading and underwriting operations — needed large amounts of capital to finance both businesses made worse by the bear market that year.

Though Lehman Brothers was running into the red, the partners continued to spend money lavishly — on the best hotels, on first-class air travel, on entertainment. They behaved as if their clients were wedded to the firm forever. Instead of focusing on their own shortcomings, they formed cabals and looked about for someone to blame. Soon after Peterson's arrival, the firm was further rocked by Glucksman's surprising trading losses.

In the summer of 1973, Glucksman made a bad bet. He had loaded down the Lehman trading account with government bonds on the hunch that interest rates would drop, increasing the price of these bonds and making them more valuable. Throughout his career, he had displayed an unerring talent for knowing in which direction the bond market was going — until now. An erratic government economic policy was in large part Glucksman's undoing, and his bond portfolio was battered. As a consequence, Lehman Brothers suffered losses believed to be in excess of $6 million, amounting to nearly half of its own money and a sixth of its total capital.

At last, Ehrman had a reason to get rid of the one partner he seemed to detest most. On the surface, Glucksman's fate seemed to hinge on the market. In reality, he was the architect of his own destiny. Like many of the New Crowd, he had pursued financial success with a fierce determination. What he had accomplished during his six years as a Lehman partner had been done solely on his own — not through connections. He had little time or desire to soften his aggressiveness. Glucksman wasn't going to sit back and wait passively for matters to take their own course.

"I'm sick and tired of everybody talking about firing me," he yelled at a board of directors meeting. "I'm hearing it in the bathrooms, in the halls, everywhere. Now if you're going to fire me, do it. Don't talk about it and do it now. I'm going to the bathroom. I'll be back in five minutes. You let me know then."

When Glucksman returned, no one challenged him. Booting him out wouldn't solve the problem of the trading losses.

With the pressure off, Glucksman concentrated on removing Ehrman. Events moved quickly, and there was no shortage of support. Among the most eager were president Warren Hellman and George

Ball, another powerful executive, who had been under secretary of state in the Kennedy and Johnson administrations and ambassador to the United Nations.

While Ehrman and several of his key supporters were out of town in mid-July, eight of the twelve board members convened at Ball's duplex apartment high above the East River, at the United Nations Plaza building, to discuss Ehrman's ouster. After Hellman made it clear he wasn't a candidate, Peterson was quickly appointed the new chief, with Hellman and Glucksman (still executive managing director) ranked just behind him. Ball and Hellman were given the unpleasant task of informing Ehrman.

By the end of the summer, interest rates started to decline, and a measure of calm returned to Lehman Brothers because the value of its bond trading account rose. Peterson took drastic but necessary steps to rebuild the firm. With the help of the board, he developed strategies to raise capital, recruit new business, and build Lehman into a full-service financial corporation. Glucksman concentrated on strengthening and expanding the firm's trading department. By 1975, Lehman was profitable again, earning $24 million before bonuses and taxes, but what was most startling about the comeback was that three-quarters of those profits had been generated by Glucksman and his traders. Yet even with Glucksman's brilliant recovery, Peterson, the new chairman, fueled his antagonism.

Peterson was aloof, too involved with selling the image of Lehman to the business world to keep track of the daily minutiae of running a growing company. His overriding concern was his campaign to control costs. He sent out memos detailing his ideas. Glucksman thought the memos were absurd and pretentious and revealed Peterson's ignorance of Wall Street. To Glucksman, costs were an essential part of doing business. All the Peterson memos that came his way were instantly filed in the wastebasket.

When the job of president of the company became open in 1975 (Hellman, like Sage before him, withdrew from the management of the firm), Peterson could have made his chief trader a peace offering and awarded him the post. But Peterson was hardly even aware that he was at war, and took the title of president himself. Glucksman was outraged. By then, he had assumed more responsibility for the daily operations of the firm but hadn't received the credit he felt was well deserved. Even without the title, Glucksman was the de facto second to Peterson. When the day of reckoning came, Glucksman would have the better hand.

# CHAPTER TWELVE

# To Build an Empire

*I*n the early seventies, Sandy Weill went through what were for him typical cycles of triumph and failure accompanied by equally strong swings of elation and anxiety that were related to fluctuations in the market. In October of 1971, he became a millionaire. By Christmas of that year he was terrified of having his reputation destroyed and even the possibility of being convicted of fraud.

The chain of events that had made him a wealthy man began the day Cogan, Berlind, Weill & Levitt acquired Hayden Stone and the number of accounts held by the combined firm increased tenfold — from about 5,800 to 57,100. Weill's most anxious moment came shortly after the merger was completed, when he had to face the twenty-eight Hayden Stone office managers at CBWL's Fifth Avenue headquarters in the General Motors building. While his three partners made some welcoming remarks to the new employees, Weill, who hated giving speeches, was too uncomfortable to address even this modest audience. He still felt more at ease in front of his stock quotation terminal or visiting his back office.

And his terminal was giving him reassuring news. The stock market had recovered from the slump of 1969–70 and was doing well. In June 1971, CBWL-Hayden Stone showed a tidy $3 million profit for the previous twelve months.

Buoyed by the success of their first major acquisition, the four principals now wanted to take the firm public. At one time, CBWL-Hayden Stone had actually handled the fifth largest block trade in history. But to do that on a regular basis — and to diversify in an uncertain market — required ready capital, not merely for the purpose of growing but also in order to survive against bigger, better financed competitors such as Merrill Lynch. Moreover, they were eager to capitalize on their success. And they were moving up in class.

Joan and Sandy Weill were moving up in terms of status symbols, too. They bought a sunny fourteen-room co-operative apartment at the corner of Sixty-seventh Street and Fifth Avenue. But they weren't extravagant in decorating their new home. (To save money, Joan Weill decided to make-do in the living room with her basic red, yellow, and black print fabric, which was moved, along with much of the other furniture, from the Great Neck house.) They were now living in a stuffy building whose tenants didn't include many Jews. On moving day, Joan, dressed in jeans, with her hair tied back for comfort, was in the basement when she encountered a fellow resident who was an elegant Lehman Brothers partner.

"Are you Mrs. Weill?" he inquired.

"Ma'am is upstairs," she lied, feeling mortified. Life on Fifth Avenue was more formal than the life she was accustomed to, but there were advantages for Sandy's work: the building was a short distance from the CBWL-Hayden Stone headquarters.

Like many of the new breed, Weill's moves over the years to different homes and neighborhoods marked clear stages in his passage from limited means and obscurity to financial success and a high profile. The East Rockaway apartments and the attached house in Baldwin had been the residences of the young married couple with small children; Brookville, Long Island, the upscale home of the budding entrepreneur; Great Neck, the stepping stone of the nouveau riche; and finally, home became Fifth Avenue, the most fashionable address in New York City.

The Weills took advantage of the dizzying array of restaurants, stores, and services that the city offered. Joan Weill, who had always been interested in clothes, began dressing even more stylishly. Occasionally Sandy accompanied her to the designer department at Henri Bendel and bought her dresses. In the summer they rented a house in the wealthy town of Bedford, New York, and Weill played tennis at the nearby Armonk Tennis Club. But their closest friends were still largely the CBWL-Hayden Stone crew; their synagogue still the one in Great Neck for the high Jewish holy days. When they invited people for dinner, Joan prepared the meals herself, and their maid served.

That fall, their dining room adorned with pumpkins, the Weills threw the largest party of their married life for all the officers and high-ranking members of CBWL-Hayden Stone; about one hundred people attended. It served as a sort of coming-out party for the Weills. The business family — with Sandy as the father figure and Joan as the gracious corporate hostess — would become the Weill trademark. It marked a great change for the compulsive stock watcher, and it was the first glimmer of Weill as a leader. His newfound sociability, not surprisingly, came not long after his firm's public debut.

In June 1971, CBWL-Hayden Stone filed a registration statement with the Securities and Exchange Commission, offering one million shares — a week after Merrill Lynch became the second New York Stock Exchange firm to sell its own shares to the public.* An air of anxiety permeated CBWL-Hayden Stone's main office; Weill and his partners were worried that they might be left behind in the race for outside capital. If the public bought the offering Weill and his colleagues were underwriting themselves — at $12.50 a share at the time it was sold — then each of them would be worth $3.6 million (over seven hundred thousand of it in cash from the sale of part of their holdings).

There was a catch. The SEC was opposed to insiders cashing in their own shares when a company went public for the first time. With the offering ready, the principals had to do something — fast — to get the SEC to change its mind. Weill and Levitt caught up with SEC chairman William Casey, who was in New York for a meeting with officials at the New York Stock Exchange. As Casey was leaving the building, Levitt ran up to Casey, whom he had known from the days when he had sold cattle tax shelters; Casey had been one of his best customers. Levitt and Weill talked themselves into the cab with Casey. For the whole $68 ride to Bethpage, Long Island (where Casey was headed for another meeting), they tried to induce him to let them cash in some of their shares. At the end of the ride they still had no commitment.

Yom Kippur was a few days later, and Weill observed the solemn occasion anxiously awaiting the SEC's decision. Just before the offering was made, a call came from the SEC. The four principals would be allowed to sell some of their own shares. They were rich. As luck would have it, the market, which had been in a slump during the filing period, turned up, and their entire stock issue sold out quickly.

Throughout the summer of 1971, as they were preoccupied with going public, Weill and Berlind were unknowingly sitting on a powder keg. For three years they had served as investment bankers for and sat on the board of the Topper Corporation, a high-flying toy company with a strongly promotable licensing agreement for making toys using the Sesame Street name. That connection, plus some glowing reports from management, had pushed the stock up sharply. But there were numerous signs, as 1971 wound down, that the company was being operated, at the very least, by an overly optimistic corps of executives.

---

* First Boston, a publicly held company since its creation in 1934, joined the Stock Exchange later than Donaldson, Lufkin & Jenrette and before Merrill went public.

Topper and another toy company, Mattel, had run into trouble with the Federal Trade Commission over false-advertising claims. Furthermore, a number of Wall Street analysts had expressed the opinion that Topper's finances were in poor shape. That hadn't stopped Weill and Berlind from aggressively, and successfully, promoting Topper's stock. Among Topper's biggest promoters, in fact, was Bernstein-Macaulay, CBWL-Hayden Stone's own investment management subsidiary.

More serious danger signs were apparent to anyone who bothered to analyze Topper's sales. Topper had counted all its shipments as final sales, ignoring the possibility of returns, but had delivered too late in the year for stores' Christmas inventories. Inevitably, many of its toys would still be sitting in the stores in January, waiting to be shipped back to Topper. Both Weill and Berlind claimed they were unaware of that until it was too late.

They arrived at the annual CBWL-Hayden Stone's Christmas party in a state of shock, having just come from Topper's board meeting, where they had been told that the toymaker would be reporting a critical loss of as much as $10 million. In knots of twos and threes, the principals and other senior executives whispered about the possibility of standing trial for fraud. In the middle of the party, Weill phoned his wife. "There's no Christmas this year," he said. "Christmas was just wiped out."

Legal actions brought by the SEC and shareholders dragged on throughout 1972. In November, declaring that CBWL-Hayden Stone either knew — or should have known — about Topper's dreadful financial condition at the time it made the offering, the SEC charged Topper and CBWL-Hayden Stone with fraud. CBWL-Hayden Stone denied any wrongdoing and maintained that Topper, in fact, had intentionally defrauded it along with its auditors and lawyers.*

It was a devastating experience for all of them, the worst moment in Weill's career. "It caused me to do a lot of thinking about my judgment," Weill recalled ruefully. "People didn't believe we hadn't known. But how do you protect yourself against fraud?"

Weill himself was financially hurt by the Topper mess. "I had

---

* Officials of the American Stock Exchange, where CBWL-Hayden Stone's stock was listed, were among those who apparently weren't convinced of Weill's and Berlind's innocence. They fined CBWL-Hayden Stone $20,000 for failing to make an independent inquiry into Topper's actual financial status. Nor were stockholders convinced. They sued.

34,000 Topper shares," he said later. That sum didn't represent his net worth, but it was a lot of money.

By 1973, CBWL-Hayden Stone had changed its name to Hayden Stone because its former name was awkward. Also, since two of the partners were under investigation and the subject of a lawsuit, the change had the salutary effect of avoiding further association of their individual names with the firm's name.

Cogan, Berlind, Weill, and Levitt had all taken separate offices at the company's headquarters. After eight years of togetherness, the camaraderie among them had worn thin. Each was on edge, sizing up the others. In many ways, Roger Berlind was chief executive officer in name only. It was time for a change in leadership. It was increasingly evident that the growing company needed one strong general. Arthur Levitt wasn't a contender: he had consciously removed himself from the competition. Only Cogan and Weill were in position to take charge, but Cogan's vision was at odds with that of the others. His old desire to go into merchant banking, which he considered potentially more profitable than brokerage, surfaced again. Weill, on the other hand, was committed to expanding the company's retail brokerage.

According to his partners, Weill acted as if he were campaigning for the post. The social whirl at his home was one example. His regular visits to his colleagues' offices were another. He prodded and probed them on important business matters. Weill doesn't remember it that way. "I supported Marshall [Cogan] to be CEO. I enjoyed having the veto on anything that was going to happen so I had the ability to stop things, but I was afraid of being the leader because the leader can be wrong." Levitt, the kingmaker, wasn't ready to take a stand, but he was leaning toward Weill.

Despite the hard times and the internal politicking, all four remained committed to their acquisition strategy. The takeover early in 1973 of H. Hentz & Co., a 117-year-old prestigious Jewish retail firm with a strong commodities business, which had suffered a capital setback almost overnight and was on the selling block at a cheap price, boosted Hayden Stone's capital to about $32 million — a 50 percent increase. The twenty-nine offices they acquired, seventeen in cities where Hayden Stone already had branches, were merely a bonus.

The foursome were becoming more seasoned in purchasing firms for virtually nothing. Each man had his clearly defined role. Once again Weill was in charge of brutally laying down the terms of the deal and working out the details. "I did what had to be done," said Weill. "It was never easy. I didn't sleep well until it was over." He closed many of the offices, laid off hundreds of employees, and appointed the Hentz management to posts in Hayden Stone many thought insignificant.

One evening in mid-August, the four men convened in their conference room to pick a new CEO. Though he was closer to Cogan personally, Levitt considered his friend too brash to run a major publicly held corporation. As Levitt presented the case for Weill, Weill himself sat quietly, feeling a conflicting surge of anxiety and excitement. For his part, Cogan was strangely subdued. The consensus was for Weill.

In the end, Cogan decided to leave the company.* He had a ready opportunity waiting for him: a partnership with an old friend, Jimmy Ling, the former head of LTV, who was now running the miniconglomerate Omega-Alpha. Weill, tapped as leader of the firm, wondered whether he could do as well without Cogan. He now had to find some help. He turned to Peter Cohen, a twenty-seven-year-old securities analyst who had been an assistant to Cogan.

The choice, while not obvious at the time, revealed that Weill had one of the most important qualifications of a leader: the ability to pick the right man for the right job at the right time. The hyperkinetic, emotional Weill could count on the cool, cautious Cohen to keep watch over the voluminous minutiae involved in running a brokerage house.

When Weill approached him, Cohen assumed he was going to be fired, since he had worked in the firm for Weill's rival, Cogan. Instead, Weill took Cohen out to lunch and confessed that he was intimidated by the prospect of having to keep track of details.

"Will you help me with the day-to-day operations?"

Cohen agreed. His presence would free Weill to pursue the avenue of leadership that would change Weill from a man who undervalued his own capabilities to a powerful contender on Wall Street.

---

* Weill later had reason to be glad that Cogan had departed. In October of 1973, the SEC launched an investigation of Seaboard, a West Coast mutual fund management firm that CBWL had underwritten three years earlier with Cogan handling the assignment. In March of 1974, the federal agency charged Seaboard and twenty-eight others with bilking more than $9 million from investors when its managers sold shares in marginal companies like Omega-Alpha to the mutual fund for their own profit. In a related suit, the SEC charged Hayden Stone and Marshall Cogan with violating securities law in the stock's public offering. Cogan consented to a nine-month suspension from the securities business, while Hayden Stone agreed to set up a $300,000 fund to reimburse Seaboard investors.

* * *

Sandy Weill had watched Arthur Carter bully, Marshall Cogan sell, Arthur Levitt speak effectively before a group, and Roger Berlind administer the firm. Now forty and the father of two adolescents, he would use all that he had learned from them and his own talents to lead the company.

In 1974, he made his first acquisition as head of the firm, and it was a perfect fit. Seventy-four-year-old Shearson Hammill, a privately run retail house slightly larger than Hayden Stone, had been desperate for a merger partner after losing $2.6 million the year before. It was a bold move on Weill's part. His own company had run $1.3 million in the red during that same period, but he could raise money in the public markets that were denied to the privately held Shearson. His exuberance and pride were tempered by Shearson's plight. "If we hadn't gone public three years before, we might have been in the same position," he said later. "It taught me humility."

Again, Weill and his team had a ruthless task to perform. Only half of Shearson's 2,400 employees survived the merger. It was triage, and Wall Street had never seen anything like it. Weill, who still desperately wanted to be liked and who hated bearing bad news, turned to Alger ("Duke") Chapman, Shearson's low-keyed chief and son of the former chairman of Squibb; he gave Chapman the assignment of traveling around the country firing employees, often one at a time.

On Wall Street, where respect and fear are often synonymous, Sandy Weill's reputation was established. The newly merged brokerage firm, now known as Shearson Hayden Stone, became the tenth largest house on the Street.* (Hayden Stone had been twentieth.) More importantly, it was the sixth largest retailer at a time when the last barriers to negotiated commission rates were crumbling, making the institutional business far less profitable.

Even more than investment banking, retail brokerage was dominated by Gentiles. Of all the New Crowd leaders, only Weill had spent his entire professional life in retail. Going to a stockbroker was all most Americans knew about Wall Street. The names of the mightiest retail firms were household words: E. F. Hutton, Dean Witter, Paine Webber, Bache, and the largest of them all, Merrill Lynch.

---

* Shearson's name came first because it rated higher in underwriting syndicates.

According to friends and associates, Weill harbored a dream that someday Shearson would pass Merrill Lynch. He denied this. "I wanted to be the best," he said later. "If becoming the biggest followed, that was fine, but I never coveted the title." Taking the lead from Merrill Lynch would be an incredible achievement, since it had nearly nine times the capital of Shearson. Begun by Charles Merrill and built up through his market savvy and several astute mergers, Merrill was so much the dominant firm in retail brokerage that Donald Regan, who headed it then, could concentrate his efforts on adding investment banking strength to Merrill's retail brokerage strength.

Such lofty plans were out of Weill's reach. The Shearson chief spent much of his energy preparing for the end of fixed commission rates. Competitive fees would mean that the small customers Weill serviced would pay more for their transactions than the institutional investors.

Finally, on May 1, 1975 — a date that would go down in history as Wall Street's Mayday — freely negotiated commission rates were instituted. Not since Donaldson, Lufkin & Jenrette went public had the financial Establishment suffered a more devastating blow. It was good-bye to the old Wall Street. That a lowly retail broker like Sandy Weill could profit with record earnings of $4.4 million in 1975 after two losing years was a telling sign. Now Weill, whose little CBWL had objected to negotiated rates back in 1970, could chomp on his cigar and say, "I was always for competition."

* * *

Weill's control over the business was virtually total. The new order at Shearson Hayden Stone reflected the distance he was putting between himself and his old partners. Peter Cohen had become Weill's technician, taking care of the details for operations and mergers. In the new company, Weill blurred the issue of who was number two by splitting up the titles of chief operating officer and president — usually one and the same — between Chapman and Levitt, respectively. Berlind, meanwhile, was fading. He had dropped into the fourth slot as vice chairman.

A highly intelligent man with a perceptive sense of business matters, Berlind in the early years had been a balancing influence in the firm, but didn't fit the concept of the new Shearson team. In a sense, it was a case of reverse snobbery; Berlind was too soft, too much the gentleman, and he rarely fought back. Weill used to shout at him, deprecate his fine manners, and, on occasion, blow smoke in his face. More to the point, Weill and the other top executives agreed that he was no longer pulling his own weight in the firm and would have to go. Even if Berlind hadn't then suffered a devastating personal tragedy, his future in the company probably would have been the same.

On the night of Junc 24, 1975, Berlind's wife, Helen Polk, whom he called Polky, their daughter, aged twelve, and two of their sons, nine and six, were killed when their Eastern Airlines jet crashed while making its final approach to Kennedy Airport during a heavy rainstorm. Berlind, who had been waiting in the baggage area, was informed of their deaths. For weeks he went around in a state of shock. Unable to concentrate on anything to the point of almost getting hit by a car while crossing the street, he spent most of his time at home with his two-year-old son, William.

Although Weill was deeply upset by the tragedy, the firm had an agenda, one that didn't include Berlind. Later that summer Berlind left.

Of the three partners Weill had originally started out with, Potoma and Carter had long since departed. Berlind had been the last link with that part of his life. Now there was no looking back. A new — and forceful — Sandy Weill had stepped out of the shade of the past.

# CHAPTER THIRTEEN

# Rohatyn City

L ife with Hélène Gaillet de Barcza brought Felix Rohatyn a dramatic change from the often predictable domestic routines of marriage. Although she moved in with him, she still maintained her old apartment and never pressed him to marry her. She had become a sought-after photographer, and her interests outside of her work were far-ranging — from avant garde art to disco to Far Eastern culture.

With Hélène, Rohatyn roamed the city with pleasure, eating in trendy restaurants, going to movie previews, art openings, concerts, and dance performances. New York was a tonic for him, a welcome relief from the pressures and disappointments of investment banking.

They spent many evenings with a small, eclectic group of friends: among them, Clay Felker, then publisher of *New York* magazine; Peter Maas, author of the best-selling *Serpico;* Mike Burke, head of Madison Square Garden; Jim Lipton, screenwriter and producer, and his exotic wife Kedakai, a Revlon model. The city offered a wealth of possibilities. In the midseventies the theater was aglow with such shows as *Equus, Short Eyes,* and *A Little Night Music.* The bar scene in Manhattan was lively, and it was chic for the affluent to escape from the haute cuisine and expense account restaurants to frequent the more pedestrian burger, pasta, quiche, and avocado bistro circuit and celebrity haunts such as Elaine's — the determinedly run-down Second Avenue eatery made famous by Woody Allen and well-known journalists and writers — where talk of the financial world was virtually off-limits.

But the wall separating work and play would soon come tumbling down in a way that Rohatyn could not have imagined. In April of 1975, a broker offered him New York City bonds that paid nine and a quarter percent interest — an exceptionally high rate for municipal notes. Rohatyn's curiosity was piqued: he knew that the city had to be desperate to pay that much. It was the first insight he had into the city's financial condition. Up to then, he had been no better informed than most New Yorkers. He knew from reading the newspapers that the city's financial health was, at best, poor, and that it was getting worse. But the city had always managed to scrape through.

This time the situation was different. For years the various mayors had kept the city running by using creative accounting. The banks and Wall Street had winked and had provided the financing by marketing even more of the city's securities. But the city was short on gimmicks, as spending outran revenues. In February of 1975, Mayor Abraham Beame's 1975–76 budget had been released with an anticipated deficit of $1.7 billion out of a total budget of $12 billion.

Rohatyn did begin paying more attention to the growing crisis, but merely from a banker's point of view. He said later, "I had no involvement with politics at the local level. I had never met a mayor, a comptroller, or a governor then. I don't think I had ever met a city or state official. My municipal virginity was total. I understood, of course, that eventually the city would have to default to its bond holders, and this might cause the city to declare bankruptcy."

The following month, Rohatyn became increasingly alarmed as news of the city's fiscal crisis was given widespread coverage in newspapers and on television. The city and the state (which had loaned the city $800 million to tide it over March and April) had been viciously humbled in Washington. Mayor Beame and Governor Hugh Carey made a desperation visit to William Simon, who had left Wall Street for Washington in 1971 and was now secretary of the treasury, in the hope of getting some federal aid for the city. They couldn't have spoken to a more unsympathetic listener. Though Simon had made his fortune in New York as a partner of Salomon Brothers, he could easily have qualified as the city's archetypal enemy. New York City, he told Carey and Beame, could stew in its own excesses, as far as the federal government was concerned.

The equivalent of turning over the last stone had a devastating impact. Bankruptcy seemed inevitable now. Several days later, when Rohatyn was in Washington as part of his work on an SEC advisory committee, he spoke over breakfast about the city's crisis with Democratic National Committee chairman Robert Strauss, a friend since his Muskie days. Strauss asked him, "What do you think will happen if New York City goes bankrupt?"

"I think it would be very bad," Rohatyn answered, "not only for New York, but for the dollar, and for our international posture, and for eighty-seven other reasons."

"Do you mind if I tell Carey what you think?" Strauss asked.

"Hell, no. Be my guest."

Governor Carey was looking for outside advisers who might have a fresh approach to the city's crisis. Not surprisingly, the well-connected Rohatyn had already been mentioned more than once. When Rohatyn met with the governor at Carey's request, he was asked if he would be willing to help. Rohatyn agreed to temporary service.

Carey assembled a blue ribbon panel of four advisers: Former federal judge Simon Rifkind; Metropolitan Life Insurance chief Richard Shinn; Macy's boss Donald Smiley; and Rohatyn. The group, which hadn't had any idea of the extent of the problem, quickly realized it was far too great for the city to handle alone.

One Friday Rohatyn was given a copy of the city's financial records, which he took with him to study over the weekend at his rented house in Wainscott, Long Island. That night Rohatyn, the Liptons, and Mike Burke went to see a murder mystery at the East Hampton Cinema. It was what his friends called a "terrible Felix movie." He found escape in such films. They sat alone in the balcony; the theater was almost deserted. Rohatyn seemed agitated and distracted. He finally said, "I've just reviewed the city's financial records. The city is going under. It hasn't a prayer."

Over Memorial Day weekend, the panel met at Shinn's Greenwich, Connecticut, home with some of the city's top bankers to map out its next move. The most immediate problem was the $280 million debt payable by June 11, just two weeks away, and the banks would no longer act as underwriters or lend the city any more money unless an overall recovery plan was in place. After much discussion, the idea of creating a state agency to raise money for the city was formulated — the Municipal Assistance Corporation or Big MAC, as it was soon to be known throughout the country. It would be an independent state agency backed by the credit of New York, which would raise money for the city and act as a watchdog on how it was spent. Its main function would be to try to sell some $3 billion worth of bonds to repay notes that would come due during the following three months. The banks would deal with nothing less. Rohatyn told Mayor Beame that if the agency was not in place in five days, the city would owe its creditors and employees $1 billion, with no means to pay.

Cornered, Beame could only argue that as mayor of the city, he wouldn't bow to the banks, which he accused Rohatyn of doing.

"We're trying to keep the patient alive," replied Rohatyn, meaning the city, "so we can treat him."

For the majority of politicians and businessmen in the city, bankruptcy was unthinkable. Rohatyn, Beame, and Carey all believed the city would collapse from the repercussions. "Everybody would be lining up before a judge who didn't know what to do," Rohatyn said later. "Services would go to hell, corporations would move out in droves, no one would do business with New York any more, and it wouldn't be able to borrow for years."

Rohatyn had only to allude to the word *bankruptcy* to stir up support for MAC among the various factions — city and state government, commercial and investment banking, and labor unions. In five days the agency was in place.* With its formation, power over the city had been taken away from Beame and every other local politician. Not one of the nine members of MAC was an elected official.

*  *  *

The MAC meetings usually started early in the morning and lasted well into the evening. Frequently the day would end with dinner and drinks. At night, Rohatyn and Hélène would stop at one restaurant, then move to another, and sometimes even to a third to meet with various groups of people involved in the city crisis.

In July, MAC unloaded $1 billion of debt through its two principal underwriters — Salomon Brothers and the Morgan Guaranty Trust Company. MAC planned to raise another billion in August. But after the police organized marches and the sanitation workers union staged a wildcat strike during the week of July 4 to protest the job cutbacks, all hope for a second $1 billion bond sale died. In the following months, whatever financing MAC arranged was done by what Rohatyn called "monthly miracles," which involved the banks, various insurance companies, and the union pension funds.

During the first few months Rohatyn was under intense pressure to quit the MAC board. He had joined over André Meyer's strenuous objections, and Meyer wanted him to return to Lazard full time. Rohatyn was also concerned that his MAC work was disrupting his relationship with his sons, who complained about cancelled plans and insufficient time spent with their father.

Over and over again, he discussed the possibility of resigning

---

* There was some tense last-minute resistance by upstate legislators. They hated helping the city as much as any government officials in the country, but, in the end, the bill to create MAC was voted through with surprising swiftness.

with Hélène, Clay Felker, Jim Lipton, and Peter Maas. But after the bond sale debacle, he decided he couldn't just walk away.

He knew that MAC would have to allocate sacrifice and he knew it would be painful. At a MAC meeting, he threw down the gauntlet: "The possibility of revenue increases such as fare increases and tuition increases should be examined . . . it was apparent from what the banking community had said that the city's way of life is disliked nationwide."

The list would grow and become harsher. On the agenda would be the end of free tuition at the City University, the thirty-five-cent public transit fare, and thousands of city jobs that had once come with virtually a lifetime guarantee. None of the proposed cutbacks would in themselves save the city from bankruptcy, but they would decrease spending. All were popular with the banks and with Washington, which viewed these cutbacks as signs that MAC was truly independent of the city. Before they handed out any bandages they wanted to see the city bleed. In a sense, the crisis had taken a new turn, one that was ugly and divisive.

Rohatyn found himself drawn deeper and deeper into a maelstrom of controversy that would harm many people's lives, especially those of the working class and the poor in New York, before it was over. As a major partner in a small, very private and profitable firm, he was risking his professional reputation for no remuneration. But his MAC work had an undefinable reward. It was important to Rohatyn to help the city that had given him a home. There was simply no more hospitable and enriching city than New York for a wealthy, cosmopolitan Jew. "People accept the fact that a man does crazy things like falling in love with a woman," he said later. "Well, I've fallen in love with a city."

There were also some business-related returns. He would be representing another powerhouse — Governor Carey — in his cherished role as the consummate dealmaker in the biggest deal of them all — involving millions of people, billions of dollars, and countless issues. The Rohatyn network of influence would reach far into the inner circles of city, state, and national politics and he would win more admirers and clients in corporate America.

By midsummer Carey wanted Rohatyn to head the board, but Rohatyn was reluctant. He wasn't an administrator, and he didn't want to assume any deeper MAC responsibilities or commitment.

Briefed by Carey, Peter Maas (a mutual friend of Rohatyn's and the governor's), had one strong argument to use, though it was a sensitive one. Maas told Rohatyn that Carey knew how terrible he felt about the public criticism heaped on him during the Hartford acquisition, especially about the label "Felix the Fixer." Carey was also aware of the taunting his three boys had received in school and how much that bothered him. If Rohatyn successfully saw the city through its crisis, Maas reported, all that would be forgotten. He would be known as "the savior of New York City."

"He said that?" Rohatyn asked.

The stigma of Hartford hadn't totally faded. In April, the SEC had reopened its investigation of that case and the IRS had ITT locked into a tax evasion case that involved Rohatyn and Meyer.* ITT was also enmeshed in civil suits. The ITT empire that Rohatyn had been so instrumental in building was crumbling. By comparison, the city was a fresh challenge.

Rohatyn had finally agreed to step up to head of the finance committee. William Ellinghaus, the chief of New York Telephone and a member of MAC, became the board's chairman. There was no turning back now for Rohatyn. The city needed a billion dollars by mid-August, another billion by September, and on and on. If the money didn't materialize on time, Rohatyn himself would be held accountable. A date was set for recommendations of further economies — July 29 — the day the first serious negotiations with the unions were scheduled. David Rockefeller, chairman of Chase Manhattan, had made it clear that the banks wouldn't bail the city out through loans unless a "comprehensive program" — a tough budget — was put into the works. That meant Rohatyn and MAC chairman Ellinghaus had to shove a package of unpleasant sacrifices — largely wage freezes and layoffs — down the throats of the municipal workers unions and make it seem as if they were swallowing a pill to restore their health. Labor mediator Theodore Kheel briefed Rohatyn on the union leaders he'd be facing.

Ellinghaus and Rohatyn would be the spokesmen for MAC and the tough-minded Victor Gotbaum, leader of Council 37 of the American Federation of State, County, and Municipal Employees, would be spokesman for the unions. The meeting at the Americana Hotel soon turned into a media spectacle. When Rohatyn proposed a wage freeze,

---

* The reason Meyer had been able to place the Hartford shares owned by ITT with an Italian bank at the inflated price, the IRS claimed, was that they were only "parked" — that is, held by agreement, temporarily. Thus, no sale and no tax exemption. In 1981, ITT settled with the government for $18.5 million.

Gotbaum leaped up from his chair and began pounding the table. A freeze, he screamed, was unacceptable. Rohatyn was taken aback. He had never before been yelled at during negotiations. It was immediately obvious to him that the public arena was different, and Gotbaum was part of that difference. Although Gotbaum's outrage was genuine, there was also a significant element of theater in his histrionics, a way of probing his opponents' weaknesses under the watchful glare of the cameras. Then Albert Shanker, head of the United Federation of Teachers, shouted at Rohatyn, and finally, Barry Feinstein of the Teamsters jumped in with a few choice words.

The atmosphere didn't improve when the negotiators got down to business in a private suite in the hotel, where the union leaders grimly settled in for a marathon evening. Gotbaum took his shoes off, and the two police union chiefs removed their jackets, revealing revolvers strapped to their belts. "It was the first time I had ever negotiated with people wearing guns," Rohatyn said. Almost as disconcerting was the lack of harmony among the union officials themselves; they were there to protect the special interests of their members. Rohatyn had to create the image of harmony to show the financial world that the city officials and the unions were all united behind MAC. The talks dragged on until three in the morning, and when they broke up, the unions had only gotten the bare minimum in return for their support.*

The new MAC plan with its package of budget cuts and other economies looked promising, but the city's financial cupboards were bare and the banks still maintained their "show-me" stance. Rohatyn had become the town crier, sounding the alarm from New York City to Albany. Day after day, he spoke with state legislators and members of Congress, urging them to scare up some aid for the city. He became the source for many journalists who needed someone to guide them through the complexities of the city's fiscal nightmare. Time after time, he came up with pithy, quotable phrases. Perhaps the best known was his comment that default would be "like someone stepping into a tepid bath and slashing his wrists — you might not feel yourself dying but that's what would happen."

The prospect of defaulting weighed heavily on his mind. His

---

* Ultimately, the unions agreed to a wage freeze until the city's budget was balanced and the city was able to sell the bonds in the bond market. (That didn't happen until 1981.) The unions also agreed to take over some of the pension funding that had previously been carried by the city, and they eventually invested large sums from their pension funds in MAC bonds.

relationship with Hélène became more distant, although she was ever-understanding. But even when they were together it was as though he weren't there. The intensely private man was also stepping through the invisible barrier between private and public selves.

By late August, as far as Rohatyn was concerned, default was a near reality. The patient was already in the tub filled with tepid water and now was holding a razor to his wrist.

Carey and Rohatyn believed that the state and federal governments had to make a huge commitment to the city. They put together a complicated $2.3 billion financial plan that depended heavily on a state loan to see the city through the end of November and also on subsequent federal aid.

Rohatyn knew the plan was a gamble. He didn't know that he would be the one making the bet. Ellinghaus resigned as head of MAC to become one of the three businessmen on the Emergency Financial Control Board, newly created by Governor Carey to supervise the city's budget and to allocate the funds raised by MAC. Ellinghaus's move made it inevitable that Rohatyn would take over MAC's top post. He was beginning to feel comfortable in the spotlight. He had eased into the role of a public figure and, in fact, had become something of a celebrity. At restaurants such as Elaine's and "21," the best tables were offered to him. At the Alrae, daily messages were left for him from numerous reporters needing information on the crisis. He could influence and direct people's thinking and action on a larger scale than ever before.

Throughout September and into October the financial cliff-hangers continued. Four hundred fifty million was needed by October 17. On the evening of October 16, Rohatyn met at the governor's office with Albert Shanker and two other trustees of the teachers union and negotiated with them well into the night. The teachers were being asked to buy $150 million in MAC bonds, but they felt they were getting no concessions in return. Time was running out. The deadline, set for midnight, passed without the teachers' yielding. On the morning of October 17, New Yorkers awakened to learn that the city, in effect, was bankrupt. Finally, that afternoon Shanker gave in. Another crisis in the melodrama of the city had been surmounted.

Rohatyn lived this life of confrontation every day. Perhaps the most brilliant aspect of the plan to save the city had less to do with raising money than building a consensus for it. Many of the city's most powerful institutions, including the *New York Times,* bought MAC bonds and thus were motivated to cheer Rohatyn on. His few critics were unable to influence events.

The only villains in the game from this point on were in Washington, the chief one being President Gerald Ford. On October 29, Ford made a forty-minute speech on why he would veto any legislation that provided New York City with a bailout. It was in the best interest of the country, the president claimed, for the city to declare bankruptcy. The next day, the *New York Daily News* summed up the president's views in the memorable headline, "Ford to City: Drop Dead."

Rohatyn and Governor Carey were sitting in Elaine's that evening, when someone thrust an early edition of the *News* under their noses. They had already been informed of the Ford speech and had been completely overwhelmed. The headline didn't change anything except their spirits. They still had to find a way to obtain help from Washington regardless of the president's stand. They decided to put the city on a more restrictive diet. It was so severe and punitive that Carey and Rohatyn didn't even consult Mayor Beame in advance. As a last, desperate measure, they instituted a moratorium on repayment of principal in the city's short-term debt, which amounted to a euphemism for default.

They had to send a clear message to Washington that the city would do anything to avert bankruptcy. It seemed to work. Congress was impressed. Finally, on November 25, even President Ford went along. New York City had the additional $2.3 billion it needed so desperately for the short term.

\* \* \*

Governor Carey had been right in his prediction. Rohatyn was a celebrity now, not just in New York, but across the nation. *People* magazine had done a profile on him. The man or woman in the street knew him by sight. Caught in traffic on his way to see a business client out of town, Rohatyn had been escorted by a police cruiser to the East Side heliport. In the minds of many Americans, he was already the Man Who Saved New York City.

The day after Ford guaranteed the federal loans, Rohatyn was off on a Thanksgiving ski trip with one of his sons at the western resort of Alta, Utah. There he was introduced to a striking divorcée from New York named Elizabeth Vagliano. She knew of Rohatyn's work on the city crisis, and while they only spoke briefly, it was the start of a new relationship.

# CHAPTER FOURTEEN

# Hardball Politics

The general feeling in New York City was that the pressure of the fiscal crisis was subsiding — at least temporarily — and the timing couldn't have been better. Adding to the air of optimism about the city's future and its position as the world's financial capital were the good news about the U.S. economy and the stock market upswing in the winter of 1975–76.

Perhaps nowhere was the renewal of faith more evident than at the Regency Hotel on Park Avenue and Sixty-first Street, where the ritual known as the "power breakfast" was flourishing. What the Polo Lounge in the Beverly Hills Hotel was to the world of film celebrities and dealmakers, the Regency was to the New York world of political and business leaders. Part of the giant Loews Corporation controlled by the wealthy brothers Laurence and Preston Tisch, the luxury hotel had become the "in" place for business breakfasts. It was the way to get the jump on the business day. More than any other group, the New Crowd gave the power breakfast at the Regency its cachet. The brighter investment outlook contributed to the expansive mood of the room.

By 8 o'clock on any weekday morning, the limousines were lined up two deep outside the Regency's Park Avenue entrance. Inside the mirrored dining room with its paintings of French châteaus, deal-makers of every stripe were seated and financial transactions were percolating. Among the New Crowd regulars, Felix Rohatyn breakfasted there with leaders from both the city and investment banking communities. "You see the politicians hustling and the hustlers politicking," he said at the time. Merger lawyers Joe Flom of Skadden, Arps, Slate, Meagher & Flom and Martin Lipton of Wachtell, Lipton, Rosen & Katz were also regulars. Usually found on opposite sides during a merger contest, Flom and Lipton sometimes could be seen at the same table. Now and then, state comptroller Arthur Levitt, Sr., would join his son Arthur Levitt, Jr., and Sandy Weill.

The Regency crowd that paid extraordinary prices for ordinary breakfast fare also put up with slow service and the din of voices and clanging silverware. The food was the least important part of the power breakfast. Conversing intently under the noise of the room, the power brokers and would-be power brokers, Jewish or not, were masters at mixing business with *schmoozing,* a Yiddish term for small talk. It required practice and concentration. No one had risen very far without that talent.

The small talk often included gossip, and part of the gossip late in 1976 was rumors about what William Simon would do next. With the November defeat of Gerald Ford, the man New Yorkers loved to hate, the secretary of the treasury was out of a job.

The obvious answer was that Simon would return to Wall Street. Everyone assumed he would eventually wind up at Salomon Brothers. At Salomon headquarters downtown, John Gutfreund, who didn't breakfast at the Regency, didn't seem to respond to the speculation that went on there or anywhere else. But those who knew him well believed he wasn't ready to cede half of the Room (the firm's trading floor) to Simon — who had been his only real rival as Billy Salomon's heir apparent — without a clear understanding of Gutfreund's dominance in the firm.

\* \* \*

Billy Salomon wanted Simon back. Having been the nation's number-one money man in Washington, Simon couldn't be taken lightly. For a Wall Street leader, perhaps no other title had a nicer ring — or offered more promise of new business — than secretary of the treasury. But four years had passed, and Simon couldn't simply pick up at Salomon Brothers where he had left off.

No longer an underdog in any sense of the word, the firm had just completed its best year ever (its fiscal year ended on September 30). To Wall Street's surprise, the negotiated commission rates instituted in May of 1975 hadn't proved a disaster for institutional brokers after all. At least, not yet. The business had simply become more concentrated in the hands of larger firms as more of the little research boutiques dropped out, unable to cope with the competition.

In 1976, the record $70 million earned by Salomon Brothers made even the most junior partners well off. But for a risk-taking firm like Salomon, the uncertainties of the seventies (the firm also lost money one year) sharpened the internal tensions and competition to the point of open feuding. Standing nose to nose in the middle of the trading floor, two rivals for one of the top spots in the firm — the volatile Jay Perry, the legendary block trader, and the equally temperamental Richard Rosenthal, one of the Street's premier arbitrageurs — screamed and cursed at each other as others looked on, expecting a fistfight to break out.

That was enough for Billy Salomon. He liked contention when it fostered competition, but he didn't want an all-out civil war on his hands. He relocated Perry, limited Rosenthal's responsibilities,* and began to lean more heavily on Gutfreund, who never seemed to let him down. At times Gutfreund groused about going back to Oberlin to teach, but few took him seriously. He was always consistent. The hours, the dedication, the stoicism — these were constants for him.

According to a number of high-ranking partners, Gutfreund would have accepted Simon back, but only under *his* set of conditions. Morgan Stanley's syndicate chief, Frederick Whittemore, who knew both men well, played the role of peacemaker. "Father Fred," as Whittemore was known around the Street, tried to impress on Gutfreund that he and Simon could work well together. Gutfreund conceded the possibility but seemed to feel he would have to remain at least a cigar length ahead of Simon. He had earned that edge, not only because of his years of labor while Simon was away, but also because he had once apparently gone against his political conscience to please Simon.

In 1971, Simon had pressed Salomon Brothers' executive committee for a $100,000 contribution to help finance Richard Nixon's reelection bid. Pledging $15,000 himself, he had asked the rest of the executive committee and other senior partners to come up with the balance.

At Salomon Brothers and elsewhere the unspoken understanding was that partners and other top executives reciprocated when it came to raising money for charities and political candidates. For many of the partners, donating money to Nixon's campaign was politics as usual. But not for Gutfreund. He seemed to revel in the fact that he was one of Wall Street's unabashed liberal Democrats. Still, he contributed several thousand dollars.

---

* Rather than putting the firm's block trading and arbitrage departments under one man as he had planned, Salomon dispatched Perry to Texas to head the Dallas regional office, confined Rosenthal's authority to arbitrage, and selected thirty-three-year-old Michael Bloomberg to run stock block-trading operations.

Simon's fund-raising efforts were not a mere show of support for the president. Attorney General John Mitchell was a close friend. As one of the foremost municipal bond traders, Simon had come to know Mitchell well when Mitchell had been one of Wall Street's most prominent municipal bond lawyers. After Mitchell moved to Washington, the two men maintained contact. Simon even threw a bon voyage party for Mitchell and his wife, Martha, when they went on a cruise. With a friend like the attorney general in his corner and a generous campaign contribution to Nixon, Simon became more influential in Washington at a time when he was somewhat hemmed in at Salomon Brothers. After two years on the executive committee, he was still running a step or two behind Gutfreund.

As Simon drew closer to the Republican power elite, Gutfreund was becoming identified with the man who would oppose Nixon for the presidency, Senator George McGovern. By now Gutfreund had caught the spirit — and style — of the McGovern supporters. In apparent defiance of Wall Street's conservative code, he grew a beard that made him look like an English professor. And for the first time, he became a vocal supporter of a candidate. "I'm not normally known as a political person," he told the New York Times, but he said he frankly felt appalled by the decline in civil liberties. He also deplored the continued bombing in Indochina.

Several days before the election, the New York Times carried a previously secret list of large contributors (more than $2,500) to the Nixon campaign, the result of a drive made by McGovern and others for full campaign contribution disclosure. Among the names mentioned was Gutfreund's. In the last week before the election, Gutfreund — who had contributed only $7,200 to the McGovern campaign — gave an additional $16,300 and his wife Joyce another $1,000 to the hopelessly doomed candidacy. On election eve, he was one of the few faithful to show up in Sioux Falls, South Dakota, to sit with McGovern and watch the Nixon landslide.

Apparently, Gutfreund's support of both sides of the campaign was confusing even to his family. As a consequence, Gutfreund, according to Simon, felt compelled to explain to his son Nicholas his donation to Nixon: "Some day you'll understand what being a partner means. Bill Simon is a friend and partner, and when he came and asked me to contribute, I never thought twice."

A month after Nixon's reelection, Simon was appointed deputy secretary of the treasury, and in 1974, he became secretary of the treasury. That pleased Billy Salomon, who loved having his firm's name as well as his own linked with the celebrated rich and powerful. Despite Simon's unpopularity among the Salomon partners, most felt proud that one of their raffish boys had finally attained that kind of national status.

For his part, Gutfreund thrived in Simon's absence. He solidified his position, moving Salomon Brothers farther up the ranks of Wall Street underwriters, giving it more muscle in bond issues than it had ever had before, and raising it to third place in total underwritings by 1972.

In the biggest shake-up in the forty-year history of the "bulge group," as the top-bracket underwriting firms were referred to, Salomon Brothers, along with Goldman Sachs and Merrill Lynch, had elbowed aside Dillon Read and Kuhn Loeb to join Morgan Stanley and First Boston in the lead ranking of debt underwriters. Soon after, when American Telephone & Telegraph (AT&T) decided to split the responsibility for raising its capital between Morgan Stanley and Salomon Brothers, the loss for Morgan Stanley was far greater than merely losing money — its bankers had always insisted on being the lead underwriter.

For all the high-stepping Salomon Brothers was doing, Gutfreund remained a reclusive figure on the Street. He attended occasional business gatherings but rarely socialized with clients. After work, he focused on his family. The Gutfreunds and their three young sons lived in a traditionally furnished Lexington Avenue apartment containing a few antiques and a serious library. Occasionally Gutfreund and his wife, Joyce, enjoyed going to good restaurants, small dinner parties, concerts, plays, and events at the Century Country Club — nothing very elaborate or formal. They saw a tight circle of friends (primarily successful Old- and New-Crowd Jews) whom they had known for years — the men worked on the Street or were involved in corporate law or finance: Bob Bernhard, Hugh Lowenstein, Don Stone, Marty Lipton, Larry Tisch, and their wives. Gutfreund played tennis with these men at the Century Country Club and at Don Stone's home in Scarsdale.

It was a serious, stable life — a good life — but one without excitement or glamour. John Gutfreund joined the board of trustees at Montefiore Hospital, thanks to his childhood friend Bob Bernhard, and Joyce Gutfreund became very involved with Blythedale Children's Hospital in Westchester. A strong, civic-minded woman, she wasn't a professional corporate wife like Virginia Salomon. Her world was her family, her home, and her charities. Rarely did she entertain business people and never on short notice. One evening, at Gutfreund's invitation, a Salomon partner and a client stopped by the apartment after dinner. Joyce Gutfreund greeted them, chatted for a few minutes, and then left the room. Some partners noted that Gutfreund seemed increasingly bothered that his wife was not as sociable as Virginia Salomon. It was perhaps a kernel of personal dissatisfaction with his marriage that would take root and grow.

But for the present, at least, his personal life was on hold and he could relish his firm's achievements and his own role in making them happen. The 1972 election was over, Simon was established in Washington, and Gutfreund's beard was gone.

\* \* \*

After the election of November 1976, Simon met quietly several times with Billy Salomon. From the start, it was clear that they had different ideas about Simon's place at Salomon Brothers.

Under Billy Salomon, the firm was a loosely structured partnership. He himself held the only title, managing partner. All he offered Simon was a position as a "very important partner." Nothing more. That apparently didn't satisfy Simon's specific needs, among them his desire to sit on corporate boards. Salomon, who had made it a policy not to allow partners to serve as directors, believing the practice would create a conflict of interest, was not going to make an exception for Simon. There were other sticking points as well. Salomon made no effort to reach a compromise. By the end of the winter, all talk of Simon's rejoining the firm had ended. The former secretary of the treasury took on a variety of posts before starting Wesray, which became a highly lucrative investment company.

After a twenty-three-year climb, John Gutfreund finally had a clear path to the summit. Billy Salomon would never pit anyone against him again. With Salomon only three years away from his self-imposed mandatory retirement age of sixty-five, it seemed that Gutfreund could soon claim the firm as his own.

Yet not long afterward, Gutfreund's lustrous prize diminished dramatically in value. Wall Street proved a rough place to turn a profit in 1977, despite a healthy economy and a decline in the unemployment rate. That spring, with the dollar weakening and inflation, oil prices, and interest rates rising, the stock market took a nosedive. It was the fourth debilitating bear market in less than a dozen years. Big investors looked elsewhere — rushing into real estate, art, antiques, and bank money market accounts.

As trading and underwriting volume fell, Salomon Brothers was hard-hit. Its profits were further squeezed when investors took advantage of the slump — and the advantage granted to them on May-day — by driving down the negotiated commission rates on securities transactions. In general, the bulge group was taking a beating. At Morgan Stanley, a latecomer to trading, the back office was in shambles during the pinch. The only major firm that had an even greater back office mess was the perennially number-two firm, First Boston. Its underwriting business fared so poorly in 1977 that it barely qualified for its bulge group ranking.

Goldman Sachs was bogged down in its own set of problems. The previous fall, its leader, Gus Levy, had died suddenly of a heart attack. Though he would be remembered as both a giant on Wall Street and a legendary philanthropist, part of his legacy had been two fraud convictions just two years earlier for the firm's trademark commercial paper operation.* Of the bulge firms, only Merrill Lynch was doing well; it had started a real estate operation and had acquired the prestigious investment banking house of White Weld.

Problems in the bulge group were more than matched lower down on the Street. Many firms went out of business. By spring 1978, the number of firms with seats on the New York Stock Exchange had dropped from 505 at the time of Mayday, three years earlier, to 465. Throughout the financial community, talk was widespread about the need for more capital to survive over the long haul and for diversification into other businesses.

Gutfreund dug in his heels for a tough fight.

---

* In October 1974, a federal jury had found Goldman Sachs guilty of defrauding its customers of $30 million by selling them Penn Central commercial paper in 1969 and 1970, even as the railroad was going broke. Much of the paper had been sold by Levy himself. After the trial, Goldman Sachs had to face dozens of claims totaling more than $30 million, which took months to settle out of court.

# CHAPTER FIFTEEN

# At the Top of the Crowd

*T*he first time he had attended a partners' year-end party was in 1958, when the celebration had amounted to little more than pitchers of beer in the back room of a steak house after the close of the stock market. Twenty years later, in April of 1978, Alan ("Ace") C. Greenberg, a poker-faced man of fifty, was about to take over the leadership of the only firm for which he had ever worked — the institutional brokerage house of Bear, Stearns & Company.

Although known as "Boys Town" for its scrappy history, this Jewish-led firm was a highly efficient trading partnership that didn't miss many opportunities to profit from trading securities. Over the years it had built a lucrative business in arbitrage, block trading, and institutional and retail sales.

Alan Greenberg had built up Bear Stearns's risk arbitrage department. Salim ("Cy") L. Lewis, the man Greenberg was formally replacing that evening, had shepherded the firm into the institutional business through block trading. Lewis stood in a little cluster of people, drinking scotch, and talking loudly. For nearly forty years, he had run Bear Stearns like a self-made autocrat. He was a giant of a man, standing six feet two inches tall and weighing more than 250 pounds, with an uncommonly large head, a thundering voice, and a jolting temper.

When they first opened their business in 1923 at 100 Broadway, the partners of Bear Stearns were far from a bunch of rough-and-tumble risk takers. Throughout the early years, particularly during the Depression, this retail brokerage house devoted most of its energy to conserving the $500,000 of capital that its founding partners, Joseph Bear, Robert Stearns, and Harold Mayer, Jr., had originally invested. They were joined in 1928 by the young V. Theodore Low, the scion of a wealthy German-Jewish family and a Princeton graduate, who became a general partner after his uncle had bought him a position in the firm. In its early days, Bear Stearns's clients were mainly rich Park Avenue German-Jewish widows.

Eager to start an institutional bond business, in 1933 Low hired Cy Lewis, who had attracted his attention while Lewis worked for Salomon Brothers. The son of Eastern European Jewish immigrants, as well as a former semipro football player and shoe salesman, Lewis began asserting himself during the war years, while Low was away in the service. Under his stewardship, Bear Stearns was transformed from a standard brokerage firm that acted only as an agent for its retail clients to a maverick trading firm that bought and sold bonds for major institutions and also risked some of its own capital. Lewis, along with a small group of savvy traders led by David Finkle, gambled on big arbitrage plays, particularly those involving utility company breakups and railroad reorganizations. A formidable trader, he spent his later years competing with his old friend Gus Levy for huge blocks of stock.

* * *

By 1949, when Ace Greenberg arrived at Bear Stearns, Lewis had taken charge of the firm, if not by title or seniority, then by the force of his personality. The trading room, where Lewis presided in a thronelike leather seat from the center of a huge U-shaped arrangement of desks, held a special attraction for Greenberg. It was the big time, from the vantage point of a young man from Oklahoma City.

Greenberg, whose father was a women's clothing retailer of Russian-Jewish ancestry, came to New York from Oklahoma, hoping to find work in the brokerage business. He had graduated from the University of Missouri with a bachelor's degree in business administration, but his real interests in college had been playing bridge and performing card tricks. He loved gambling and magic. (He first became hooked when he was eight years old, after seeing a performance by Blackstone the Magician.) Greenberg saw Wall Street as the biggest and most challenging "card game" of them all.

In a sense, he made his first bet with the $2,000 given to him by his father to cover his expenses while he was in New York. He gambled that a letter of recommendation written by a friend of his uncle's — a businessman whom he had never met — would land him a job. He was interviewed at six Jewish brokerage firms, all of which turned him down, and was almost ready to take the train back to Oklahoma City when Bear Stearns offered him a spot as a $37-a-week clerk.

At first, Greenberg's tasks consisted mostly of reading technical journals and sticking pins into a map to show where new oil rigs were located. But he soon gravitated to the trading floor, where he spent his lunch hours watching the stock ticker and becoming absorbed in the action. The sight of a group of arbs, brokers, and traders — all in a state of constant animation, calling buy and sell orders and talking excitedly on the phone — was infectious. He soon came to the attention of John Slade, a German-Jewish refugee and head of the arbitrage department, who arranged to have Greenberg work for him.*

Being part of the pressure-cooker atmosphere was quite different from just watching it. On Greenberg's first day in the arbitrage department, the breathtaking pace, combined with a verbal lashing by Slade, made him violently sick. With the help of another partner, he managed to get to the washroom just before throwing up.

That was arguably the first and last time Greenberg ever suffered from a nervous stomach. He learned quickly, and when in 1956 a desk opened up next to Lewis, the senior partner, Slade convinced Greenberg that it would be good for his career to sit next to the firm's boss.

Like some strong-willed men, Lewis had a supportive, kind side. One of his great strengths was encouraging young people to stake out their own turf in the firm. Nevertheless, if Slade hadn't prodded him to work next to Lewis, Greenberg never would have gone willingly. Although a solidly built "Jewish six-footer," as Greenberg jokingly referred to himself (he was actually five feet ten), he saw Lewis as a Goliath, someone to be avoided. Being seated next to Lewis meant suffering the full force of his frequent titanic rages. If anyone disagreed with him, it was virtually a no-win situation. Lewis had an ego as large as his physical proportions. If you were wrong, he would never let you forget it. If you were right and he was wrong, then Lewis would hold a grudge.

Worse, from Greenberg's point of view, Lewis had a habit of falling in love with almost every stock he bought, which made it difficult for him to sell the securities, even when their prices dropped well below what had been paid. That was contrary to what Greenberg had been brought up to believe constituted good business practice. "If something isn't moving," his retailer father had told him over and over again, "sell it today, because tomorrow it will be worth less." Greenberg privately asked some of the other partners how they felt about

---

* John Slade had joined the firm in 1936 as a runner. Originally his name had been Hans Schlesinger, but he became John Slade at Low's request in 1940. Low had previously changed his name from Lowenstein, which he felt sounded too German and too Jewish.

Lewis's reluctance to unload securities. Many shared Greenberg's view, but no one would stand up to the boss. As a young man without seniority, Greenberg wisely chose not to challenge Lewis. Instead, under Slade's watchful eye, he honed his own skills as a trader, making more and more profitable plays in arbitrage for Bear Stearns. (In good years, arbitrage accounted for 30 percent of the firm's profits; in bad years, it accounted for almost all of them.) Even Lewis came to admire Greenberg's growing talents.

Greenberg lived with his wife (the former Anne Lieberman, whom he had married in 1953) and their two young children in an apartment on the Upper East Side. John Rosenwald, a Bear Stearns institutional salesman who sat on the other side of Cy Lewis in the trading room, lived in the same building, and John Gutfreund, who was still a bachelor, had an apartment across the street. Since the three young men were friendly, they often rode downtown together in Gutfreund's green Oldsmobile convertible. In 1958, at the age of thirty, Greenberg was made a partner at Bear Stearns.

Though his personal dissatisfaction with the way Lewis ran the trading desk remained, a crisis in Greenberg's life forced the issue into the background. A year after making partner, he was diagnosed as having colon cancer and underwent surgery at the Mayo Clinic in Rochester, Minnesota. The odds were not the kind Greenberg liked to play. He was given less than a fifty-fifty chance of surviving. For a year or so after the operation, he was uncharacteristically pessimistic and behaved as though he were living on borrowed time. "I don't know if I can afford to buy any long-term stocks at this point," he confided to one friend.

As his health improved and his spirits rebounded, his old frustrations with Lewis's stock holdings surfaced again. In the early sixties, Greenberg, who was no more patient than Lewis, couldn't take it anymore.

"I'm quitting," he told Lewis one day.

"You're what?" Lewis bellowed.

"I'm leaving," Greenberg said flatly. "There's nothing to talk about," and he strode out of the room.

That evening, Lewis called him at home and asked him to come to his apartment for a talk. Reluctantly, Greenberg went. When Lewis demanded to know why he was resigning, Greenberg mentioned the name of a stock — Rudd Melikian, a vending machine manufacturer — and asked if Lewis had ever heard of it.

"No," Lewis replied, puzzled, "Why do you ask?"

"Because we own 10,000 shares," Greenberg replied. "It's down ten points, and you didn't know we own it. And that's why I'm leaving — because you won't take losses. You buy these things and you won't sell them."

The next day Lewis called Greenberg into his office.

"All right," Lewis said. "I'll make a deal with you. You're right. I'm a terrible seller. I hate to admit I'm wrong so you can sell anything you want at any time. I promise I won't interfere."

Greenberg immediately sold off the 10,000 shares of Rudd Melikian, and, after scanning the position book, gave the order to dispose of a dozen or so other losing stocks. He put the proceeds into a huge arbitrage play that was under way in shares of the American Viscose Corporation (Avisco). The chemical company had long been the subject of takeover rumors, and Greenberg thought the time was right to take a big position in the stock. For months, nothing happened, and he had reason to be concerned: if his bet didn't pay off, his showdown with Lewis could ultimately cost him his partnership. But the situation was saved by a bid from the FMC Corporation, which took over Avisco in 1963.

Greenberg's confrontation with Lewis marked the turning point in his career. He was the only one who could stand up to the senior partner and win. Over the next decade, he began to be seen as Lewis's successor. He wanted to move the firm in new directions, and from the midsixties onward he pushed to expand the firm's retail business, against the opposition of both Lewis and Low. He correctly anticipated that some form of negotiated commission rates was inevitable, threatening the profitability of Bear Stearns's thriving institutional business.

In 1973, the firm further expanded its retail brokerage department at Greenberg's insistence, but only after Bear Stearns had moved its headquarters to much larger offices at 55 Water Street in a year when many firms were retrenching. Because the back office was already in operation and generating expenses and there was so much excess office space available, Lewis finally agreed to Greenberg's plan of establishing a securities clearing business and leasing the unused space to other traders.

Lewis's acquiescence was perhaps his last major show of power. Within a few years, he was the firm's leader in name only. Greenberg was virtually trailing him, telling everyone to ignore any orders the senior partner issued. There was no alternative. Lewis was disintegrating before their eyes, both physically and emotionally.

By that time, Lewis had had two heart attacks and suffered from cancer. Because of varicose veins, one swollen foot was always encased in an open sneaker. His nose was raw and bulbous: a testament to the bottle of scotch that he drank daily. His marriage of four decades to the former Diana Bonner was in shambles, and his relationship with his four children — he had largely been an absentee father — was strained to the breaking point. To compound his woes, his mistress of many years, Valerie Dauphinot, had committed suicide.

Meanwhile, Greenberg was also undergoing a transformation. In 1975, nearing fifty and the father of grown children, he had divorced his wife of twenty-two years. He kept the capacious apartment on Fifth Avenue. More of a base than a home for the new bachelor, the apartment was still filled with some of the French furniture purchased by his ex-wife. A few personal touches of his own, which would have been noticeable in any room, stood out in bold relief here, including the head of a trophy-sized antelope that he had hunted down with a bow and arrow while on vacation in Africa. (He would say with a smile that he hadn't used a gun because "arrows were longer than bullets.") But perhaps his most significant possessions in the apartment were the more than three hundred books on magic that he had collected over the years. These books reflected the intensity and meticulousness with which he approached any undertaking that interested him. He trained dogs, made wood carvings, and enjoyed fresh-water fishing, but nothing held quite the fascination of magic.

At dinner parties, the ageless boy magician was apt to pull out a deck of cards or a handkerchief to perform a trick or two, and he prided himself on the fact that he never did the same one twice. He was, in a manner of speaking, the wild card in a social setting. There was a certain guileless charm about him. Although he had a dry wit and seemed highly approachable, he was neither glib nor polished.

Greenberg started dating again. He was drawn to glamorous women who were financially and socially independent. They would soon learn that there were no ties that bound.* His uncommitted life allowed him more time to pursue another long-held interest. A bridge player since he was a teenager, he and James Cayne, also a Bear Stearns partner, won a national championship.

The ties that bound him were to Bear Stearns. When the partners met for their annual dinner in May of 1978 to commemorate the end

---

* In 1987, Greenberg married Kathryn Olson, a young lawyer.

of the fiscal year, there was no question that Greenberg was in reality running the firm. Otherwise, the sixty-nine-year-old Cy Lewis would never have allowed the dinner to be turned into his own retirement party.

It must have been only a small consolation to Lewis that the party was being held at the Harmonie Club, where he and Greenberg were both members. When he had first applied for membership, the unpopular Lewis had been rejected. Determined to join, he had reapplied and been admitted. Actually, the party setting had more to do with convenience than with any personal tribute to Lewis, who was hardly the main issue on the partners' minds. For many partners, he was already part of their past — or more to the point, a tyrant whom they wished would leave quietly. The standard gold watch (albeit a Piaget specially ordered from Switzerland) was their pro forma gift to him. Indeed, there was little time for sentimentality. The close of that fiscal year had confirmed that earnings had slipped from the previous year. Reversing that trend was the primary issue for everyone at that party.

During the ceremony honoring Lewis's retirement, John Slade made a short speech, recalling his own earliest days at the firm when he had made $15 a week. Like many others, Slade had developed under Lewis's guidance. He told the audience that he owed "everything" to Lewis. Indisputably, Lewis had made all of the partners rich. Slade presented the watch to Lewis, who then returned to his seat. As he started unwrapping his gift, Lewis began to shake violently. He was having a stroke. An ambulance rushed him to the hospital, with partners Ted Low and Dick Fay at his side. Two days later, and one day before Greenberg officially took over, Lewis died. Some partners speculated that his fatal stroke was triggered by the finality of his retirement from the firm that had been almost his entire working life.

At the time of his death, Bear Stearns was one of the premier trading firms on Wall Street. In the 1970s, along with the significant growth of its retail and clearing operations, it set out to expand its international finance department (founded by Slade in 1948). John Rosenwald, who had built the firm's institutional business, took over the firm's corporate finance department.

Yet in many ways, toward the end of the 1970s the firm was only beginning to enter the modern age. The man who "pissed ice water," as Lewis had said of Greenberg, and who had proved himself over and over again, went about his work, adding new businesses such as private placement financing and mergers and acquisitions — fields that Lewis, the hidebound trader, wouldn't have considered. And the firm had the capital to back up its expansion — $74 million — good for seventeenth place on the Street, up from the thirty-fourth spot eleven years earlier.

But the essential character of the firm wasn't going to change dramatically. If anything, Greenberg seemed determined to maintain its slightly rebellious image in a world where a college education, even an MBA, had become commonplace. For him, Bear Stearns's partners and employees need possess only two qualities: the motivation and the ability to make money. In later years, only partly in jest, he once issued a memo to all the partners, stating that Bear Stearns wouldn't discriminate against a job applicant if he or she had an MBA, but that what the firm really sought were people with P.S.D.'s — "which stands for poor, smart, and a deep desire to become rich." Only one group would be discriminated against in hiring: relatives. Nepotism was frowned on at Bear Stearns. Talent and performance were what counted.

Before 1978 was over, there would be one more final break with the past for Greenberg. Late in the year, Ted Low died. His death symbolized the end of the old Bear Stearns. Throughout most of the tenure of both Lewis and Greenberg, Low, as the only surviving founding partner, held the title of managing partner. Yet the quiet and conservative Low had been too much a gentleman to exert any real influence. By the seventies, he had become a limited partner, and his old-fashioned manner was barely tolerated. At his funeral, however, the partners, led by Greenberg, showed up in force among the mourners.

*    *    *

One of the speakers who delivered a touching eulogy was Low's son-in-law John Gutfreund, though Gutfreund's marriage to Low's daughter, Joyce, seemed even then to be dissolving. Coincidentally, the same year Greenberg took over Bear Stearns, Gutfreund was to assume control of Salomon Brothers. And coincident with that change the life of Ted Low's son-in-law would change in ways that no one who knew him could have anticipated. The catalyst was Joyce Low's apparent opposite, a statuesque blonde former Pan Am stewardess. There was a hard-edged quality to Susan Penn's attractiveness and she had a will to match. They would soon become known in the fashion tabloids as "Social Susie" and "Solemn John." The social metamorphosis of John Gutfreund had only just gotten under way.

## Before the New Crowd

Arthur, Herbert, and Percy Salomon (*left to right*), who founded Salomon Brothers in 1910. (*Courtesy of Salomon Brothers*)

(*Left*) Sidney Weinberg ("Mr. Wall Street") with his wife, Helen, outside their Scarsdale home. (*AP/Wide World Photos*) (*Right*) Gus Levy, pioneer trader and Wall Street powerhouse. (*AP/Wide World Photos*)

(*Left*) John Loeb, "Our Crowd" investment banker. (*AP/Wide World Photos*) (*Right*) Billy Salomon, longtime managing partner of Salomon Brothers. (*Courtesy of Salomon Brothers*)

Support for President Lyndon B. Johnson in the 1964 election came from some of the country's top business leaders, including Wall Street bankers Bobbie Lehman (*standing behind Johnson, sixth from right*), John Loeb (*seated on the president's left*), and André Meyer (*seated on Loeb's left*). (*AP/Wide World Photos*)

# The New Crowd

(*Left*) John Gutfreund in 1963, when he was made a partner of Salomon Brothers. (*Fabian Bachrach/Courtesy of Salomon Brothers*) (*Right*) Saul Steinberg (the "Boy Wonder"), in 1969. (*AP/Wide World Photos*)

Arthur Carter, Roger Berlind, and Sandy Weill (*left to right*) of Carter, Berlind & Weill, in 1968. (*Edward Hausner/*The New York Times)

Richard Kleindienst (*left*) and Felix Rohatyn, the Lazard Frères banker, at the U.S. Senate hearings on the nomination of Kleindienst as the U.S. attorney general in 1972. (*AP/Wide World Photos*)

Felix Rohatyn ("The Man Who Saved New York City") with New York Governor Hugh Carey and New York City Mayor Abraham Beame, at a press conference in 1976. (*AP/Wide World Photos*)

Mike Milken ("Mr. Junk Bond"), Drexel's junk bond trader, in his New York office in 1978. (*Neal Boenzi*/The New York Times)

Ace Greenberg, chief of Bear Stearns, at his trading desk. (*Fred R. Conrad*/The New York Times)

Ace Greenberg, big-game hunter. (*Courtesy of Bear Stearns*)

Lewis Glucksman when he finally won sole possession of the top spot at Lehman Brothers, in 1983. (*Chester Higgins, Jr. / The New York Times*)

American Express chairman James Robinson III and Sandy Weill (*right*), in 1981.  (*AP/Wide World Photos*)

Felix Rohatyn flanked by dancer Judith Jamison and Alvin Ailey, founder of the Alvin Ailey dance company, at a dinner in 1984 honoring Felix Rohatyn for his contribution to the cultural and business life of New York City.  (*AP/Wide World Photos*)

The Room at Salomon Brothers. John Gutfreund (*standing at extreme right*) is talking on the phone. (*Courtesy of Salomon Brothers*)

# CHAPTER SIXTEEN

# Epitaph for Loeb Rhoades

S andy Weill had a selective memory. Stored in his mind were the equivalent of huge neon signposts that recalled a few landmarks in his life that he would never forget. Among the most important was "The Papers" — the contract that, if it had been signed in the fall of 1977, would have made Kuhn Loeb a part of Shearson Hayden Stone. Although the 110-year-old Our Crowd firm's resources had been depleted, Weill would have gained a significant investment banking business. For months he had been closing in on the deal, and just when he thought the seventy-three-year-old John Schiff, grandson of Jacob Schiff, was ready to complete the merger, Weill read in the newspapers that he had been jilted. Kuhn Loeb had agreed to a marriage with Lehman Brothers. "I couldn't believe it," he recalled. "I had to read it twice. When it finally sank in, I was very angry and hurt, but there was nothing I could do about it." Weill was the only Wall Street leader who didn't receive an official announcement from Lehman Brothers of the proud match. The message was clear to the Street: Weill's firm didn't count among the major houses.

Until then, his life as a chief executive had proceeded on a steady course upward. In the past two years, he had acquired Lamson Bros., a Chicago-based commodities broker, and Faulkner, Dawkins & Sullivan, an institutional brokerage house. He could boast that Shearson's earnings were racing ahead at record levels and that, as of 1976, Shearson was listed on the New York Stock Exchange. That year, he had also resolved the four-year-old Topper mess, in which he had been charged with criminally negligent behavior in his duties as a director of the toy company. Three suits against Shearson were settled out of court for $1.7 million.

The bitter disappointment that came from being rejected by Kuhn Loeb was followed by a series of defections at Shearson. Though that had nothing to do with Kuhn Loeb, the timing made it all the more painful for Weill. Arthur Levitt was the first to leave, to become head of the American Stock Exchange. Next, former U.S. energy czar Frank Zarb, the Shearson senior executive vice president who had set up CBWL's back office with Weill and had arranged the first meeting with Kuhn Loeb, went to Lazard Frères. Finally, Peter Cohen resigned to work for Edmond Safra, an extremely wealthy Sephardic Jew, at Safra's Republic National Bank.* Cutting all ties with Shearson, Cohen even sold his stock in the company, which made Weill furious. During Cohen's farewell party, Weill, who rarely could conceal his strong feelings, called Cohen a "traitor" before his office colleagues.

Weill's flashfire reaction was revealing. He behaved as though Cohen was personally deserting him. Yet whatever disappointment he felt about the loss of Kuhn Loeb and the defection of his closest associates, he would not lose his sense of direction.

Weill had changed from the days when he felt he had to lean on others. "I'd done a couple of gutsy deals and they'd all turned out well," he said. His early doubts about his abilities were allayed, despite some setbacks, by his string of successes, and he derived strength from that. "I'd become more confident, more sure of my judgment." Even his appearance had improved. His suits were made for him in London and Hong Kong, where Shearson had an office, or were purchased with his wife's help at the fashionable Paul Stuart in New York City. Now he felt that building an empire was what he knew how to do best. In line with other empire builders, he turned his attention to acquiring financial companies — attractive targets in a nation that was fast becoming a service economy.

Dozens of Wall Street houses, weakened by post-Mayday negotiated commission rates and a flagging stock market, were scooped up easily. "What makes you successful yesterday is not what's going to make you successful in the future," he said. "You've got to throw the bait out farther and keep trying. When you stop trying, the dead weight sets in like my waistline."

---

* When Arthur Levitt left, the position of Shearson president became available. Weill offered it to Frank Zarb, who instead went to work for Lazard Frères. According to Weill, Peter Cohen resigned because the position wasn't offered to him. Cohen saw things differently. "The firm didn't need a president," he said later. "Sandy and I had a major disagreement over that. At my age, I didn't think I was entitled to it, but I didn't think anyone was more entitled than I was. I left because it was time to get out of Sandy's shadow and do something on my own."

In early 1979, Weill swung into action with two quick financial acquisitions, the California-based Western Pacific Financial Corporation and half the outlets of the midwest brokerage firm of Reinholdt & Gardner. By spring, he was zeroing in on his greatest target ever, Loeb Rhoades, Hornblower & Co.

For some time, he had been stalking the venerable investment banking and brokerage firm that had been built by John Loeb in Our Crowd's image. Weill played tennis regularly with Loeb's nephew Thomas Kempner at Weill's eight-acre estate in Greenwich, Connecticut, which he had purchased for $500,000 in 1977. Both men had excellent games, sat on a corporate board together, and lived in apartments only a block apart on East Seventy-ninth Street.* Yet, except for common business interests, there was little to draw them together.

Fifty-one-year-old Tommy Kempner was Our Crowd and acted it. Educated at Yale, he was a bright, athletic man who was known as something of a dilettante. His seemingly arrogant manner was accentuated by his tendency to be a loner. His tall, fashionably thin and elegant wife more than compensated for his aloofness.

Nan Kempner (née Schlesinger), a member of a wealthy Jewish San Francisco family, was at the center of New York Society, even though her husband was often absent from the constant round of fundraising dinners and gala evenings she attended. She had once joked, "I'd show up for the opening of a refrigerator." But this mother of three and former editor of *Harper's Bazaar* had her favorites. She was a major fund-raiser for some of New York's most prestigious Establishment causes, including Memorial Sloan-Kettering Cancer Center and the American Ballet Theatre.

By contrast, the social world of Sandy and Joan Weill still rotated around Wall Street and the extended Shearson "family." Socializing often meant entertaining employees and their spouses at their Greenwich home with a picnic, barbecue, or cocktail party. Joan Weill, a gracious, attentive hostess, knew the name of virtually everyone. She had a large wardrobe and was generally the best dressed woman at these gatherings. Unlike Nan Kempner, who ordered many of her clothes at the couture collections in Paris, she sometimes saved money by buying her dresses wholesale on Seventh Avenue.

---

\* In 1976, fearful that New York City's mounting financial crisis would result in a drop in real estate prices, Weill had sold his fourteen-room Fifth Avenue co-op and bought an eight-room one on Seventy-ninth Street off Madison Avenue.

With two grown children, Joan Weill, the former school teacher, felt she had more time to pursue her own interests. She started a course in counseling at the Bank Street college in Upper Manhattan but failed to complete it because of a recurring painful back ailment that required surgery and that led her to take up swimming — which became her chief form of exercise and relaxation.

Over the years, Weill had made some effort to enlarge his business and social contacts. Part of that effort included joining the Harmonie Club, which, though it had lost its elite standing among Our Crowd Jews, still had potent appeal as a place to meet and mingle for successful members of the New Crowd, who could now gain admission and enjoy the steam room, sauna, exercise room, squash courts, and swimming pool. Joan Weill swam her laps there.

Each time Weill and Kempner played tennis, Weill brought up the possibility of a merger between their two firms. Kempner, who for the past two years had represented the Loeb family in the management of the firm his uncle and grandfather had founded, dutifully relayed the message to John Loeb. Over and over, the patrician banker had turned down Weill's suggestion. But by the beginning of 1979, the prospect of a merger couldn't be rejected out of hand. The great Our Crowd firm was in trouble.

Early in the previous year, Loeb Rhoades had taken over Hornblower, Weeks, Noyes & Trask, the huge century-old Wasp brokerage firm that had been facing extinction. Loeb Rhoades, Hornblower became the fourth largest firm on Wall Street. John Loeb had hoped to turn it into a house that would rival any on the Street, but the merger hadn't worked out as he had envisioned. By the end of 1978, the merged firm was losing millions fast, as would be revealed later. Loeb needed to stop the hemorrhaging if he was to save the firm and, even more important, his own capital and the capital of the Loeb family and other partners.

At the time, Weill had no way of knowing the extent of the losses — as a private partnership, Loeb Rhoades didn't report its earnings — but even if he had known, his interest would likely have remained the same. Here was a chance to more than double the size of Shearson in a single stroke and to build a strong investment banking department that would bolster Shearson's skeletal one. Losing Kuhn Loeb to Lehman still rankled; gaining Loeb Rhoades would more than make up for that loss.

By the fall of 1978, the prize was beginning to seem attainable. In his own fashion, John Loeb began making overtures to Weill. At a black-tie dinner sponsored by the Economic Club of New York, he went out of his way to praise Weill in the presence of a top Shearson executive. Ironically, this was the same John Loeb who, ten years earlier, had rebuffed Weill and his partners when they had pleaded with him to have Loeb Rhoades clear for their little-known firm of Cogan, Berlind, Weill & Levitt.

Loeb was reluctantly coming to the conclusion that he had to go outside for help. He didn't want to see Loeb Rhoades simply die, nor was he willing to cut back substantially to save it. But he wouldn't virtually give it away either. It meant too much to him. What had been started nearly fifty years before, in part as a way to help his mother get his father, Carl Morris Loeb, out of the house, had become the family's legacy.

* * *

The son of a middle-class dry goods merchant and a hausfrau who was devoted to her family, Carl Loeb had been born in 1875 in Frankfurt, Germany. At the age of seventeen — with $250 advanced by his employer, a German metal-fabricating company — he came to New York City to work for its American trading subsidiary, the American Metal Company. He was soon transferred to its St. Louis office, which he helped transform into the firm's largest American branch.

When he first arrived in St. Louis, young Carl was a boarder at the home of two genteel maiden ladies named Moses, descendants of one of the wealthiest and most prominent Jewish families in the South. He soon met and married their niece Adele Moses, whose father, respected banker Alfred Huger Moses, maintained close ties with the Lehman banking family.

Advancing rapidly within American Metal, Carl Loeb provided his wife and growing family with a comfortable home. Several years later, American Metal sent him to New York, where he eventually became president of the company and led it into a new era when it split off from its German owner at the end of World War I. Now that he was rich and powerful, Carl Loeb adopted the style of Our Crowd. His children — John, Carl, Henry, and Margaret — grew up in a New York town house attended by servants. They traveled with their parents to Europe accompanied by two nurses and mountains of luggage; spent summers at large rented houses in Westchester; took tennis, riding, and dancing lessons; and learned at an early age the importance of breeding and good manners.

Carl and Adele Loeb entertained lavishly and sought to establish themselves in German-Jewish High Society. But Loeb's money and his wife's connections took him only so far. In many ways the Our Crowd

German-Jewish bankers viewed Carl Loeb less as an aristocrat than as an early technocrat. It was through his eldest son, John, that the family finally entered that elite world dominated by the older German Jews.

After graduating from Harvard, John Loeb went to work for American Metal in Pittsburgh before his celebrated marriage to Frances ("Peter") Lehman. He persuaded his father, who had retired in 1929 from American Metal, to buy a seat on the New York Stock Exchange, and thus at the start of the New Year in 1931, father and son headed a new firm. Six years later, it acquired Rhoades & Co., an old Wasp firm that had been devastated by the Depression. Eventually taking charge, John Loeb employed family members, relatives, and friends as partners and built Carl M. Loeb, Rhoades & Co. into a major Wall Street house.

By the time of his father's death in 1955, John Loeb, now the official leader of the firm, was well on his way toward recognition as a senior statesman in the world of finance — alongside Bobbie Lehman, Sidney Weinberg, John Schiff, and the Wasp Establishment led by Henry Morgan. To his employees, he was a benevolent dictator, kind to those who met his exacting sense of propriety — which covered everything from the proper standards in doing a deal to how an employee behaved in the office. No one ever removed his suit jacket, loosened his tie, or dared to smoke during lunch in his presence.

In a business where impeccable timing was crucial, John Loeb was a master. He completed the sale of his firm's major holdings in Cuba in 1959, for example, one day before Fidel Castro assumed power. But he was above the ordinary concerns of day-to-day management. The senior partners, who flourished under him — entrepreneurs who ran their own operations with spectacular success — had the same strengths and weaknesses. They all ignored the operation of the back office, where the brokerage transactions were processed. As long as the firm remained profitable, the lack of tight management from the top didn't seem to matter.

If ever there was an era that belonged to John Loeb, it was the sixties. Loeb Rhoades seemed to be on an uninterrupted climb upward. The title of a 1963 profile in *Fortune* said it succinctly: "Wherever You Look, There's Loeb, Rhoades." As the decade progressed, that became even more true. The firm's operations included its securities clearing business, institutional sales, underwriting, investment management funds, and venture capital. With its growing retail business, Loeb Rhoades moved up in capital rankings past such regal Wasp peers as du Pont, Goodbody, and Dean Witter; by the end of the decade, it had become the fourth-largest house on the Street.

The empire, though, showed visible signs of cracking under the strains of expansion and the limitations of the star system fostered by John Loeb. The vast number of mundane but necessary back office operations had to mesh smoothly for a firm to succeed in the modern age. Equally important, Loeb made no substantial effort to develop a corps of capable middle managers.

He seemed less involved with the concerns of actually running the firm than with other causes. He worked hard at raising funds for his good friend Vice President Hubert Humphrey when he ran for president. On Wall Street, Loeb fought the leading Establishment fights of the period. First, he spoke out against public ownership of brokerage firms and then against negotiated commissions. He served on the Board of Governors of the New York Stock Exchange, was a member of the prestigious Council on Foreign Relations and, through his mother's bloodlines, belonged to the Sons of the American Revolution.

He was a man with such an unshakable sense of confidence that even a million-dollar loss in 1969 would not alter his determined course for the firm. As the seventies were ushered in, he was preparing for the next generation of leadership. In 1971, at sixty-nine, John Loeb stepped down as the active head of the firm and turned over its management to his forty-one-year-old son, John junior, to work with fifty-one-year-old Carl Mueller, a partner and a former vice president of Bankers Trust. Loeb planned to become an elder statesman of finance, a part he understood. Modeling himself after the great older Our Crowd leaders, he gave away millions. His beloved alma mater, Harvard, was the major beneficiary.*

John Loeb had gone well beyond Our Crowd. *Time* magazine, in fact, described him as having qualified as an "honorary Wasp." He had the breeding, speech, dress, manners, and devotion to public interests of an upper-class Anglo-Saxon. In short, he was identified with Our Crowd and Wasp High Society, and mingled with America's top tier in philanthropy, business, and politics.

Within two years of Loeb's semiretirement, the problems he had put behind him intruded into his life. Mueller began to chafe under the younger Loeb's leadership of the firm and presented Loeb senior with an ultimatum: either he or Loeb's son would have to go. John Loeb had never given his son real authority. A handsome, yet insecure,

---

* By 1986, John Loeb was reported to have given over $10 million to charity, including an $8.5 million gift to Harvard and more than $2 million to New York University for its Institute of Fine Arts.

man who had always been in his father's shadow, John Loeb, Jr., had shown good strategic judgment about the firm, but his personality irritated many people. "He's the worst spokesman for his own case," said a relative. "Every time, he shoots himself in the foot. Even the people he tries to help get angry with him." John Loeb, Jr., was opposed to the direction in which Mueller wanted to take the firm; he thought it should be turned into a private banking house like Lazard Frères. Most of the senior partners sided with Mueller, and John Loeb felt compelled to choose Mueller. John Loeb, Jr., left the ranks of management to become a limited partner. "For John Loeb, Jr., and the Loeb family," says a former partner, "it was a tragedy," and it was made worse by Mueller's inability to deal with the firm's problems.

It didn't help that the seventies provided the stiffest test for survival. Loeb Rhoades's clearing business — so vital to the firm's profitability — suffered, partly because Loeb Rhoades had opened branch offices in cities all over the country, thus competing with the very regional firms for which Loeb Rhoades cleared. Not surprisingly, many of them took their business elsewhere. A deep rift developed among the partners as to what to do next.

In 1977, Loeb ousted Mueller and told several people in the firm that he never should have given in to the partners who had insisted that he select Mueller over his son. By now Loeb Rhoades was clearly floundering. Some partners, like his nephew Peter Loeb, wanted to sell, but John Loeb wouldn't consider it. He turned the operating reins over to his nephew Tommy Kempner (chairman) and Sherman Lewis (president) and appointed them as co-CEOs. About a month later, in November, Loeb launched one last large deal: the takeover of Hornblower, Weeks, Noyes & Trask.

As it happened, Hornblower's back office proved to be in sorrier shape than Loeb Rhoades's, which caused endless foul-ups in processing orders and recording transactions. It soon became evident — as the capital of the combined firms was leeched out — that the merger was a failure. Years later, Loeb would acknowledge that he had not been up to the task. He was a "speculator," the term he used to describe himself, but the firm now required a modern corporate manager. Before long he called Sandy Weill.

\* \* \*

In the winter of 1978–79, John Loeb invited Weill to meet with him at his midtown office for a more formal discussion. Loeb immediately stated that he wouldn't do the actual negotiating, but there was no question as to who would be making the important decisions. If the two firms were to join, Loeb made it clear, it wouldn't be a merger or takeover. He insisted that it be called a "combination," and that the negotiations be handled by Kempner and Sherman Lewis. For weeks the talks seemed to go nowhere. It was a feeling-out period for both sides.

The question of who would work out the numbers on the Shearson side was resolved when Peter Cohen returned. Soon after he had gone to work for the Republic National Bank, Weill sent signals through an intermediary that he was no longer angry and would welcome Cohen back. He missed Cohen, and Cohen, who felt too comfortable as the bank's chief operating officer, missed the big deals and Shearson's fast pace. His wife, Karen, found that he had become "boring."

One evening in the fall of 1978, Joan Weill prepared a convenient dinner of homemade chopped liver, cole slaw, potato salad, rugelah, a noodle pudding from her grandmother's recipe, and ordered the rest of the food from Eli Zabar's EAT, an exorbitantly expensive takeout shop on Madison Avenue that had just opened. The Cohens and several dozen other couples had been invited to the Weills' apartment to break the Yom Kippur fast. The meal was a yearly event and ostensibly a social occasion — the kind of informal entertaining for friends that made everyone feel at ease — but Weill and Cohen both knew that they had something on their minds.

In front of the other guests, Weill said to Cohen, "You made a mistake."

Cohen replied, "No, you made a mistake."

Weill then said, "If you tell me you want to come back, I want you to come back."

Another layer of resistance in this adult but adolescent relationship had been broken down.

In December, the two men met for dinner in the Oak Room of the Plaza Hotel. Weill kept ordering gin and Cohen, who rarely drank, had several vodkas. Around ten o'clock, they started discussing Cohen's return. At one o'clock, when they left, both men were very drunk, and in the morning, very sick. One year to the day after he had resigned, Cohen resumed his old position as senior executive vice president at Shearson.

Meanwhile, Shearson and Loeb Rhoades Hornblower had stepped up their discussions when word of the talks leaked to the press. Late in the day on May 13, the Friday before Mother's Day, the news was out, and both sides decided to work over the weekend in an effort to hammer out an agreement. Weill suggested that they convene at his country estate in affluent Greenwich, Connecticut — a community that in former years had been virtually off-limits to Jews. He felt the comfort of meeting at his own estate was to his advantage. He was also aware that the estate's landscape — the garden, tennis court, and swimming pool — proclaimed his success. Inside the thirteen-room Normandy-style house, the marble-floored entrance gave way to a spacious, traditionally furnished living room with sofas and chairs covered in a pink and blue printed linen, comfortably arranged on a beige rug. The showcase of the house was the dining room. On two sides of the room, flanking the gleaming glass table, banks of windows overlooked the beautiful perennial garden and woods. On many occasions, the estate had been the setting for business discussions about Shearson. Now it would provide the gracious backdrop for a potential merger — Weill's largest so far.

When the two sides assembled that Saturday morning, the Shearson executives delivered their demand that the merger had to be announced by Monday: the deal was either on or off. Cohen's return was well timed for Weill. He welcomed backup support and had never liked working out the fine details. He padded around the house in casual pants and a T-shirt, offering the guests some of his wife's abundant stock of chicken salad and only occasionally making his presence felt.

On Saturday afternoon, an angry John Toolan, former Hornblower chief and part of the three-man team then running Loeb Rhoades Hornblower, arrived on the scene, apparently shocked that he had been deliberately left out of the talks that had been going on all morning; only the day before he had been denying that a merger was under way. Whipping out a notebook, he wasted no time laying out his demands. Weill pulled Kempner and Cohen aside. "Get this guy out of here."

Toolan went upstairs to phone Jansen Noyes, Jr., one of the Hornblower faction's largest investors. "We're being sold out," Toolan was heard screaming before he hung up and stormed out of the house.

The Shearson and Loeb Rhoades contingents continued their discussions well into the evening, touching on lines of responsibility — titles for various executives, consolidation of branch systems, and such — but made no mention of the finances involved.

The next morning, Mother's Day, the meeting resumed early. By then, the various factions had staked out headquarters in the upstairs bedrooms. Joan Weill replenished her supply of chicken salad and distributed it around the room as the day wore on, jokingly reminding the negotiators to call their mothers.

In the afternoon, Jansen Noyes showed up. "I'm Jan Noyes," he announced, "and I've got five million dollars invested in this company."

Cohen welcomed him and directed him to the Hornblower headquarters: "Upstairs, third bedroom." But it was clear the Hornblower forces were being squeezed out of the negotiations. The name would be dropped from the new firm.

The talks grew strained, but by the end of Sunday evening the two sides reached a basic agreement on the financial structure: in exchange for most of Loeb Rhoades's assets, Shearson would issue $90 million of securities ($63 million in debt instruments and $27 million in common stock). In turn, Loeb Rhoades would invest $90 million in Shearson. The new name would be Shearson Loeb Rhoades, Inc. Weill would be chairman and chief executive and John Loeb honorary board chairman.

*   *   *

The passing of the last great German-Jewish banking firm out of family control would be a slow and costly death for Loeb Rhoades, whose offices were to come into the Shearson fold in a series of four minimergers. A deadline of June 22 had been set for the first of these — when forty-four of the one hundred and fifty branch offices as well as the investment banking division and half a dozen other departments were to be integrated into the Shearson network — but on that day Shearson still didn't have a signed contract.

Weill was incensed. He, Cohen, and George Sheinberg, Shearson's chief financial officer, convened in Cohen's office. Weill was so exhausted he fell asleep on Cohen's sofa. They attempted to reach Kempner and the others for a conference call, but no one at Loeb Rhoades seemed to know where they were. After both sides couldn't agree on an issue, Sheinberg shouted into the phone, "Where the fuck is that son of a bitch Kempner? He's never around!"

Sherman Lewis, a tall, barrel-chested Chicagoan — who was on the Loeb Rhoades Hornblower phone and who had been told Weill had left for the day — exploded: "Don't give me that shit. Where's that asshole Weill?"

No one in Cohen's office said anything until Weill finally acknowledged from his background seat on the sofa, "I'm here. I'm here."

At four o'clock, Weill, still extremely tired, departed for Greenwich, delegating to Cohen the responsibility for getting the contract signed somehow. At five, the telephone company disconnected the phones of the forty-four Loeb Rhoades Hornblower branch offices and transferred the lines to Shearson's back office. Feeling grubby and tired,

Cohen and Sheinberg took a dinner break at a Greek restaurant before moving on to the offices of their lawyers, Willkie Farr & Gallagher, to hammer out a final agreement. The Loeb Rhoades Hornblower contingent arrived with three sets of lawyers — a total of fourteen people to Shearson's four-man team. Kempner, who had been unavailable for the conference call earlier in the day, arrived immaculately dressed in a sports jacket and slacks, fresh from a workout at his gym.

At the outset, Kempner looked at his watch and, in effect, said, "We have four hours. Either we reach an agreement on all the issues or the deal is off." The threat was more show than substance, because by the next working day, a third of the firm would, in fact, be in Shearson's hands — a piece of information denied Kempner. All the telephone lines would be hooked up. But Kempner's bluster set the tone for the rest of the evening. It wasn't until four o'clock in the morning that the contract was finally signed.

Racked with exhaustion, Cohen hired a limousine and was driven out to Amagansett, Long Island, to join his family at their country home. The next day, he called Weill and briefed him on what had happened. Weill was elated; Loeb Rhoades was his. "I felt fantastic and excited. My fatigue disappeared," Weill remembered. In mid-July, the second minimerger was closed.

Throughout the summer of 1979 and into the fall, the meshing of the two firms went along its tortured course. In the process, about 2,500 of the 10,800 employees were fired. "Sandy Weill takes no prisoners" was the line heard at Loeb Rhoades Hornblower. Weill agreed and held fast.

For him, the deal became almost magically better and better as it progressed. Toward the end of the year, the terms of the merger were revised — at Kempner's request — to take advantage of certain tax benefits. Therefore, instead of being issued stock, Loeb Rhoades would take $30 million in cash, which it would reinvest in Shearson, plus a guarantee of 15 percent of any pretax profits for its investment.

Weill added a new wrinkle of his own for the revised terms, one that greatly improved the deal for Shearson: once Loeb Rhoades's investment dropped below a certain percentage of the merged firm's total capital, Shearson would have the right to buy out the Loeb Rhoades partners. Inevitably, the Loeb Rhoades percentage would drop, because the partnership was going to withdraw its profits, but Shearson would plow its profits back into the company. In short, Weill set things up so that if the combined firm did poorly, Loeb Rhoades would suffer along with everyone else. If the firm did well, the Loeb Rhoades interest would be eliminated quickly.

At the time, this change in the agreement didn't seem conse-
quential, since there was no reason to think that Shearson would perform any miracles with the Loeb Rhoades acquisition in the near future.
Everyone focused on finishing the deal. On December 3, the last sixty
Loeb Rhoades offices were turned over to Shearson. All that remained
was a victory celebration.

Two weeks later, the creation of Shearson Loeb Rhoades became official the day the board met at the Harmonie Club. At the
reception prior to the luncheon meeting, the cigar-chomping young
brokers boasted about the great times that lay ahead. All of them,
especially Weill, took pride in what they had already accomplished.

Shearson Loeb Rhoades was now second in size only to Merrill
Lynch. But the most impressive fact was the bottom line. In 1980, the
first year of the merger, Shearson Loeb Rhoades's profits reached a
substantial $55.7 million, up from $19.9 million for the year ending
June 30, 1979. Weill's bonus was $250,000. (As chief executive, he also
received a salary of $227,000.)

Weill bought Loeb out at the end of that first profitable year
and would soon drop his name as though it were a dusty old hunting
trophy. (Years later, in the sanctuary of his office in the Seagram's
building provided by Shearson, Loeb would say quietly that he had
made a tragic mistake in selling his firm: "In looking back, we should
have cut back in size. The deal we made with Shearson reflected a lack
of imagination on our part. We didn't realize what a valuable asset we
had. Properly managed, it was a gold mine for Sandy.")

Despite its humble beginnings and its relative newness, the firm
that Sandy Weill helped build could no longer be labeled an upstart.
Looking back on the sale, a Loeb Rhoades banker reflected on the extent
to which the old-line Wall Street underestimated a new-breed man like
Weill: "This could have been a much better deal for us. The partners
didn't realize they had a real winner in Sandy Weill. They didn't believe
he could build a profit center from the combined companies. Otherwise,
they never would have given up stock for cash."

Crowning his triumph, in August of 1980 Weill moved Shearson's headquarters to the top six floors of the south tower of the World
Trade Center high over lower Manhattan and the Hudson River. "It
was a terrific move for us. We got a penthouse on top of a great building,
with our own elevator bank," he recalled. But the space — which was
supposed to be large enough to house the entire company — was inadequate by the time they were relocated.

Weill would have his setbacks, but there was less likelihood
that anyone would seriously underestimate him again.

# CHAPTER SEVENTEEN

# Starting Over

Success propelled Felix Rohatyn into the New York social milieu that embraced the rich, powerful, accomplished, and famous. As one of the most influential and interesting bachelors around, he was besieged with invitations. But the sophisticated bachelor and consummate dealmaker who remained cool in heated takeover contests for his corporate clients somehow seemed restless in private.

Though his professional life was exciting and rewarding and he was a role model for young dealmakers on the way up, his personal life took on aspects of his uncommitted, freer years as a Lazard apprentice in Paris, London, and Zurich. His willingness to reside at the faded Alrae Hotel, which he claimed was merely "convenient," may also have been an act of defiance, as well as a coded message that he wanted to keep his options open in his living arrangements. Although Hélène Gaillet de Barcza was the woman he escorted about town most frequently in the first half of the seventies, he saw other women as well — a situation Hélène was willing to put up with. Close friends said he had no wish to remarry then.

One woman who knew him well in that period described him as "an extremely complex, intelligent man with intense interests" but a man unwilling to make a commitment. "In those days, Felix tried to be very counter-Establishment, very tough, smart, and independent," she recalled. "He used to say, 'I only own two suits, the one I'm wearing and the one that's at the cleaner's.' The first night we went out, we drove through Central Park in his beat-up car. It was spring, and the apple blossoms were in bloom. 'Do you see those flowers?' he asked me. 'Take a good look, because I'll never send you flowers. I don't believe in things like that.' "

His attitude began to change after he met Elizabeth Vagliano on his ski vacation in Alta, Utah, in 1975. Soon afterward he broke off with Hélène, whose unconventional life-style, by her own admission, made her "too wild" for him. He was in a transitional period.

Elizabeth Vagliano's warm, gracious manner captivated Rohatyn. A tall, aristocratic-looking woman in her late forties, she had light brown hair (which she made blonde later), a graceful figure, and refined features; her quick wit and sharp insights were a spur to his own lively humor. He seemed exceptionally animated when they were together. The daughter of a prominent Episcopalian Memphis family, Elizabeth had graduated from Foxcroft, an exclusive boarding school, and had attended Brillantmont in Switzerland. Twice divorced, she had one daughter, Nina Griscom, a beautiful blonde model. Elizabeth Vagliano was very comfortable in the world of power and money.

One sign of the way Rohatyn's life began to change was that, not long after they met, he at last moved out of the Alrae, where he had lived for most of the seventies, into a comfortable two-bedroom, duplex co-operative apartment on Park Avenue. "Elizabeth and I were already seeing a great deal of each other when I bought it," he remembered. "In fact, she indicated that unless I moved out of the dump where I was living, our relationship would be more tenuous. I told her that I had no time to look. I was still involved with the City crisis. If she could find an apartment, I would move. She found one which I bought immediately, the occupant having died the same day."

He was still too busy with city and corporate affairs to furnish the apartment. He left that to Elizabeth. With the help of a decorator friend, she chose the furnishings, which she described as "fairly minimalist, modern, and masculine, with a bottle-green rug, a tobacco-colored sofa, and a green marble coffee table in the living room."

Even as their relationship deepened, the situation at Lazard was deteriorating. For some time André Meyer, who was riddled with cancer and the ravages of old age, had stopped being an important force at Lazard. The firm slumped badly in the midseventies when Meyer started neglecting the business, causing some major clients to drift away.

By 1977 it was clear that something had to be done — fast. The old banker had cherished the wish that Rohatyn would don the mantle of senior partner, but Meyer's protégé remained firm in his resolve to stay independent; he wanted to concentrate on his dealmaking activities and on his financial work for New York City.

Meyer was deeply disappointed. "Of all the people I've seen in my very long career, I think Felix has always been the best, and I would have liked to have him take the full job and the responsibility," he said in one of his last interviews. "And at certain moments I had the hope, the illusion that he would. But he has never expressed any desire to do that."

By mutual agreement, Meyer and Michel David-Weill, the senior Lazard partner in Paris and the fourth generation of the founding family, decided that David-Weill would assume the senior partnership reins in both Paris and New York. The forty-four-year-old David-Weill took immediate steps to strengthen the firm. He was a decisive, demanding leader, but his style of management wasn't manipulative and smothering like Meyer's. He and Rohatyn got along well. Both men paid deference to Meyer, consulting him on major decisions, but that was all. After a quarter century of working for the imperious Frenchman, who had tried to keep Rohatyn and all his other Lazard partners on a tight leash and whose unbankerlike outbursts sometimes drove him to distraction, Rohatyn had become the dominant one in their relationship.

"The last fifteen years he needed me more than I needed him," Rohatyn acknowledged later. "I had relationships with his peers, the governor [Hugh Carey], Arthur Sulzberger [publisher of the *New York Times*], and Bill Paley [the head of CBS]."

Rohatyn was now far better known and more widely respected than Meyer, in large part because of his work on the New York City fiscal crisis. In the summer of 1978, he decided to give up his most impressive power base; he resigned as chairman of MAC, which had occupied the bulk of his time and energy, and returned full-time to Lazard.

"The city was beginning to finance itself," he explained at a later date. "The budget wasn't in balance and the city wasn't in the market yet. But I felt that with the long-term federal loan guarantees, which everyone said couldn't be done but which began that summer — along with the four-year package we had put together in combination with the loan guarantees — that would get the city from here to there. And it did. Besides, I always thought one should leave early."

His farewell at the MAC meeting of January 1979 was covered by the press. Rohatyn spoke softly, almost in a whisper, and at moments appeared overcome by emotion as he ended his three and a half years in the center of the city's power structure.

Adding to the wear and tear of the job were his ongoing verbal skirmishes with New York City mayor Ed Koch, who was renowned for his sharp tongue and comedic delivery of his barbed lines. Shortly after the mayor's election in the fall of 1977, while the city's fiscal situation was still critical, the two men clashed. On one occasion Koch complained in print that Rohatyn, as chairman of MAC, was getting credit for work that he, Koch, had done. More than once, Rohatyn rebuked the mayor for not being tougher in handling labor contracts.

The hostilities didn't end when Rohatyn left MAC. He was soon stung by another Koch barb. "He [Rohatyn] has to have his place in the sun, but all day?" the mayor cracked.

But the most serious battle took place in March, after Lazard was awarded a $250,000 contract to advise the city on fiscal matters. (When Rohatyn was the unsalaried chairman of MAC, Lazard did the work without a fee.) Koch accused Lazard of having a "moral conflict of interest" over the deal, in light of Rohatyn's connections to the city.

The mayor's charge incensed Rohatyn. For three and a half years he had worked without compensation. He felt that it was unfair to ask his partners to continue working for nothing — now that he was no longer chairman of MAC. The next morning, after reading Koch's remarks in the newspaper, he said to his partners, "What are we doing this for? Is it worth it?"

"I was completely outraged," he said years later. "Koch made his comments about 'this moral conflict' to a reporter on the day of a black-tie dinner in my honor for some five hundred people at Lincoln Center, where he was one of the speakers. At the dinner he said that I was one of the greatest things that ever walked the streets of the city. And the next day his criticism was published. It was a cheap shot."

Lazard resigned its advisory role. Two months later, an apparently refreshed and seemingly tougher Rohatyn returned as MAC chairman when his successor suddenly quit.

"One thing I learned from that experience was how quickly people want to kick you around as soon as you're out of a position of influence — which was a powerful incentive to come back as chairman of MAC when George Gould decided that he wasn't going to run it any more," Rohatyn recalled wryly.

Koch never said so publicly, but he reportedly told aides that he regretted having started the ruckus about the contract. When Rohatyn resumed his MAC post, Koch's stance toward Rohatyn changed: "I'm delighted the governor asked him." After a conciliatory breakfast at Gracie Mansion, the mayor's residence, Koch, in his best stand-up-comedian manner, summed up the gist of their conversation: "He told me he had no desire to be the mayor and I told him I had no desire to be chairman of MAC." Beneath the humor was an acknowledgment that Rohatyn was a true powerhouse in city affairs.

At the time, Rohatyn stated he was returning as chairman on

a temporary basis, but the job became a permanent one. In 1980 his efforts were rewarded; the city's budget was balanced for the first time since the start of the crisis. The strong recovery the city was enjoying made his skills and talents much in demand. He turned up frequently in Washington to testify before Congress on a wide range of economic matters, and he was responsible for Lazard's becoming financial advisers to Washington, D.C., Cleveland, and Detroit, and to Governor James Thompson of Illinois on the Chicago school system's fiscal crisis. He sat on the board of MCA, the giant Los Angeles–based entertainment company run by his friend Lew Wasserman. He was, in the words of his friend labor leader Victor Gotbaum, "going national."

*   *   *

At the time he returned "refreshed" to the MAC board, Rohatyn and Elizabeth Vagliano were deeply attached to each other. Over the years of their courtship, they had found they had many common interests — tennis, skiing, art, and politics. Their conversations ranged from serious discussions to light banter that often reduced the normally soft-spoken Rohatyn to hearty laughter. They attended concerts together, and he introduced her to one of his favorite pastimes, ice hockey. "Sometimes we went to two hockey games a week," she recounted. "Felix is a great Ranger fan. We went to a club at Madison Square Garden; Felix was friendly with Mike Burke [head of Madison Square Garden] and a marvelous group of men was there. We sat around and talked and joked."

They also found they liked each other's friends. Rohatyn had formed a close friendship with the tough-talking municipal union chief, Victor Gotbaum, whom he had come to know through their work on the New York City fiscal crisis. Both men shared a passionate commitment to save the city from bankruptcy. After many angry confrontations, they had gradually learned to trust each other. Both had endured the strain of ending long marriages. Rohatyn and Elizabeth Vagliano and Gotbaum and his second wife, Betsy (the daughter of the former chairman of the J. Walter Thompson advertising agency), became a foursome — going out to dinner, playing tennis, and even traveling together. One time the two couples met in Italy for some sightseeing in Florence and Venice. When they were together, there was always a lot of spontaneous humor. They joked about their different social and religious backgrounds. Rohatyn and Gotbaum were both Jews; Rohatyn was involved with an upper-class Protestant named Elizabeth and Gotbaum was married to one.

Despite his obvious attachment to her, Rohatyn procrastinated in proposing marriage. One early spring day in 1979, Victor Gotbaum took him aside, as the two couples were walking on the beach in Southampton. Gotbaum felt that Elizabeth was a very traditional woman and that if his friend didn't commit himself, he would lose her.

"Who's the most important person in your life?" Gotbaum asked.

"You know," Rohatyn replied, "Elizabeth is."

The blunt-spoken Gotbaum laced into him. "You don't realize it, but you're really fucking her over. You're not facing up to what you have to do. You really have to make a commitment."

Shortly afterward, Elizabeth Vagliano and Felix Rohatyn were married in a civil ceremony at his apartment. The bride wore a short blue silk Oscar de la Renta dress and carried a single rose. Victor Gotbaum served as best man. Among the small group of family and close friends in attendance were their children — his three sons and her daughter — Rohatyn's mother and stepfather, banker Walter Wriston, Governor Hugh Carey, Betsy Gotbaum, Jane Engelhard, widow of Charles Engelhard, and André Meyer. As a wedding present, Meyer presented the couple with a Pierre Bonnard painting.

On this festive occasion there was one disquieting note. Rohatyn was concerned about Meyer's health. The frail eighty-year-old banker, who now walked slowly with the aid of a cane, was clearly dying. He rarely ventured out anymore, spending most of his time at home heavily sedated. Soon he would be leaving for Switzerland, where he traditionally spent the summer. Rohatyn was pleased that the old man who had meant so much to him was able to be there to see him happily remarried.

* * *

By the end of 1979 aspects of Rohatyn's past were receding like images from a train window. His wedding celebration was the last time he saw Meyer. On September 10, a week after his eighty-first birthday, Rohatyn's first great mentor died in Switzerland. Two memorial services were held, one in France and the other at Temple Emanu-El in New York, where David Rockefeller paid tribute to his old friend and financial adviser. But perhaps the most emotional of the eulogies was delivered by the usually steady Felix Rohatyn. His voice cracking at times, he recalled how he still from habit reached for the phone to call his mentor, and he revealed how much Meyer had meant to him:

"Behind the stern, forbidding, and sometimes theatrical facade lay a man who was really yearning for affection. . . . In my youth, he was an Olympian figure, Zeus hurling thunderbolts. Then he was my teacher. He taught me not only to achieve perfection, but to do it in style."

His relationship with his other great mentor, Harold Geneen, was undergoing a transformation, by dint of circumstances. Over the past number of years, Geneen had come increasingly under attack — both from outside and from within ITT. The trait that had made him a legend in his lifetime — his insatiable appetite for producing higher and higher earnings, no matter what manipulations were involved — was at the heart of his troubles. By the seventies ITT had become an unwieldy behemoth, expanding recklessly around the globe. The most damaging allegation against Geneen that surfaced in federal investigations and in the media was that his actions as head of ITT somehow may have led to the overthrow of Chilean leader Salvador Allende, whose socialist government, Geneen apparently feared, would nationalize ITT's business in Chile.

A federal grand jury had been gathering evidence since 1975 that ITT had joined forces with the Central Intelligence Agency during the 1970 elections in Chile to keep Allende from the presidency. Allende was elected but was ousted in a 1973 coup that resulted in his death. Later that year Geneen denied under oath before the congressional committee conducting the Watergate hearings that ITT had made a series of payments to Allende's right-wing opposition candidate prior to the election. Further investigations by the Justice Department revealed that the right-wing candidate had received a total of $350,000 from ITT. Geneen was forced to acknowledge payments had been made but told the stockholders he hadn't known about them. But the ITT board wasn't appeased. The prospect of Geneen's indictment, let alone his conviction, on perjury charges was too much for them.*

Rohatyn wasn't in the vanguard of the ITT board members who wanted to curb Geneen. He had defended Geneen when the Chilean connection had first been aired in the media several years earlier: "He can run any company I'm a director of until he's ninety-two years old." Though they had never been close friends outside their business relationship, Rohatyn remained loyal despite the ensuing hearings and press

---

* No charges were ever filed against Geneen. The Justice Department investigation into his activities mysteriously died.

coverage, perhaps in recognition of the great debt he felt he owed Geneen. "I've always said," he would remark years later, "had I gotten acquainted with the chairman of U.S. Steel instead of Harold Geneen, I would still be doing studies down there somewhere."

Still, when the ITT board decided to replace Geneen as chief executive officer, Rohatyn bowed to the exigencies of good business sense: "The directors had gone through the trauma of Hartford and Chile," he later explained. "I frankly thought it was now time for Harold to leave."

Geneen, ousted as CEO, managed to hang on to his position as ITT chairman and board member, but he sniped at his replacement and kept meddling in ITT's affairs. In November 1979, his presence at ITT effectively came to an end when he was forced to resign as chairman. He remained on the board until 1983 but had lost his authority. Rohatyn would leave the board even sooner, to accept a position in 1981 as a director of Schlumberger, the international oil-drilling service company, passing on his ITT seat to Michel David-Weill. By then Rohatyn had outgrown ITT — and Geneen.

* * *

While Meyer was dying and Geneen was losing his last vestiges of power at ITT, Rohatyn could look forward as well as backward. He was happily becoming domesticated again. The rebel who had "owned two suits" was on a steady progression upward and outward socially. Though he wasn't an eligible bachelor any longer, the number of invitations to social events didn't diminish. As a couple, the Rohatyns filled their calendar with many kinds of functions, from political and philanthropic dinners to glamorous benefits and galas to entertaining at home.

After their marriage, Elizabeth had the Park Avenue apartment redecorated in more traditional style that included some English and French antiques. The duplex offered little natural light, so the living room was painted a soft yellow to create the illusion of brightness; yellow, rose, and green were the predominant fabric colors. There was no library, but bookcases covered the walls of the dining room.

Elizabeth was an imaginative, stylish hostess and Rohatyn was soon playing the lively, attentive host. Invitations to their New York dinner parties for twelve to fourteen people, given several times a month, were widely coveted among the city's political, business, publishing, and social elite. Stimulating conversation, rather than elaborate food, was the focal point, and sometimes a special guest, such as a politician or foreign visitor, was asked to discuss a specific issue informally at dinner. The guests at any given time might include Henry Kissinger, William Paley, noted political pundit Joseph Kraft, and Barbara Walters. "There was always a great mixture of people," commented Walters, "and you went there knowing you would have one of the best and most interesting evenings you could have."

The Rohatyns in turn were invited to some of the most exclusive social gatherings in New York City. Rohatyn, a self-styled Democrat, even found a welcome in Reagan country. A few weeks after the 1980 election, he and Elizabeth attended a private dinner party on Park Avenue given by society doyenne Brooke Astor, as one of a hundred select guests — among them, David Rockefeller, Tom Brokaw, Arthur Ochs Sulzberger — honoring President-elect Ronald Reagan and Mrs. Reagan.

The Rohatyns spent weekends at their Southampton home. They kept a low profile and unwound from the frantic pace of the week. Here they almost never attended benefits or elaborate parties, although they often bought tickets and donated them. Their two-story gray-shingled house — with its sprawling lawn and mature trees — was located on a little more than two acres in one of the resort's most desirable areas. Maintaining the house and grounds was Elizabeth's responsibility. "Felix is absolutely useless" is how his wife described his household and gardening skills. "He can barely change a light bulb." She enjoyed doing the cooking herself: local help handled the rest. Throughout the rooms a mixture of country furniture and modern pieces were attractively arranged. In the white-washed living room, comfortable sofas and chairs — covered predominantly in an off-white-and-raspberry Indian print — were arranged in two groupings. A French armoire stood against one wall. Paintings by local artists with national reputations, such as Robert Dash and Jane Freilicher — featuring the Hamptons landscape of dunes, fields, and flowers — brought the spirit of the outdoors inside the house.

In Southampton, Rohatyn took care of business matters on the telephone. "Felix is an enormous telephone person," said Elizabeth. "On the weekends, he calls all over the country and the world, and people all over the country and the world call him."

Not infrequently, the calls were about deals. Whatever else Rohatyn was involved in, he was first and foremost a merger maker and he hadn't been so busy since the late sixties.

\* \* \*

A merger wave of unprecedented dimensions had been gathering momentum from the midseventies onward. It was triggered by a series of economic tremors resulting in the worst stock market tumble in thirty-five years during 1973–74. Strong, steady growth, the hallmark of the postwar era, appeared to be over. Corporate leaders sought a strategy to cope with what they perceived as the vagaries of the economy.

The acquisition of another company — formerly an activity of the maverick raiders in the sixties — seemed as good a move as any to the top managements of many companies. Plowing the earnings into expanding one's own facilities was less appealing than branching out into something new — the acquisitioin of a company in the same field or, preferably, in an entirely different one. Going into different fields offered managers the opportunity to spread their business risks. Savvy corporate leaders, financial analysts, and financiers began to identify dozens of companies in which the stock price languished far below the value of underlying assets. Bargains were everywhere. Though the blue-blooded investment bankers initially hesitated to join the common raiders, the barrier was breached in 1974 when Morgan Stanley, represented by Robert Greenhill, helped the proper old International Nickel Company of Canada acquire ESB, the Philadelphia-based battery company, in an unfriendly deal.

As the country emerged from the 1974–75 recession, the pace of mergers quickened for the first time since the heyday of the conglomerateurs in the late sixties. Corporations were piling up earnings, yet their stocks remained undervalued. As the economy overheated and inflation continued to rise in the later 1970s, it became risky to hold on to cash for very long. Hard assets, in contrast, generally increased in value, and chief executives could do well by going into debt to purchase a bigger company, because the size of the loan, in effect, shrinks during inflation. Debts are repaid in depreciating dollars.

If all that weren't enough, there was another compelling reason: survival. If corporations didn't invest their cash, they could become takeover targets themselves. The hunger to ingest new companies became insatiable, greater than during the peak of the Go-Go Years. Purchase price and fit would no longer be the only major considerations. Personal incentives were involved: the sheer pleasure of winning a contest, high monetary rewards, bigger empires to run, instant gratification. The deal that was to prove the harbinger of the new hostile era was Colt's raid on Garlock in 1975, in which Rohatyn served as Colt's adviser.

For some time, Rohatyn had kept his eye on the gasket maker as an acquisition for his friend David Margolis, the head of Colt, who was turning the century-old manufacturer of the famous handgun into a diversified defense contractor and automobile equipment maker. Rohatyn felt certain that Garlock would resist a friendly offer, so he suggested a hostile bid.

He persuaded Margolis to hire Joseph Flom as Colt's outside lawyer. At fifty-one, Flom was the star partner of Skadden, Arps, Slate, Meagher & Flom, the most seasoned legal veteran of the merger wars and part of the winning International Nickel team in the ESB battle.

Surprise was the key in Colt's pursuit of Garlock. As a consequence, Rohatyn needed to keep in close touch with Margolis. Despite his heavy MAC schedule, Rohatyn had many opportunities to see him, since Margolis was a member of the city's control board that watched over how the city spent its money, and they met on city fiscal matters. (At one point during the negotiations, Rohatyn actually handed Margolis some pertinent papers about Colt's raid on Garlock to sign outside the mayor's office.)

In mid-November Colt took out newspaper ads to announce its tender offer for Garlock;* the bid would expire a week later — the day before Thanksgiving. As soon as Colt announced its bid, Garlock hired forty-three-year-old Martin Lipton of Wachtell, Lipton, Rosen & Katz to head its legal defense. Lipton was quickly gaining the reputation as the only counter to Flom. Garlock also retained investment banker Stephen Friedman of Goldman Sachs. The following day the Garlock team filed suit to enjoin the tender, charging that the takeover would violate both antitrust and securities law.

"Lipton decided that the way to really get under my skin was to take depositions from me all the time," Rohatyn recalled, "and we were going through one of the endless crises about the city's finances. Once I was deposed on a Saturday night, unshaven and looking awful, as I came out of a labor negotiation. The television crews were outside waiting to grill me — not about Garlock but about the unions."

Garlock searched frantically for a white knight — a company that acquired the target of a hostile takeover — and opened talks with AMF, the sporting goods company. Shortly into the negotiations, the potential white knight began to look more like an unfriendly one. Garlock did a sudden about-face and accepted Colt's offer.

---

* In general, a tender offer is a public notice expressing a willingness to acquire a company by buying its stock.

The Garlock acquisition worked out well for Colt and enhanced both Rohatyn's and Flom's reputations. (Friedman and Lipton also benefitted by making the best deal possible.) But what everyone would remember most about the raid was the phrase "Saturday Night Special" — coined by a witty public relations man for Garlock's chairman — that was published under his name in newspaper ads rejecting Colt's initial offer. "We don't think your rush 'Saturday Night Special' tender offer is a credit to American business, and we don't think it's in the best interests of our shareholders."

The term Saturday Night Special immediately became synonymous with a lightning-fast tender bid. It was one of the first words in the new argot of colorful, evocative, and warlike terms spawned by the takeover movement that captured media and press attention. Shortly afterward, the general public became caught up in the frenzy of merger contests both as observers and investors.

Rohatyn was ready for the subsequent takeover frenzy, even as his most important client — Harold Geneen — was fading in importance. The Lazard dealmaker knew a whole new generation of CEOs who were becoming his firm's clients. A few of them had grown up under Geneen's tutelage as executives at ITT. David Margolis, Colt's chief executive, had earned his stripes there. So had Michel Bergerac, the new head of Revlon. But perhaps the most significant addition to Rohatyn's network was someone who hadn't even become a CEO yet — Edward Hennessy, the president of United Technologies.

At the time of the Colt raid on Garlock, Rohatyn also advised United Technologies in its successful hostile bid to acquire Otis Elevator. He brought the idea to Hennessy, who liked the proposal. They then met with Hennessy's boss, Harry Gray, in Rohatyn's office. Gray had failed in his attempt to rescue ESB from International Nickel the previous year and was under considerable pressure to win on a grand scale. Gray was impressed with Rohatyn. "He was someone you could share your innermost thoughts with," he said.

Rohatyn, a friend of Otis chief Ralph Weller, arranged for the four of them to meet for lunch. Weller told them that the time wasn't right for an offer, but Rohatyn recalled that his demurrer "wasn't very strong." When the talk turned to specifics about price, Weller balked, and the friendly bid turned hostile overnight — but only in the newspapers.

The four men kept the talks under way behind the scenes while Otis countered with several lawsuits and searched for a white knight. The battle raged on for weeks, until Rohatyn advised Gray to raise his offer. This time Weller accepted. Gray and Hennessy couldn't have been more pleased. It was the largest hostile takeover until then; they would set another record when they did their next one with Rohatyn.

In 1978, he helped Gray and Hennessy launch the first billion-dollar hostile raid. After many months of bitter struggle in and out of the courts, United Technologies finally acquired Carrier, the giant manufacturer of air conditioners. Like Otis, it was one of the best acquisitions United ever made. "He has a long-term outlook," Hennessy would say of Rohatyn.*

Rohatyn finished the seventies as the undisputed champion of dealmaking, but the competition was heating up for the title. As the legal and financial tactics grew more complex and vicious, he would be forced to grapple on the same level with most of the other takeover warriors — or lose his clients.

He was strategically positioned to stand the heat. He had the know-how and the client contacts and he could depend on the younger partners at Lazard for help in the nitty-gritty of number crunching and other details. His personal life was anchored by his marriage and a rewarding social life, and his range of interests were an antidote to the tensions of the business day. But when it came to the interests of his clients, he wanted it known that he was still in top form.

---

* By the time Carrier had joined United Technologies, Ed Hennessy had left to become chief of Allied, the former Allied Chemical, a company that would come to rival United among the upper ranks of corporate America. And Rohatyn would continue to advise both Hennessy and Gray.

# CHAPTER EIGHTEEN

# Superbroker

I t was a fantasy of modern design: a huge, sleek, black wood-and-stone fireplace spreading warmth throughout the room. But there were no dancing flames, only billowing smoke that filled Sandy Weill's vast new corner office on the top floor. To install a chimney, the construction crew had channeled through the ceiling all the way to the roof of the World Trade Center tower. Despite their prodigious efforts, the fireplace had failed to draw properly. Because Weill had insisted on having a fireplace that worked, everything was dismantled and reassembled three times — at considerable time and expense to Shearson — until at last the smoke could be drawn upward. Now, on a clear day, Weill could get up from his chair at the eighteenth-century English hunt table that served as his desk, gaze out through his floor-to-ceiling windows, puff contentedly on a Te-Amo, and enjoy his crackling fire. To the West, he could see New Jersey and Pennsylvania, to the North, New York City past Central Park, and to the East, the Brooklyn Bridge, beyond which lay the streets where he was born. He could even look directly down on Merrill Lynch's offices.

Getting the fireplace just right was perhaps the last touch needed to complete the new Weill image. But Weill was still known around Shearson as a "shirt-sleeve manager," who monitored the Quotron terminal on the hunt table with undiminished fascination as it flashed out stock and bond quotations. His door was open to any employee — from secretary to vice president — who wanted to see him. He was the accessible chief executive, the homey Brooklynite in the corporate suite. But visitors had to walk past the guard stationed in the reception area on Weill's floor, and proceed down a long beige corridor past a row of secretaries to reach his office.

On the walls mementos called attention to Weill's status, including a photograph of him beaming with Gerald Ford, now a Shearson director. Weill, easily impressed by people in high places, had met

Ford through a family friend and had welcomed the opportunity to have a former U.S. president on his board.

Even before the Loeb Rhoades deal was put into play, Weill himself had overseen the critical plans for the move to the new Shearson headquarters, smoothly transformed into a showplace seven times the size of the old offices in the General Motors building. In retrospect, the transfer seemed like a stockbroker's study in perfect timing. A market rally that had begun in the spring of 1980 continued throughout the year.

Weill's favorite customers, the small investors, played their greatest role in a decade by rushing to buy and sell securities. Some 30 million Americans owned shares of stock directly or indirectly through mutual funds, the largest number since 1970, when there were 31 million shareholders. In an economy heated up by inflation, they had a lot of money to invest. But that wasn't the only reason for celebration among retail brokers. Small investors also jumped with gusto into the phenomenon of "money market" mutual funds, which accorded some hedge against inflation without considerable risk. For the first time, they could earn the high interest rates on debt instruments such as Treasury bills and commercial paper that previously had been available only to much larger players. Investment in these funds skyrocketed from $8 billion in 1978 to $40 billion in 1979 to $75 billion in 1980. It was a financial bonanza for most brokers. But it wasn't enough for Weill. He wasn't finished building his empire.

*  *  *

One day in late August of 1980, while having breakfast at the New York Stock Exchange Luncheon Club, Weill had been presented with a striking idea — to sell Shearson to American Express. The combination of Weill's diversified brokerage house and American Express, with its global charge-card and traveler's check service, international banking division, and Fireman's Fund Insurance Company, would create a financial empire that would rival any in the world. In short, a superbroker. The proposition was the brainchild of forty-one-year-old Salim ("Sandy") Lewis. Until then, Weill had had only a nodding acquaintance with Lewis, who ran his own trading outfit. But Weill's breakfast companion had a calling card that could not readily be ignored: he was the son of Cy Lewis, Weill's unforgettable first boss. Although Sandy Lewis had little else in common with his father, the tall, gangly redhead did have his father's abrasive personality, which contributed to a checkered career at such firms as Merrill Lynch, Salomon Brothers, and White Weld.

Weill was surprised at Lewis's proposal, but he was neither shocked nor ready to accept it. In fact, he had once approached American Express himself. Back in 1975, Weill had spoken with the company's then president, Roger Morley, about having his firm acquired by Amexco, but Amexco's management was just ending a disappointing relationship with Donaldson, Lufkin & Jenrette, the first Wall Street firm to go public, in which Amexco had owned a 25 percent stake. There hadn't been much hope of Shearson or any other brokerage catching American Express on the rebound.

Now, after the passage of five years that had seen the remarkable growth of Shearson, Weill was no longer so eager to part with his firm. He countered with a startling trial-balloon proposal of his own — he would entertain the notion only if he became president of American Express. Lewis pulled back. He couldn't promise anything, except that he would set up a meeting between Weill and Amexco chairman James Robinson III, a friend of Lewis's since their days together at White Weld.

In September Weill's chauffeur-driven Mercedes pulled up in front of American Express's headquarters overlooking the East River, bringing him to a luncheon meeting with Lewis and Robinson. The security guards in the lobby directed him to the elevator that took him to the top floor of the white-ribbed skyscraper. There he was met by another security guard wearing a sky-blue blazer with the American Express logo emblazened on the breast pocket, who escorted him to Robinson's private dining room.

The environment at American Express reflected a corporate culture that seemed worlds apart from the fraternal life at the top at Shearson. At the brokerage house, executives hopped from office to office, trying out ideas on one another, putting out fires, arguing, and kibitzing. The voices of Weill, Cohen, and Sheinberg could be heard in the long executive corridor, and the smell of cigar smoke was omnipresent. The offices were sleek and functional; none was particularly grand except for Weill's.

At American Express, by contrast, the walls were adorned with a golden-hued fabric, the dark wood was polished, and the carpeted corridors were usually empty. Soothing landscapes and imposing portraits of past chairmen were framed on the walls. The silence was intimidating. An ornate chandelier hung over a broad spiral stairway that wound down to the floor below, where a battery of executives carried out the orders from above. Robinson's corner office overlooked New York City's harbor. Weill, though he was loath to admit it, found the whole atmosphere intoxicating.

Robinson, the forty-four-year-old chairman of American Express, fitted into that environment like a set piece. Stocky and of average height, with dark wavy hair, soft smooth skin, and a cherubic smile, he conveyed an unshakable sense of assurance and calm. Born and bred into the Wasp Establishment, he had been around executive suites his entire career. It had been an orderly progression upward for him, fulfilling a lifetime of expectations.

His father, grandfather, and great-grandfather had been prominent bankers in his native Atlanta. After graduating from the Harvard Business School, Robinson had worked at the prestigious Morgan Guaranty bank, then at White Weld, before joining American Express. From the very first, he had been treated like someone special, a man who was being groomed for a top spot. After only seven years at the company, in 1977, he was named chairman of one of the most prestigious corporations in the world.

For the first time in some years, Weill was about to begin negotiating with a corporate chieftain who was not only strong financially, but was deeply confident about himself and his future. Robinson wouldn't be pressured into a deal unless the terms suited him and American Express. Weill, accustomed to moving quickly and aggressively, had to adjust his approach that morning to a more measured pace. That initial meeting was merely an opportunity for Weill and Robinson to size each other up. They carefully avoided the suggestion that one or both executives might be interested in a possible merger of their two firms.

Weill never mentioned his previous talks with American Express; nor did Robinson reveal that American Express was now ready to get back into Wall Street. They talked politely about the state of the market and about reciprocal financial services — such as an American Express card for Shearson customers — that each company might provide for the other. When Weill reached for a cigar, Robinson, a nonsmoker, didn't object.

The meeting lasted a little over an hour. And there the matter rested for some months. Robinson then flirted briefly with the heads of Dean Witter, Merrill Lynch, and E. F. Hutton. From time to time, he would talk to Weill, but they spoke exclusively about financial services. Weill played the dating game so close to the vest that not until the spring of 1981 did he tell Peter Cohen what he had in mind. By then, events beyond his control forced him out into the open.

Bache was the catalyst. In 1979, the Our Crowd firm had celebrated its one hundredth anniversary. It wasn't the most auspicious occasion. Despite an extravagant centennial luncheon at the Hotel Pierre on Fifth Avenue, Bache was on the defensive. In truth, it had limped through the seventies.

At the time, it was led by Harry Jacobs, a bald, avuncular broker and a fierce loyalist. Long known as "Harold Bache's little boy" (his actual father was the architect of Century Country Club in Westchester), Jacobs was quick to point out his connection to Our Crowd. But the Our Crowd days were over. What's more, the house of Bache had never recovered from the excesses of the sixties, and Jacobs could hear the wolves prowling outside the door, waiting for the right moment to attack.

The most determined foray was made in 1980 by the Belzbergs, an extremely wealthy Canadian-Jewish family. The three brothers — Samuel, Hyman, and William — ran a raffish industrial, real estate, and financial empire. Frightened and angry, and preferring to make his own decision, Jacobs sold Bache to the Prudential Insurance Company for $385 million in March of 1981. In theory, the combination created an international financial organization that had the potential to provide almost every service — from banking to insurance to real estate to brokerage — under one roof. It would be known as Wall Street's first superbroker.

Sandy and Joan Weill learned of the Prudential-Bache deal the morning after it was announced, from a newspaper article in the *South China Morning Post,* which was delivered to their suite at the Mandarin Hotel in Hong Kong. The Weills were there with Gerald Ford, visiting the local Shearson office. Joan Weill sensed from the excited and alarmed look on her husband's face that something momentous had happened. From his point of view, it had: the balance of power on the Street had shifted.

For some years, Bache had not been a serious competitor for Shearson. But now Bache would be owned by one of the world's biggest financial institutions, one with more than $60 billion in assets. Knowing Wall Street's herd reaction, Weill was convinced that other firms would sell out to large corporate entities in order to remain competitive in the new world of financial superpowers.

Meanwhile, Peter Cohen, who was vacationing in Israel, learned about the Prudential-Bache deal from a telegram sent to him by George Sheinberg. Cohen immediately phoned Weill at his hotel suite in Hong Kong and asked what Weill thought the Bache sale meant for the future of Shearson. Weill replied vaguely, "It means we've got to get bigger." He wasn't yet ready to share with Cohen the fact that he had already had secret talks with Robinson. Weill and Cohen merely agreed to talk further as soon as both returned home.

That day, Weill had one other phone conversation about the Bache takeover, but this one was far more specific. Sandy Lewis called to find out if Weill was interested in talking hard facts with Robinson about a merger with American Express.

"Sure, set up a meeting," said Weill, acting deliberately non-committal. For the remainder of his trip in the Far East, he thought incessantly about the pros and cons of a merger with Amexco. The prospect would provide Shearson with far more capital for expansion and would narrow the gap with the number-one brokerage house, Merrill Lynch. But deep down, he felt ambivalent about his plans to sell out to American Express. "I'd helped build Shearson from scratch into a major Wall Street firm and was very proud of what we'd accomplished," he admitted later. "If it was sold, we'd lose our independence." But his ambition and common sense told him that things couldn't stay as they were.

Back in New York several days later, he broke the news of his talks with Robinson to Cohen and Sheinberg, who also felt ambivalent about a possible merger. But there was obviously no harm in a meeting of both sides.

Shortly afterward, Sandy and Joan Weill invited Robinson and his wife, Bettye, to their Connecticut home for a Sunday brunch. It was the first time the two couples saw each other socially. Bettye Robinson loved the house and the garden. Joan Weill cut her a bouquet of forsythia. Later, when the two men talked alone, Weill dropped the posture of the genial host.

He said he wasn't interested in a merger that would simply fold Shearson into American Express. He demanded to know what his role would be in the combined company. He didn't want to get lost in a huge corporation. Robinson was evasive: Weill would have to prove himself to the Amexco board. Weill's ardor for the deal quickly cooled. He sat atop one of the most profitable publicly held securities firms in the industry. The obvious question: what more did he have to prove? Since Robinson had another appointment that day, the conversation was left hanging.

But Weill wasn't ready to give up. In their ongoing talks, he let Robinson know that he wanted to be president of Amexco. Conveniently, the post was vacant. Put on the defensive, Robinson deflected the request, suggesting that the board would not approve his appointment. Clearly, with Weill exerting so much pressure, Robinson couldn't afford to leave the post vacant long.

For many at American Express, no candidate was more suitable than vice chairman Alva Way, who had been the chief financial officer at General Electric before moving to Amexco in 1979. Robinson himself leaned toward Way as the choice for president, but showed no inclination to appoint anyone chief operating officer (a position normally held by the president, and the real number-two slot in most companies). By leaving the post of COO vacant, Robinson was tempting both Way and Weill.

Weill brought Cohen, who would work out the details of the deal, with him to the American Express headquarters in early April. They discussed the issues to be resolved, who would handle them, and other details. Almost at once, the two teams were working sixteen-hour days. All the while, Robinson and Weill kept in regular touch with each other. Before they could work out a deal, Shearson and American Express had to perform "due diligence" — an examination in depth of each other's business. That wasn't problematic, since both companies had enjoyed record years. The ticklish issues were the total price, titles, and the number of American Express board seats allotted to Shearson executives.

The name for the new brokerage arm was easy: Shearson Loeb Rhoades became Shearson/American Express. Finding the right slot for Weill was harder. The best he could extract (in addition to his remaining chairman of Shearson) was to be named chairman of the executive committee at Amexco, a meaningless post and title filled, according to Robinson, "if the other titles are taken." With the COO slot left vacant and with Alva Way the obvious choice as president, Weill was given one concession. George Sheinberg jockeyed successfully to ensure that Weill's signature on the annual report would follow Way's, in recognition that Weill was Amexco's third-ranking executive. American Express countered by adding two more of its executives to the photograph over the signatures. This gang of five was known as the "chairman's office." (The two extra Amexco officers were dropped the following year.) The first bell had sounded in the game of cat and mouse between American Express and Sandy Weill.

Price also required some maneuvering. American Express offered to exchange 1.1 shares of Amexco stock for each share of Shearson stock for a package worth $864 million. Weill had some 450,000 shares, making his stake worth more than $25 million. Cohen objected fiercely, demanding 1.3 Amexco shares for each share of Shearson stock, or $915 million. The Amexco team wasn't responsive to Cohen's demands and held its ground.

The number of seats on Amexco's board of directors that

would be allocated to Shearson men also had to be resolved. At first Robinson seemed to agree that three seats would be awarded: two for Shearson insiders — Weill and Cohen — and one for an old friend of Weill's who was an outside Shearson director. But as the talks progressed, Amexco's signals suggested that the third seat might not be available.

The negotiators didn't have much time to resolve these differences. Keeping the momentum going was important, and this merger was supposed to be very friendly. Suddenly, on April 17, 1981 — Good Friday — the pressure to wrap it up increased. The *Wall Street Journal* and the *New York Times* had gotten wind of the talks. Both sides had told reporters that they were negotiating a joint financial marketing venture, not a merger. The two teams decided that they were close enough to a deal to iron out the remaining details over the weekend and thus avoid further divisive speculation by the press.

At around five o'clock Friday afternoon, both teams reported to Amexco, where Robinson and Weill were conferring privately. Cohen was fairly sure he had at least moved American Express up to the $903 million mark, if not up to the $915 million mark, and he believed that all opposition to his getting the third board seat had been dispelled. But he was wrong. When Robinson and Weill joined the others, they were smiling. Robinson told the two teams they had an agreement. Weill had sealed the deal at $915 million, and everything else was assumed to follow from that.

(Cohen has a totally different recollection from Weill's as to how the $915 million figure was reached. According to him, "Robinson walked out of the conference room and said, 'Sandy and I've agreed to 1.1 shares.'" Cohen and George Sheinberg immediately informed Robinson, "In all due deference to our chairman, that won't sell back at the World Trade Center. You have no deal with any of us at 1.1. We can assure you that when we get together tomorrow our group will vote against it. The deal will get done only if it's 1.3." The atmosphere became heated. In effect, Cohen was negotiating against Weill. Finally, Robinson increased the amount to 1.3.)

With an agreement for 1.3 shares in his pocket, Weill shook hands with Robinson. The price increased Weill's personal holdings by $1.5 million dollars. Weill, Cohen, and Sheinberg left American Express headquarters together and shared a cab to their Upper East Side apartments. For all the disagreements and tensions, they were well satisfied with the deal they had negotiated. Weill was the first one out of the taxi. He walked over to the front of the cab where Cohen was sitting. "By the way, you're not going to get a board seat," he said to Cohen. He then turned and disappeared into his building.

When Cohen got home, he exploded with anger. Rarely had Karen Cohen seen her husband so agitated. Cohen considered his boss, Weill, a good friend and was outraged by his behavior. The two couples saw each other socially. The Cohens were always invited to the Weills' party to break the Yom Kippur fast and were at many other family events, such as Jessica Weill's sweet sixteen party. Every summer the Weills spent a weekend at the Cohens' home in the Hamptons.

Later that evening Sandy Lewis, who had played the role of mediator throughout the negotiations, phoned Cohen and asked how he felt about not getting the board seat. "I've been sold out," Cohen told him bitterly. "I don't know what I'm going to do tomorrow."

Cohen received another call, this one from Weill. "I know you're very upset. We should talk about this face to face. Come to Greenwich early tomorrow."

The next morning, Weill explained to Cohen that the American Express board had decided to give only two seats to Shearson and tried to persuade Cohen that, with stock options, it was a great deal for him despite his loss of the board seat.

No matter how hard Weill tried, Cohen remained unconvinced and told Weill that he might leave after the end of the year. That ended the discussion. They finished breakfast and waited for the other Shearson executives to assemble.

*   *   *

Spring had arrived early in Greenwich, Connecticut. The apple trees on the Weills' property were starting to bloom; fresh-leafed Norwegian maples lined the driveway, and there was a wash of daffodils. Joan Weill had prepared her standby, chicken salad. By midmorning the top echelon of Shearson were gathered in the living room. Weill told his executives that he had been talking to American Express about acquiring Shearson, but that he needed a consensus from them. Apart from Cohen and Sheinberg, none of the other five had the slightest inkling that Weill and Robinson had already shaken hands on the deal.

The executives had to feel they were part of the decision-making process. To Weill, not surprisingly, that was no lie. The handshake, he felt, was a conditional handshake, awaiting his executives' approval. In reality, the matter had been settled for Shearson. It only remained for the American Express board to ratify it.

None of the five spoke up in favor of the deal. As for Cohen and Sheinberg, their support stopped short of being enthusiastic. Cohen was prepared to back Weill all the way because he felt it was in the interests of Shearson, but he was not at his best that morning. Something between him and Weill had been lost.

Weill would have to push for the deal himself. "Imagine waking up one morning," he told his executives, "and reading in the papers that American Express has acquired Hutton. How will you feel? We'll have to do something sometime — in two or three years, who knows. American Express is unique. The offer is a special opportunity. If we don't make the move now, they won't be around in the future."

In a sense, holding up American Express as a savior was a little like waving a red flag in front of a charging bull. Weill was dealing with a Shearson gang who, temperamentally, were bullish on themselves. The Dow was making every broker happy in the merry month of April. It had already spent seven days over the awesome 1,000 mark. First breached in November 1972, the Dow had rarely crossed the barrier since then.

"We don't need them," insisted Hardwick ("Wick") Simmons, a senior executive vice president and the most vocal opponent of the merger. Of the five, only Dwight Faulkner, a vice chairman, and Sherman Lewis were for it. Alger ("Duke") Chapman, the quiet cochairman of Shearson, had a growing sense that it was a done deal and that protests were irrelevant. The executives expressed doubts about whether the ways of Shearson and American Express would be compatible. They were worried that they would be bogged down in memos and red tape and that their bonuses would shrink. Self-interest mixed with cynicism over Weill's grand design. Before long, a deep-rooted concern surfaced: Weill's ambition.

"What about you?" one of them asked Weill.

"I'll never leave Shearson," Weill protested.

"Bullshit!" came the resounding chorus. It seemed apparent that Weill would move over to the American Express tower the moment he had the chance and would leave Shearson to fend for itself as just another division of Amexco, and that his secret, unarticulated ambition was to be the high man in the Amexco pecking order. Yet Weill had carried them this far — from one successful merger to another on sheer energy and bravado. He continued to press hard, and his constant pounding, cajoling, and pleading wore down their resistance. Weill, the shy man who had at one time preferred to recede into the shadows, had become formidably persuasive, more and more so with every successful move he made.

In fact, they suspected that his sense of security was undermining him. They could accept his arguments for the merger with Amexco, but they found it disquieting that Weill seemed unable to grasp what they considered the unalterable truth: that there would never be room at the very top for him within American Express itself. Worse still, he would never see why. Cohen and Sheinberg talked about it privately. In a quiet moment, they took Weill aside and pointed out that they didn't know of a single Jew on the American Express board and certainly not in its upper management. Jews would not be easily accepted in that environment. Cohen said, "There's no way this company is going to have a Jewish chairman."

Shearson president Sherman Lewis told Weill much the same thing, only more delicately: "The type of people on Amexco's board are very different in style and background. I think as a practical matter, it would probably be impossible for you to run American Express."

Weill was clearly uncomfortable with such talk — half the men in the room weren't Jewish. His response was predictable: he didn't feel his religion would hold him back. "It's not an issue," he said in a quiet, but firm, voice. And he would never make it into one.

In that respect, Weill wasn't facing up to reality. The division that had separated Jewish and non-Jewish firms for decades continued in the eighties. Though such Jewish firms as Goldman Sachs, Shearson, Bear Stearns, Lazard Frères, and Salomon Brothers now had a number of non-Jews in important positions, the Wasp firms had few Jews, as was true virtually everywhere else in finance. Certainly no Jew had risen to the helm of a Wasp firm, as John Whitehead had done in reverse at Goldman Sachs, where he was co-managing partner with John Weinberg. And not until the seventies had the imperial Morgan Stanley conferred a partnership on a Jew, awarding it to Lewis Bernard, a young man with impeccable academic credentials. Bernard had attended Princeton with the son of the firm's chairman and had joined Morgan Stanley virtually as its "Jewish Jackie Robinson."* He had since become one of the more prominent partners at the firm — and the exception that proved the rule. Most of the other Wasp firms didn't even have a "Bernard."

Since Passover began at sundown, it hastened the end of the

---

* A black man hadn't made the partnership level or its equivalent at any major house. Moreover, there were no top-ranking women executives at any of these firms.

meeting, ironically cutting off the discussion of religion as a barrier to Weill's chances of making it to the top in the Wasp world. Whether or not the rush to finish had any influence on the outcome of the meeting is difficult to measure. In any case, Weill got his consensus.

After the meeting, Cohen headed for his brother's house on Long Island for the traditional Seder, while Sheinberg stayed to observe the holiday with the Weills. They listened as Weill's daughter, Jessica, read the four *kashas,* broke matzoh together, and drank kosher wine. It was the only relaxation they would get. The next day the tension would start all over again.

* * *

The following morning, which was Easter Sunday, Weill met with Louis Gerstner, a plump, Harvard-educated wunderkind who ran Amexco's flagship travel business. Weill was at his best with Gerstner, who, he thought, would not go as far at Amexco as Weill himself would. As it happened, Weill's assessment was to prove wrong, along with other assessments he would make about the alien world he was soon to enter.

The evening of Easter Sunday, Weill, Cohen, and Sheinberg met at the offices of Skadden Arps, which had prepared the contracts for both parties to read.

At least for the moment, Weill didn't brood about what title he would hold at American Express. After all, he still ran Shearson, and he felt he got along well enough with everyone who mattered at Amexco. Cohen was more relaxed, too, having exorcised all his demons late Saturday night in a phone conversation with Robinson. The Amexco chief, who had been told by Lewis that Cohen was wildly angry about losing the board seat, had called him and tried to rekindle his enthusiasm for the deal.

"Save your breath," replied Cohen, cutting Robinson short. "I think we're going to do this thing. And I go along with it, because I think it's the right thing for the company. I don't know if it's the right thing for me. You have an end-of-the-year commitment and that's it."

From that point on, Cohen was gone from Shearson, at least in his mind. He was mentally prepared to show up for work on Monday as if nothing had happened. Monday was Weill's turn for doubts.

That day the American Express board met to deliberate on the deal. Instead of a two-hour-or-so meeting, as most expected, it dragged on for five hours. The directors still had reservations about whether

American Express should be in the brokerage business. The company — started in 1850 by Henry Wells and William Fargo, the men who also founded the legendary Pony Express and the Wells Fargo bank — had built a reputation for stability for over 125 years. Now it was being asked to take a large risk, beginning with Sandy Weill.

Meantime, a humbled Shearson team, along with the anxious matchmaker Sandy Lewis, sat expectantly at Shearson headquarters. Sandy Weill, alone in his office, also nervously awaited the outcome. They were all at the mercy of the Amexco board.

Finally, Robinson called and told Weill that the board had approved the merger. But Weill wasn't quite ready to make an announcement. He wanted to talk to Robinson first. At 8:00 P.M. Robinson and his negotiating team arrived at the World Trade Center, just as Joan Weill entered the building. They rode up together to the 106th floor. If he was going to take the final steps and give up his firm, Weill wanted his wife with him. He closeted himself with Robinson and Joan in a sitting room adjacent to his office. The deal had been structured and approved. Now it came down to whether Robinson and Weill could get along. Weill was overwhelmed by doubts. His identity was closely tied to Shearson, but he was risking it for the gamble of greater rewards — and more power. What if the gamble didn't pay off?

Robinson had further news for Weill. The American Express board had changed its mind and agreed to make Cohen a director. That would satisfy Cohen, but Weill was quick to grasp that nothing concrete had been provided for him. One last time, he asked to be named president of American Express or at least given some other assurance that only Robinson would rank above him. Robinson wouldn't promise, except to say, "Your time will come." Weill would have to trust him, but it wasn't easy to read this cool, polished diplomat.

If the merger went through, Weill's holdings of Amexco stock would be much greater than Robinson's; 600,000 shares to Robinson's 15,000. Weill wondered if that would cause serious conflicts and jealousy, since on Wall Street success is measured above all else by someone's net worth.

"What are you worth?" Weill hurled the question at Robinson.

It was a typically blunt Weill question, one intended to get to the heart of the matter — and it was reminiscent of the old Arthur Carter refrain: "How much money did you make today?"

Robinson was clearly taken aback. "Not nearly as much as you," he answered. But he assured Weill it wouldn't affect their relationship. He also maintained that Weill would advance quickly in the American Express hierarchy. Weill was still uncertain. He took Joan aside. He prided himself on never making a tough personal decision or evaluating any individual of consequence without consulting her. And this was the most important decision of his career.

"Should I trust him?" he asked.

"Yes," she answered without hesitation. For weeks she had vacillated — concerned about what her husband would give up if he sold Shearson. Now she was encouraging him to press ahead with Robinson, convinced in her own mind that "Sandy was ready to expand."

Weill turned to Robinson.

"Okay, let's do it," he said.

\*     \*     \*

Around midnight there were steaks, champagne, and tears. The Shearson kitchen staff served food to more than forty people, but not many had the appetite for more than a few bites. Both sides were exhausted. They didn't know how close they had come to losing everything they had worked so hard to achieve in recent weeks, as Weill teetered back and forth during the final moments before agreeing to sell. He didn't say so but he was thinking, "Have I done the right thing?" He was on the verge of crying, even as he lit up a victory cigar. Cohen was torn by his own conflicting emotions. After being told he had been given the board seat, he had agreed to stay on, but the memory of Weill's behavior lingered. The other Shearson executives clung to Robinson's assurance that they would all keep their jobs and that the brokerage firm would remain autonomous.

On Tuesday at 9:00 A.M., April 21, 1981, Weill addressed Shearson's some two hundred and forty offices over the squawk box, the speakerphone that carried his voice all over the country. He hesitated before delivering the news of the sale to most of the ten thousand people who worked for him. In a halting voice, he explained the rationale behind the merger and what the benefits were for Shearson. In the middle of the explanation, he broke down and began sobbing.

The following day, news of the merger was carried by major newspapers throughout the country. A week later, Alva Way, who had been a virtual nonpresence during the course of the negotiations, was officially named Amexco's president. That was hardly how Weill had envisioned the start of his odyssey into the brave new era of the superbrokers.

He would have to wait two more months, until June 29, when the shareholders of the two companies would vote their proxies in favor of the deal, before anything remotely resembling "his time" would come. The Shearson executives and shareholders were his people; dozens of them had become millionaires because of him. Most of them would gladly follow him into an even more profitable future. In the meantime, Weill was in a netherworld. His wife had already had a hint of what the new era would bring.

The wives of the top executives of the two firms were invited to celebrate the merger at a get-together luncheon at the River Café in Brooklyn, where, looking across the East River, one could see a postcard view of the American Express tower. The Shearson women were picked up at their homes in limousines. As the senior Shearson representative, Joan Weill drove downtown with Bettye Robinson, while Karen Cohen rode with Robin Gerstner, the second-highest-ranking Amexco wife attending. After the luncheon, Karen Cohen wanted to ride back with her friend Joan Weill, since they were going in the same direction.

Bettye Robinson would not hear of it. "You came with Robin Gerstner," she said, "and you will go in that car."

Karen Cohen looked at Joan Weill in disbelief. Neither had ever been forced to observe such rigid protocol before, but they followed orders. When Joan Weill told her husband what had happened, they both dismissed it as of little consequence. Certainly Weill knew things were done differently at American Express, but he wasn't worried. He could adjust or, at least, he would reserve judgment until he was there.

\* \* \*

The Shearson shareholders' meeting on June 29 was held in the ballroom of the Windows on the World restaurant at the top of the other World Trade Center tower. Weill had taken great pains to make sure that his former partners Marshall Cogan and Arthur Levitt attended. (Roger Berlind came as a matter of course, since he was on the Shearson board.) Standing behind the podium addressing the shareholders, a nervous but excited Weill joked, "It's amazing what one has to do to get a crowd." The audience broke into laughter. Then he said, "Welcome to the wedding." Weill was clearly enjoying his return to center stage.

He recapped Shearson's extraordinary growth for a receptive audience. "We've survived — and prospered — through too many market cyles to count. Always charging like bulls, never hibernating with the bears. We've accomplished eight mergers or acquisitions — each one bringing new strengths, a new expertise, and most importantly, new people with ideas. We've changed our name three times since then, but never lost our identity as a growing, evolving, dynamic force in the financial services industry."

Cogan and Levitt, who had remained large shareholders in Shearson, had assumed that Weill would publicly recognize their role in helping to build the company. But Weill wasn't sharing the spotlight with anyone. When they realized he had ignored their contribution completely, they stormed out of the room. The relationship between Weill and his former partners was seriously damaged.

But Weill simply saw things as he wanted to see them, and, at this point in his life, it was hard to disagree with him. He had been right so often. By the time he actually turned in his Shearson shares, along with all the other stockholders, on June 29, their value had risen. Shearson was now worth $988 million, and Weill's shares were up $2 million from the time in April when the merger had first been announced.* His Shearson stock was worth nearly thirty million dollars. The jump in Amexco stock reinforced his conviction that the sale of Shearson to American Express had been right. The future seemed bright and limitless. Anything was possible for him at American Express. Or so he thought until he had to face the inescapable truth: Sandy Weill, the free-spirited entrepreneur, was trapped.

---

* For his efforts as a matchmatcher, Sandy Lewis received a finder's fee of $3.5 million.

# CHAPTER NINETEEN

# New Alliances

S ixty-eight years of family control of Salomon Brothers, interrupted only in the midfifties by Rudolph Smutny's brief reign,
ended in 1978, when Billy Salomon called John Gutfreund into his
office and handed the mantle over to him — without receiving even a
thank you from Gutfreund. At sixty-four, a year shy of the mandatory
retirement age he himself had initiated and after a decade and a half as
head of the firm, Salomon felt no obligation to stay on. Gutfreund was
his choice as successor. Later he would deny that he minded Gutfreund's
lack of a display of gratitude. Their parting was typical of their per-
functory relationship — they had never been personally close — and
of the no-frills way things were done at Salomon Brothers.

At the partners' annual meeting later that year, Gutfreund did
make an appropriate speech, paying tribute to Billy Salomon's long
years at the firm. And a chair was endowed in his name at the Salomon
Brothers Center — part of the New York University Graduate School
of Business Administration. But only when he passed his title and
authority to Gutfreund did Salomon begin to learn how little he knew
the man.

Under Billy Salomon, the partnership had become a major force
in stock trading, underwriting, and risk arbitrage. None of that would
have been possible if it were not for his original decision to shore up
the firm's capital by limiting the partners' ability to withdraw their
share of the profits. When Salomon stepped aside officially in October,
John Gutfreund, whose name was to come to epitomize the house of
Salomon's way of doing business, held sway over the fifth-largest house
on Wall Street. He was the same tough-minded boss with superb business instincts. It was his life-style that would change, and with that,
he would change radically as well. The man who had married the quiet,
civic-minded Joyce Low, sported a beard, and endorsed George
McGovern hadn't disappeared entirely. But increasingly that man

would recede into the background. The most startling indication was the Gutfreunds' unpredicted divorce.

A few Salomon partners had sensed that Gutfreund seemed ready to be more socially accessible than he had been, but they hadn't sensed that those indications signaled anything deeper. The Gutfreunds' marriage could be characterized as stable and dependable — they had been married for twenty years. Thus, their friends and associates were taken by surprise when John and Joyce Gutfreund announced that they were divorcing. To their friends' knowledge, John had been a constant husband, one who had never participated in the "summer festival" of affairs and alliances with other women while the wives were staying at their summer homes, and Joyce certainly, like Caesar's wife, seemed above suspicion. Neither of them ever gave a reason for their action and preferred to remain intensely private about what happened and why. Sometime later, Gutfreund met Susan Penn, and his personal life was never quiet again.

The divorce was coincident with Gutfreund's becoming the head of Salomon Brothers. Pushing the firm to the top wouldn't come easily. For all its success in underwriting, the Salomon partners couldn't persuade corporations to think of them as the "right sort" of investment bankers, though Billy Salomon had hired one of them in 1976 to head up its corporate finance department: James Wolfensohn, an Australian Jew who was a graduate of the Harvard Business School and former head of a London-based merchant bank, Schroders. Major corporations still largely ignored Salomon. But the firm made something of a name for itself in 1978 when Lee Iacocca turned to Wolfensohn and his department to help raise money for Chrysler, then virtually bankrupt.

When Gutfreund took over the reins, perhaps the most lucrative business of the firm was its eleven-year-old investment in a "side deal" in the Gulf of Mexico. The $8 million oil and gas venture was now reaping returns that totaled more than $100 million. Gutfreund had to prepare for the day when the wells would run dry, which meant making Salomon Brothers outstanding. Like the other members of the New Crowd, he acknowledged that he was "competitive" and that he wanted to be "the best." Along with achieving his goal, in the next few years, of making Salomon "the best" — that is, the number-one trading and banking firm on Wall Street — he would increase his net worth by millions.

Gutfreund, the assertive "outsider," had by 1978 joined the select company of proud security industry "insiders" (Robert H. B. Baldwin, the erudite head of Morgan Stanley; Donald Regan, the tough-talking chief of Merrill Lynch; and the pair of Harvard MBA graduates who ran Goldman Sachs, John Whitehead and John Weinberg, the son of the legendary Sidney Weinberg, among others), but he hadn't yet proved that he belonged in their league.

As it happened, he soon had the opportunity to outflank Wall Street's number-one firm: Morgan Stanley. When Morgan Stanley declined to underwrite a massive $1 billion debt offering in 1979 — then the largest in corporate history — by its longtime client IBM, Salomon Brothers took over the deal, which helped propel it past Morgan Stanley to the top of the underwriting heap for the first time.

But the impressive victory came at a stiff price. The Federal Reserve "tightened" — decreased — the money supply, which led to sharply higher interest rates, making the fixed yields of all bonds, including IBM's, less attractive. The subsequent drop in bond prices created heavy losses for the underwriters of the IBM issue, and that was just the beginning. By the spring of 1981, double-digit interest rates had become a frightening norm and made borrowing money more costly. As a consequence, stock and bond trading became an even more volatile, chancier business than usual for Salomon, putting the firm's capital at greatest risk.*

Salomon partner Henry Kaufman, a member of the executive committee, was particularly concerned about the rising volatility in general and the difficulty of competing in a rapidly growing debt market with limited capital and he was not someone who could be ignored easily. A widely respected economist whose views, especially on the bond market, could trigger a rally or start a tailspin, he was most widely known for forecasting downdrafts, for which he had earned the nickname of "Dr. Gloom."† And now, the professorial German-Jewish refugee was living up to his sobriquet. Predicting that the already high interest rates were headed even higher, Kaufman warned that the rates

---

* Salomon often held in inventory securities worth billions of dollars ordinarily bought with its own and borrowed capital. Higher interest rates increased the cost of borrowing money and led to a sharp drop in the stock and bond markets. These two factors — more expensive money and lower securities prices — made it harder for firms like Salomon to earn a profit. A long losing streak could seriously deplete a trading firm of its capital, thus leaving it with insufficient funds for a rebound.

† There was also a "Dr. Doom," economist Albert Wojnilower of First Boston, who, like Kaufman, was concerned about rising interest rates.

would drive bond prices down even lower. Apart from his pessimistic prognosis, some members of the executive committee believed the firm was undercapitalized to begin with.

As the perception of Salomon's vulnerability deepened, Gutfreund and the executive committee began to think seriously that it might be better to sell out to a rich benefactor rather than face such high risks. The limited partners — including Billy Salomon, who jealously protected the firm's traditions — were dead set against selling, as were all the employees who hoped to win a partnership eventually. As they wrestled with the idea of being acquired, a very impressive suitor appeared: the Phibro Corporation. Phibro already had close connections with Salomon; the two companies had done business together for twenty-five years. Moreover, Kaufman and another executive committee member were friends of Phibro's president, Hal Beretz.

* * *

In terms of its history, people, and culture, there seemed no better match for Salomon Brothers than Phibro. The commodities firm had been launched in the 1890s by two German-Jewish brothers, Julius and Oscar Philipp, who peddled scrap metal and brokered small deals on the Hamburg Metal Exchange. Philipp Brothers was a classic Jewish business at a time when metal trading was ripe with opportunity.

The Philipp brothers became the most successful metal traders in Europe. In 1914, Siegfried Bendheim, a cousin, opened a Philipp Brothers office in New York, just four years after the Salomon brothers had opened their doors for business. He was the guiding force in establishing the culture of Philipp Brothers in America. Like him, most of the traders were Orthodox Jews who wore yarmulkes and ate kosher lunches brought in paper bags from home. Many of them came from immigrant backgrounds and were wary of outsiders but deeply loyal to one another. Commodities trading was a secretive and competitive business revolving around shipping schedules, mineral finds, and financing. It required being exacting and agile under pressure. The traders hired apprentices on the basis of personal references to help ensure continuing fealty to the firm. Family members were always a reliable source of fledgling employees. One of them was Ludwig Jesselson, who some day would run the firm.

The son of a struggling businessman and farmer from a small town near Heidelberg, Jesselson learned the commodities business early, as a teenage apprentice working for one of the largest international metal firms in Germany. In 1936, when he was in his midtwenties, he emigrated to America. Already an experienced trader, he fitted easily into the Philipp culture.

In the postwar period, Jesselson and his mentor, Siegfried Ull-mann — the distant cousin who had hired him — brought Philipp Brothers into worldwide prominence. They merged first (in 1960) with Minerals & Chemicals, in a deal engineered by André Meyer of Lazard Frères, and seven years later (again with the help of Meyer) with En-gelhard Industries, a fabricator of gold, platinum, and other precious metals, owned by Meyer's friend and sometime business partner Charles Engelhard, the legendary inspiration for Ian Fleming's Gold-finger.

The huge new company, known as Engelhard Minerals & Chemicals, with a billion dollars in sales and offices worldwide, was seen as a consolidation of perfectly matched interests. But the combi-nation never quite jelled. Charles Engelhard wasn't an active manager. The Princeton-educated scion of a wealthy family, he had built an even greater fortune of his own and lived in grand style. He spent much of his time breeding racehorses and socializing with the idle rich and the political elite of the world.* The Engelhard executives, mainly well-educated Wasps, tended to look down on the Philipp Brothers traders as scrap metal dealers. The Philipp traders, for their part, resented the Engelhard people who, they felt, didn't work very hard. When En-gelhard died in 1971, the need for a chief executive acceptable to both sides produced a compromise candidate: lawyer Milton Rosenthal, whose most significant achievement was keeping peace between the two disgruntled factions.

Jesselson, who ran Philipp after Ullmann's death, wasn't an aggressive leader. In his sixties, he understood that there was wide-spread concern about the firm's future and tapped a dark horse to become president — David Tendler, head of the Philipp office in Tokyo.

Short, dark, and roundish, Tendler was a trader in the classic Philipp mold: tenacious, smart, and loyal. The son of a "rag trade" merchant, he had grown up on Manhattan's Lower East Side. At the Baruch College of City University, he had studied international trade and economics. Following a brief stint in the Army, he went to work for Philipp Brothers in 1960; he became head of the new Tokyo of-

---

* Some claimed Engelhard lived a life of bizarre excess. He was an obese man who ate butter with his fingers and washed it down with Coca-Cola.

fice when he was still in his thirties and president of the company in 1975.

By 1977, the thirty-nine-year-old Tendler and other younger Philipp executives were restive and ready to take over. By then, everyone concerned knew that Philipp would separate from Engelhard. The only question was when. The actual split-up in the spring of 1981 was largely pro forma. Originally paired as an equal, Engelhard had become dwarfed by Philipp, whose sales and profits were more than seven times greater. But fourteen years of anonymity had left their mark. The secretive trading firm, now called the Phibro Corporation, was perhaps the biggest unknown company in the world.

Both Tendler and Hal Beretz, the number-two man at Phibro, wanted to expand. They hired Salomon Brothers to help them look for an acquisition, and almost immediately Salomon became Phibro's hottest prospect. There seemed to be no valid reason for Salomon not to sell out to the commodities traders. Jesselson, Tendler, and Beretz were the kind of men the Salomon executive committee members thought they understood. As Jews and traders — outsiders to both the Wasp and Our Crowd Establishments — the Salomon partners knew what it meant to succeed on one's own in a hostile environment. And the Salomon executive committee had the benefit of example: by selling to American Express, Sandy Weill had made the major Shearson shareholders and the firm very rich very fast, and the previously troubled Bache looked remarkably more solid after having become an arm of Prudential.

At Salomon there was an almost overripe eagerness to sell out among the members of the executive committee. They wanted to get their share of the action — and none, according to several people close to the Salomon chief at the time, wanted that more than Gutfreund. Salomon Brothers needed the money, and so apparently did he. John Gutfreund was transforming himself.

*   *   *

To some degree, the money-conscious climate of the eighties simply made it easier for Gutfreund to go along with the real stimulus for his transformation: the social ambitions and whims of Susan Penn, who had once been an airline stewardess. The Chicago-born daughter of a retired Air Force pilot, Louis Kaposta, she was the only girl in a family of five boys. As the thirty-three year-old former wife of wealthy Texan Roby Penn (a man much older than she), she had arrived in New York apparently eager to meet rich, eligible men. Through Sandy and Hugh Lowenstein, who lived in River House on Sutton Place, she was introduced to John Gutfreund, who at the time was living a bachelor life in an apartment on Park Avenue and was at loose ends. (In future years, according to several friends, she would not be forthcoming about her background or about the circumstances through which she and Gutfreund had met at River House. She would tell people, among other things, that she had met him while traveling in Europe.)

A casual observer might have thought they had little common ground for a relationship. After his marriage had broken up and before he met Susan Penn, Gutfreund had, according to one friend, "dated women whom he had met through business or women with an intellectual bent — like art curators." By contrast, Susan Penn was a talkative, gregarious woman whose life revolved around shopping, ladies' luncheons, and parties. She loved expensive clothes and jewelry, and pampered herself regularly at the hairdresser, skin care salon, and exercise studio. Although Gutfreund had come to enjoy certain luxuries over the years (a good bottle of wine at a fine restaurant), he had always been critical of people who squandered their money.

Still, he seemed to be captivated by her. On their first date, they stayed out until four o'clock in the morning. She exuded a certain magnetic glamour. It was said that before long, she moved in with him. Gutfreund's friends, relatives, and partners were stunned by the sudden change in him. The formerly conservative, often dour, executive was seen kicking up his heels on the dance floor at various benefits — seemingly enthralled by his fashionably dressed, bejeweled girlfriend.

Even as they attended social and charitable events, Susan seemed to have bigger things in mind. Her sights appeared to be set on moving into a showcase apartment in the building in which they had met, River House, a co-op named for its location on East Fifty-second Street overlooking the East River. Few apartment buildings in the city could compare for sheer luxury with that limestone-and-gray-brick edifice. A block wide and rising twenty-six stories to a crowning tower, it was an urban castle. Residents and visitors entered through an imposing pair of private gates to walk through a large cobblestone courtyard into a black-marbled lobby filled with expensive carpets and art objects. In the rear, visible through floor-to-ceiling glass doors, was a formal garden with a working fountain. A staff of thirty-one employees — two for every five of the seventy-nine oversized apartments in the building — was ready to meet the occupants' needs.

But most of all, what River House had to offer was exclusivity.

From the time it was opened as a co-operative in 1931, the apartment
building had, by design, been the home of very rich and socially prominent people. Among those living there in 1981 were such bastions of
the Establishment as Rodman Rockefeller, the great-grandson of John
D. Rockefeller; Carter Burden, a member of a wealthy old Society
family; and Angier Biddle Duke, the tobacco heir and former ambassador. While all their apartments were large and impressive, few
matched the vacant one that Susan Penn wanted Gutfreund to buy.

It was a tower duplex on the twenty-fourth and twenty-fifth
floors, with an asking price of $1.1 million. The apartment's pedigree
was as glorious as any in the building; it had once formed the bottom
two floors of a triplex penthouse owned by Marshall Field III, the late
department store and newspaper magnate. It had another distinction,
not of the kind welcomed by River House tenants. In the spring of
1980, a squabble over its ownership won national coverage in newspapers and magazines.

At the center of the controversy was Gloria Vanderbilt, a "poor
little rich girl" who was the great-great-granddaughter of Commodore
Cornelius Vanderbilt and who was famous in her own right for her
designer jeans. The River House board of directors rejected her, claiming she couldn't afford the apartment because of the volatile nature of
the fashion industry and that she would attract unwelcome publicity.
Vanderbilt, who claimed her net worth was $7.6 million, offered to
put the entire purchase price in escrow and countercharged that she
was the victim of discrimination because of her friendship with Bobby
Short, the popular café society pianist, who is black. The board remained singularly unmoved.

Enter John Gutfreund and Susan Penn, who had been waiting
in the wings. No fuss was made by the board over their social qualifications or the finances of a Jew whose father had been in the wholesale
meat business and who now lived with a former airline stewardess. In
the power-broker world of the eighties, where new fortunes often
dwarfed the size of old money, the head of a major banking house with
his Salomon bankroll behind him was a more suitable candidate than
Gloria Vanderbilt. River House already was home to Amexco's Jim
Robinson and new-style financial potentate Pete Peterson, head of Lehman Brothers. New Jewish money was represented by Hugh Lowenstein of the investment banking house of L. F. Rothschild and Muriel
Siebert, head of her own brokerage firm. But no one could get in unless
the old guard gave its blessing. None was more important to passage
into River House than its board chairman, Carl Mueller. Now the vice

chairman of Bankers Trust, Mueller had once been John Loeb's most trusted lieutenant as a partner at Loeb Rhoades.

Two weeks after Vanderbilt withdrew in defeat, John Gutfreund wrote out a check for the 10 percent down payment of $110,000. (The maintenance on the $1.1 million co-op was a relatively paltry $41,000 annually.) Without the slightest to-do, the five thousand-square-foot duplex — with its sixty-foot living room, two fireplaces, spiral staircase, four maid's rooms and one butler's room, and views north, south, east, and west — was his. Gutfreund, who had rarely spent money extravagantly, now found himself scooping it out by the barrelful. First, he paid the balance of the $990,000 in August. Then, he hired the high-priced decorating team of MAC II, run by socialites Mica Ertegun and Chessy Rayner, to supervise a total renovation of the apartment.

Living on that scale of opulence and being a visible candidate for acceptance among the socially elite may have been a departure from his former way of life, but the process of winning acceptance was familiar to him. Making a big splash socially was not very different from succeeding on modern Wall Street. Both required power, drive, and, of course, money. Pour enough of all three into a project and a lot of ground could be covered fast. Susan Penn's drive was a match for John Gutfreund's power. The two forces came together, officially, in February 1981.

While the River House apartment was being gutted and re-modeled, fifty-one-year-old John Gutfreund and thirty-five-year-old Susan Penn were married at City Hall in a brief ceremony witnessed by Sandy and Hugh Lowenstein. Afterward, the two couples had lunch at Le Cirque, a chic East Side restaurant. That evening the newlyweds hosted a party for about sixty people at "21"; it was attended by Gutfreund's three sons, a few of his old friends and their wives (Marty Lipton, Edmond Safra, Larry Tisch, and Don Stone, among others), and some of their new friends such as Mica and Ahmet Ertegun, Chessy and William Rayner, and others from the worlds of fashion, decorating, and the record industry. The tables were decorated with white lace cloths and napkins and bouquets of yellow roses. Susan Gutfreund wore a white lace dress by the French designer Karl Lagerfeld.

After the marriage, only one ingredient was missing for the ascension of the former Susan Penn to the social stratosphere: serious money.

Strangely enough, for a Wall Street money man, John Gutfreund seemed to know little about it, at least not in the ways that were important to his new bride. He would find out. One evening at a private yachting party, Susan Gutfreund confided to a woman whom she had just met that Gutfreund had no idea of what good clothes and jewelry cost. "He was shocked," she claimed, when she took him to designer Mary McFadden's Seventh Avenue showroom and bought several pleated evening dresses at wholesale prices of around $700 each. (In those days, Susan Gutfreund was willing to buy her party frocks wholesale. Later, she would buy couture clothes, at many times that price.)

The education of John Gutfreund had only just started. Like other Wall Street chieftains, he had amassed enough money to buy a million-dollar apartment and designer clothes wholesale. But the kind of money required to put his bride and himself on the social map was buried in the Salomon Brothers' partnership. Susan understood that lots of money was needed by people who otherwise lacked the social credentials for a beachhead in celebrity society and perhaps even in High Society.

In the summer of 1981, the lock Billy Salomon had placed on the partnership's capital still held fast. For the moment, it kept John Gutfreund from getting his hands on his millions and his wife from enjoying the kind of life-style those millions could buy.

# CHAPTER TWENTY

# The Road to Tarrytown

By mid-July of 1981, John Gutfreund and the Salomon executive committee were ready to break the news of the deal with Phibro inside the firm. Each partner received a brief memo instructing him to report for a weekend meeting two weeks later, on Friday, July 31, at the Tarrytown Conference Center near the Hudson River, some twenty miles north of New York City. Everyone had to check in by 6:30 P.M. No one was told why he was summoned. Attendance was obligatory. Every partner — from London to San Francisco to Tokyo — had to drop whatever he was doing to be there. Vacations were cut short and business trips canceled or rescheduled. The men (there were no women partners) asked one another, "What's going on?" No one knew. They would know soon enough.

The secrecy was airtight and the operation was carried out with military precision. The board of directors at Phibro had no more of an inkling of what was going on than the Salomon partners. Not until a meeting shortly before the Tarrytown conference did the Phibro board learn of the proposed takeover. John Gutfreund was introduced to the Phibro board members, who had assembled in the large circular board-room at the company's headquarters in the McGraw-Hill building. Typically, there was no glitzy hard sell from Gutfreund. If anything, he may have been somewhat embarrassed to be there. Mark Kaplan, who was on the Phibro board, felt that Gutfreund avoided eye contact with him. When Kaplan had joined the commodities firm's former parent company, Engelhard, four years earlier as its president, Gutfreund, a friend of his, had said, "I don't understand how you can get along with those people." Kaplan soon lost the post in a power struggle. Now Gutfreund would be dealing with the very same people. Kaplan thought that the deal was a "brilliant maneuver that would allow the firm to get a lot of money out." In a brief speech, Gutfreund told the board in essence that he wanted to be part of the Phibro organization, that he thought they would work well together.

"It was the kind of presentation of a deal that had already been wired," Kaplan said later. "Not the kind of thing you expected to be informed about casually. It was a major acquisition, with few numbers given."

The speech, despite its vagueness, was effective. Gutfreund was excused, and after deliberating only half an hour, the Phibro board gave the merger its blessing. Now it was on to Tarrytown.

*  *  *

Most of the sixty-two Salomon partners arrived in time to check into their rooms, which were located in the estate's former tennis complex and in a Greek Revival plantation house — both a short walk from the main building, where dinner would be served.

As the partners followed directions into the auditorium, the level of anxiety rose. They clustered in small groups, speculating wildly about why they had been brought together. Some were aware that more executive committee meetings than usual had been held recently, but that was all. The executive committee members took their places behind a table at the front of the room. At precisely 6:30 P.M., Gutfreund stood up. He was wearing a three-piece suit, unlike most of the partners, who were dressed casually.

Gutfreund was formal and serious. Too serious, even for him. He was hunched over as he read from a prepared statement, another sign of the meeting's obvious importance. The words came out muted. He began by announcing that the firm had just concluded the most profitable ten-month period in its history. "We can't hear you," a partner called out.

"My wife always tells me to stand up straight when I speak," Gutfreund retorted to ripples of laughter.

There was some confusion over what he said next, but the word "sell" hung in the air.

"What did he say?" the partners asked.

Gutfreund started over again, and this time there was no confusion. Salomon Brothers had a proposal to merge their partnership with Phibro. The executive committee had approved the merger, and Gutfreund had brought the Salomon partners together to attain a "critical mass" in favor of the offer. The purchase price would be approximately $550 million. The Salomon partners would get all their own capital out of the firm in one lump sum when the partnership was dissolved, and Phibro would recapitalize Salomon Brothers. The size of each of the general partners' share would be determined by the percentage of the Salomon profits to which he was entitled. Booklets would be available after dinner that would spell out in detail how much each partner would receive. Not everyone would be invited to join the new company, he added, almost in passing. There was a stunned silence. Most of the partners were so shocked that they could remember little else of what Gutfreund said in his brief remarks.

Since they had been told that the executive committee had already recommended approval of the merger, the overwhelming majority of them didn't believe that they were actually being consulted. Obtaining a "critical mass" was a pro forma gesture, many thought. In their eyes, Salomon Brothers had already been sold. Very few of them knew much about Phibro, other than that it was a major commodities house. Some found a slight measure of reassurance when Gutfreund informed them that there would be no real attempt at synergy, such as blending the two firms' trading operations into one.

When he was finished, he asked if there were any questions. At first, no one said anything. Then a few junior partners asked deferentially what compensation there would be for those who had worked long and hard to become partners and now were losing the opportunity. Gutfreund merely said some would leave and others would be promoted to an equivalent rank in the new company. Although that was hardly the same as becoming a partner, no one questioned him rigorously. Henry Kaufman rose and made a short speech about the importance of having a greater reservoir of capital. Jay Higgins of the M&A department stood up and called it a great deal for Salomon Brothers. By then, the reality of the sale had set in.

If one thought ran through each partner's mind it was: "How much does that booklet say is there for me?" The sixty-two partners would split up more than $550 million, or an average of close to $9 million each. The first $300 million was their capital, which had accrued over the years and would be theirs as of October 1, when the deal would be completed officially. The remaining $250 million would come in the form of stock options in Phibro.

No one publicly questioned the desirability of the groom, who, after all, was recently divorced, or the terms of the marriage. The wily Phibro team had given the Salomon partners a smaller premium for their firm than American Express had awarded Shearson or Prudential had given Bache. The deal Salomon Brothers had negotiated for itself could have been a better one and years later Gutfreund would concede as much. At that moment, though, it would have been hard to convince many Salomon partners that it wasn't a great deal. They had just been made instant millionaires, and they were eager to get their hands on their money.

But what would the demise of the partnership mean for the firm? Few thought much about it. They were too dazed by the news and too eager to learn about their net worth. Within an hour, the meeting was over. Most appeared openly elated as they wandered out of the auditorium. Some, however, had mixed emotions: excitement about their newfound wealth, but a sense of foreboding that something precious had been lost. "This is the end of the Salomon Brothers that I've known and loved to work for," thought Jon Rotenstreich. A few of the partners were openly distraught. Lewis Ranieri, a rising star who had begun in Salomon's mail room, complained angrily to his mentor, Bob Dall: "They sold my firm."

Despite all the money that was being distributed, some were apprehensive about which partners would be asked to leave. There was little talk about who might be fired — as if to do so was to invite dismissal. They would have to wait until morning to be told. Over dinner that evening, as the partners searched for other topics of conversation, one name kept cropping up. It soon spread — like the rustling of the wind — throughout the dining room.

"What does Billy think?" a partner finally asked Gutfreund.

The head of Salomon Brothers turned to another member of the executive committee seated at his table. "You hear that?" Gutfreund said, with a half smile on his face. "He wants to know what Billy thinks."

\* \* \*

After dinner, the partners grabbed their booklets and found out exactly how rich they were. On Saturday, they met individually with the members of the executive committee to discuss their future roles with the firm. For some, there was none. James Wolfensohn, a member of the executive committee and an articulate, charming, socially-at-ease man who had never adapted to the aggressive, informal striving that characterized Salomon Brothers, was going. Everyone had known that before Tarrytown. Wolfensohn had already announced his intention of leaving the firm at the end of September. His single main achievement had been helping to spearhead the federally subsidized bailout of Chrysler in 1980. His outside interests, including his duties as chairman of Carnegie Hall and playing the cello, which he had brought to Tarrytown to practice, made too many demands on his time for him to want to continue as a full-time partner. He apparently was departing with the blessings of Gutfreund. The Australian-born banker had come to Salomon hoping to get rich, and he was leaving the firm with $12 million.

Michael Bloomberg, who had survived five years as head of block trading, making him second only to the legendary Jay Perry in length of service in that position, had been prepared to leave a year earlier, when it had become clear that Richard Rosenthal was going to win the territorial battle with him, just as Rosenthal had driven Perry off. But Gutfreund had convinced him that he should stick around for a while. The time had been well spent. He would also leave a wealthy man.

Meanwhile, the other partners waited anxiously for their turns. A few lackluster games of tennis were played. Some strolled along the grounds; others sat around and talked. They were told they could call their wives but no one else. Kenneth Lipper phoned both his wife and his elderly parents in Brooklyn. "Momma, Kenny's rich," his father yelled out.

As the day dragged on, the body count mounted. In all, five partners besides Bloomberg were told they were fired. One was old-timer Stanley Arkin, who was too beaten by the unending sunrise-to-sunset battles, the strain on his personal life, and the knowledge that he would never make the executive committee to want to stay on anyway. Four others, Craig Stearns, Norman Levy, David Osborne, and Robert Bernhard, went sorrowfully.

The ousting of Bernhard came as a great shock. He was unusual among the partners in that he was a descendant of an Our Crowd family. He had been brought into Salomon Brothers by Billy Salomon, who had known him for years through the Century Country Club. What made his firing even more disturbing was that Gutfreund had delivered the bad tidings, and Bernhard was his only close friend at the firm. They had grown up together in Scarsdale and they had even been formerly related through marriage; Joyce Gutfreund was a cousin of Bob Bernhard's wife.

In addition to his obvious discomfort in addressing large groups, Gutfreund displayed a lack of grace and sensitivity when he had to deliver unpleasant news. Since the task evidently made him uncomfortable, his manner was brusque. "We're going to have to let some people go," he told Bernhard, who had traveled eleven hours from his summer retreat in Maine to attend the meeting, "and you're one of them."

By dinnertime on Saturday, everyone knew who was staying

and who was leaving. For many, the shock and euphoria of Friday had given way to uneasiness and exhaustion. Strings were attached to the deal, unwelcome strings, that would mean the end of the firm as they had known it. Despite all of the intense infighting and jockeying for power, Salomon partners had always shown a certain fraternal spirit. No matter what they thought of the respective competence of each of the six men being let go, many of the remaining partners were horrified by the sudden and public way in which the hatchet jobs had been handled.

The next morning, they would have their first meeting with their new Phibro bosses. They had become another company's employees. It was a disturbing thought — something every partner knew in his bones Billy Salomon never would have permitted. By now, they all were aware that Billy Salomon had not been informed or consulted about the sale. During dinner that evening, some of them talked in hushed tones about him. Word got around that Gutfreund and two other partners were flying to Southampton Sunday afternoon to break the news to him. One of the partners finally screwed up the courage to ask Gutfreund how he felt about telling Salomon that he had sold the family firm and recalled his response.

"After firing your best friend, everything else is chickenshit," Gutfreund replied flatly.

* * *

On Sunday morning, David Tendler, Hal Beretz, and Thomas O'Malley, the three senior executives at Phibro, arrived at the conference center and met with their new employees.* The session was upbeat. The Phibro executives gave their view of the merger and answered a few questions about money that were lobbed as softly as the ones that had been thrown to Gutfreund Friday night. When it was over, all except the departing partners signed employment contracts that barred them for three years from working for competing firms. They then gave Gutfreund a standing ovation.

After lunch, Gutfreund, Henry Kaufman, and Richard Schmeelk, who at fifty-seven was the senior member of the executive

---

* O'Malley was the Irish exception to the Jewish rule at Phibro. He took over the oil trading department in 1974 after its head, Marc Rich, left because of a dispute with the firm's leader, Ludwig Jesselson, over money. O'Malley exploited the oil crisis of 1979 as successfully as Rich had the one in 1973.

committee in age and years spent at Salomon Brothers, flew to Southampton, where Billy Salomon had a country home. It was the last act
of the Salomon sellout.

\*   \*   \*

For Gutfreund himself, the professional implications of the sale
would be just as dramatic as those for the firm. On the one hand, he
would be giving up control of Salomon Brothers. But on the other
hand, the partnership could now tap into Phibro's $2 billion reservoir,
and Gutfreund's authority at Salomon Brothers would be greater than
ever. Instead of being first among equals, he would now be Salomon's
chief executive officer, with the same power to hire and fire, to set
policy, and to make executive decisions as any other chieftain of a major
corporation.

It was a timely switch. Before the Phibro deal, Gutfreund had
wanted to add more junior partners because there was an expanding
need for them, but the general partners resisted splitting the profit pie
into smaller pieces. At the other extreme, the elderly limited partners
had wanted a greater return on their own investment, which the general
partners had also resisted. When Gutfreund became chief executive
officer, there would be no partners, only employees. As for the limited
partners, they would be bought out and given an honorary title and
an office — all nineteen of them, including Billy Salomon.

Gutfreund had called Salomon at his country home early in the
weekend to arrange the Sunday meeting. As usual, the conversation
between them was brief and impersonal. Gutfreund offered no explanation on the phone and Salomon asked for none. The man whose
family name had been on the door for seventy-one years assumed that
Gutfreund wanted to discuss something important, but it never dawned
on him that it had anything to do with the sale of the firm. In the three
years since his retirement, he had continued to show up regularly at
the company's headquarters, where he still had an office and a secretary
but no responsibilities.

Salomon and Gutfreund actually had little contact. Gutfreund's
divorce and remarriage had caught Salomon by surprise. He had not
been invited to the wedding. He had thought the changes taking place
in his protégé were odd but had no reason to dwell on them until the
events of recent weeks were revealed to him that Sunday.

From the Southampton airport, Gutfreund, Kaufman, and
Schmeelk traveled by taxi to Salomon's home facing the ocean on
Meadow Lane, one of the most exclusive, staunchly gentile sections of

Southampton. Thick, mature evergreens and shrubbery concealed most of the Salomon property from view. After turning up the curved driveway, the taxi stopped in front of an imposing modern structure.

Salomon greeted them at the entrance, which was flanked by hydrangea bushes. He was outfitted in typical Southampton daytime attire, a casual shirt and brightly colored slacks. The visitors wore business suits. Salomon offered them coffee, but the blunt-talking Gutfreund wasted no time in coming to the point.

"I know you'll possibly be shocked by this," Gutfreund is remembered saying, "but this is what has transpired."

The former chief found it hard to believe what he was hearing. He listened as Gutfreund spelled out the terms of the sale. Salomon said little. "I was surprised and shocked and upset," he said years later, in recalling what had passed through his mind at the time. "I felt betrayed. I had accorded them my trust and they hadn't returned it. They had presented it to me as a fait accompli."

They hadn't informed him, he thought, because they knew that if he had been told beforehand, he would have done everything within his power to persuade the other partners not to sell out. He would have warned them that they were acting out of fear and greed. He had set up the capital preservation rules specifically so that Salomon Brothers could continue as a private partnership into the indefinite future.

The real reason they did it, he thought, was to get their hands on some very important money.

But he didn't say it. The meeting was over in a mere fifteen minutes. Gutfreund, Kaufman, and Schmeelk shook hands with Salomon, then left. Salomon was seething. He thought of the decision to sell the firm and all the recent changes in Gutfreund's life — from his divorce from Joyce and his remarriage to Susan to his extravagant living. In Salomon's view, they all derived from one simple explanation: "middle-aged menopause." And the conclusion made him furious.

"In my intimate knowledge of John, over a period of years, he lived not only conservatively, he lived ultraconservatively," he said in retrospect. "John did not frequent the most expensive restaurants. In fact, he was somewhat critical of any of our younger partners who did what we considered a little showboating or were extravagant or maybe living beyond their means." In those days, Salomon believed, John Gutfreund would no more have gone to "21" or Le Cirque out of choice than he would have withdrawn all his capital from the firm.

Salomon himself, however, could hardly plead poverty from the sale. As a limited partner, who had retired only three years earlier, he still had a stake in the firm. He would receive almost $10 million. But that was only a fraction of what Gutfreund was to pocket as his share of the partnership. After being at the helm a mere two and a half years, he would realize a windfall of more than $32 million. As for the other members of the executive committee, they would receive, on average, roughly half that sum.

No matter what Salomon thought, there was no looking back for Gutfreund. Later in the day, he began telephoning the limited partners to give them the news.

The call to Daniel Kelly, one of the older limited partners, came late that evening.

"I wanted you to hear this before it hits the newspapers," Kelly recalls Gutfreund saying. "You know, you're going to have your office and all your privileges, the dining room, and the barber shop."

But what Kelly really wanted to know was how much money everyone was getting. Gutfreund told him that the limited partners would receive $125,000 annually for ten years.

"John," Kelly exclaimed. "I've been screwed."

Gutfreund replied that he hadn't done the negotiating. The terms had been worked out by executive committee members Ira Harris and Richard Rosenthal. To Kelly those words meant nothing. The deal was done.

\* \* \*

By Monday, when the news hit the wires, Gutfreund had wrapped up most of the loose ends. The sale of Salomon Brothers to Phibro was treated as a page-one story. One of the world's largest commodities traders had merged with the fourth-largest securities house to create a giant corporation that could compete with any financial organization in the world. On Tuesday, though, it was apparently business as usual at Salomon. The firings, the confrontation with Billy Salomon, and the calls to the limited partners were over. Gutfreund returned to his managerial role.

In many respects, Gutfreund's share of the money from the sale would have a far greater impact on his personal life than on his professional life. Like an oversized, shining jewel, the opulent duplex apartment purchased by the Gutfreunds a year before would soon be ready to be displayed. The entire apartment had been gutted and was being rebuilt, decorated, and furnished — at a cost estimated at several million dollars.

Susan Gutfreund's plans for the duplex involved more than

merely having a lavish home. She also apparently saw it as a means to propel herself into the role of one of New York's reigning hostesses at a seemingly nonstop succession of dinners and parties replete with fashionable guests. Their dinners and parties would be chronicled in the social pages and fashion tabloids. What she wore, whom they entertained, even her menus and table service would inspire imitation, gossip, and envy. In the small world of New Society, the Gutfreunds' extravagant life-style would give them local status as celebrities, and they would receive far more publicity than even Susan Penn could have hoped for, much of it unfavorable. The fireworks were about to explode.

# CHAPTER TWENTY-ONE

# "Do You Know Me?"

*W*hen Sandy Weill handed control of Shearson over to American Express, he ached to belong and would have given virtually anything to be accepted in the top tier of the venerable corporation. The big question among Wall Street handicappers was: how long before the Brooklyn firebreather would overthrow the patrician Robinson? Certainly, Weill, the confident corporate leader, seemed to be making many of the right moves to put himself in the driver's seat at Amexco.

He quickly began cultivating the American Express executives and board members. His suggestion that spouses be included at out-of-town weekend management meetings was soon adopted, and as a result, Joan Weill got to know and became friendly with the key American Express wives. She always found it easy to get along with people. Sandy Weill admired that quality in her. "Joan listens," he said. "She cares about what people say. She's somebody with a lot of feeling."

When he was honored at the 1981 Man of the Year Awards dinner given by the Anti-Defamation League, he paid homage to her in his acceptance speech: "I've got an incredible wife who's the best asset in my life, which is blessed with so many assets." The previous year, in celebration of their twenty-fifth wedding anniversary, he had presented her with the most sumptuous gift of their marriage: a matching sapphire and diamond necklace, bracelet, and earrings.

Joan Weill now had the opportunity to wear such impressive jewelry. She and Sandy attended all the major American Express social functions and were stepping out in style at a number of benefits. Their new social friends included former U.S. president Gerald Ford and his wife, Betty. They were invited to the Fords' thirty-fifth wedding anniversary celebration. But being entertained by a former president could be intimidating. Even some years later, though by then they had seen the Fords on a number of occasions, Joan Weill was nervous about visiting. The Weills were scheduled to be house guests for several days at the Fords' vacation home in Beaver Creek, the exclusive Colorado ski-and-golf resort, where the Gerald Ford Golf Tournament was held. Joan phoned her mother, seeking advice.

"What do I do as their guest?" she asked.

Her mother replied, "You make your bed and clean up like you would anywhere else."

As it happened, the Fords had a very relaxed style that put the Weills immediately at ease. "In the morning we sat around in our bathrobes," Joan recalled. "Jerry would come in after playing golf, take off his shoes, serve us ice cream, and we would all gossip. It was a lot of fun.

"And Betty Ford had a way of making you feel her warmth and friendliness was directed especially toward you. She asked lots of interested questions about our children and she obviously liked her own kids."

The Ford's house had an indoor swimming lane. In the morning Ford swam laps and Joan did the same in the afternoon. A friendly rivalry developed between them. At lunch, Joan would ask, "How many laps did you swim this morning, Mr. President?" Whatever the number, she would swim twice as many in the afternoon. She was capable of doing sixty consecutive laps.

\*　\*　\*

Befitting a man who hobnobbed with a former president, Weill was becoming better known by the end of 1981. His job at American Express and the times demanded it. The age of the superbroker was being heralded throughout the financial world. The future of the securities business, it seemed, would be in the hands of a few giant firms offering a cornucopia of financial services to all sorts of investors. Not only did Shearson, Bache, and Salomon Brothers align themselves with powerful benefactors: so did Dean Witter, the fifth-largest broker, when it teamed up with Sears Roebuck in October of 1981.

In terms of money, clout, and fit, Weill may have cut the best deal of all. When he had sold Shearson that spring, he had caught the Dow near its all-time peak and consequently had made Amexco pay mightily for his brokerage house. Now the "Shearsonization" of American Express seemed to be under way. Soon after the merger was completed, George Sheinberg of Shearson was named Amexco's treasurer, Duke Chapman became vice chairman of Amexco's international banking arm, and Robert Riley moved over to Amexco as a senior vice president in charge of planning. But the most significant Shearson transfer was Weill himself. By early 1982, he was ensconced in a corner office on the fortieth floor of the American Express tower, diagonally across from Robinson's suite.

Memorabilia of Weill's career hung on the walls. A framed photo — taken by his chauffeur — of the modest house in Brooklyn where he had spent much of his childhood served as a reminder of how far he had traveled. There was no fireplace in his new office, nor could he build one. The only Weillian architectural feature was a sundeck. However, in keeping with the high opinion the Street had of him, Weill expected to warm things up at Amexco's headquarters. He certainly didn't have to trumpet his arrival. Shearson spoke volumes for him. In 1981, the brokerage house had easily outperformed the other three main branches of Amexco — travel services, insurance, and banking. And, in case anyone forgot his power base, Weill still held onto his aerie in the World Trade Center. He was also back on the acquisition trail, this time as a loyal Amexco soldier carrying home a brokerage firm (Foster & Marshall). But, in truth, he was still no more a part of the American Express power echelons than he had been back in June when he had first joined that company.

His wife and colleagues cautioned him against giving up his hold on Shearson. Whatever happened at American Express, he would still be the boss at the World Trade Center. But Weill seemed to have abandoned his customary caution. It was one of the few times he was deaf to Joan's advice. He stubbornly set his course and wouldn't veer from it until he was forced to. Though he still clung to his titles of chairman and chief executive officer at the brokerage house, he calculated that Robinson and the Amexco board would respond favorably if he demonstrated that his first loyalties were to the parent company. The strategy seemed to pay off quickly.

In a matter of weeks after Weill moved over to American Express, Robinson gave him the responsibility for capital planning. It was a staff position without real projects or management function. Just the same, Weill interpreted it as a personal commitment to him by top management. In return, in 1982, he voluntarily turned over the day-to-day running of Shearson to Peter Cohen.

Two small acquisitions — Robinson-Humphrey, a brokerage, and Balcor, a real estate business, required some attention, but he had less and less to do at Amexco, and, in fact, had only one ongoing project to keep him busy.

He embraced Peter Cohen's plan to sell the American Express building and lease another office tower in the new World Financial

Center complex being constructed on the Battery Park landfill by the Hudson River. The building project was a way of putting Weill's mark on the company for a long time. The capital gains expected from the sale of the current American Express building, which was sold for $160 million, would greatly enhance Amexco's investment portfolio, and the new skyscraper would become the cornerstone of the most impressive development in New York City since the creation of Rockefeller Center half a century earlier. Robinson bought the idea at once, and Weill enjoyed his first major coup at Amexco, one that was in keeping with the dramatic, entrepreneurial style set at Shearson.

But if he had had his antennae up, he would have noticed that Robinson was displaying some of his managerial skills. He set the tone for his relationship with Weill: comfortable without being intimate — in contrast to the way Weill dealt with close associates. Robinson's actions worked to divert Weill from the presidency and the hauntingly elusive job of chief operating officer, while at the same time making use of the Shearson chief's talents. This had the added benefit of soothing a board of directors that had never liked Weill, finding him abrasive.

As Weill's first year at Amexco drew to a close, it became increasingly apparent that Robinson was not just a southern gentleman who could be brushed past easily. Amexco was his court, and everyone played by his rules. Weill had tried making up for having no real authority the only way he knew, by becoming involved in the running of the company.

He took to speaking with subordinates of high-ranking Amexco executives, pressing them with questions about their work. When word got back to their bosses, he was viewed as meddling in their territory, and tempers began to flare. Whereas others might have restrained themselves, Weill faced up to the complaints and told everyone exactly what was on his mind. That approach — so effective at Shearson — was little understood at Amexco, where executives shunned direct confrontation. Even at meetings on the highest level of the corporation, Weill asked probing questions that others avoided. He tried to introduce a sense of urgency into Amexco's way of doing business. Instead, his actions merely served to disturb American Express's rather fastidious culture.

For all these reasons, Weill was no more loved and no farther ahead in 1982 than he had been in 1981. Robinson told him that he would have to back down for the time being. With Robinson keeping a firm grip on the company, Weill might as well have appeared in a commercial for the American Express card asking, "Do you know me?"

Perhaps because of all the time on his hands and his inability to make a real impact at Amexco — he lavished even more attention on what was already a very special occasion, the marriage of his twenty-two-year-old daughter, Jessica, in June of 1982. He would do it in style — *his* style.

The wedding, held at the Weills' Greenwich estate, was a black-tie affair. Two large white tents had been festooned with pink, white, and lavender flowers. The two hundred guests were for the most part relatives and Weill's business friends, primarily a large contingent of Shearson executives and their wives. Jim and Bettye Robinson also attended, along with a few other top American Express executives. The Weills were glad Bettye could come. A heavy smoker, she had suffered a stroke during the last weeks the Shearson–American Express deal was being worked out, and Robinson had shuttled back and forth between her hospital bedside and the negotiating sessions.

The decided chill in the weather that drizzly June night couldn't be dispelled even in the heated tents. Dozens of women in evening wear returned to their cars to put on a sweater or a shawl. Joan Weill noticed that one woman was wearing a red wool jacket similar to the one she owned and then realized that it was her jacket. Sandy Weill had been handing out wraps from his wife's well-stocked closet upstairs. He even loaned his green down parka to a shivering guest in a strapless dress.

In the Reform Jewish ceremony that began at 7:30 P.M., a beaming Weill walked down the aisle with his daughter, who was wearing an elegant silk bridal gown — Victorian style — with full sleeves and a high collar. Joan Weill — her daughter's matron of honor — attired in a pale-pink silk-organza dress, stood by proudly. After Jessica and Nathan Bibliowicz, an architect, exchanged vows, a lavish dinner was followed by dancing. When Sandy Weill stepped out on the dance floor with his daughter, a video camera captured his exuberance. As the band played on, the gloom of the weather outside and his problems at American Express were temporarily forgotten.

*     *     *

The summer of 1982 was a long, hot summer for Weill, and time at American Express seemed to stand still. Then, Peter Cohen presented him with an exciting acquisition candidate that immediately revived his spirits. Cohen's old boss, Edmond Safra, might be willing to part with the foreign operations of his Geneva-based Trade Development Bank (TDB) and might even come to work for Amexco, a move that could revitalize the ailing international banking division of American Express.

The idea was tantalizing to Weill. At American Express headquarters, he had been the chief advocate of retaining the international banking arm. The acquisition of TDB would put Amexco in a brandnew banking league. Though Weill had some initial concerns about adding another executive to the company, particularly a heavyweight like Safra, he also saw the advantages of having an entrepreneurial ally who might help him break into the steely American Express monolith.

The fifty-one-year-old Safra, a Brazilian citizen who had been born in Lebanon, could trace his family's roots in banking back to the Ottoman Empire. He ran his international banking network quietly and almost single-handedly, often referring to his banks as "my children." His customers generally were rich Europeans and South Americans, who valued his carefully run operations. One of the richest men in the world, Safra had a personal fortune estimated at some $500 million.

Why, then, would he be interested in making a deal with American Express? Cohen felt that he understood the reasons. Safra, who had no successor within his own organization, also believed that the number of financial firms in the world was shrinking and that ultimately American Express would remain as one of the leaders. Still, to win him over, American Express would have to move quickly.

Meetings weren't actually scheduled till late November. Cohen's plans to see Safra at his Paris apartment were made in secret. The Trade Development Bank and American Express were called Copper and Tiger, respectively, and the whole operation was given the code name Mazel Tov, Hebrew words chosen by Safra that mean "good luck" or "congratulations." Robinson subsequently met with Safra in Geneva. The two men got along well and agreed that a merger could be worked out.

Weill, chosen to open the negotiations, was back in his element. Even if this wasn't his deal, he was working on a major acquisition that might total around half a billion dollars.

*   *   *

As 1982 drew to a close, the market was in the midst of a sensational rally. For the traders, there was a veritable gold rush on the floor of the New York Stock Exchange. Volume and the Dow were skyrocketing; the blue chip index topped 1,000 by mid-October. By the end of the year, 16.5 billion shares had changed hands on the Big

Board alone, more than all the shares traded in the first two decades of the postwar era and nearly 50 percent above the record 11.4 billion the previous year. What had started as a sluggish year became a bonanza — the best in the history of Wall Street to date. (By mid-1983, some forty-two million retail customers would own shares listed on the Big Board, up a third from mid-1981.)

Weill celebrated the end of the spectacular old year and the beginning of the promising new one with Safra in Paris. He had told friends and colleagues that he and his wife were taking a brief vacation. Joan Weill's father had died recently, Weill said, and he wanted to cheer her up. That was true, but it was also an effective cover for the talks with Safra.

Weill and Safra got along well from the start, and the deal seemed headed toward a happy ending. At 5:45 A.M., New Year's morning in Paris, the two men, both of whom had had a lot to drink, placed a call to Peter Cohen at his new country home in East Hampton, Long Island, where a New Year's Eve party was in progress, to wish him a happy New Year. The man who answered the phone fifteen minutes before the start of 1983 wasn't Cohen but Thomas Strauss, a member of the executive committee at Salomon Brothers and an old friend of Cohen's. "It's Edmond Safra," Strauss told Cohen. John Gutfreund, Strauss's boss at Salomon, was not only Safra's friend but also his long-time banker. Though Safra had already promised Cohen that he wouldn't discuss the merger with the Salomon chief, Cohen worried that Strauss might guess what was going on. Thinking quickly, Cohen told Strauss that the call must be for another guest at his party, Jeffrey Keil, an executive of Safra's bank, and managed to sneak into another room to take the call himself in private. For the moment, at least, the danger seemed to have passed.

With the three key American Express executives — Robinson, Weill, and Cohen — backing the deal, Safra was satisfied that a merger between the two firms would work. As a precaution against leaks, Cohen arranged for the two sides to meet in Montreal the following week in order to nail down the final details.*

With Cohen doing his usual number crunching, the details on the merger were worked out swiftly in Montreal. In the final agreement, Safra would be given American Express cash and stock worth $550

---

* Safra couldn't meet with the Amexco executives in the U.S. for tax reasons.

million, making him the largest shareholder in the company, with
3 percent of its shares, several times more than Weill held. But Weill
jumped one hurdle when Alva Way resigned as Amexco president to
take the same position at Travelers. Robinson hastily scheduled a special
board meeting at New York's Helmsley Palace on Sunday, January 16,
to ratify both Weill's promotion to president and the company's acquisition of Safra's Trade Development Bank. It looked like clear sailing
all the way — until the project hit some unforeseen reefs that threatened
to sink it.

As it happened, Edmond Safra had a bar mitzvah to attend in
São Paulo, Brazil, and would be away the entire week before the signing. While Safra was in São Paulo, a top Safra lieutenant broke the
news to John Gutfreund of the bank's pending sale. That Saturday, the
Salomon boss flew down to Brazil to try to persuade Safra not to go
through with the American Express deal. Cohen found out about it on
Sunday evening, when he sent an American Express jet to São Paulo
to bring Safra to Montreal for the contract signing.

"Would you mind if John returns with me?" Safra asked politely
on the telephone.

Cohen was still worried about Gutfreund when he received a
call from the Amexco pilot after the jet touched down in Montreal.
"There's a man named Mr. Gutfreund on the plane, and he says he
wants to go to New York. What should we do?"

"Take him to New York," Cohen replied. A relieved Cohen
learned from Safra that the deal was still alive.

On Sunday, the merger won the approval of the Amexco board,
which also approved Weill's appointment as the company's president.
At 2:10 A.M. on Tuesday, Safra signed. Once the formalities were over,
Cohen called his wife and then Weill, who was elated. It was a sweet
triumph for him inside American Express. In a matter of days, a joyful
Sandy Weill was photographed by the press standing between Safra
and Robinson — who personally and professionally represented generations of banking expertise, but two different business styles. And
Weill had joined both worlds. In the glow, he didn't seem at all con-
cerned about what he had just given up — his chief executive title at
Shearson to Peter Cohen.

# CHAPTER TWENTY-TWO

# Billions Up for Grabs

With the election of Ronald Reagan in November 1980, a new era began. The following January, as millions watched on television, the president, in white tie and tails, and Nancy, dressed in a dazzling Galanos gown, made their triumphant entrance at all the inauguration balls. The Reagan ascendancy signaled an unrestrained enthusiasm for the freewheeling free-enterprise system.

The popular culture reflected the country's obsession with money. The "life-styles" of the TV characters on "Dallas," "Dynasty," and the like were the envy of millions of Americans who could live the rich life only vicariously. Some could do more than dream: graduates of Ivy League colleges and prestigious business schools in particular had an excellent chance of realizing the fantasy. They had no shortage of real-life role models — among them, the superstar dealmakers on Wall Street.

By then, few fields rivaled mergers and acquisitions for the opportunity to make a fast fortune. In a few months, or sometimes days, dealmakers could wrap up millions in fees by helping companies on either side of a hostile takeover. Like a swarm of bees around the honey pot, newcomers tried to create their own sweet returns. They were ready to take on legendary figures like Felix Rohatyn. But they wanted to do it their way.

At the beginning of the seventies the M&A field was still dominated by Lazard Frères and Rohatyn. Only a dynamo like Ira Harris of Salomon Brothers was capable of making a fresh impression on corporate America — and it took all of his verve and ingenuity. Over six feet tall and weighing 225 pounds, Harris — who had a taste for expensive clothes, cars, and gourmet food — cultivated the wealthy Jewish investors in Chicago, including the Pritzkers and Crowns, along with the heads of midwestern Wasp corporations.

One indication that M&A would be broadening out came from

the august house of Morgan Stanley, which had started an M&A department in 1971 and put it under the astute control of Robert Greenhill, a young managing director who was considered a man-on-the-rise in the classic Morgan Stanley mold. This Harvard and Yale man with a passion for brightly colored suspenders and motorcycles would stamp the M&A world forever when he led International Nickel's hostile bid against ESB in 1974. From then on, raiding was considered respectable.

On the other side of the contest was mighty Goldman Sachs, which quickly became known as corporate America's chief defender. That was the image Stephen Friedman worked hard to build. He was the rare M&A specialist who had no flair for showmanship or interest in personal confrontations. Despite a middle-class background and the fact that he was a lawyer turned banker, he approached his job like a working man, with the sleeves of his dress shirt rolled up his thick arms. A 1961 national wrestling champion (160-pound weight class), this uncontentious man seemed ready to grapple with any corporate opponent. The smaller companies that made up a significant part of Goldman Sachs's client list were ideal targets for raiders. When the right deal came along, Friedman and his team were there to pin down the best terms.

Defending clients also became the special forte of Martin Siegel of Kidder Peabody, who fashioned a niche that suited his own purposes. A smooth, charming, and incredibly handsome Harvard Business School graduate whose politics, he himself quipped, were "to the right of Genghis Khan," Siegel was unapologetic about his pursuit of personal wealth in Wall Street's fast lane. Taking his cue from Goldman Sachs, he decided in 1976, at age twenty-eight, that defense would be his suit. After talking to Joe Flom, he instituted a retainer system at Kidder Peabody similar to the one recently begun by Skadden Arps. For $75,000 a year, the merger specialist advised companies on how to guard against and, if necessary, fight off a raider. In time, he would put his M&A skills to questionable use.

Striking out in a new direction, the innovative firm of Kohlberg Kravis Roberts opened its doors in 1975. Started by Jerome Kohlberg, a practicing attorney who had become an investment banker at Bear Stearns, Henry Kravis, who came with the fresh outlook of oil-rich Oklahomans, and George Roberts (Kravis's cousin), it helped pioneer LBOs, or leveraged buyouts: a company was taken from public to private ownership, usually through heavy reliance on bank loans and other debt. The idea was akin to "nothing down" real estate deals. The LBO would become one of the most significant dealmaking trends in the headlining, mind-boggling megadeals of the 1980s (the $25 billion RJR Nabisco LBO, for example). Spearheaded by Henry Kravis, KKR won control of the huge tobacco and food company in 1988, beating out its rivals at Salomon and Shearson. With Kravis in charge of a $5 billion war chest in the late eighties, there was no telling where LBOs would stop or what would stop them.

* * *

Rohatyn. Harris. Greenhill. Friedman. Siegel. Kohlberg. Kravis. With superstars like that to contend with, Joseph Perella of First Boston faced an uphill battle even to get his name on the boards. It was a sign of how little the white-shoe house thought of M&A in 1972 that, to start up a mergers department, it hired an "oddball," as he described himself, the son of Italian immigrants, who, though he had graduated from Harvard with honors, had been rejected by a host of Wall Street firms. The six-foot-four "oddball" was ebullient and persuasive, a superb salesman who could literally seem to be carried away by his own enthusiasm. When he became excited, he would groan, flail his arms about, and sometimes even bound around the room.

Such displays of emotion were tolerated at the moment at First Boston only because the firm was trying to remake its image from a clubby aristocracy into a modern bank, but its upper-class crust, accumulated over decades, wasn't easy to remove. Its bagpipe-playing chairman, the Scotsman George Shinn, had been brought over in 1975 from the number-two spot at Merrill Lynch to infuse some professionalism. An infusion was badly needed. First Boston's reputation in investment banking had dropped in segment after segment. But the worst area of all was its merger business. There were snickers of laughter within First Boston when the ranking of its M&A department on Wall Street was reported: "no factor at all."

The snickers would soon disappear.

* * *

It took Joe Perella, outmanned, outflanked, and outmaneuvered by the competition, five years to find the help he needed to put his laggard M&A department into the race. Perella, the former accountant who had come to Wall Street at age twenty-eight to seek his fortune, knew that it would take a lot more than the ability to add two and two. On the plus side was his good eye for people and a willingness to share credit. In 1977 he lured Bruce Wasserstein, a young lawyer at Cravath, Swaine & Moore, to First Boston for twice his $50,000 income as an attorney. Perella recognized a good man when he saw one. He spotted in Wasserstein the inborn talent to structure a deal and the ability to work under great pressure. He recalls telling a colleague, "I don't know who this son of a bitch is, but we've got to get to know him because he is some piece of work."

The two men were an oddly compatible pairing of opposites. Unlike the extroverted Perella, Wasserstein was low-keyed and precise, an innovative tactician. Patently bright, he had a quick, incisive mind that grasped a wide range of concepts and facts. With his thinning reddish-blond hair, thick glasses, and flat voice, he conveyed a Talmudic air of great intellectual intensity, but when he was plotting intricate takeover strategies, he came across more like a chess master or computer hacker, with only a trace left of the former honors scholar he once was.

*    *    *

Wasserstein grew up in a middle-class neighborhood in Brooklyn, in an eclectic and creative Jewish household. When his mother, Lola Wasserstein, a dancer and health food fanatic, wasn't stuffing young Bruce and his three sisters full of wheat germ and bran, she was teaching them to think for themselves. He attended an Orthodox Jewish elementary school, Yeshiva of Flatbush, not because the family was religious but because his father believed he would receive a rigorous education there. A self-made man whose parents were of German origin, Morris Wasserstein, along with his brothers, devised a new application of a synthetic method for making velveteen and turning it into ribbon. With the profits, he invested in real estate, grew prosperous, and moved his family from Brooklyn to Manhattan's Upper East Side.

As an adolescent, Wasserstein led a charmed life, attending the McBurney School and simultaneously taking some college courses at Columbia University. He became captain of the low-ranked McBurney tennis team (he acknowledges that he was a mediocre player), edited the school paper, and dated socialite Penelope Tree (whose eminent mother, Marietta, had held a United Nations post). He had a high enough academic standing to be admitted at sixteen to the University of Michigan, where he was eventually named executive editor of the *Michigan Daily*. At the time he thought he wanted to be a journalist. But when he was offered a job by the *New York Times* in the summer of 1967, he turned it down.

By then he had developed other goals. He went off to Harvard Law School at nineteen, and when the university opened up a dual-degree program, he enrolled in the Graduate Business School as well. He did brilliantly in both programs, graduating from his law class with honors and being selected as one of the business school's George F. Baker Scholars. By 1971, at the age of twenty-three, he had a law degree, an MBA, and a fellowship to study law and economic regulation at Cambridge University. Even so, it wasn't clear where his interests would lead him professionally.

In childhood, Wasserstein showed an unusual fascination with money. At seven, he read business magazines and pretended to invest in the stock market. He took a keen interest in his father's real estate investments and worried about becoming poor, though there was little reason to do so. The graduate business student represented that side of Wasserstein.

But he had another side: the Wasserstein who held the traditional Jewish liberal view of the world, who lived in a small apartment near Harvard with his wife, Laura, worked on the Harvard *Civil Rights-Civil Liberties Law Review,* and spent one summer as a poverty worker in the slums of Brooklyn and another on a study for Ralph Nader on antitrust law. His Nader work led to two books, coauthored with Mark Green, a Nader protégé: *With Justice for Some* (1971), which, among other matters, argued for the decriminalization of marijuana, and *The Closed Enterprise System* (1972), which excoriated the Federal Trade Commission for its confused antitrust policies "despite the alarming increase in corporate mergers" — an interesting statement for a future M&A prince. He could be described as the prototypical sixties activist turned eighties businessman dramatized in the 1984 movie *The Big Chill.*

* * *

The tradition among First Boston bankers was to sit back and wait for business to come to them, but Perella and Wasserstein knew they had to go out and actively woo M&A clients. They drew up plans, projecting where the takeover action would be concentrated in the next five years, which industries would be hot (energy and finance were two), and what clients would be most receptive to their strategies. When the thirty-year-old Wasserstein called on corporations, he was often accompanied by older bankers so that prospective clients would know that First Boston wasn't sending a raw recruit to do a seasoned specialist's job.

Wasserstein wasted no time in proving himself. In June of 1978, he masterminded the takeover of Pet, a food company valued at close to half a billion dollars, on behalf of the Chicago-based conglomerate IC Industries. The defender in that protracted battle was the Robert Greenhill team of Morgan Stanley, who failed to preserve Pet's independence, and Wall Street's interest was piqued. Perella persuaded George Shinn to elevate Wasserstein to codirector of the M&A group before another firm stole him away. In 1980, their first full year as codirectors, they doubled their 1979 figures, pulling in $25 million in fees, in another league from the mere $1.8 million First Boston had earned in M&A in 1978.

When Perella had started out, his ideal was Felix Rohatyn, but he now felt that Lazard Frères had slipped from the top of the M&A ladder because it relied so heavily on that one man. The First Boston duo were off and running, with Wasserstein the tactician primed for the gold medal; Felix Rohatyn would soon run into him.

*  *  *

In background and style, Wasserstein and Rohatyn presented a study in contrasts. If Wasserstein was the eighties counterpart of Rohatyn in the sixties — the hottest investment banker on the mergers scene — the similarity ended there. Unlike Rohatyn, Wasserstein hadn't had to please overbearing taskmasters or navigate in largely uncharted waters. In the wide-open M&A field in the eighties, a firm handling mergers and acquisitions had to build a highly organized machine that spewed out research and strategies. That appealed to Wasserstein. His meteoric rise could be traced to his skill at coming up with clever, effective game plans.

Felix Rohatyn never immersed himself in the five-year plans, marketing strategies, organizational charts, and the team approach adopted by new mergers and acquisitions stars like Wasserstein and Perella. Having established his own style as a dealmaker through two decades of spadework and network building, he was not going to change that. Rohatyn remained more than ever highly individualistic. Though still a sophisticated dealmaker, he appeared eager to take on new challenges. He played a growing role in political and civic affairs. As a consequence, some of his friends, clients, and politicians alike felt that he would make an excellent secretary of the treasury.

It was hard to imagine Wasserstein in any cabinet post. He was a man of many talents, but diplomacy and professional modesty weren't among them. He said he chose his profession because "it's fun," but his conversation was also laced with words like "better" and "smarter" when referring to First Boston's deals, its M&A department, its strategies, and sometimes even himself.

For all his worldly experience and intelligence, there was still in him something of the Brooklyn-born kid who reveled in achieving a position of power and wealth so young. He seemed to have no difficulty reconciling his business practices with his political opinions or with his former life as a poverty worker and Nader raider. He hadn't given up on his liberal politics and was active in the 1980 congressional campaign of his coauthor, Mark Green. His personal life also ranged far beyond Wall Street, but his was a more private world than the one Rohatyn inhabited.

At the center of Wasserstein's life was his family. He remained close to his parents and to his sisters, with whom he never discussed dealmaking. He was more likely to be talking about theater with his sister Wendy, the playwright, who had interested him in joining the board of Playwrights Horizon, an Off-Broadway company. He and his second wife, Chris, a psychotherapist who used her maiden name professionally, lived with their children in an Upper East Side apartment. His home was not the decorator's dream that housed many other entrepreneurs but was designed for family living. Chris's paintings hung on the walls. The Wassersteins found relaxation in reading and art and, at their summer home, in riding (she was a skilled equestrian) and tennis (he still enjoyed playing).

Summer weekends were spent at their house in East Hampton, where he sometimes walked for miles along the beach, brooding about deals and strategies, occasionally becoming so absorbed in his thoughts that he would wander as far as the next town, search for a phone, and ask Chris to pick him up in the car. He may have lost his sense of distance in his meanderings on the beach, but he never lost sight of his goals.

\* \* \*

In 1981, a number of corporations were eyeing Conoco — the oil giant and fourteenth-largest company on the Fortune 500 list — among them Seagram. Seagram's chairman, Edgar Bronfman, made a bid for it after a block of shares was sold for what he considered a bargain price. Rebuffed by Conoco (on the advice of Robert Greenhill of Morgan Stanley and lawyer Joe Flom), Bronfman turned to Felix Rohatyn for help. They had known each other since they were both young men starting out in business; in fact, Bronfman's father, Samuel, had originally advised Rohatyn to go into M&A. It was a classic Rohatyn matchup. Bronfman, an aggressive chief executive with a towering ego, needed a financial statesman like Rohatyn.

By the 1980s, Rohatyn's stamp of approval on a major takeover attempt had become a vital part of his role as a dealmaker. Rohatyn offered assurance that whatever the outcome of a contest, his client would receive the full measure of his experience. He had seen all — and used many — of the dealmakers' strategic moves. All his political and media contacts and his stature and influence in the larger world won him a measure of respect from his clients that no other dealmaker could match, but he never took Wall Street for granted. The battle for Conoco would require his concentrated talents in promoting his client's cause.

Conoco lashed back at what it saw as Seagram's raid in a series of counterattacks led by Flom and his associates. The most disturbing was a variation of the "Jewish dentist" defense that was by then part of the Flom legend. (In 1975 the lawyer had helped the dental-supply company Sterndent resist a takeover bid from a firm owned in part by Kuwaiti investors, by raising the specter of Sterndent's many Jewish customers taking their business elsewhere.) In light of Seagram's bid for Conoco, he questioned whether countries such as Libya, where much of Conoco's reserves came from, would be happy to supply oil to a Jewish liquor producer.

Conoco desperately began to hunt for a white knight. It held preliminary talks with Texaco, but the two oils didn't mix well. A more congenial possibility, Du Pont, turned up on its own without an invitation. First Boston was its advisor.

Wasserstein's strategy for capturing Conoco changed very little during the subsequent rounds of bidding. From a walk along the beach on the Fourth of July weekend came the inspiration for a battle plan that was dubbed "Big Rube" around First Boston (named after cartoonist Rube Goldberg, famed for depicting comically complicated contraptions). At its simplest, the plan offered a higher cash premium than the Seagram bid to the Conoco shareholders who tendered to Du Pont the first 40 percent of Conoco stock — which made the offer particularly attractive to the arbs. That was the first part of the two-part offer. Once 40 percent of Conoco stock had been tendered, the remaining shareholders — largely institutional investors — who owned the outstanding 60 percent of the Conoco shares were offered Du Pont ones worth somewhat less in a tax-free stock swap. The strategy displayed the technical and tactical intricacy Wasserstein excelled in. And it left Seagram and Rohatyn, who lacked Du Pont's financial resources, with little room to maneuver.

By the time Mobil, the number-two corporation on the Fortune 500 list, jumped in with a bid, Seagram and Rohatyn were planning on a winning-by-losing strategy. That ploy showed Rohatyn's skill at reversing direction quickly and making the best of a bad situation. If he couldn't match resources with Du Pont, he could at least salvage something by striking a deal with it. In exchange for the Conoco shares that Seagram had picked up in the bidding war, the liquor company would receive an equivalent amount of Du Pont stock. To help Seagram reap the maximum number of shares, Rohatyn called in his lieutenant Peter Jaquith.

Eight years earlier, Jaquith had been assigned by Meyer to be Rohatyn's assistant — and to spy on him. Jaquith ignored Meyer's command, frustrating the old banker, but he survived and became the partner chosen by Rohatyn to handle major hostile mergers. In many ways, Jaquith was to Rohatyn what Rohatyn had been to Meyer — an able, trusted lieutenant who could handle complicated technical details. Rohatyn endorsed Jaquith's decisive bid against the two behemoths, while Wasserstein outflanked Mobil.

By early August the Mobil threat had faded, and Du Pont won Conoco for $7.5 billion — more than twice the previous high for any corporate merger — and doubled its size. (The downside was that Du Pont was saddled with huge debt.)

When the Conoco outcome was announced, the bartenders and other employees at the hotel that was the temporary outpost for Perella and Wasserstein in Du Pont's headquarters city of Wilmington, Delaware, treated the First Boston pair like conquering heroes — clapping and cheering for the home team. Everyone who worked on the deal — from Perella and Wasserstein to the pilots who had ferried them back and forth from New York to Wilmington, to the Du Pont chairman of the board — celebrated at a midnight victory party with Dom Perignon champagne and caviar.

Bronfman was also pleased with the work of his dealmaker. Seagram's $2.6 billion stake in Conoco had been transformed into a 20 percent share of Du Pont — a huge legacy for the loser — and three seats on its board of directors.* And for just five weeks of work, Lazard split $7 million down the middle with Shearson, whose top investment

---

* Only with the passage of time did the outcome of the Conoco deal prove a real winner for Seagram. As Americans cut back on drinking, the liquor company came to rely more on Du Pont's earnings. Moreover, Seagram strengthened its position within Du Pont by winning more seats on its board of directors.

banker, Mark Millard, had advised Seagram in the Conoco contest. At the close of the year, when profits at Lazard were divided, Rohatyn got two percentage points more. Those two points were worth millions, pushing his share of Lazard profits up to nearly $5 million in 1982 and more than $6 million in 1983. He was rich and he became richer.

The young pair at First Boston would also eventually command seven-figure incomes. They had demonstrated their worth by earning $15 million for First Boston as Du Pont's adviser and by establishing it as a house where original and highly profitable ideas blossomed. When they left to form their own company — Wasserstein, Perella & Company — in 1988, their renown was so widespread that the firm instantly became a major dealmaking house.

*   *   *

On Wall Street, the race never let up, and the brightest, least timid rushed toward the hot center. New records became old standards almost overnight. And merger stars would find bold ways to beat those records.

# CHAPTER TWENTY-THREE

# The Junk Bond King

H e was a phenomenon from California who, more than any other financier, made the eighties Wall Street's moment in American business. Chief executives of small corporations saw him as a sugar daddy helping their companies grow: the heads of big blue-chip corporations saw him as a hydra-headed ogre threatening their independence. Yet Michael Milken remained something of a mystery, better known for what he did than for who he was.

With almost evangelical fervor, the young bond trader promoted his instrument of change — high-yield securities. A more obscure banner could hardly have been found. These securities — a grab bag of debt and preferred stock issues — offered impressive current returns but earned low marks from credit ratings services because they were perceived as risky investments. Some of them were "fallen angels," the old bonds of once solid companies that had experienced hard times. Others were newly issued bonds from small companies in emerging industries. Still others became part of the creative financing deployed by raiders in taking over corporations. Focusing only on the greater risk of default, traditional financiers called these high-yield securities "junk bonds," and the label stuck.

Institutional investors across the country weren't interested in labels. By 1983 they were lining up behind the thirty-seven-year-old Milken like soldiers in the crusades. With each passing day, corporations seemed to be supported on an ever-thickening layer of paper laid down by Milken and his company. Largely through his efforts in marketing these securities, Drexel, a middle-ranked firm, was elbowing aside Morgan Stanley from the elite bulge group in underwriting rankings. Even staid old savings and loan companies, which had built their reputations on using depositors' money for safe loans, felt compelled to buy some of these bonds.

America was on a junk bond spree except, it seemed, for some

critics on Wall Street who were no more receptive to Drexel's inno-
vation than the old Establishment had been to risk arbitrage and takeovers. The higher yields, however enticing, the critics argued, weren't
worth the risk. The bonds were still simply "junk," and Milken had
been awarded the dubious title of "the Junk Bond King."

No scrap-heap label could stop him from promoting the bonds.
In truth, the predicted massive wave of defaults never materialized.
Milken and his junk bond movement gathered momentum and, in a
business which held few secrets for very long, only what Milken wanted
revealed was circulated around Wall Street. The financial community
knew his firm well enough or at least thought they did. Drexel Burnham
Lambert had always been viewed as a likable bunch of brokers who
handled a little of everything, from institutional research and trading
to moderate-size underwriting to retail brokerage. Exactly how Milken
ran Drexel's junk bond operation remained a closely guarded secret. In
the company's annual reports, he wasn't even listed as an officer or a
director. Drexel would only acknowledge that he was a senior vice
president, which seemed almost like a convenient title designed largely
to satisfy the curious. Milken wasn't part of the closely linked world
that was Wall Street. Nor did he talk to the press.

There were precious few photographs of him, just an occasional
handout that showed a promising-looking young man with sparkling
eyes, high cheekbones, and a brilliant smile, which could have passed
for typical college yearbook pictures unless the viewer was discerning
and noticed the toupee he was wearing.

* * *

In his manner, he was different from the other mighty traders.
His voice lacked their fire — if anything, his was thin and reedy —
and his look was mild-mannered. Although he could be impatient on
occasion, and sometimes arrogant, Milken was approachable and calm
even in his pressurized trading room.

His background was also different. Born on July 4, 1946, Milken
was a child of "the Valley," Los Angeles parlance for the San Fernando
Valley. Although part of Los Angeles, it had been little more than a
quiet, low-profile suburban bedroom community in the fifties when Milken was growing up. The Valley, in the heart of southern California's
middle-class residential area, was separated from the pressures and ambitions of downtown Los Angeles and Hollywood by a wall of mountains.

Milken's youth was a slice of Valley success. He lived with his
parents and his brother, Lowell, two years his junior, on the north side
of Ventura Boulevard in Encino, where the homes were conventional

middle-class boxes — laid out on a neat checkerboard grid of streets. At Birmingham High School, a public school in nearby Van Nuys, he was on the debating team, head cheerleader of a squad that included future actress Sally Field, and prom king. He was voted the "most spirited" and "friendliest" member of the class of 1964 and finished second in ranking. Years later, Milken complained to a colleague that he was beaten out of being first by "a little squirrel who was always studying." He had a steady girlfriend; she was a classmate, a sweet Jewish girl named Lori Hackel. For all his conformity, there was another side to Milken, one that was more revealing of his talents as a future financial wizard.

At ten, he began helping his father, Bernard, an accountant, prepare income tax returns. Later he studied business administration at the University of California at Berkeley, worked for the giant accounting firm of Touche Ross on the side, and managed money for a small group of clients. (He covered losses out of his own pocket and took half the profits.) An A student, he claimed that he put little effort into getting high grades. Being known as a grind wasn't the image he wanted to convey. His college social life was very like his social life in high school. A straitlaced young man who read the *Wall Street Journal* while attending the university that was the seedbed of radical student upheaval in the 1960s, he was seemingly immune to the student ferment that was sweeping the country. He played intramural sports and served as the chairman of his fraternity chapter in his junior year. Even the company he kept was the same. Lori Hackel had followed him to Berkeley, as did his brother.

After graduating with highest honors in 1968, he went east to the University of Pennsylvania's Wharton School. There he found his mission in life. After reading two massive financial textbooks on the history of corporate bonds, he realized that the rate of default, even among the lowest-rated issuers, had actually been comparatively small. (There were two standards for bonds considered below investment grade: those rated BB or lower by Standard & Poor's or rated Ba or lower by Moody's. They were called "high-yield" bonds because they typically paid much higher interest than the investment grade ones issued by blue-chip companies such as AT&T, IBM, and General Electric.) Milken reasoned that a lot of money could be made trading high-yield, or junk, bonds because they had tremendous potential for an increase in value if their company's earnings improved, thus boosting their ratings. In the meantime, the bonds offered substantial interest payments. By borrowing short-term money at comparatively low cost, Milken could easily stockpile such bonds and, in theory, make a profit on the difference between the interest paid by the bonds and the interest paid on the loan. He soon would have the chance to test his theory.

Just one course and one paper short of obtaining his MBA (he had straight A's),* he took a job in 1969 doing research for Drexel Firestone in Philadelphia. In 1970, he was transferred to the New York office, where he became the apostle of high-yield securities. He wrote reports constantly (until he found out too many analysts were plagiarizing him), tirelessly visited prospective clients around the country, nurtured corporate contacts through regular phone calls, talked to whoever would listen, read bond prospectuses — and traded junk bonds aggressively. He was never a hard sell, but what he lacked in outward drive, he made up for in conviction and determination.

Rather than live in New York, he awakened two hours earlier to ride the bus from his home in Cherry Hill, New Jersey. Cherry Hill was also convenient for Lori, who was by then his wife; she was studying for her Master of Science degree in education at the nearby University of Pennsylvania (she graduated in 1972 and their first child was born a year later). The predawn start gave him extra time to read bond prospectuses, and the bus trip enabled him to avoid the Wall Street rail commuters who might take up his time in conversation. Junk bonds were such a small part of the debt market in the early seventies that Milken had little trouble making his presence felt.

Yet after only a few years of trading junk bonds, he was ready to give it up to teach at Wharton. His dissatisfaction was triggered by the acquisition in 1973 of Drexel Firestone by Burnham, under the combined name of Drexel Burnham.† The acquisition was a coup for the affable I. W. "Tubby" Burnham, who didn't have the Wall Street reputation of his cantankerous friends Gus Levy and Cy Lewis. The merger moved the company from eighteenth to fifteenth place in total capital and, even more impressive, from fifty-ninth to twentieth in underwriting. But in acquiring Drexel, though he couldn't have known then, Burnham's most fateful acquisition was Mike Milken. His decision to do whatever was necessary to keep Milken marked the real turning point for the firm.

---

* He later coauthored a paper with one of his professors and received his MBA degree.

† Three years later, in 1976, the name would become Drexel Burnham Lambert, Inc., following the acquisition of Lambert Brussels Witter, the holding company of the research boutique William D. Witter.

Soon after the Drexel merger, Burnham called Milken into his office for a talk and asked why he wanted to leave.

"Things have been so tough at Drexel," Milken told him, "that I'm never sure I'm going to get paid. And basically, they don't understand what I'm doing, and they don't want to give me enough capital to operate with."

"What [amount of capital] are they giving you?" asked Burnham.

"They gave me five hundred thousand dollars," said Milken, who was then twenty-seven.

"What do you want?"

"One million."

"If you stay here, I'll guarantee you'll be paid regularly, and I'll give you two million dollars the first year for your [trading] position." Milken also got a percentage of his trading profits.

His department ran like a finely tuned profit machine that became even more productive after the investment banker Frederick Joseph joined the firm the following year.

In an odd sort of way, Fred Joseph's background served as a training ground for the Byzantine world, with its traditions and turfs, of investment banking. The son of a Boston cab driver, he had been the leader of a Jewish teenage street gang known as the Vikings. Although they could hardly have starred in *West Side Story,* they had their colors — blue and gold — in satin reversible jackets, their neighborhood turfs, and occasionally they tussled with other ethnic gangs and even with another Jewish one called the Indians. Joseph was just as proud of having been president of the Vikings and boxing in the Golden Gloves competition as of being an A student at Roxbury Memorial, a hard-scrabble Boston public high school. He won a scholarship to Harvard, where, after flirting with physics, he majored in English and boxed for the university team, winning the lightweight championship three years running. After active duty in the Navy and marriage to a Wellesley student, he returned to Harvard for his MBA.

His first job on Wall Street, in 1963 at the age of twenty-six, was in investment banking at E. F. Hutton. A power struggle in 1970 forced Joseph to move on, and not too long afterward he was running Drexel Burnham's corporate finance department. But it wasn't until 1977 that he was to help distinguish the firm from run-of-the-mill houses.

*   *   *

Early in 1977, Lehman Brothers broke new ground by underwriting an original issue of junk bonds, which met with such disap-

proval on the Street that Lehman quickly abandoned the practice. For
Joseph, however, underwriting new junk bonds seemed like a golden
opportunity. With Milken trading some 1,500 existing junk bonds belonging to several hundred companies, his intimate knowledge of the
buyers for junk bonds would be invaluable in soliciting the business of
the potential sellers of those bonds. Joseph and Milken quickly teamed up.

That April, they did their first junk bond underwriting: a $30
million issue for Texas International. The market seemed responsive:
new issues of junk bonds jumped more than 60 percent the following
year, nearly a third of them brought out by Drexel. Junk bonds gave
companies with little chance at raising capital advantageously a new
way to finance themeselves. At the time, the obviously pejorative terms
"junk bond" and the nickname Mr. Junk Bond, as he was then called,
didn't bother Milken.

He was determined to make "high-yield" securities, as he preferred to call these issues, a major force in investing. Apparently Drexel
was prepared to back him wherever he went. But not even Tubby
Burnham or his firm's new chief executive, Robert Linton, could have
guessed how far that would lead.

Milken stunned everyone. He wanted to take the entire junk
bond department to his native California. At first, Linton fought it.
He didn't think Milken's people would work as hard in southern California. Milken argued that they might work even harder and certainly
better. For him, the commuting time would be less, adding three hours
to the work day. He would extend the work day of his staff as well.
Long lunches, traditional on Wall Street, simply wouldn't be tolerated.
He would see to that by paying for everyone's lunches — and breakfasts — out of his own pocket.

In truth, he had a compelling reason for wanting to move west.
His father had cancer and he wanted to be nearby. In the end, Milken
and his department of fifteen traders, salesmen, and securities analysts,
all of whom wanted to stay with him, left for Los Angeles in July 1978.

He returned to Encino and bought a house on the south side
of Ventura Boulevard, up in the hills above the valley, which was
famous as a house on the 1939 honeymoon estate of Clark Gable and
his bride Carole Lombard. By movie-star standards, the rambling two-
story brick-and-wood dwelling was modest enough. It seemed to have
been built with a family in mind, and there was plenty of room for
Milken's two children (a third would follow) to roam about. For
Milken, perhaps its single most attractive feature was that it was only
a few minutes' drive from his parents' home. Milken's brother, who

practiced law in Los Angeles, joined Drexel's West Coast office. For the first time since Milken had gone away to college, the family was united. His move to California and his brother's decision to work with him came just in time. In 1979, Bernard Milken finally succumbed to cancer.

Milken's workload multiplied in California, but it paid handsome dividends. In 1981, Drexel cracked the top ten among underwriters — a first for the firm. The junk bond team grew. From cramped space in Drexel's Century City branch office, it moved into its own six-story office building in Beverly Hills overlooking Rodeo Drive, where shops like Bijan, Cartier, and Gucci attracted the world's richest clientele. The new environment was well suited to the Drexel traders of the eighties.

Drexel's research revealed a huge untapped market for junk bonds, because more than 95 percent of all companies didn't qualify for investment-grade ratings. Month by month, year by year, more money than anyone could have predicted passed through the portals of Milken's trading and underwriting operation. The Beverly Hills trading room became Drexel's main profit center. The rebirth of the merger and acquisition field, the quantum leap in trading, and a healthy economy all contributed to the boom.

In 1983, when Drexel reached the fifth spot in underwriting, Wall Street could no longer ignore the firm or the reason for its success. Of Drexel's $6 billion in underwriting, two-thirds came from junk bonds alone, and its growth seemed assured. The junk bond market expanded at a fantastic rate — from $1.4 billion in 1978 to $7.3 billion in 1983 — when Drexel controlled more than 64 percent of the market.

Milken went from being merely Mr. Junk Bond to being the Junk Bond King, although he no longer tolerated the term junk bond kindly. But whatever the term, it brought him a royal income. Because Drexel is a private company, no exact figures were known; estimates of his income were said to be around $15 million annually, easily making him among the richest men on — or off — Wall Street.

Even with that amount of money at his command, there were few changes in Milken's personal life. His children received allowances at the time of $2 a week, with no cost-of-living adjustment. He rarely used his swimming pool or tennis court. He took few vacations. Apart from his family, his only real interest was work. There was simply no time for anything else. As he told people, reading bond prospectuses was a hobby. With few variations, his working days followed a predictable pattern.

Up each morning at 4:00 A.M., he dressed quickly, then drove to the Drexel offices some ten miles away. At 4:45 A.M., the day began with breakfast, reading the newspapers, and meetings. It wasn't unusual for a top executive of a major corporation to show up at Milken's office at the crack of dawn in order to enlist Milken's help in underwriting a company's securities. When the stock market opened at 7:00 A.M. (10:00 A.M. in New York), Milken was in his pivotal position on the trading floor, at the center of desks arranged in the shape of a large X.

His jacket off, he spent the next six hours in front of his computer terminal or talking on the phone, with the receiver pinned to his ear, masterminding trading. He gobbled down lunch at 10:00 A.M. His staff could have anything to eat at any time of the day, as long as they didn't leave their desks.

At one o'clock, following the market's close in New York, he and his staff spent another six hours or more working on internal strategy and receiving visits from corporate financial officers trying to interest Milken in their companies. On Saturdays and Sundays he would hold court in his office — and home — for corporate visitors. The pattern was repeated week after week, month after month. He kept pushing the limits of those around him. He got away with it because he always pushed himself harder. All told, the work week consumed perhaps some ninety hours. He seemed to think of everything in terms of a competitive edge, since he apparently hated being beaten in any deal. He appeared bothered when Linton or Joseph turned down a deal of his that they didn't think was right for Drexel.

Late in 1983, he came up with a proposal that would shift American business, including some of the nation's most powerful industries, in a totally new direction. Junk bonds would be used for the first time to finance hostile takeovers. Through the issuance of junk bonds, Milken would provide virtually all the leading raiders of the day with access to huge pools of capital. His power was formidable. Corporate heads and financiers willingly went out of their way to meet him. His name was known from one end of the financial world to the other. "Junk bonds" entered the popular lexicon, even though the exact meaning of the words may have baffled many. The term would become familiar to the general public through Drexel's high-intensity advertising campaign late in the 1980s that touted high-yield bonds as the savior of endangered small companies and the protector of workers' jobs. But the man who unlocked the secret of junk bonds remained as much of an enigma as ever.

# CHAPTER TWENTY-FOUR

# Greenmail

*B*efore he could enjoy the ceasefire in his personal life that began with his marriage to his third wife, Gayfryd, in 1984, Saul Steinberg had lived in the "combat zone." By the early 1980s he was a hot item in the gossip pages of magazines and newspapers, fueled by his sizzling separation and divorce from his second wife, Laura.

Before it was over, she had accused him of siphoning off hundreds of thousands of dollars of company money for his own use and for drugs (she later confessed that everything she said was untrue), and he had had her arrested. The tabloids couldn't get enough of it, but Wall Street was less interested in those steamy headlines than in his takeover battles.

The brash twenty-nine-year-old whose attempted raid on Chemical Bank in 1969 unleashed a storm had tried to quiet the fears over his next moves by proclaiming: "I'm no takeover artist. I only did one and that turned friendly in the end. My wife [Barbara] and I, we're decent people. We like tennis, art, music. We have three children. We're not really bad at all." But he hadn't succeeded in calming the business community. The onetime boy wonder had become the bad boy of business. And his reputation wasn't helped when in 1969 he was plunged into a heated contest that created an uproar in London's financial district.

Robert Maxwell, the forty-six-year-old Czech-born Jewish refugee and Labour Party member of Parliament, began the courtship by inviting Steinberg's parent company, Leasco, to acquire the Maxwell-run Pergamon Press. Steinberg was soon blasting Maxwell, proclaiming "massive fraud" when muddled profit forecasts and other apparent discrepancies were allegedly uncovered. Steinberg announced that he was withdrawing his $60 million offer.

The British cried foul. Charges and countercharges were hurled across the Atlantic and around London, where partial takeover bids or withdrawals were considered unfair — particularly since Steinberg owned 38 percent of Pergamon. The furor contributed to the collapse of Leasco's stock, and Steinberg was branded an enfant terrible on two continents. He did salvage something that was of great value to him personally — a fast friendship with the London Rothschilds.

Out of necessity, a more sober Steinberg settled down to evaluate his holdings and his future. His one great coup, Reliance Insurance (which had inspired Felix Rohatyn's ill-fated course of urging Harold Geneen and ITT to go after Hartford Insurance), had turned into quite a success story, eclipsing his losses. He had changed the insurer's name to the Reliance Group in the midseventies, which underlay the direction he planned to follow now: wheeling and dealing on Wall Street.

* * *

Steinberg's preoccupation with finance started early. The son of a plastics manufacturer who made items like kitchen dish racks, he was reading the *Wall Street Journal* by 1952, at thirteen. He had done so well in his early school years that he entered the University of Pennsylvania's Wharton School at age sixteen, but there he was a surprisingly mediocre student, partly because he was too busily engaged in business to study much. In his senior year, he had enough self-confidence to acquire 3 percent of O'Sullivan Rubber and threatened a proxy fight if management didn't diversify into automotive parts. O'Sullivan bought back Steinberg's stock for three times what he had paid for it. The lesson of how effective he could be as a gadfly and irritant wasn't lost on him.

During that time, at the suggestion of one of his professors, he began a senior thesis entitled "The Decline and Fall of IBM," but he was astute enough to perceive that the assumption was wrong. Far from being in a precarious position, IBM had a rosy future. It wasn't IBM's technological lead that interested him, but the promise of its future cash flow. He reasoned that he could buy the computers from IBM, lease them at a rate lower than IBM's but high enough to pay off the costs of the machines quickly and could keep leasing them for pure profit until they became obsolete.

His plan was anything but academic. After graduation, he set out to implement it. With $25,000 borrowed from his father (who borrowed it from a bank) he launched a new leasing company, appropriately named Leasco, in his father's Brooklyn factory. Leasco made $55,000 its first year, $110,000 its second year, and soon became IBM's biggest customer. Leasco became Steinberg's base, and with its profits, he turned his attention to acquiring other companies. Reliance was his great triumph.

Plump, with a round face and a persistent beaverlike smile, Steinberg looked insultingly young to be challenging the likes of Chemical Bank. As he grew older, his natural volubility, an impish sense of humor, and an expansive manner made his aggressiveness seem arrogant. He wasn't averse to putting his success on display. His estate, on the south shore of Long Island, boasted a beautiful colonial-style house of twenty-nine rooms, a tennis court, a swimming pool, two saunas, paintings by Picasso and Kandinsky, and a staff of eight. The Steinbergs left that home in 1973.

At the insistence of his then wife, Barbara, that they live in New York City, the family moved to a baronial triplex on Park Avenue that had once been owned by John D. Rockefeller, Jr. The apartment was splendid enough to impress any tycoon: it had 23,000 square feet of living space, thirty-four rooms, and fifteen fireplaces.

Albert Hadley, of the venerable interior decorating firm Parish-Hadley, furnished the co-op in "classic" taste. It featured a plenitude of antiques and the Steinberg's modern art collection, which included works by Kandinsky, Paul Klee, Hans Hofmann, and Fernand Léger chosen by Barbara Steinberg (who had studied art history at the Parsons School of Design and at New York University) and others by photo-realist artists such as Richard Estes, selected by her husband.

With a staff of eleven to attend them, the Steinbergs entertained four or five evenings a week. Having become meteorically successful so young, the thirty-four-year-old Steinberg didn't seem to have much in common with his contemporaries, who were still establishing themselves. Most of the couple's friends were older. Among those they saw were Joan and Sandy Weill and Larry and Wilma ("Billie") Tisch. Twice a year they hosted huge parties catered by Joe Mitchell, whose bountiful food was "in" on the affluent party circuit.

A committed Jew, Steinberg donated large sums to Jewish charities, among them the United Jewish Appeal, the Federation of Jewish Philanthropies, and Long Island Jewish-Hillside Medical Center. He was also a director of the United Cerebral Palsy Foundation and contributed to research in juvenile diabetes and to a center that taught occupational skills to the mentally handicapped.

Yet, try as he might, he was incapable of establishing a reputation as a "gentleman" of finance. Ugly incidents seemed to dog him, situations that would lead to more adverse publicity and to lawsuits. In 1969, he had pledged $375,000 to the Woodmere Academy, a private school near his Long Island home that his children attended. The money was designated to build the Barbara Steinberg Library and Computer Center, in honor of his wife. He had originally agreed to pay the entire sum by 1972. When the deadline arrived, he had come up with only $175,000, although he had managed to be one of the largest contributors to President Richard Nixon's reelection campaign, donating a then secret sum of $250,000 (and, years later, claimed to have raised $8 million more). Over the next few years, he found other excuses not to pay the balance. The school sued. He finally did pay the rest of the promised money to the Woodmere Academy in 1977, but only after the case reached the state's highest court. By that time the Steinbergs were divorced. The settlement did little to improve his image, which would get worse before it got better. Beginning in 1978, and for most of the next three years, he was mired in controversy. First, the Securities and Exchange Commission charged him with having violated federal securities laws a few years earlier in the sale of stock in Pulte Home Corp., a Michigan homebuilder. According to the SEC, Steinberg, a former Pulte director, touted the stock to people he knew while he himself was unloading his shares. As is standard in such cases, he settled without admitting or denying guilt and promised not to violate the law in the future.

Soon after that, he was caught up in a political scandal involving a bid to build public bus-stop shelters in New York City. Several years earlier, a French businessman had presented the city with a proposal: his company, Bus Top Shelters, would erect steel-and-glass bus shelters similar to the ones found in Paris, with one panel available for display advertising. The idea was that the ads would eventually generate enough revenue to pay for the shelters and their maintenance. The company and the city would share the proceeds. In 1975, Bus Top was granted a three-year pilot franchise, but ran out of money within two years and approached Steinberg as an investor. He declined. Instead, along with two associates, he formed a competing company, Convenience & Safety, Inc., and went after the New York franchise himself, leading to government investigations into whether his political contacts and contributions played a part in awarding the new franchise.

In the midst of all that, there had been one bright spot in his life, some return to normalcy, or so at first it seemed. A week before Christmas 1978, in a Jewish ceremony performed at his Park Avenue apartment, Steinberg married thirty-two-year-old Laura Sconocchia, a willowy raven-haired Italian divorcée from Rome. The marriage produced Steinberg's fourth child, a son.

By the time everything simmered down on the bus shelter front and Steinberg had withdrawn his bid (he said he lost $2 million during the fight), he was the target of federal and city probes. No proof was ever presented that he had actually done anything wrong, but when called to testify, during the city's investigation, he invoked his fifth amendment right against self-incrimination.

Against this backdrop of city politics and official investigations, his next business move might seem mild in comparison — but not to readers of the business press. Utilizing the strategy that he had first used as a college student in his fight with O'Sullivan Rubber, he now forged it into a powerful tactical weapon that would drive corporate America into a panic. Companies would be forced to reevaluate their management practices and to line Steinberg's pockets with more riches.

\* \* \*

*Greenmail*. In the late seventies, the term didn't exist and no one had tagged Steinberg with it. But, to paraphrase Supreme Court Justice Potter Stewart's definition of pornography, you knew it when you saw it. The name the Street had given to the strategy was "buyback" — a euphemism comparable to describing Orpheus's descent as a trip south.

In a buyback, a large shareholder promised to sell all his shares back to the company and not to purchase any other shares of that company for several years. In return, he was paid a higher price for his stock than the going market rate. Management was willing to pay the premium to him and not to other shareholders in the belief that a divisive threat of a takeover-from-within was being eliminated. Extracting this kind of financial blackmail was perfectly legal, which was why it had many corporate leaders scared witless. Recognition of Steinberg's clout spread quickly throughout corporate America.

He made the Williams Act of 1968, once the bane of raiders, work to his advantage. The requirement in the law that investors reveal how much they own of a company once they acquire more than 5 percent of the stock became Steinberg's shield of legitimacy: he was not a raider undertaking a covert assault, he claimed with straight-faced understatement, but an aboveboard investor seeking representation among a company's directors to make improvements — which could mean anything from getting rid of management to selling off part or all of the business. Lomas & Nettleton, the nation's largest independent mortgage company, agreed to buy back his securities — stocks and bonds — at an inflated price to induce him to go away. Those securities, listed on Reliance's books as $22 million, were worth some $30 million on the open market when Lomas & Nettleton bought them back from him for $37 million.

Penn Central, the failed railroad turned profitable conglomerate, was the next candidate on his list, and Steinberg couldn't have been smoother in his approach. He invited Richard Dicker, the company's chairman, to his Park Avenue apartment for lunch. He gave Dicker a tour of his extensive art collection and introduced Dicker to his wife, Laura, and their infant son. When the two men were alone, Steinberg talked about his former spouse, Barbara. After the divorce, Steinberg said, he had invited her to move whatever furniture she wanted from the triplex into her new apartment. To his surprise, she had cleaned him out except for the art. "She got thirty-four rooms into ten," Steinberg joked. "Now tell me, how is that possible?"

Dicker enjoyed the lunch, but the two men were soon at lawyer's length from each other. Penn Central filed a complaint claiming that Steinberg was involved in an "unlawful scheme" to take control of the conglomerate. With counsels ready to do battle, a settlement was reached, and Steinberg emerged an even richer man for his efforts. In February 1980, Penn Central bought back his stock for $26.25 a share, $5 more than he had paid for it and $1.50 more than it was selling for on the market — or a greenmail payment to Steinberg of $2.7 million on top of $5.3 million in ordinary market profits for his 1.8 million shares.

Laura Steinberg may not have known in exact dollars and cents her husband's net worth, but when their marriage of less than two years exploded in 1980, money became a hotly contested issue in the bitter divorce proceedings. When they separated, he kept the apartment, and she reportedly set up temporary quarters in a $1,000-a-day suite in the luxurious Pierre Hotel on Fifth Avenue. Two weeks later, she returned to the apartment and barricaded herself inside. Steinberg promptly had her arrested for trespassing. Laura, who owned 14,000 shares of Reliance, retaliated in equally dramatic fashion by filing a suit against him.

Her complaint accused him of misappropriating funds from Reliance's $3 billion coffers, but it was what she claimed he did with the money that really opened eyes, even among longtime Steinberg watchers. Along with other allegations, she charged that he had taken at least $100,000 of Reliance money to help maintain their lavishly furnished apartment and its eleven-member staff, to pay for the company jet for his private use, and to hire his own security force; and further, that he had siphoned off another $190,000 to purchase illegal drugs, including cocaine.

In a separate court action, she charged Steinberg with arranging an illegal cash contribution to the campaign of Harrison J. Goldin, the comptroller of New York City, in exchange for Goldin's support in going after the city's bus shelter franchise. The court papers weren't accompanied by corroborative documents, and Steinberg vehemently denied the charges. "She's a liar — an outright liar," he insisted. The Reliance board backed him, announcing it was convinced the allegations were baseless. By the end of the year, the charges were dismissed. A New York State Supreme Court judge concluded that Laura Steinberg had a conflict of interest because of the simultaneous divorce proceedings.

But Laura Steinberg wasn't going to go quietly. She brought another court action — this one directed against Steinberg, his lawyers, and the entire New York City Police Department — asking for $14.5 million in damages for the trauma of being "treated like a common criminal" at the time of her arrest. So rich was the dirt that it was even reported in the normally dry and impersonal financial press.

In December, *Fortune* ran an article entitled "Fear and Loathing in the Corporate Boardrooms," which dredged up all the Steinberg scandals and controversies of recent years. One unnamed Steinberg associate described him as "a genius who has led a notorious and sleazy life." A friend was quoted as saying, "I assume Saul will self-destruct."

There was, of course, far more to his business and personal life than the scandals indicated. Despite his recent troubles, his massive, well-run insurance enterprise had expanded into a money-making machine. Yet his freewheeling style of doing business added an element of volatility to whatever he undertook. Even when a corporation could have profited from his advice, it was generally Steinberg and not his proposals that became the focus of controversy.

\* \* \*

Saul Steinberg was working hard at dissociating himself from all the ties that had brought him so much negative publicity. He wasn't going to remain an open target for his critics forever. After his friend New York State Senator Jack Bronston went to jail for his role in the New York City bus shelter contract dispute, Steinberg signaled in a letter written in August 1981 to the *New York Times* that he hadn't "the faintest inclination to do business with the City of New York. So think about what you have accomplished, as you stand out in the rain waiting for your bus."

No longer was anyone going to tell him how to run his business. Soon after the start of 1982, he took the Reliance Group private (the

Steinberg family offered a cash and securities package worth some $550 million to purchase all the Reliance shares they didn't already own) — a move designed to allow him to make even more money and to free him from the restraints imposed by public ownership. That would mean fewer instances of greenmail or bruising confrontations with corporate managements — at least for the present. His good behavior as a New York Times Company shareholder paid off handsomely in ways not measured in dollars: he won the friendship of the chairman, Arthur Ochs Sulzberger, who was among New York City's political, social, and Jewish elite.

Steinberg assumed the stance of an established financier. His younger brother, Robert, was put in charge of the day-to-day operations of the insurance side of the business, while he himself focused on investing. For his own reasons, Steinberg stopped talking to reporters. In his office at the sleek, modern headquarters of Reliance Group Holdings off Park Avenue, two gray marble tablets inscribed in English and Hebrew hung on a wall behind his desk to serve as a warning:

THE ELEVENTH COMMANDMENT
DO NOT TALK
ON THE TELEPHONE
TO THE PRESS

The only intentional publicity was the favorable kind that showed him in the role of the generous philanthropist. By his own estimate, he had given away millions to the Metropolitan Museum for various projects, including the Frank Lloyd Wright Room and the restoration of several European galleries. He donated $1 million to his alma mater, Wharton, where he endowed a chair for a dean and embarked on a project to donate another $10 million for a building on campus to be named after him. These magnanimous gifts helped to soften his image as a greenmailer.

At the same time, his reputation as a serious art collector grew when he sold his collection of German Expressionist paintings and other art — for a disappointing $4.2 million — to devote himself to buying Old Masters and the works of other renowned artists. His acquisitions weren't confined to established tastes. Over the years he had purchased works by up-and-coming artists, only to see them later become famous — two examples were Francis Bacon and Richard Estes. "I buy a lot of *hard* art," Steinberg has said more than once. "Definite. Not wishy-washy."

And he was leaving the steamy strains of his personal life behind.

He had been seeing a number of women and was linked in gossip columns with a covergirl. But it was thirty-three-year-old Gayfryd Johnson, a tall, slim Canadian with a model's figure and short dark hair, who finally captured the forty-three-year-old financier's undivided attention. They met in November of 1982 at a dinner party hosted by art dealer Richard Feigen. Twice divorced and the mother of a son, she had known great wealth in her second marriage and was a successful businesswoman in her own right, as the owner of a company that distributed tubular steel to industry. She was more impressed by Steinberg's energy than by his money. The relationship flourished, though Gayfryd refused to move in with him until he was free to marry her.

By late 1983, the four-year Steinberg divorce battle finally ended. Laura received $10,000 a month in alimony and dropped the stockholder suit. ("I was hurt, upset, and confused," she later wrote her former husband. "All of the charges and lawsuits that I instituted were totally untrue.") Very soon thereafter — in January 1984 — Saul Steinberg and Gayfryd Johnson were married in a Reform Jewish ceremony at Central Synagogue in Manhattan attended only by family members and close friends. (Honoring her husband's request, Gayfryd had converted to Judaism after receiving weekly instruction for many months from a rabbi.) For the occasion the bride wore a Zandra Rhodes off-white-and-silver dress. After the ceremony the newlyweds were feted at a formal dinner given by the groom's brother and his wife, Kathy.

Even before their marriage, Gayfryd had taken complete charge of Saul's home. With the help of designer Tom Collum, she redecorated the thirty-four-room triplex, which she had considered "impersonal" and "plain-Jane" despite its size. Long gone were the elephant tusks and leopard skins that were the hallmark of the Laura Steinberg era. What was left, according to Gayfryd, was "an enormous warehouse on Park Avenue for Saul's art collection." She had something else in mind. "In the great English country homes, they live with extraordinary art and make a house a home. That was my goal."

The living room was redone with crimson Fortuny printed cotton on the walls to show off Old Master paintings: among them, Rubens's "Venus and the Three Muses Mourning the Death of Adonis" and Titian's "Salome with the Head of Saint John the Baptist." The library, Steinberg's favorite room, was also highlighted by great artworks, including Hals's "Portrait of a Man Holding a Book" and two bronze hands by Rodin. The dining room — with an English Regency table that seated twenty-four — contained Jacob Jordaens's massive "The King Drinks" over the sideboard. Near the canopied bed in the sumptuous master bedroom hung Kees von Dongen's "Woman with Pearls." The magnificent eighty-foot entrance hall displayed a dazzling array of paintings and sculpture that included Rodins. (Steinberg's art collection was so large that it even spilled over into the bathrooms. In the ladies' powder room, the rare Louis Seize wallpaper was highlighted by a Louis Seize mirror and a Renoir landscape.)

The redecorated apartment also contained a gymnasium, half a dozen bedrooms, a poolroom for relaxing with a cue stick — "Our one crazy room," Gayfryd explained. "With its gray flannel walls, it's like a giant security blanket" — a French country kitchen, an upstairs sitting room for Saul and Gayfryd, and a second, smaller, dining room with a round Regency table, where the Steinbergs ate when they weren't entertaining formally.

Friends now said that Gayfryd was responsible for "domesticating" Steinberg. A staff of fifteen helped her run the household smoothly. For the first time at the Steinberg residence, meals were served on a regular schedule. Steinberg, who had always suffered from a weight problem, gave up sodas, candy, and other junk food, although, his wife conceded, "we still have Häagen-Dazs ice cream occasionally." At night, Gayfryd locked up the kitchen to prevent her portly husband from making midnight raids.

Despite his pressured business schedule and their busy social life, they had breakfast with the three youngest children in their blended family* and were at home with them for an early dinner, even though they often went out afterward to dinner parties or benefits. They attended synagogue at least twice a month and observed all the significant Jewish holidays.

No sooner had Steinberg put his personal life in order than he returned to one of his favorite pursuits: greenmail. The timing was ripe to shake up corporate management, whose jobs and whose companies' independence had never been more at risk. The year 1984 saw a new high of $122 billion, up 50 percent from the record set three years earlier. Steinberg sank a $36 million investment into the stock of Quaker State, which gave him ownership of nearly 9 percent of the motor oil company. He threatened to take control.

---

* Steinberg had two sons and a daughter from his marriage to Barbara and a son with his second wife, Laura. In 1985, he and Gayfryd had a daughter of their own. Gayfryd's son from her former marriage (whom Steinberg had adopted) lived with them, as did Steinberg's youngest son for most of the year.

In the middle of the battle, a buoyant Steinberg addressed students at Wharton and spoke fondly of the market: "It's the largest gambling casino in the world. It continues to play an important part in my life as well as my family's, as we have $400 to $500 million in equities at all times and we make a lot of money on them. . . . I love what I do and I have to say it is really a lot of fun."

Two days later, he extracted $11 million in greenmail profits from Quaker. It served as a warm-up for his raid on Mickey Mouse.

If ever there was a company that Steinberg thought could profit from his expertise and thereby make him an even richer man, it was Walt Disney Productions — a conclusion he came to after his research staff prepared a profile of Disney's extremely valuable assets. The theme parks, Disneyland and Disney World, were estimated to be worth as much as $2 billion, the company's film and program library might fetch another $1 billion, and Disney held underused or totally unused properties, such as the seventeen thousand acres of raw land surrounding Disney World in Florida. None of these assets were reflected in the price of Disney's shares, which were falling as earnings dropped 10 percent in 1983. The message was clear: Disney was vulnerable to a takeover.

"I think that this was a know-nothing, do-nothing management," Steinberg said years later. "I thought they were rather stupid but maybe hardworking. In fact, what we found out afterwards was that they were stupid and lazy, which is the worst combination of all."

From March through May of 1984, his Reliance Group kept raising its stake in Disney until it owned some 4 million shares. It was the same strategy that he had employed in the past.

As its primary defensive maneuver, Disney — which traditionally carried little debt and had never made an acquisition — negotiated to buy other companies and to issue new stock so that Steinberg's shares would be diluted.* The frantic search for acquisitions was code-named "Project Fantasy."

Those moves only angered Steinberg, who viewed them as additional examples of Disney's incompetent management. As he wielded his financial and legal guns, Disney began reinforcing its barricades around the Magic Kingdom. The hostilities escalated into a major battle, which prompted Steinberg to enlist the help of Drexel

---

* Disney purchased Florida-based Arvida, a real estate development company, for $200 million in stock.

Burnham Lambert's Mike Milken. Milken had just demonstrated the potential of junk bond financing for a hostile takeover in T. Boone Pickens's raid on Gulf Oil. The mere threat of deploying junk bonds as a weapon had chased the nation's ninth-largest company into the arms of a white knight, Socal, in what was then the largest takeover ever — $13 billion. Pickens lost, but he also won: he and his backers emerged with a profit of $750 million by selling Socal the Gulf stock they already owned. Such lucrative corporate raids landed Pickens on the cover of *Time* magazine. Life in the fast lane became associated with doing deals in the eighties. None traveled faster than Steinberg; a few months later he took junk bond financing of hostile takeovers to a new level.

Steinberg had known Milken and his Drexel associates for a long time. In fact, the previous year Reliance and Drexel had formed a special investment partnership. Now they were ready to operate on a much larger scale. They decided that they needed $2.4 billion for the Disney takeover. Steinberg figured that Reliance's investment portfolio and other sources could take on nearly a billion of the total package, while Drexel could raise the remaining $1.5 billion from investors. For Drexel's portion of the war chest, Steinberg promised to pay investors a 1 percent commitment fee for the use of their capital. Once Milken told prospective investors that, the money poured in.

On Friday June 8, Saul Steinberg made his tender offer for Disney. Petrified by the amount of money Mike Milken and his investor group had put at Steinberg's disposal, Disney's management became obsessed with finding a way to stop him. They turned to lawyer Joe Flom, who led the Disney legal team and was prepared to meet Steinberg head-on with the only defense that had a chance: a "poison pill." Nothing else quite so drastic could be used by a corporation under siege. In fact, Flom himself had spoken out against the poison pill, saying it unfairly prevented corporations from making acquisitions.

Developed only a year earlier by his arch rival, Marty Lipton, the poison pill was a ploy by a target that could, in effect, bring about its self-destruction. In its brief history, it had achieved an excellent record of success in warding off unwelcome acquisitors. Flom's and Lipton's conflicting positions on the poison pill caused such unpleasantness between them that it undermined their long-standing friendship.

Despite his negative assessment of the poison pill, Flom was willing in this instance to use any measure to mount the best possible defense for his client. Through complicated maneuvering, he plotted to saddle Disney with an unbearable debt level if Steinberg's efforts to take over the company succeeded.*

The prospect of the dreaded poison pill confronted Disney's management with a remedy that was almost as bad as the condition: being acquired by Saul Steinberg. But Steinberg had more than one string on his bow. Greenmail. A Flom lieutenant, Donald Drapkin, had reason to believe — from a conversation with an unnamed source close to Steinberg — that for the right price Steinberg would leave Disney alone. That was not a choice Disney wanted to face. But given the hole into which management had dug itself, paying off Steinberg now seemed the only possible alternative to a takeover.

Friday evening, Drapkin called Laurence Tisch, chairman of Loews and a friend of Steinberg's, and Tisch, in turn, called Steinberg, who was relaxing at his giant white country home in Quogue, Long Island, that resembled a luxurious ocean liner. Tisch relayed the news that Disney was "out of control." If Steinberg refused to sell the stock back to the company, Tisch told him, then Disney would "do dangerous and stupid things."

Here was the perfect face-saving opportunity for Steinberg to be bought out. If Disney was a company gone berserk and was ready to swallow a poison pill, there was, after all, no taint in not pushing farther — particularly since, by selling his stock back to Disney, he would walk away with $60 million more than he had paid for it. No investor, Steinberg could argue, could blame him this time for accepting greenmail.

A lot of money would be paid to greenmailers in the future.

\* \* \*

Despite his identification as a greenmailer, in many ways Steinberg changed with his marriage to Gayfryd. She had a calming and stabilizing influence on him. Not only was she committed to providing a happy home life for their blended family, she was determined to

---

\* Steinberg's offer came in two parts. He would pay stockholders $67.50 a share in cash until he owned 49 percent of Disney. Then he would buy the other 51 percent by issuing junk bonds of uncertain value. Flom wanted to borrow $2 billion so that Disney could buy 51 percent of the stock, then retire it, thereby leaving Steinberg with 100 percent of the outstanding shares, ownership of Disney, and the unfortunate burden of $2 billion in debt.

establish a niche for Steinberg and herself in New York Society and to play a serious role in philanthropy.

Perhaps because she was Canadian and new to the social scene, in the eyes of certain entrenched New York hostesses she seemed at first to be trying too hard. One well-known socialite, who attended a ladies' tea at the Steinberg residence and was greeted by the hostess dressed in a long mousseline gown with diamond bracelets wrapped around both wrists, commented: "She was very nice, but she'll learn in time that she doesn't have to bring out her artillery in the afternoon."

Gayfryd Steinberg was learning. She could command a table at Le Cirque, New York's most fashionable restaurant for lunch, "anytime I want." As a patroness of Scaasi, couturier to her generation of party-going women, she was frequently reported on in the fashion press. She made a lasting impression in the social philanthropic world as cohost in April 1987 of a glamorous $750 a ticket black-tie benefit at the Metropolitan Club, an exclusive Wasp bastion, for a very needy and worthy organization that had never benefited from such an event before. The recipient was the PEN American Center, a nonprofit organization of writers that fights for freedom of expression as well as other causes.

Though outside the mainstream of society, PEN was an undervalued social asset, to paraphrase a term Steinberg often used to describe his financial investments. It was also the special interest of Gayfryd, who had been working diligently for several years to raise money for it. The benefit brought together what the *New York Times* called "the literati and the glitterati."

Among those present were some of America's most celebrated writers, including Norman Mailer, Arthur Miller, William Styron, Kurt Vonnegut, Joyce Carol Oates, Joan Didion, and E. L. Doctorow. New York's power brokers, celebrities, and philanthropists — old and new — flocked to the event. Hobnobbing with the writers were banker Henry Kravis and his wife, fashion designer Carolyne Roehm, Brooke Astor, Donald Trump, Patricia Lawford, Shearson's Peter Cohen, and Calvin Klein. The novelty of the event gave a special lift to the evening. The Steinbergs had raised $250,000 for a worthy cause and scored one of the social coups of the year. "Anything that enriches and enhances literature is very positive," writer Joyce Carol Oates said later. "I have good memories of the Steinbergs."

When the Steinbergs adopted a fifth-grade class in a Harlem school, whose college tuition they would eventually pay, she visited the children weekly and sometimes took them on outings to the country. She sat in 1988 on the undergraduate executive board of her husband's alma mater, the Wharton School. One magazine saw her as the logical successor to the doyenne of the ancien régime, Brooke Astor, and she also won the accolade of "queen of Nouvelle Society."

To some, her crowning achievement in the realm of New York Society was the lavish wedding reception she arranged in the spring of 1988 for the marriage of Laura Steinberg, daughter of her husband and his first wife, Barbara, to Jonathan Tisch, son of Preston Robert Tisch, president and co-chief executive officer of the Loews Corporation and former postmaster general of the United States (and nephew of Laurence Tisch, now chief of CBS as well as Loews chairman). The cost was rumored to be $2 million (which Gayfryd Steinberg denied and refused to discuss). The wedding joined two superrich Jewish families that in one generation had carved an exalted place for themselves in New York's twin worlds of high finance and new society. A ranking socialite remarked, "There has been nothing like it since a Vanderbilt married an Astor." At the couple's engagement party the previous year, a family member had quipped, "If they get married, it will have to be cleared by the SEC."

Planning for the wedding, largely carried out by Gayfryd with Laura's help, began more than a year in advance. Everything had been thought out, down to the most minute detail. The function was scheduled for Monday, April 18, when the Metropolitan Museum of Art was closed, so that extensive preparations could be completed for the reception and dinner that were to be held there. (Reliance was a corporate patron of the Museum and Steinberg had personally donated millions of dollars.) The previous evening, some seventy men worked double time to transform the Museum's Great Hall and restaurant into a glamorous French Directoire setting.

The wedding day dawned chilly and rainy, but that didn't impede the festivities. Several hours before the ceremony, limousines brought family members and attendants to Central Synagogue, where their carefully pressed clothes and accessories were ready. Hairdressers with blow dryers and hair spray were on hand, along with makeup artists and a manicurist, to provide the finishing touches.

Even the landmark Moorish-style synagogue had been embellished. Spotlights illuminated the East Fifty-fifth Street entrance, creating the illusion of sunlight streaming through the stained-glass windows. The radiant bride, who walked down the aisle escorted by her father, wore a Scaasi draped off-the-shoulder off-white taffeta dress delicately embroidered in a Tudor flowered design of white silk threads outlined in gold and a seven-foot train, along with a tulle veil held in place by a diamond and pearl tiara. Gayfryd Steinberg was dressed in a Galanos two-piece outfit: a fitted beige lace jacket — embroidered with beads — over a strapless floor-length gown. The ten bridesmaids were attired in Scaasi off-white moiré dresses shot with gold, young women from both families were flower girls, and Laura's two young half brothers served as ring bearers, carrying satin pillows that Gayfryd Steinberg had decorated herself.

The Reform Jewish ceremony was performed under a *chuppah* (canopy) fashioned of antique bronze palms installed for the occasion. The altar was banked with masses of white lilies, glowing candelabra wrapped with garlands of flowers, and Jewish antiquities lent by the Steinbergs.

After the service, attended largely by family members and close friends, a fleet of limousines ferried the wedding party to the reception at the Metropolitan Museum, to which some 500 people had been invited. Tuxedo-clad attendants holding umbrellas escorted the arrivals at the Fifth Avenue entrance up the steep bank of steps to the Museum's Great Hall. The information desk, camouflaged with trompe l'oeil painted dressmaker's muslin to simulate limestone, had been turned into a champagne bar. A row of female harpists draped in ivory satin togas played on gold-painted harps adorned with white garlands. Abundant pink-and-white floral displays of French tulips, roses, and branches of dogwood and quince — ordered by party florist Robert Isabell — filled the permanent hexagonal-shaped planting beds surrounded by benches, now covered in ivory fabric trimmed with tassels, situated at each end of the hall.

The grand staircase leading to the second floor was bathed in a pale blue light that filtered down to potted white tulips arranged at the foot of the stairs — providing a striking backdrop for the receiving line. Among those being greeted were some of the most famous names in the spheres of business, entertainment, real estate, fashion, art, and society: Donald and Ivana Trump, Prince Albert of Monaco, Beverly Sills, Norman Mailer and his wife, Norris Church, Barbara Walters, Lord Weidenfeld, Carolyne Roehm and Henry Kravis, Helen Gurley Brown, Lewis Rudin, Eric de Rothschild, Vartan Gregorian, David Mahoney, Carter Burden, Leonard Lauder, Liz Smith, Tina Brown, and New Crowd members Sandy Weill, Peter Cohen, "Ace" Greenberg, and Martin Lipton — and others.

At 8:30 trumpeters in white medieval costumes summoned the guests to dinner. The walls of the Museum's restaurant were covered in cream-colored muslin fabric and hung with wreaths painstakingly fashioned of hundreds of hand-dipped gilded magnolia leaves. An all-white carpet had been laid for the evening. The tables were draped and swagged in cloth trimmed with rosettes and tassels. Lush arrangements of peonies and other flowers formed the centerpieces. At the far end of the room an area had been squared off into a trompe l'oeil marble dance floor decorated with a leaf-and-bow border, wreaths in the four corners, and a central wreath entwined with the couple's monogram. "It was like walking into a fantasy world," according to one guest.

A battalion of staff kept everything flowing smoothly. The guests dined on poached salmon in champagne aspic, trio of veal, lamb, and chicken, orzo with porcini mushrooms, and spring vegetables produced by society caterer Glorious Food, and a seven-foot-high Grand Marnier wedding cake festooned with sugar flowers prepared by the dean of such confections, Sylvia Weinstock. They drank vintage wines — Corton Charlemagne, Château Latour, and Roederer Cristal Champagne — all from Saul Steinberg's private collection.

Between courses, they danced to the music of Hank Lane's orchestra and to a spirited rendition of the traditional Jewish wedding music for joining hands to dance the hora. The bride and groom were enthusiastically lifted in chairs and carried around the room — a general custom at Jewish weddings.

Making the only toast of the evening, a glowing Saul Steinberg congratulated the newlyweds and thanked Gayfryd for planning such a memorable party.

"The most beautiful wedding I've seen since Grace Kelly married Prince Rainier," was the comment of Ann Siegel, wife of Chris-Craft mogul Herb Siegel and a friend of the late princess. It was discussed and written about for months, receiving the kind of attention that had for previous generations of the newly rich established their social presence.

The Steinbergs had demonstrated what wealth, energy, and savvy could accomplish in the social sphere, just as Saul had demonstrated what those attributes could accomplish in the financial sphere.

# CHAPTER TWENTY-FIVE

# Squeeze at the Top

P eter Cohen sensed the opportunity to capture a prize for Shearson, one that included in its package an acquisition that had eluded Sandy Weill seven years earlier. Before going to bed on Friday evening, March 30, 1984, he picked up the current issue of *Fortune* and read a brief article about Lehman Brothers that began: "In Lewis Glucksman's first six months as head of Lehman Brothers Kuhn Loeb, the firm became so deeply split that the board decided to sell it." The article went on to note that seven potential buyers had already decided to pass on the troubled firm. Cohen could have easily done the same.

At thirty-seven, Peter Cohen had little to prove. He was powerful and secure and had more money than he had ever known in his life. The previous year, with an income of $1.2 million, he had surpassed the salaries and bonuses of every other American Express executive, including Robinson and Weill.

He had always lived comfortably, but, in a process which could be called "leveraging up," he was now living graciously. From a two-and-a-half-room apartment in Brooklyn Heights, the Cohen family had moved into a two-bedroom apartment on Manhattan's East Side and, eventually, into a luxurious eight-room co-op on Park Avenue. (In 1987, the Cohens would move again, to a thirteen-room co-op on Fifth Avenue with a spectacular view of Central Park.) They also had a four-acre weekend estate in East Hampton, Long Island, not far from the valuable acres of beachfront property belonging to Bruce Wasserstein. Hidden from view, the Cohens' strikingly modern copper-roofed, glass-walled stone structure consisted of two parts separated by a kitchen and entrance that formed a bridge over a decorative pool and waterfall. The estate, with its man-made pond and vegetable garden, was Peter Cohen's escape from Wall Street. He spent most of his time there unwinding with his wife, Karen, and their two children, Lauren and Andrew, working in the garden, or building furniture.

The Cohens were part of an affluent Hampton social set composed primarily of Jewish businessmen and their wives in their midthirties to midforties who played tennis together and went to one another's cocktail parties, buffet dinners, and clambakes. It included Jeffrey Keil, president of Republic Bank and Bruce Wasserstein. On weekends Peter Cohen made an effort to put the pressures of running Shearson aside. But some business opportunities couldn't be ignored. Lehman Brothers Kuhn Loeb was one of them. Weekend or not, Peter Cohen appreciated the necessity of remaining involved with his work.

Even as a boy growing up in middle-class ease on Long Island, Cohen had displayed an unusual passion for work. Every Saturday, he assembled cardboard boxes for $1.50 an hour at the Brooklyn factory of his father, Sidney, founder of Andover Togs, one of the largest manufacturers of children's clothes. His choice of work over play proved helpful. A bicycle-fall injury when he was twelve aggravated a congenital bone defect and forced him to spend two years on crutches, keeping him from much of the usual social and athletic activities of the early teen years.

If he could have had things his way, he would have gone to work at Andover Togs after high school, but his father insisted that he attend college. At Ohio State University, Cohen, a business administration major, realized he could make money supplying beer to fraternities. The venture was so lucrative that he could afford to buy a Corvette in his favorite color for a car — midnight blue.

After he obtained an MBA at Columbia University, father and son sat down to discuss his salary at the family factory. When they couldn't agree on a figure, Peter Cohen headed for Wall Street. Two years as a securities analyst for Reynolds & Co. led to his job with the growing research department of CBWL-Hayden Stone, to his relationship with Sandy Weill, and to his becoming head of Shearson. The acquisition of Lehman Brothers would be a milestone for him and his brokerage.

* * *

Lewis Glucksman, the man *Fortune* had cited as contributing to the split at Lehman, was, for all his success, still engaged in a titanic personal struggle. The trader who for years had been at war with the world still numbered among his enemies the Wasp Establishment, Our Crowd, and the Lehman investment bankers and chairman Pete Peterson. His hatred for what he considered their arrogance and prejudice had never abated.

In recognition of his contribution to Lehman Brothers, Peterson had named him president in 1981; as far as Glucksman was concerned, it was five years too late. He felt he should have been given the job in 1976, when Peterson had taken the title for himself and kept it even when his work load grew following the acquisition of Kuhn Loeb in 1977. Title or not, Glucksman had assumed more and more responsibility in the firm, which was making an excellent profit. When the books closed in September for 1981, it had reached a record $118 million in pretax earnings.

Lehman was among the leaders in mergers and acquisitions largely through the efforts of partners Eric Gleacher and Stephen Schwarzman and was once again competing with the most successful Wall Street houses in underwriting, after falling out of the race in the midseventies. But the real star was Glucksman's trading department, which earned more than the entire banking operation put together.

Although earnings were piling up, the partners couldn't withdraw the money they had made. Even more frustrating, the capital structure, which the partners had designed themselves, was not bringing them the best possible return on their money — a source of embarrassment to men who prided themselves on their considerable financial acumen. They speculated on where the firm would fit in the age of the superbroker. Its total capital — twelfth on Wall Street in 1981 — might leave it too big to fill a specialty niche and too small to compete with the largest houses in the future. They also speculated on how much Lehman could fetch if it were acquired. In February 1982, rumors blew hot that a group of investors led by Harold Geneen was interested in buying the firm for some $600 million.

But by December, nothing had happened. Eric Gleacher of Lehman arranged a meeting with his former brother-in-law, Sherman Lewis, Shearson's president; Peter Solomon, an important Lehman executive; Peter Cohen, who in a few weeks would take over Sandy Weill's job as chief executive of Shearson; and Herbert Freiman, a Shearson executive. The purpose was to probe Shearson's interest in acquiring Lehman. Secrecy was of utmost concern. Neither Peterson, chairman of Lehman, nor its president, Glucksman, was informed before or afterward of the meeting. The quintet went out to dinner at a quiet Italian restaurant in Brooklyn to make sure no one from Wall Street would spot them.

Ironically, the possibility of acquiring Kuhn Loeb — the firm

Sandy Weill had wanted so badly — and the whole Lehman package didn't interest Cohen at the time. In a bull market, he would have to pay a steep price, and the acquisition might prove to be more trouble than it was worth. Shearson was a retail firm, very much an informal operation, whereas Lehman was a traditional Our Crowd investment bank still run by its proud and haughty investment banking partners. But perhaps his greatest reservation concerned the prospect of having to deal with Glucksman and Peterson — both willful, ego-driven men.

Cohen, considered something of a Wall Street wunderkind, had other goals in mind. He was working on the biggest deal of his life then: the pursuit of Edmond Safra's Trade Development Bank. The dinner ended with a flat no.

\* \* \*

The promotion to president of Lehman didn't satisfy Glucksman. He still had his eye on the top spot, chief executive. By 1983 his resentment was about to spill over. He was going to take what he thought was rightfully his, and he wasn't going to let anyone stand in the way, especially Pete Peterson.

In May Peterson named Glucksman co-chief executive, in response to mounting pressure from Glucksman for greater recognition. Among the board members the once strong opposition to Glucksman was long gone, and by then he virtually managed Lehman. The promotion seemed inevitable.

From Peterson's viewpoint he was being generous by making Glucksman co-CEO. Glucksman, on the other hand, saw the promotion as simply "acknowledging the actual position I had had for a long time." Far apart as they were in their thinking, for the moment the two chiefs and most of the senior executives could live with the arrangement.

But before long the tensions between the two men became disruptive. Their differences served to widen the division between the firm's traders and bankers. In July, the situation exploded.

As told in Ken Auletta's book, *Greed and Glory on Wall Street,* the trigger was a luncheon given by John Carter, chief executive officer of the Equitable life insurance company. Peterson was invited to speak and in turn suggested Glucksman also attend, in case they could interest Carter in a joint venture of some kind. They arrived separately at Equitable's private dining room high atop a midtown skyscraper, greeted each other perfunctorily, and mingled with the other seven guests prior to sitting down to dine. Glucksman began to seethe as soon as they were seated: Peterson was at the head of the table, next to Carter, while Glucksman was parked at the other end in what he considered "the bleachers." Then he had to sit through "the speech," as Glucksman derisively referred to the talk Peterson gave on the burgeoning federal deficit, in which he managed to work in, on a first-name basis, references to his friends Henry (Kissinger, former secretary of state), Paul (Volcker, then chairman of the Federal Reserve), and Art (Buchwald, the columnist). Glucksman lowered his head, played with his silverware, and banged his chair closer to the table.

The next day an extremely agitated Glucksman met with Peterson and in a conversation lasting five hours made it clear that he wanted the chief executive's job for himself and implied that he had the support of the board. Peterson was astounded. He found it hard to believe that Glucksman thought he could run Lehman alone. He suspected that Glucksman was bluffing about having the board's support, but he couldn't be certain, and he didn't have the stomach for a fight.* He suggested that George Ball, who had retired from the firm, serve as mediator. The fissure between them was so great that Ball, the former ambassador to the United Nations, was forced to talk to each man separately.

Peterson desperately wanted to stay on for a few years until he turned sixty, but Glucksman wouldn't stand for it. His only recourse, Peterson decided, was to accept a generous severance settlement. On July 25, the board members were stunned by the news, as were all the partners when they heard it at a general meeting the next day. In the interest of the firm, Peterson made an effort to be supportive of Glucksman, but Glucksman was savoring the moment he had waited for so long and asked Peterson to leave the room.

Glucksman would officially take over the CEO job on October 1 and the chairman's post on January 2. After swimming against the tide for thirty-six years, the fifty-seven-year-old Lew Glucksman finally had achieved his goal.

As soon as he ousted Peterson in July, he made his presence felt, departing from precedent by allocating bigger bonuses to the trad-

---

* Peterson had been through a series of traumatic experiences in recent years — surgery in 1977 for a brain tumor that was benign and a difficult divorce. He later married Joan Ganz Cooney, the producer of the popular children's TV program "Sesame Street," who subsequently underwent surgery for breast cancer.

ers than the bankers, some of whom even found their partnership percentages cut back. By the fall Glucksman's people headed most departments. Without consulting anyone, he appointed as president of the firm his closest ally, Robert S. Rubin, a dour banker with limited management experience, and as head of investment banking, he chose Sheldon Gordon, a diplomatic, capable executive whose career had been largely in sales and trading, rather than in investment banking.

A growing number of partners began to bridle under Glucksman's autocratic rule, comparing him to Captain Ahab, Captain Queeg, and Richard Nixon. Six left, taking with them their capital. Glucksman's way of conducting himself didn't help: he saw himself as "the toughest guy on the Street."

He claimed the changes taking place in his personal life had nothing to do with his ascendancy at Lehman, but they coincided. He was in the process of shedding both his wife of twenty-six years and his excess weight. Still short and heavy, at least he could no longer be called obese. He bought more conservative, expensive new clothes to replace the ill-fitting ones of old, a sporty Chrysler convertible, a house in East Hampton with a flag out front that read "Don't Tread on Me," and a five-room co-op in the luxurious Museum Towers atop the Museum of Modern Art in Manhattan, where apartments sold for between $500,000 and $5 million. With his homes in Florida and New Jersey, where he kept pleasure boats, he now had four residences, not counting the one his ex-wife and two daughters lived in on the Upper East Side of Manhattan.

The changes in his personal life didn't change Glucksman's style at Lehman. In response to the unhappiness of the executives about Lehman's management and its bonus system, he made a strategic decision that would prove unwise for him. He set up a bonus compensation committee to meet on its own without him. At the first meeting, the talk turned to a forbidden subject, the sale of Lehman Brothers. From that point on, the committee set out independently and secretly to find a buyer. Those efforts — combined with growing financial losses that made the capital issue urgent, the unstable climate at Lehman Brothers among the bickering partners, and Glucksman's failure to be a diplomatically effective leader — all brought matters to a climax.

*  *  *

The morning after he read the *Fortune* article that had piqued his interest in acquiring Lehman Brothers Kuhn Loeb, Peter Cohen returned from a trip to the supermarket with his wife and son, fighting a bad cold and feeling terrible. As the station wagon pulled into the driveway, he saw his neighbor Steve Schwarzman waiting for him.

"I want to talk to you about the firm," the Lehman executive began. Sensing that Schwarzman wanted to talk to him about Shearson's acquiring Lehman, Cohen replied, "I read the [*Fortune*] article last night."

"Well, can you buy it now?"

"Why would I want to buy it?" Cohen asked. "What do I get? I'm interested, but tell me why."

For the next two hours they weighed the arguments for and against Shearson's taking over Lehman, and the potential timing of such a deal. In 1982 the price for Lehman Brothers would have been too steep, but in early 1984 Cohen was in a better position to bargain. The great bull market had been dealt a sharp blow by a renewed bout of inflation, and Lehman was hurting. Schwarzman told Cohen that the situation at Lehman was chaotic. The time to approach Glucksman was now.

"Call him," Schwarzman advised. "Tell him you read the article. Don't tell him you spoke to me, because he hates me, but I'll make sure people know, so he won't be able to hide it."

Over the weekend Cohen consulted with a few of the Shearson executives, who felt the acquisition would make sense, provided Glucksman wouldn't be a factor in the combined firm. On Monday, Cohen obtained a go-ahead from Jim Robinson and Sandy Weill. He then called Glucksman.

* * *

Glucksman had read the *Fortune* article and had found it "scurrilous." While he recognized the need for a capital infusion, he fumed at what he saw as his Lehman brethren's "open-mouth policy" with the press and deplored their greed in wanting to sell out in order to grab all their money. He felt he had "more money" than he "would ever need" and the people on Wall Street, including himself, were "the most overpaid people relative to the value of the service provided."

The *Fortune* article, he felt, had made his position untenable. "I had an obligation to act quickly," he said years later, "before any damage could be done, which was a shame."

When Cohen phoned him, Glucksman agreed to a meeting to discuss the possible sale of Lehman Brothers Kuhn Loeb. It was the toughest decision he had been forced to make in his brief reign as chairman.

On Tuesday, April 3, he found himself sitting in Jim Robinson's private dining room at a breakfast meeting with several of his Lehman partners and an American Express contingent that included Robinson, Cohen, and Weill. Looking around the table, Glucksman thought: "This is the best of a bad bunch."

The following day he quickly removed the last major obstacle to the deal. He knew what was expected of him. "Look, I'll make it easy for you," he told Cohen. "You don't have to worry about me and Bob Rubin. We won't work for American Express." Now Cohen and Glucksman could begin talking about price.

That night, at a meeting in Cohen's office in the World Trade Center, the Lehman people asked the Shearson team for a firm proposal. The Shearson group, which left the room to talk over the deal, spent no more than five minutes. "Why are we wasting our time," Dwight Faulkner said. "We know we want to do this." Sherman Lewis echoed that sentiment. "We're deal junkies. It's time for a fix."

The American Express board met on Tuesday, April 10, and approved the purchase of Lehman Brothers for $360 million. Lewis Glucksman's shares in Lehman Brothers netted him more than $15 million personally. Having reigned for a mere 101 days as chairman and chief executive of the only firm for which he had ever wanted to work, Glucksman was gone. And after 134 years in business, Lehman Brothers, the proud Our Crowd firm, was history. A new chapter had started on Wall Street for Shearson.

*　*　*

Until the acquisition of Lehman Brothers, Shearson was trailing well behind Merrill Lynch in retail brokerage. Among the other giant nationwide firms that had dominated the retail business during the Go-Go Years, only Dean Witter, E. F. Hutton, Bache, and Paine Webber had survived with their businesses relatively secure in the mideighties. Yet none had done more than that.

Bache might not have lasted if Prudential Insurance hadn't acquired it (it was renamed Prudential-Bache Securities). Almost at once Harry Jacobs was bounced from the position of chief executive (while remaining chairman) in favor of Hutton alumnus George Ball. Ball began rebuilding Bache from the ground up with Prudential money. Virtually single-handedly Ball restructured Wall Street salaries by launching a bidding war for talent.

Hutton chief Robert Fomon (Ball's former boss and the man who had stood between him and the top spot at Hutton) was angered that Ball was raiding executives from other firms and complained to Prudential. But the real problem for Hutton, which had remained independent, was the competition from retail brokerage houses that had found rich benefactors. In selling out to Sears in 1981, Dean Witter had bounded past Hutton in terms of capital, number of offices, and number of employees. Independently operated Paine Webber, the fourth member of the quartet, fell behind Bache in size, even after completing two substantial acquisitions.

For all these houses, the prize was a greater market share of the bull market. In both size and earnings, Shearson now had more in common with Merrill Lynch than with the other four. By the end of 1984, Shearson boasted $1.9 billion in capital and $103 million in earnings compared to Merrill Lynch's $2.2 billion and $95 million in earnings. Shearson could also now lay claim to being the only other retail firm besides Merrill that was a major investment banking house. (But in some ways Merrill had been going through difficult times of late and would have its third chief executive in three years. After Donald Regan had left the firm to become President Reagan's chief of staff, his replacement, Roger Birk, was soon ousted in favor of William Schreyer.)

Shearson's future looked even more promising. Its management was stable; Peter Cohen had a lock on his position as chief.

# CHAPTER TWENTY-SIX

# Solemn John

The internal tensions that John Gutfreund and Billy Salomon had fostered at Salomon Brothers were more readily evident now that the company had to answer to a board of directors and to shareholders. While the sale of Salomon Brothers to Phibro in the fall of 1981 brought together two groups of successful Street-smart traders, from the moment the papers were signed, the union was headed for trouble.

Neither Gutfreund nor anyone else at Salomon thought in terms of forming fast or lasting alliances. That notion ran counter to the combative and competitive spirit that had enabled the Salomon partners to succeed in the first place. In truth, Salomon hadn't married Phibro; it had agreed only to live under the commodities broker's roof. Given all they seemed to have in common, the two sides thought they could coexist peacefully. Instead the combination known as Phibro-Salomon proved incendiary. After the merger, Salomon Brothers was having trouble enough preserving old loyalties in what was now a public company.

Former partner Edgar Aronson, who had left the firm in 1979, sued for $4.5 million, alleging that he had been paid less than his fair share of profits from the firm's lucrative oil-and-gas venture in the Gulf of Mexico. Another former partner, Vincent Murphy, sued for the $1.25 million limited partners received from the merger with Phibro, claiming he had been illegally denied his share. In addition, several top partners left soon after the sale, among them Richard Rosenthal, the high-strung arb who departed presumably because of ill health. Then the independent-minded legendary dealmaker Ira Harris suddenly stepped down from the executive committee. The moves by Rosenthal and Harris, who had played key roles in the Phibro-Salomon merger, seemed like an open rebuke of the deal — coming less than two years after its completion. And Billy Salomon remained on the sidelines, still carping that the merger had been a terrible mistake.

As Salomon Brothers distanced itself from its new owners, tensions increased between the two sides, tensions that soon became the talk of the financial press. Rumors began to circulate that Salomon Brothers wanted to undo the Phibro merger. Gutfreund told *Fortune* that the speculations were "nonsense," but he didn't have nice things to say about the rule of David Tendler, who was chief executive of the merged firm, or about the commodities business. "It's been a very difficult year for Philipp Brothers," he stated. By contrast, Salomon was responsible for most of the corporation's combined earnings — $337 million — except that its record-high profits were being funneled now into Phibro-Salomon Inc and not to the Salomon partners. Something had to give. Gutfreund seemed primed for a shakeup in the company.

\* \* \*

After they moved into their renovated River House duplex, the Gutfreunds had a showplace for lavish parties. Throughout the duplex, marble was used extravagantly — in the entranceway, in the butler's pantry, and in the vast master bathroom with its cavernous circular tub, twin Jacuzzi, and mirrored ceiling, causing one Society wag to dub the apartment "marble minimalist." The guests were entertained in the two-story, starkly modern living room adorned with French and Russian antiques and boasting a Robert Adam rug that reportedly cost a million dollars. Exotic, expensive orchid plants adorned the apartment, and fresh flowers were always in full display. In the early days of her marriage to Gutfreund, Susan threw a lot of theme parties. One was what she referred to as "a Proustian evening." Elaborate gilt candelabra adorned each table, and bouquets of herbs were tied to the back of each chair. A staff of five kept the social whirl humming at the seemingly nonstop succession of dinners and parties.

The regulars included Mica and Ahmet Ertegun, Chessy and William Rayner, Oscar de la Renta, Sid and Anne Bass, William and Donna Acquavella, and Hollywood agent Swifty Lazar. Susan Gutfreund didn't need to know someone well to host an event in his or her honor. For her new friend, heiress Patricia Cisneros, she threw an impromptu birthday party with balloons decorated with fresh orchids and a cake in the shape of a gift box festooned with a glistening sugar bow.

There were to be so many of these evenings that Gutfreund once quipped to a friend, "When I come home, I have to ask Susan, 'Who's coming for dinner?' It doesn't matter if I ask her because I don't know most of them."

But there was more to the social whirl than compulsive enter-taining. It represented a determined effort on Susan Gutfreund's part to boost her husband and herself into New York Society through social networking on the highest level.

Her first social forays were promising enough. In September of 1982, she became a member of the Citizens Committee for New York City, a service organization providing financial aid to the city's neighborhood associations that brought together many prominent New York men and women who shared a common interest in revitalizing the city. Among the other women who belonged to the Citizen's Committee were Marietta Tree, socialite Blanchette Rockefeller, dress de-signer Mollie Parnis, and Carol Sulzberger, wife of *New York Times* publisher Arthur Ochs Sulzberger.

Susan Gutfreund hosted a luncheon for the Citizens Committee at her home. The table was set with Royal Copenhagen china, Bohe-mian hand-engraved crystal glasses from the estate of the late heiress Barbara Hutton, seventeenth-century German silver flatware, hand-embroidered linens, and an elaborate centerpiece of orchids, which had become Susan's signature flower.

Through an accident of good timing, Gutfreund was able to complement his wife's efforts. Since 1974, he had been a trustee of the renowned New York Public Library, whose financial resources were at a low ebb. In the fall of 1981, the library held its first Literary Lion black-tie fund-raiser. Twenty patrons, each of whom contributed $10,000 for a table, played dinner hosts to some 200 guests, including such noted authors as Norman Mailer, Lillian Hellman, Robert Penn Warren, and Louis Auchincloss, along with former and future first ladies Jacqueline Onassis, Lady Bird Johnson, and Barbara Bush. The gala was a smash success and instantly became one of the highlights of the New York social calendar, comparable to fund-raisers held on behalf of such preeminent recipients of High Society largesse as the Metro-politan Museum of Art, the Metropolitan Opera, and Memorial Sloan-Kettering Cancer Center — which in the past hadn't welcomed new Jewish money on their boards of directors. The second annual Literary Lions dinner was sold out well in advance, and the Gutfreunds were again patrons of one of the coveted tables, which put them in the midst of the old monied crowd.

Their frequent appearance on the society circuit earned the stiff, unsmiling Gutfreund the nickname of "Solemn John." (His wife was called "Social Susie.") Yet he seemed to enjoy being at the center of this social scene. According to one friend, "Before he married Susan, John had led a staid, conventional life. Now he was meeting famous,

elegant, and dazzling rich people. He found that interesting and fun."
He accompanied Susan on shopping trips not only around town but
also in Europe. As he later told one magazine writer, "She collects
things. I don't. She's enriched my life." His wife took care of everything, the furnishings and the friends. The trouble started over the
former.

Late in the fall of 1982, Susan Gutfreund met one of her upstairs
neighbors for the first time. Joan Postel, an opera singer, lived in the
penthouse above the Gutfreund's apartment with her husband Robert,
a lawyer, real estate developer, and former city councilman, and their
young son, Darren. The two families shared a common space — the
twenty-fourth-floor hallway landing on the Gutfreund's lower floor.
From this landing the Postels had to climb five steps to an elevator that
took them up to their apartment. One day the two women encountered
each other on the landing. Both were slim, attractive, and in their
midthirties. Susan Gutfreund ignored Joan Postel. There seemed no
provocation for this haughty treatment or for what the Postels' son
told his parents that Susan Gutfreund had said to him — that he didn't
deserve to live at River House because he was "from the wrong side
of the tracks." The two families retreated into opposing camps. By
Christmas, the Gutfreunds and the Postels would engage in a battle
royal.

The fight centered around a Christmas tree. It wasn't just any
Christmas tree. Susan Gutfreund was determined to have a special one
for the holidays. Very important guests would be coming, including
Felix Rohatyn and Saul Steinberg. She called on the florist ZeZe, who
located a magnificent twenty-two-foot Douglas fir from the same
source that had provided the White House with two Christmas trees.
The Gutfreund tree weighed a quarter of a ton and cost $400. There
was one hitch. The tree simply wouldn't fit into the River House
elevator. Someone came up with a solution. It could be hoisted up the
side of the building by a crane mounted on the rooftop terrace belonging
to the Postels. Given Susan Gutfreund's frosty attitude toward her
neighbors, it wasn't surprising that she delegated the chore of asking
permission. Concerned about the possibility of an accident while the
tree was being hoisted, the Postels requested that the Gutfreunds obtain
insurance. No notice of insurance was received and no permission
granted, according to one source. Susan proceeded anyhow, without
the Postels' consent or knowledge.

The layout of the building made it relatively easy to use the
terrace. A fire stairway led to the roof. At the Postels' floor, the rear

fire door was often left open because their own apartment was undergoing massive renovations and their construction crew needed easy access to the apartment.

On the eighth of December, "operation Christmas tree" was launched. A Gutfreund scout, disguised as a Postel workman, was sent ahead to check that the coast was clear. Joan Postel caught him in her apartment. Her workmen were on a coffee break, and she was alarmed to find a man there who clearly was not one of her construction crew.

"Who are you?" she demanded.

"I'm a workman," he muttered.

"What's your name?" she said.

"I'm a workman," he repeated. "Just looking for some nails." Then he disappeared.

He returned soon, this time with eight confederates, including the building superintendent, who brought along the hoisting equipment. They worked quickly, setting up an outrigger pole with ropes and pulleys. The tree was hoisted up the side of the building and eased through the Gutfreund's twenty-fourth-floor window. (The fee for the job would be $3,000.)

During this entire maneuver Joan Postel had been posted behind her fire door, watching and listening. She had called the police. But the tree gang was about to make its escape. In a rage, she barred the way, assisted by her workmen, who had returned from their coffee break. A standoff ensued long enough for a patrolman to arrive. He made the Gutfreund's crew leave the premises immediately without removing their equipment.

A truce followed. It was, after all, the Christmas season. At their lavish holiday festivities, the Gutfreunds' tree dazzled their guests, including Jerome Zipkin (escort to Nancy Reagan and many socialites), Felix Rohatyn, and Saul Steinberg. It was decorated with magnificent satin ribbons, antique lace, and costumed dolls representing characters in Russian ballets. Orchids and mimosa hung from every branch. On Christmas day the resplendent Christmas dinner was highlighted by an appetizer of coral of scallops — scallop caviar.

The New Year saw no letdown. For Susan Gutfreund's thirty-seventh birthday in January, the Gutfreunds were treated to dinner by French designer Emanuel Ungaro; Susan Gutfreund bought his couture dresses in Paris.

Soon thereafter, new hostilities erupted between the Postels and the Gutfreunds, with Susan Gutfreund again taking the offensive. The renovations on their co-op finally completed, the Postels moved into River House. They soon discovered that Susan Gutfreund always turned off the light in front of the elevator that led to the Postel apartment. With the light out, the Gutfreunds' visitors exiting from the main elevator wouldn't know they hadn't reached the top of the building — in other words, the penthouse. Apparently, that pleased Susan Gutfreund. She reportedly told many people that she and her husband lived in the penthouse.

The struggle over who controlled the light switch continued until, one evening, Bob Postel stumbled and broke his toe on the darkened steps. In an effort to come to some resolution, a summit conference was arranged between the two husbands on Valentine's Day at the River Club located in the building. At the club, the two men talked politely, but nothing was resolved. There the matter rested for the time being. Postel's toe healed.

Meanwhile, Susan Gutfreund's extravagant style of entertaining became the talk of New York Society. At a dinner for Ungaro attended by twenty-three guests, she served chili, chicken, ribs, and monkey bread flown up from Angelo's, one of her favorite restaurants in Dallas. That was followed in May by the most exclusive of several sixtieth birthday parties for Henry Kissinger, their River House neighbor. Among the twenty-five guests seated at two large round tables were Mrs. Johnny Carson, Greek shipping magnate Stavros Niarchos, Lord Soames, and Yitzak Klabin, an extremely wealthy Latvian industrialist from Brazil. For dessert, the Gutfreunds' chef spun sugar into iridescent green apples, a technique, Susan Gutfreund announced, that he had acquired from the glassblowers of Murano, Italy.

That summer the Gutfreunds rented Blenheim Palace in England to entertain 350 of Salomon Brothers' clients and social acquaintances, including a few shipping magnates, dukes, and lords. Engraved invitations read, "Mr. and Mrs. John Gutfreund, At Home, Blenheim." Soon after, the party yielded social dividends. When Susan returned from London, she reportedly told friends that they had been entertained by, among others, publishing mogul Lord Weidenfeld.

With each step up the social ladder, there appeared to be a commensurate push up for Gutfreund in business. Salomon Brothers profited not only from the bull market but also from a 1982 regulation passed by the Securities and Exchange Commission. Commonly called Rule 415, the regulation permitted a corporation to register all the securities it planned to issue over the next two years and allowed that company to take the securities "off the shelf" whenever it saw an attractive window of opportunity in the marketplace.*

Rule 415 had been passed in response to the growing need on the part of corporate chieftains to compete in a volatile market environment. They wanted to be able to move quickly to take advantage of a sudden shift in interest rates, gold prices, and dollar values in the fast-changing climate of the eighties. Because it took days, if not weeks, to organize a syndicate, old-style investment banking had become less valuable to them. In short, the types of investment bankers who had made up the Wasp Establishment and Our Crowd had virtually been regulated out of business. Salomon metaphorically danced on their graves, marketing an incredible array of complex and imaginative securities — from zero-coupon bonds to mortgage-backed securities. Following the passage of Rule 415, Salomon came to dominate the underwriting field in the eighties in the way the aristocratic Morgan Stanley had during the Depression and the early postwar years. In 1983, the Gutfreund-led troops would underwrite nearly $13 billion worth of securities, $2 billion more than its nearest competitor, Merrill Lynch.

Gutfreund, nonetheless, seemed restless. It wasn't enough to be the most powerful financier on Wall Street if he couldn't take the reins and steer Phibro-Salomon in the direction he thought it should take. Phibro continued to perform miserably: its profits were only half what Salomon Brothers earned from one tenth as much revenues as its big brother.

* * *

When the Christmas season again arrived, Susan Gutfreund's social activities generated their own share of press coverage and gossip, and there was little Gutfreund could do to prevent it. She planned to bring another gigantic Douglas fir into their apartment, the same way she had done the previous year. On December 9, 1983, the Postels were notified that on the thirteenth of December the hoisters and riggers were once again scheduled to use the Postel terrace. Susan Gutfreund must have been shocked to learn on the twelfth of December that she and her husband — and River House — were being sued by the Postels

---

* For a few years prior to the passage of Rule 415, firms such as Salomon Brothers and First Boston had already done a number of underwritings that closely resembled the "shelf" issues. These were "bought" deals, meaning that one underwriter took on the entire issue itself.

for injunctive relief plus monetary damages of more than $35 million. Furthermore, she was being charged with terrorizing the Postels' son and with causing Robert Postel's broken toe, among other complaints. River House was in an uproar at the prospect of being sued, but that didn't sway the Gutfreunds from their plan to hoist a large tree into the apartment.

Because a temporary restraining order stopped them from sending their workers to the Postels' roof, the hoisting crew was forced to use the Gutfreunds' balcony instead. Susan Gutfreund complained that the job "necessitated the removal of almost all of our living room furniture as well as a window and door to get the tree inside and resulted in approximately seven moving men being in our apartment for most of a day." The cost of hoisting the tree was $6,000, twice what it had been the previous year.

* * *

Gutfreund hadn't been reticent in voicing displeasure with Tendler at Phibro board meetings in the summer of 1983, suggesting that better controls be put on Phibro's operations. Essentially, that meant firing people, an action that would not be welcome among board members of a family-oriented firm like Phibro. The swing vote had to come from the outside directors. In September, the board had voted to make Gutfreund co–chief executive.

The next spring Gutfreund focused on taking the last step up at Phibro-Salomon. The "two-headed monster," as Gutfreund later described his job-sharing arrangement with Tendler, wasn't working. Tendler blundered in May by proposing a spinoff of all the commodities business, except for oil, to a group of executives and employees, a plan that would effectively separate Phibro and Salomon into autonomous companies once more. Gutfreund sprang into action, and ten days later the plan collapsed.

Rejecting Tendler's offer, the board sealed his fate. He was trying to leave the ship; instead the ship sped away without him. A board member soon proposed that Gutfreund be named sole chief executive of Phibro-Salomon. Again, the outside directors held the swing votes. On August 6, in a stunning reversal of fortunes, the board gave Gutfreund the job Tendler had once held alone. The Street called the overthrow the "coup of coups."

Gutfreund was at the peak of his power and so was Salomon Brothers. The mightiest firm on Wall Street was now under his sole command, and it was a staggering empire to behold. Many billions passed through the hands of Phibro-Salomon traders every year. The company boasted assets of $42 billion, revenues of $30 billion, profits of $470 million, 6,700 employees, and 25,000 shareholders. It also had the capability of trading virtually everything from wheat to U.S. Treasury bonds. In the underwriting race, the signature business of investment banking, Salomon was so far out in front with $21 billion of securities sold that it had no ready competition even among the bulge group of Salomon, Morgan Stanley, Merrill Lynch, First Boston, and Goldman Sachs.

Gutfreund faced the challenge of trying to make the two halves of his merged company finally jell. When Tendler officially quit in October, Hal Beretz, president and chief operating officer of Phibro-Salomon, left with his friend. The way was now clear for laying off a large number of employees in the commodities end of the business, which Gutfreund had long wanted and Tendler had resisted. The day Tendler left, 115 people were fired in New York and around the world.

Susan Gutfreund hosted a party for her husband in Paris afterward. That same month he made plans to put behind him the one arena where he had lost a battle, River House. The Postels were unbowed and intent on pursuing their lawsuit. Susan Gutfreund was now pregnant, and the Gutfreunds sought another apartment, plunking down a reported $6.5 million for a twenty-five-room duplex at 834 Fifth Avenue, one of New York's most exclusive co-op buildings, whose tenants included a Rockefeller.

Before they could move out, the Gutfreunds were forced to spend one more Christmas at River House, but reportedly without any fuss: they seemingly chose the simplest option, one that had always been available to them. A tree was sawed in half, brought up in the elevator, and bolted together in the apartment.

Gutfreund rarely resorted to such compromises. Although he was sensitive to criticism about his personal life, especially when it involved his wife, he continued slashing his own path through business, politics, and society. True to his character, he would remain aloof, arrogant, honest, shrewd, and brutally competitive. Reflecting the personality of its boss, Salomon Brothers was the firm most feared by its rivals. It was the prototype of the modern investment bank, "the not-so-benevolent king of the Street," as *Business Week* would dub it in 1985.

Gutfreund, the firm's uncontested ruler, had developed the stature of a Wall Street monarch, and he looked the part as well. His receding hair was completely gray now, his jowls deeply creased, his face a hardened mask. He was driven to assume new challenges. "I am addicted to the business," he once said. But the man who seized the throne had spent his life working in "the Room" — a place known for its aggressive internal competition and squabbling — and would need to develop other skills: diplomacy, sensitivity, and leadership to rule his international empire. Staying on top, he always claimed, was the most difficult task.

# CHAPTER TWENTY-SEVEN

# Endstopped

The annual meeting of American Express, held in late April 1983, at the Colony Park Hotel in Atlanta,* was a serious, self-congratulatory affair. But Sandy Weill couldn't seem to maintain the proper decorum. From his front-row seat on the stage of the hotel's auditorium, where he sat with other members of the board of directors, he spent much of his time fidgeting and mugging at some friends in the audience while Amexco chairman James Robinson addressed the shareholders. Even stripped of his cigar for the duration of the event, Weill was having the time of his life attending his first Amexco annual meeting as the corporation's president.

For a twenty-four-hour period, he was enveloped by power. The names of those assembled around him read like a top council of the Wasp Establishment. Among the board of directors were Gerald Ford, former president of the United States; Charles Duncan, Jr., former secretary of energy; Rawleigh Warner, Jr., chairman of Mobil; Richard Furlaud, chairman of Squibb; and Joseph Williams, chairman of the Williams Companies. Appropriately enough, Weill and his wife stayed in the hotel's presidential suite. That evening, he dined with two former presidents, Ford and Jimmy Carter, who was Amexco's guest.

Even the weather cooperated with Weill's ebullient mood. As the sun rose over the magnolia trees outside the hotel, it was the start of a perfect spring day. A chauffeur-driven stretch Cadillac Seville waited as Weill wrapped up a brief conversation with Jimmy Carter,

---

* Occasionally, the annual Amexco meeting was held outside New York City. Since American Express had recently acquired the Atlanta-based brokerage firm of Robinson-Humphrey, Amexco chairman James Robinson III (no relation to the founder of Robinson-Humphrey) took the opportunity to have this meeting in his hometown.

who had returned from a sunrise jog. Then the limousine took Weill and his entourage to the airport for a flight in his eight-passenger Amexco jet. When the plane touched down in Westchester three hours later, a minifleet of limousines collected Weill and his party.

Although by no means was every twenty-four-hour period like this one, there were now many occasions when, as president of Amexco, Weill basked in the rarified corporate atmosphere. Only a few weeks earlier, he had met briefly in his office with David Rockefeller, former chairman of Chase Manhattan, who had used the American Express boardroom to honor an artist whose work was being displayed on Wall Street. Weill had met the banker several years before on a plane taking them both to Cornell, Weill's alma mater, for a speaking engagement. Their subsequent conversation in his office left Weill fairly aglow.

"Do you think he remembers me?" Weill wondered aloud after Rockefeller had departed.

The office of corporate president — with all its status and perks — was merely a diversion. He had just come through the winter of his discontent when he had failed to be appointed the chief operating officer. He wanted to make policy and management decisions that would shape the future of Amexco. But he had few responsibilities in the day-to-day management of the firm. He handled superficial chores, odd problems, and corporate projects as they arose. He supervised the building of the new Amexco tower; lunched with promising young company executives; approved (in Robinson's absence) the press release on the firm's quarterly earnings; and spread good tidings for the company to the media and press. One day he wandered into the office of his old friend George Sheinberg, now treasurer of American Express, who was talking with some visitors, and exclaimed disconsolately, "I don't have enough to do."

He had little leverage to break out of his tight box. Although he had benefited from the bull market of 1982–1983, it didn't have the impact for him as president of American Express that it would have had as head of Shearson. Ironically, the brokerage business — which had allowed him to expand his domain and had served as his springboard to power and influence — was, for all its success, still not very important in the context of the total Amexco picture. He was working on a broader front now and had drawn out his supply lines until they were uncomfortably thin.

By comparison, Peter Cohen, as chief executive of Shearson, was his own man, firmly in charge of the brokerage house. Weill, the president of Amexco, merely rubber-stamped decisions about Shearson that had already been made by Cohen. And Weill didn't even have the satisfaction of being the largest shareholder of the Amexco board, now that Edmond Safra had joined him.

In fact, the only significant difference between being chairman of the executive committee of Amexco and being president was that his profile had been pumped up. Weill, who had prided himself on being a man of substance, was in effect more of a paper tiger.

Just as gardening had been an outlet for his energies at other times of stress, the renovation of the apartment he had bought in 1982 became a major preoccupation. It was a seven-room penthouse on the Upper East Side overlooking Central Park. After the apartment was stripped down to its bare walls, his wife, Joan, called it "Dresden after the war." Following months of plaster dust, a few unforeseen decorating disasters, and delayed deliveries of furniture, the hexagonal foyer was floored in a pattern of white, beige, and dark-stained wood; the paneled library was graced by an antique English desk; the traditional English-style living room was done in shades of blue and apricot; and the dining room was adorned with handpainted Chinese-inspired wallpaper and an English Regency table. It would provide the Weills with an elegant cosmopolitan setting for entertaining, a setting that befitted the president of American Express.

Reflecting her more mature taste and affluent circumstances, Joan had banished former traces of red, yellow, and black for a more subtle palette of pale pink, apricot, lavender, blue, and a soft yellow. The one exception was in the library, where the chairs and small sofa were covered by a red-and-chocolate-brown floral fabric in the same pattern used in Brooke Astor's library. "I'm a big flower person," Joan said, "and our decorator, Janet Leroy, helped me choose some wonderful floral patterns."

For all his ambition, Weill saw no signs that he was James Robinson's heir apparent or that he even had a shot of taking the job away from the Amexco chief. He laughingly referred to himself as Jim Robinson's "deputy dog," but the joke was a poor one. He had to do something. The question was, what?

\* \* \*

Although Weill would have fiercely denied it, he needed a power base of his own if he was to be more than a paper president. He slowly but insistently launched an all-out bid to acquire Investors Diversified Services, the venerable Minneapolis-based mutual fund. The offer was to be $1 billion in American Express stock.

At first blush, IDS seemed the perfect match to advance his

superbroker vision of American Express. It had the potential to tap markets and provide services that had largely been missing from his company's fold, and its acquisition might also add a division to Amexco that would report to Weill himself. But IDS was basically an unknown quantity. Its conservative middle-class, midwestern customer base was outside Weill's Wall Street milieu. Moreover, it was controlled by the very private and extremely wealthy Fred Kirby II, sixty-four, who was the chairman of Alleghany corporation, a New Jersey–based holding company, which had IDS as its principal asset.

A soft-spoken man, Kirby had to be brought along carefully. He had always rebuffed the many other firms that had bid for IDS. He didn't need them. Aside from his Alleghany riches, he was an important shareholder in Woolworth's, which his grandfather had helped to found. If he did sell IDS to American Express, he would join the board and become, like Edmond Safra before him, a larger stockholder than Weill. Despite this consideration, Weill was persistent. Talks proceeded sporadically for the next three months. Although Kirby provided him with copious information and arranged for IDS executives to meet with Amexco's management, he refused Weill's request for a large-scale investigation of IDS's operations before an agreement was reached. His concern — and Weill's — was to keep the talks a secret. They met at times at Kirby's retreat in the Adirondack mountains, where the only way to keep in touch with the outside world was through a radiophone that Kirby switched on only at certain times of the day. Weill made the most of these hours.

Their obsession with secrecy wasn't frivolous, but it was futile. The news of the impending deal leaked and pushed up the price of Alleghany's shares sharply, eventually forcing a halt in the trading in the stock — and thus putting IDS in a seemingly unenviable bargaining position. But Weill, overly eager to make a deal, failed to take advantage of this edge. He and Kirby shook hands on a billion-dollar purchase price for IDS and some other Alleghany assets without Weill's really knowing what Amexco was acquiring for its money. However, a handshake from him as number-two man in Amexco was different from a handshake from Jim Robinson, as Weill would find out soon.

At first, Robinson backed Weill, at least publicly, subject to a more thorough investigation of IDS's assets. Peter Cohen, George Sheinberg, and Howard Clark, Jr., headed the investigative task force that was quickly dispatched to Minneapolis. They swarmed all over IDS headquarters. Weeks and hundreds of thousands of dollars were spent reviewing the company. Weill joined them in Minnesota and asked Cohen what he thought of the deal.

Cohen told him the price was too high. Weill exploded, lacing into Cohen in front of a roomful of people. Turning on his heels, Cohen flew back to New York. Round two took place in Jim Robinson's office, where Weill, Cohen, Sheinberg, and Clark met with the Amexco chief for the final review. For Cohen and Sheinberg, the moment was awkward because they were put in the position of having to critique their mentor's work in front of him.

"With all due respect to Sandy, we think the bid is priced too high," said Cohen. Sheinberg agreed.

Weill stood firm, "I never said it was a bargain, but I think acquiring the company would be good for us."

But the bottom line was price. Weill had agreed to pay too much. Robinson nixed the deal.

Weill was furious. He reacted as though Cohen and Sheinberg had been personally disloyal to him. But after he calmed down, his relationship with Cohen settled into its familiar wary pattern. As for Sheinberg, Weill simply stopped talking to him. The loss of Sheinberg's friendship was a real loss. As the treasurer of American Express, Sheinberg had been Weill's only ally in the Amexco hierarchy.

Despite the setback, Weill soon revived secret talks with Kirby, and eventually the two men hammered out a $773 million agreement for IDS alone that closely reflected the assessment of the due diligence team.

Soon after the IDS negotiations ended, Weill found himself suddenly faced with another assignment: rescuing Amexco's Fireman's Fund. To many of his old friends at Shearson, it appeared that he was moving farther away from the power base at American Express and that Robinson was responsible.

From December of 1983 through March of 1984, Weill, though still the president of American Express, spent three-quarters of his time in California as the new chairman of Fireman's Fund. Occasionally Joan joined him there. Sometimes he flew home for weekends. In what some called the "December debacle," he fired 1,150 of the 14,000 Fireman's Fund employees, including virtually all of the senior executives. At IDS the carnage was far less extensive, but no less brutal. After the IDS deal had been completed that same month, Robinson praised IDS's chief executive officer. Then Weill took the man out to dinner and fired him.

As Weill was making his mark on IDS and Fireman's Fund, another link with Shearson was severed. Robinson had directed the brokerage house to report to him and not to Weill. It was not a situation Weill relished at this bleak stage of his career at American Express, where his advancement seemed virtually blocked.

When Cohen acquired Lehman Brothers for Shearson four months later, Weill was not even a principal player in the acquisition. His contribution was merely a footnote. In October, he hired Glucksman, the man Robinson and Cohen couldn't accept at Shearson, as an executive vice president at Fireman's Fund. Hiring Glucksman was one of Weill's few remaining prerogatives of power.

*  *  *

As 1984 drew to a close, IDS was being run virtually independently, as had been the case before the merger, and earnings were up sharply. The new chief executive installed by Weill required little supervision. Nor was Weill needed as much at Fireman's Fund as he had been in the past. He had tightened operations, brought in new management, and laid off employees. His emergency tour of duty was over. With his role at American Express increasingly circumscribed, he sought to reassert some of his former authority at Shearson, which infuriated Cohen and exacerbated their long-standing friction. Typically, Robinson acted as peacemaker and, just as typically, Weill got nowhere.

His isolation at American Express was brought home later that month by the resignation of Edmond Safra. According to several Safra intimates, the banker felt that he had been treated in bad faith by the Amexco management — but they wouldn't elaborate. One thing was clear: Safra's highly personalized, idiosyncratic, independent style hadn't meshed with the stiff corporate culture at Amexco.

The same could be said of Sandy Weill. It was becoming harder to imagine the day when he would take over Jim Robinson's job. Rumors began to circulate freely on the Street that Weill was going to quit, rumors that were fanned when Weill decided that he had been too loyal in holding on to so much American Express stock for such a long time and sold off a huge block.

Weill worried that the gossip would hurt his relationship with Robinson, especially when he heard stories that Robinson was bothered by all the media attention Weill received, including a mention on television of his having played golf with former president Gerald Ford. Robinson reassured Weill that there was no substance to the rumors. Though Weill asserted that such public notice didn't negatively affect his relationship with Robinson, he had to ask himself whether there was any truth in it.

When Glucksman, after only five months as executive vice president of Fireman's Fund, left to start his own business, Weill was infused with a renewed sense of entrepreneurial spirit. He began to entertain the idea of going out on his own again. Fireman's Fund could be the vehicle, since American Express wasn't any longer really interested in building it up. Weill quietly put together a leverage buyout proposal for Fireman's Fund, with American Express keeping a stake. He presented the scheme to Robinson, who, in turn, brought it to the American Express board for consideration.

Amid these developments, as Sandy Weill saw his star dimming at American Express, Jim Robinson and Peter Cohen hosted a black-tie party in May 1985, in Weill's honor, to celebrate the twenty-fifth anniversary of the firm that had begun as Carter, Berlind, Potoma & Weill. Some 170 Shearson employees, wives, and friends gathered for the occasion at the 143-year-old Federal Hall National Memorial on Wall Street. They had come from as far away as Geneva and London. Despite the unpleasant circumstances surrounding their departure, co-founders Arthur Carter and Roger Berlind were both present. They had no need to harbor a grudge, since both men had done extremely well. By his own estimate, Carter's prosaic utilities and real estate business had made him worth $130 million, some of which he had used to pursue special outside interests, which included the newspaper he had started in Connecticut and taking over the long-established, controversial left/liberal magazine, *The Nation*. Berlind had returned to his first love, the theater, and had coproduced such Broadway hits as *Amadeus, Sophisticated Ladies,* and *Nine*.

Conspicuously absent were Marshall Cogan and Arthur Levitt, the first and last letters in CBWL (Cogan, Berlind, Weill & Levitt), the successor to Carter, Berlind, Potoma & Weill. Like Carter and Berlind, Cogan and Levitt had continued to be forces in business and elsewhere. Cogan had become extremely rich from his carpet-backing business (General Felt) and his office furniture company (Knoll International). He had used his wealth to make a name for himself in the art world as a noted collector of twentieth-century paintings, and he was one of the new owners of "21." Levitt had become a highly visible presence on Wall Street as chairman of the American Stock Exchange. He felt it was outrageous that the party was being given in Weill's honor alone.

"Did you ever hear of an anniversary party for a firm given in honor of only one of the founding partners?" was the gist of his complaint and the reason he boycotted the event. If Weill were sensitive at all to other people's feelings, he maintained, he wouldn't have gone along with it.

But, in truth, neither Levitt nor Cogan had been original partners in the firm that had grown up to become Shearson Lehman Brothers, and Sandy Weill wasn't the host of the event. Many of the Shearson people missed Weill and were happy to honor him.

After cocktails, the guests trooped into the giant rotunda for dinner. Round tables were covered with silver lamé cloths and decorated with vases of lilacs and dogwood. Huge white helium balloons hung in clusters overhead. With dessert came the speeches. First the Weills' children, Jessica and Marc, both of whom worked for Shearson, said a few words about their father and how wonderful it was to be part of the Shearson family.*

Peter Cohen described the growth of the firm: how it had expanded to 22,000 strong because Arthur Carter, Sandy Weill, and Roger Berlind had come together in 1960. (He didn't even mention Peter Potoma, who had more serious legal problems after he left the firm.) Cohen then presented Weill with a silver loving cup inscribed:

> THE GRAND MASTER SANFORD I. WEILL MASTERMIND, MASTER BUILDER AND MASTERFUL CHAIRMAN OF THE BOARD OF SHEARSON/AMERICAN EXPRESS INC. 1960–1985. PRESENTED BY THE BOARD OF DIRECTORS ON MAY 2, 1985 IN GRATEFUL APPRECIATION FOR THE CREATIVITY, VISION, INSPIRATION AND MOTIVATION YOU GAVE THE PEOPLE OF WALL STREET'S NUMBER ONE FIRM.

American Express chairman Jim Robinson introduced himself as a newcomer. "I say I'm from southern Brooklyn," drawled Robinson. Delivering a parody of the Gettysburg address, he proclaimed gleefully, "One score and five years ago, Carter, Berlind, and Weill brought forth in Brooklyn a new firm dedicated to the proposition that all money is created equal. . . ."

He presented Weill, Berlind, and Carter each with a 2,300-year-old coin — a tetradrachma from the Macedonian Empire. "Like Shearson, Macedonia was created in twenty-five years," Robinson explained.

Weill came to the podium and introduced Arthur Carter. "You were always the big shot," Weill told his old friend, the former leader of the firm, and the man Weill had helped to oust.

"We were three young men who had a dream," Carter said.

---

* Weill, who had in common with Our Crowd a strong belief in nepotism, employed both his children at Shearson. Marc Weill, twenty-nine, was a financial consultant with Shearson Asset Management: Jessica Weill Bibliowicz, twenty-five, worked in the division's marketing department.

"It seems like only yesterday I was sitting in Roger Berlind's house on the right side of the tracks in Woodmere. He was going off to Princeton. I remember my son John and Sandy's son Marc playing together in our apartment in East Rockaway. I remember honing my investment banking skills by playing monopoly with Roger Berlind. One day Sandy Weill joined the game. While I was collecting railroads and Roger was amassing hotels, Sandy wasn't doing very well. But at the end of the game, he had half the board and half the money."

Then it was Berlind's turn. "The harder we worked, the luckier we got," he said simply.

By the time Weill came to the podium to speak, he seemed overcome by emotion and too many drinks. So much of his life had been played out with the people in this room. "Arthur Carter lived across the hall from me," he said in a subdued voice that could hardly be heard across the vast rotunda. "We bought a seat on the New York Stock Exchange for a hundred and sixty thousand dollars. . . . And here we are."

Finally, at 1:00 A.M., the party was over. Later it would be remembered as Sandy Weill's farewell party.

Early in June, Weill was absent when Amexco executives met at Robinson's home in Greenwich, Connecticut, to decide what was to be done with their half-interest in Warner Amex Cable. Weill was also excluded from meetings in which the future of Fireman's Fund was discussed. It was another sign that Weill was being pushed aside.

Shortly afterward Weill and his wife went to the south of France to celebrate their thirtieth wedding anniversary. At the Hotel du Cap in Cap d'Antibes, Weill received a call from Robinson, who told him that the board had rejected his plan to acquire Fireman's Fund. He was deeply disappointed. The implication was clear. The Amexco board was willing to risk the chance that Weill would resign and it seemed that he had no other choice now.

On June 25 he walked into Robinson's office and listened politely as Robinson suggested that he run Fireman's Fund as an employee after a portion of it had been sold to the public. Weill quietly tendered his resignation. "I didn't want to be part of a process that I wasn't enjoying," he said much later. But the hardest part was that, in walking away from American Express, he was also cutting the thin silver thread that still tied him to Shearson. "I had put so much of my life in that company — and now it was all behind me. It was a very hard thing." He left American Express "flat-out exhausted," emotionally and physically, and unsure of what he would do next.

# CHAPTER TWENTY-EIGHT

# The Calling of the Cards

T he best year of Alan ("Ace") Greenberg's life always seemed to be the current one. He didn't dwell on the past or worry much about the future. He had never taken for granted his incredible good fortune in achieving such great success on Wall Street. Indeed, the Bear Stearns chief seemed to marvel that he had become a millionaire many times over, especially since his immigrant grandparents had arrived in America penniless at the turn of the century.

For the most part, Greenberg enjoyed his success quietly. As long as Bear Stearns was a private partnership, he didn't have to make his income publicly known, and he was not the kind of man who had any need to broadcast his wealth. He donated millions of dollars to various charities without fanfare. The extent of his wealth was highlighted in 1985, when Bear Stearns became a public corporation. (It sold 22 percent of its stock and was listed on the New York Stock Exchange.) Greenberg's stake in the company was worth more than $60 million. Moreover, the switch from private to public ownership made him the highest-paid chief executive on Wall Street, at $5.3 million annually, $1.5 million more than his old commuting pal John Gutfreund, with whom he had regularly driven down to Wall Street when they were young men, earned, and more than three times as much as the heads of Merrill Lynch and Morgan Stanley each earned.

As part of the balance he maintained in his life, the money he earned was closely related to the money he dispersed. For him, that had less to do with the world of private jets and multiple homes than with charity. After five years of resisting attempts to recognize his generosity, the fifty-eight-year-old Greenberg finally allowed the Wall Street division of the combined campaign of the United Jewish Appeal-Federation of Jewish Philanthropies to honor him. The occasion was their private gala dinner held each December in the grand ballroom of the New York Hilton — the Super Bowl of Wall Street fundraisers.

* * *

On a damp, chilly Wednesday evening in December 1985, some 1,200 highly successful bankers and brokers began arriving at the Hilton. The securities professionals brought with them the same sense of purpose and vitality that they usually carried to work every day. They were part of a community of money men who moved in the same circles on Wall Street. But that night, instead of making money, they were giving it away. They exuded a glow of well-being that came from being rich enough to donate thousands and hundreds of thousands of dollars freely.

The early arrivals, most of whom had come directly from their offices, gathered for cocktails and kosher hors d'oeuvres in the lobby of the Hilton's grand ballroom. Drinks were served from two open bars. Waiters passed trays with canapés of pressed duck, miniature shish kabobs, sliced beef with pineapple, and asparagus spears. At tables positioned around the room, other waiters sliced roast beef, corned beef, and Nova Scotia smoked salmon and offered tempura, pasta, and blinis with caviar. Representatives from some seventy-five firms attended. Most were companies known historically as having been run by Jews. The New Crowd were among the largest contributors, including stars from the former upstart firms of Oppenheimer, Salomon Brothers, and, particularly, Bear Stearns.

At Bear Stearns, Ace Greenberg had played a pivotal role in fostering the spirit of giving — and not just to Jewish causes. It was estimated that he himself had donated more than five million dollars to charities over the years. He was a generous contributor to the United Way, New York University, the University of Oklahoma, and Johns Hopkins University — along with his substantial contributions to the American Jewish Committee and the UJA-Federation campaign. His firm was the largest per capita donor on Wall Street to the United Way, as well as the largest per capita donor in the country to the UJA-Federation. Since 1982, all the managing partners had been required to give a percentage of their pay and bonuses to charity. For Greenberg, as a member of a community, donating to charity was not a voluntary act but an obligation (from the Hebrew *tzedakah,* the word whose root meaning is "to be just"). Jewish tradition holds that everyone, including the poor, has the right to a decent life. The more privileged are obligated to help, each according to his means.

In America, the spirit of *tzedakah* has been used as a springboard for an unusual — but extremely effective — method of fund-raising that the Wall Street division of UJA-Federation had refined almost to a science. It is known as the "calling of the cards." Prior to a fund-raising event, each potential donor is solicited to submit a card listing the amount of his or her pledge. At the event itself, when the card caller reads each name, the individual stands and announces the pledge. The presence of their peers exerts pressure on donors to exceed or at least match the previous year's gift.

The dinner for the Wall Street division of UJA-Federation was held in December — traditionally the month that financial firms determined bonuses — when most successful bankers and brokers were known to be flush with cash, which increased the pressure on them to give more. Whatever reservations some individuals had about the means being employed, the ends were impressive, particularly in the highly competitive world of Wall Street. The previous fiscal year (the year ran from July through June 30), the members of the Wall Street division of UJA-Federation had donated an average of $10,000 each, for a total of more than $12 million — a staggering ten percent of the charity's annual fund-raising effort in New York.

At 6:10 P.M., the doors to the ballroom opened, and the Wall Street financiers filed in. Twenty minutes later, they had gotten down to the business of the evening. The goal was to beat the past year's contribution. In the front of the room was a blue placard that read, Share Your Pride-UJA-Federation in gold letters. Below that were the words, Wall Street, flanked by a stylized bull and bear.

There were several brief speeches, including one by Israel's ambassador to the U.N. Then Stephen Peck, a onetime member of the New York Stock Exchange Crisis Committee and a former senior partner of Weiss, Peck & Greer, a brokerage firm, came to the podium in front of the placard and began the roll call. "I'd like you to help me by repeating each gift, loudly and clearly. The first privilege of having the honor of calling the cards for the Wall Street division is to call your own card. My wife, Judith, and I are happy to announce a gift of one hundred thousand dollars."

The next card read was the guest of honor's. "I'm delighted to call on Alan Greenberg," Peck said. "He's the man who leads the others in his firm. His firm is dedicated to being successful, but it's important to everyone there to participate on the other side in the kind of thing we're doing tonight."

Greenberg stood up near Peck. "One million dollars," he said.

"That's terrific," Peck said. "We couldn't be more appreciative."

And on it went, interrupted by rounds of applause after each gift was announced.

John Rosenwald, head of corporate finance at Bear Stearns, pledged $250,000.

Alvin Einbender, of Bear Stearns, announced $165,000.

Jack Nash, who, along with Leon Levy, had built the brokerage house of Oppenheimer & Co. and now ran the venture capital firm of Odyssey Partners with Levy, pledged $180,000.

J. Morton Davis, head of the brokerage firm of D. H. Blair & Co., committed $100,000.

As the roll call of Jewish Wall Street continued, with a couple of pledges besides Greenberg's for a million or more, it became apparent that not only was there a strong turnout by the New Crowd but that the descendants of Our Crowd were a minor factor at the event. They had been replaced in Jewish philanthropy, just as they had been replaced on Wall Street.

Federation had been launched in 1917 by New York's German-Jewish investment bankers as an umbrella social service organization whose primary purpose was to provide assistance to poor Jewish immigrants in the New York City area. Later, it came to serve New York State residents in need, regardless of their religious or ethnic background. Federation remained an Our Crowd charity — and the dominant Jewish cause — for half a century. As the German-Jewish financiers gradually assimilated, they began to spread their philanthropic donations more widely, and their involvement in Federation declined.

By contrast, the United Jewish Appeal, founded more than two decades later, was the charity of Jews who were not part of Our Crowd. It was started in November of 1938 in response to *Kristallnacht* (night of the broken glass), when Nazi thugs burned synagogues and smashed the windows of Jewish-owned stores throughout Germany. Until the end of World War II, it provided assistance to Jewish refugees. With the formation of the State of Israel in 1948, UJA became its prime source of American funding.

For many years, UJA's fund-raising efforts ran a distinct second to Federation among Wall Street's Jewish community, but by the mid-sixties, UJA's Wall Street division began to take off — largely because of the growing involvement of New Crowd members, who were beginning to make their mark in philanthropy. The energy of the organization was epitomized by the irrepressible and tireless leadership of Gus Levy of Goldman Sachs, who was also a leader in Federation. Ace Greenberg also typified the New Crowd's commitment to UJA. He became an associate chairman of its Wall Street division in 1965. With the outbreak of the Yom Kippur war between Israel and Egypt in 1973, Federation and UJA put aside their differences for the greater good of

Jews around the world. At the first combined Wall Street dinner —
held in 1974 — the guest of honor was Gus Levy. In succeeding years,
the UJA-Federation honored such New Crowd superachievers as Salomon Brothers arb Richard Rosenthal, John Gutfreund, Jack Nash,
Stephen Friedman, Ivan Boesky — and now, in 1985, Alan Greenberg.
As their net worth increased, the New Crowd leaders upped their annual
contributions to UJA-Federation.

In less than an hour, the calling of the cards was over. Not
every one of the 1,200 names was called, but most of the big pledges
were mentioned. Greenberg's $1 million gift was one of the largest
individual contributions of the evening. In all, $13.5 million —
a healthy 10.7 percent increase over the previous year — would be
raised by the end of the fiscal year.

The time had come to honor Greenberg. His longtime friend
and partner at Bear Stearns, Alvin Einbender, spoke glowingly of his
exemplary generosity and presented him with an engraved Star of David
to commemorate the event. Then Greenberg came to the microphone.
The previous year Greenberg had stood up at the same podium, calling
the cards. Chomping on his cigar and coughing occasionally, he had
performed the task in the same brisk manner with which he did everything — making it obvious that time was precious. Now he was expected to deliver a speech, but in characteristic fashion his remarks were
brief.

"I have to confess something to you," he told the audience.
"When I pay my pledge every year to UJA, I don't feel like I'm giving
to charity. I'm really paying a tax or an obligation or dues that I owe.
Frankly I can never understand why other Jews who have prospered
in this unbelievable country don't feel the same way that I do.

"I'm in this great country because my grandparents took a long
voyage, left their relatives knowing that they might never see them
again, came to this country with no money, didn't speak the language,
and settled here and gave me a remarkable opportunity. I'm just plain
lucky and I know it."

Gedale Horowitz, a member of the Salomon Brothers executive
committee, read an invocation and *motzie,* a prayer, and the meal was
served. By 9:10 P.M., less than three hours after the fund-raiser had
begun, the evening was over and the ballroom was virtually empty.
Tomorrow was another day on Wall Street.

# CHAPTER TWENTY-NINE

# Eye of the Storm

Until 1979, Carl Icahn had been a nobody. For fourteen years, he had frequented the "21" Club, a restaurant in midtown Manhattan where almost everybody was somebody or was trying to be somebody. Icahn didn't care about status. The tall, lanky arbitrageur usually went there simply to pass the time with his uncle Elliot Schnall, as much a friend as a relative, who did care passionately about VIPs. Schnall knew who was "in" and who was "out," who came for drinks and who ate there, who was seated where, the whole history of the place, and the traditions and quirks that gave the "21" Club its cachet.

Begun in 1921 as a speakeasy, the "21" Club became one of the early outposts of Café Society. Through the decades the rich and famous — from the Astors and the Vanderbilts to Bernard Baruch, Ernest Hemingway, and the Marx Brothers — made it a regular drinking and dining stop on their evenings out. The food was poor and the prices were outrageous. And the main gathering spot was a dark, dingy bar/restaurant downstairs done in red and white, its low ceiling hung with hundreds of objects, including toy trucks, autographed footballs, and model airplanes. Nonetheless, the rich and famous remained loyal to the club (the regulars never considered it a restaurant). Richard Nixon, Sammy Davis, Jr., and many other notables kept bottles of wine in the club's wine cellar. The favorite tables of Humphrey Bogart and Robert Benchley were each marked with a plaque. General Motors had its own table, where every chairman since the end of World War II had eaten; it was located in the most exclusive area, known as "21."

Schnall, thanks to a wealthy father-in-law, was able to secure a table in the section next to "21" and hungered to be promoted. For his part, Icahn wouldn't have minded if they had been "exiled" to seating in "Siberia" — the most remote section of the room and the fate of the anonymous. But he wouldn't remain anonymous — his success as an arb over the past five years and the new attention to the once quiet but now bustling business of arbitrage would bring him into the public eye. Participating in the arbitrage game had become so established that such unlikely players as Morgan Stanley and Merrill Lynch were developing arbitrage departments, and flocks of mere amateurs were also entering the competition. By conservative estimates, the arb community had amassed a total of at least $1 billion in its war chest, waiting for takeovers to be announced. That was hardly enough in itself for more than a few big mergers, but the money could be split up many times — and borrowed against — to tip hundreds of scales.

For a while Icahn was lost in the crowd; then in February 1979, the *Wall Street Journal* ran an extremely favorable front-page story about his activities. The forty-two-year-old arb had agreed to the interview, but even the favorable notice made him uneasy. Too many players were already attracted to arbitrage for him to want to publicize it; the number of investors seemed to be growing faster than the potential profits. It was enough to send him looking for another line of work, one with fresher money-making possibilities. Shortly after the article appeared, he discussed his latest financial idea with his uncle over drinks at "21."

"I'm going to invest in undervalued assets," he revealed, meaning that he wanted to invest in companies whose stock, for a variety of reasons, was selling for less than it was worth, or at least less than Icahn thought it was worth.

"What, are you crazy?" Schnall said, not even sure he knew what his nephew meant. "You're doing terrific. You've got your name in the paper. Stick to what you're doing. Don't go looking for trouble."

"When things get too crowded," Icahn said, "I get out."

In fact, Icahn was already putting his new plan into action by zeroing in on two targets, and his techniques would attract more attention than ever before. No longer just an arb, he was becoming a greenmailer, a raider, and, in the process, perhaps the most successful financial predator of them all.

\* \* \*

Nothing in Carl Icahn's background seemed to set him on the road he would follow.

His father, Michael Icahn, an indifferent lawyer who had given up his legal practice because of ill health, was a cantor in a Conservative Jewish temple in Cedarhurst, Long Island — an occupational choice that may have had less to do with religion than with finding something he could do. He had learned Hebrew from his father, who had learned it in his native Russia. Moreover, he loved to sing. His fondest dream was to perform at the Metropolitan Opera House, but being a cantor was the closest he would ever come. Carl's mother was a schoolteacher and, in her son's eyes, a meek woman, "afraid to venture out in the world." Home for the Icahns was a modest, yet comfortable, row house in the bayside community of Bayswater in Queens, near the father's synagogue. Except for ethnic variety — Jews, Italians, Irish, and blacks — the neighborhood had the air of a small town far removed from Manhattan.

There was little to distinguish Carl Icahn from the other boys his age other than his keen interest in chess. Routinely, he pursued the classic American-Jewish dream of becoming a doctor, because that was what his parents wanted. He studied hard in school and his diligence paid off. According to him, he was the first graduate of Far Rockaway High School to attend Princeton University, where he majored in philosophy.

After college, he enrolled in medical school at New York University, but found he wasn't interested in his studies. For two years he slogged through his courses, dropping out three times, until he finally told his parents that he had had enough. He enlisted in the Army, where he exercised what he thought was some talent as a card player. After his discharge in 1960, with $5,000 he had won in poker games, he headed for Wall Street.

His uncle Elliot found him a job as a $100-a-week broker trainee at Dreyfus. With his $5,000 stake, plus a small inheritance from his grandfather, Icahn started playing the market. The year was 1961 and stocks were rising sharply. In a short time, he had earned $50,000. The novice confidently expected his winning streak to last forever. It didn't.

When the market broke sharply in the first half of the following year, he lost everything. He was forced to sell his cherished white Ford Galaxy convertible to pay the rent. From that point on, he vowed never to play the market again. At least, not with his own money. Instead, Icahn became an expert in options — the right to buy or sell securities at a certain price over a set period — before the field became respectable and popular. He headed the options department first at Tessel Paturick and then at the larger Gruntal. He was extremely successful because there was no organized exchange at the time for trading options. Taking advantage of this vacuum, he issued a comprehensive weekly report that became regular reading for option investors across the country. One of his best clients was Elliot Schnall, who had become a prosperous manufacturer of loose-leaf binder notebooks.

Icahn, a bachelor, and his uncle, who was only fourteen years older and divorced, often double-dated and attended parties together. Icahn wasn't socially ambitious. He lived a disorganized, quiet life. His simple one-bedroom, high-rise apartment on Second Avenue was decorated with furniture provided by his mother and uncle. History books — his favorite reading material — were scattered about. Dinner was often a quick hamburger or take-out from a deli, pizzeria, or Chinese restaurant. Only his work provided some sort of rhythm and regularity. In 1968, when the opportunity he had been waiting for arose, he was ready to take advantage of it. That year his uncle sold his company for several million dollars.

"What are you going to do with the money?" Icahn asked.

"I don't know," replied Schnall. "I haven't decided yet."

"I want to start a business. Will you loan me the money to buy a seat on the [New York] Stock Exchange?"

"You got a deal."

In February 1968, Icahn and Co., Inc. opened as a small general brokerage firm at 15 William Street. The cost of operating the office — $100,000 — was paid with money Icahn had amassed on his own. Two months later, with funds provided by Schnall, Icahn successfully bid $400,000 for a seat on the New York Stock Exchange.

Business was good from the start, and Icahn prospered. Within a few years, he moved to a two-bedroom apartment on Sutton Place that overlooked the East River. In the summer, he followed the singles scene to the Hamptons, sharing houses with several other bachelors and dating a variety of women. Well into his thirties, he quipped, "I can't get married. I already am — to my work."

The options business served him well until the midseventies, when the Chicago Board Options Exchange (CBOE) opened. No longer at the center of the game, Icahn began to look around for other opportunities. Risk arbitrage seemed the natural route to follow. Options had taken him into traditional arbitrage, that arcane business of exploiting slight discrepancies in securities pricing.

Traditional arbitrage was becoming less lucrative. The Chicago options exchange, the general fine-tuning of securities prices, and the growing sophistication of markets around the world — all contributed to its decline. The opposite was true of risk arbitrage. The pace of merger activity often kept Icahn up well beyond midnight, poring over stacks of annual reports. But the payoff, at least financially, was worth it. His original $100,000 investment had grown to $5 million by 1979. But Icahn liked to take on a new challenge. He found it in corporate raiding. He had actually attempted to take over the small Highland

Capital Corporation three years before but had failed badly. He simply didn't have the experience and financial strength then. This time he would not back down.

Early in 1979, he unloaded twin-barrel shots, one aimed at Baird & Warner and the other at Tappan. Both attacks displayed the Icahn style: it was combative, uncompromising, and, most of all, unrelenting. In each case, he acquired large blocks of stock and launched a proxy fight to land seats on the company's board of directors.

Not even a change in his marital status slowed him down from the corporate chase. That spring, Icahn and his thirty-year-old bride, Liba, were wed in a small civil ceremony at his Sutton Place apartment, followed by a reception at "21" for some fifty people. Icahn and his wife, a slim Czechoslovakian with high cheekbones and dark eyes, who had been a ballerina in her native country, had first met several years earlier at a summer party in Quogue, Long Island, when Icahn was just trying out arbitrage and she was an assistant to an interior decorator. They had lived together for several years before marrying, and Liba had grown accustomed to Icahn's ways. Thus, it wasn't unanticipated that there would be no honeymoon. The groom returned to work the next day to continue the corporate battle begun several weeks earlier.

Baird & Warner, a real estate investment trust, not only lost its proxy battle to Icahn, it surrendered to him without putting up much of a fight. (He renamed it the Bayswater Realty & Capital Corp., after the neighborhood where he had grown up.) However, Tappan, the century-old manufacturer of stoves, mounted stiffer resistance to the syndicate Icahn put together.

W. Richard Tappan, chairman of the company and grandson of its founder, wanted to have nothing to do with Icahn and urged him to abandon what he called Icahn's "short-term, fast-buck, turnover approach." That was his polite request. Then Tappan got rough. Management brought up the fact that Icahn had been fined — $25,000 — by the New York Stock Exchange for violating federal securities laws. Icahn dismissed that problem as a bookkeeping error and counterattacked with a full-scale proxy battle to gain a seat on Tappan's board. In May, he claimed victory, which, under his relentless pressure as a board member, was the same as putting a "for sale" sign on Tappan. It sold out to the giant Swedish appliance manufacturer, AB Electrolux. Within just twelve months, Icahn had increased the value of Tappan's stock from $8 a share to $18. Selling his shares, he pocketed $4.1 million on an initial investment of $1.4 million.

A couple of proxy fights, a small takeover, and a forced sellout — these were just the beginning of Icahn's assault on corporate America. In his next foray, the mere threat of a proxy fight caused Saxon Industries to buy him out quickly at a premium — in other words, to pay him greenmail.*

Because of his raids, Icahn became a rich man in a very short time. He found ready investors for his syndicates. Among his financial backers in his attack on Saxon was none other than W. Richard Tappan, who had first-hand evidence of Icahn's know-how and clout. And in the ensuing years many other investors and corporate leaders would come to know him all too well.

* * *

December 22, 1984. Car after car turned off the road by the country club golf course and passed through the stone and iron gates of Carl Icahn's thirty-seven-acre estate located in the wealthy enclave of Bedford, New York, thirty miles north of New York City. Late-comers had to park far down the long, winding lane, then walk up past dozens of cars to the twenty-room stone mansion that stood majestically at the top of the rise. It was late afternoon — crisp and pleasant — three days before Christmas.

From the house the visitors could look out over a Currier and Ives landscape of woods and snow-covered fields, actually the fairways of the neighboring golf course, which shimmered in the setting sun. Inside the house, a festive scene unfolded. Guests entered a warmly lit, comfortable living room filled with plump sofas covered in floral chintz and surrounded by book-lined shelves, where they were greeted by Carl and Liba. In the center of an adjoining room, called the gallery, an ornately decorated Christmas tree reached to the ceiling. Scores of guests — Icahn's friends, neighbors, business associates, and employees — drank vintage wines and ate holiday fare served buffet-style. The Icahns' two young children played among the crowd. A German shepherd watched dolefully from an enclosed porch while an ensemble performed classical music.

The party capped a period of unparalleled calm in Icahn's life.

---

* Very likely Icahn's talents were not the only factor in winning a quick settlement with Saxon. The company's chief executive had committed a then undisclosed fraud in running the business, for which he would ultimately go to jail. Thus, he may have preferred to pay greenmail to Icahn rather than risk exposure in a public battle.

For eight months, he had launched no hostile raids, fought no proxy contests, extracted no greenmail from besieged corporations. None of this conformed to the Carl Icahn Wall Street knew: the steel-edged raider who had hung framed annual report covers from the companies that had made him millions — like trophies — in the reception room of his Fifth Avenue office. His estate was named Foxfield after the secret code word he had used in his takeover bid for Marshall Field, the department store chain. His German shepherd was called Shiloh — a Civil War victory for the North — to commemorate the fortune he had extracted from Dan River, a southern textile company. He seemed to revel in his steeliness. Icahn was fond of saying to those who pointed to his lack of popularity in corporate boardrooms, "In our business, if you want a friend, buy a dog." He was brash in his analysis of the profit motives: "If the price is right, we are going to sell. I think that's true of everything you have, except your kids and possibly your wife."

Yet there was a quirkiness in even his most outrageous remarks that exposed his earthy, human side. A kibitzer, a complainer, and a rambler, he was also thoughtful and straightforward in person. His favorite charity was a center for abused children. Sometimes he wondered aloud about his newfound wealth.

"Maybe I'm just another Jew who has made a lot of money," he told an acquaintance. (Icahn doesn't recall making the remark.) He sought to justify his aggressive behavior in business by talking about his "outrages" — the poorly run companies that he felt should be taken over and made to run right. Still, his sense of "social responsibility" never deterred him from accepting greenmail. When Marshall Field, the department store giant, had sued him, calling him a "racketeer" for buying stock in the company, Icahn drove it into the arms of a white knight and managed to emerge with $18 million more than he'd invested. When he took over ACF Industries, a maker of railcars and oil field equipment, he considered the management one more of his "outrages."

For most of his adult life, the forty-eight-year-old "Icahnoclast" had been a lone wolf, who professed to abhor all kinds of social rituals. He never staged postraid victory parties. He didn't even celebrate his own birthday or, more recently, his wedding anniversary. (Both he and his wife claimed they had forgotten the date.) Although he observed the Jewish high holy days, he was "not a believer in organized religion."

Following the birth of his two children, Icahn had mellowed to a certain degree. A devoted New Yorker who maintained a luxury two-bedroom apartment on Park Avenue, he seemed to be growing comfortable in the role of the genial country squire. His annual Christmas party, first given a few years earlier, was becoming a tradition at the estate.

Icahn had purchased the estate for $1.25 million in 1981 from actress Jennifer O'Neill, subsequently adding a tennis court, library, and, near the swimming pool, a cabana the size of a small house. He bought two adjoining properties, adding eight acres to the original twenty-nine. The serenity of country living appealed to him and his wife liked the outdoors. His athletic activities were confined to weekend tennis — she enjoyed downhill skiing. They vacationed with their children at Western ski resorts where Icahn generally avoided the slopes.

But he hadn't given up his maverick independence, which was manifested in the way he handled his business and in the way he handled his life. He had no real interest in the social scene — either in New York City or in Bedford. The atmosphere at the Christmas party was largely devoid of the intense social posturing of the monied striving for recognition. Though rich and powerful businessmen were gathered there, few were from Wall Street.

Icahn considered himself something of an alien on the Street, and certainly he was an alien among the corporate bureaucrats in whose companies he invested. His disdain carried over to investment bankers and lawyers, often the raiders' most determined aides, except when he absolutely needed their services. He prided himself on negotiating without their help most of the time, believing he could best any of his target CEOs one-on-one. He also felt he had little in common with his New Crowd brethren who, he believed, cared too much about social status and were not truly self-made men; he considered himself one of the latter. However, if anyone were to mention the obvious financial boost he had received in his start-up days from his rich uncle Elliot Schnall, Icahn acknowledged it.

Now, after the lull, he was ready to strike again at a target few others would dare to attack.

*   *   *

On Sunday, the day after Icahn's Christmas party, Mesa Oil company chief T. Boone Pickens ended his hostile takeover bid for the mighty Oklahoma-based Phillips Petroleum, the sixteenth-largest industrial corporation, by agreeing to have management buy him out at a premium. The view from the Street was that there was more money to be made from Phillips. Enter Icahn.

After the holiday he started buying Phillips's shares. A few weeks later, Icahn called Mike Milken in Los Angeles to discuss a Phillips takeover. He had only recently made his Drexel connection. Early in December Drexel had issued $400 million in junk bonds to pay off the bank debt Icahn had incurred in his acquisition of ACF. Now, he would really see what Drexel could do.

In forty-eight hours, Milken was prepared to raise billions for Icahn. The next move was Icahn's and he acted swiftly. He announced that he was ready to take over the company for $55 a share, or $8 billion, and threatened a proxy fight. He warned that he would use his stockholder power if necessary to win the vote against the company's recapitalization plan that was meant to boost its stock. Though management's bid was lower than Icahn's, it counted on shareholder loyalty to approve the plan and defeat him.

On February 22, the day shareholder voting on the recapitalization plan came to a close, schoolchildren were out in force in Phillips's headquarters city, Bartlesville, Oklahoma, waving heart-shaped balloons and carrying I Love Phillips signs. In the window of one store a sign read: I CAHN YOU CAHN/WE ALL CAHN/LICK ICAHN. To the people of Bartlesville the battle revolved around keeping Phillips alive under local management, pitting their concerns against the major investors' interest in a higher value for their stock. Icahn never appeared. The night before, he claimed, he had passed out on the floor of his New York apartment — one of the rare times he had caved in from total exhaustion. He didn't have the strength to fly to Oklahoma. But it didn't matter.

Two weeks later, when all the proxies had finally been tallied, Phillips's management had lost. In a startling development for American business, the shareholders had stood up to management and defeated the recapitalization plan.

Faced with the prospect of Icahn's taking over, Phillips sweetened its package. Now the shares were worth about $55. For his two months of work, Icahn walked away with a profit of $50 million — plus $25 million in expenses to cover, among other things, the commitment fees, the money owed to his backers, and Drexel's fee for raising the money.

"I'm happy the shareholders benefitted," Icahn said. "But I'm no Robin Hood. I enjoy making the money."

Indeed, Icahn never had made so much money so fast. He seemed almost indomitable until he entered the eye of the storm several weeks later.

* * *

Icahn allowed himself no respite. He turned his attention immediately to one of his little stock positions — Trans World Airlines — that had been percolating on a back burner while he was involved with Phillips. One of the cornerstones of modern American business, the St. Louis–based carrier was the country's third largest after American and United. It had a long and prestigious history. Launched in 1929 with Charles Lindbergh at the controls, TWA had been christened by Mary Pickford when its first scheduled flight had taken off for the East Coast.

Amelia Earhart was a TWA pilot. Wiley Post set around-the-world records in its planes. For many years, the bashful billionaire Howard Hughes controlled the airline. In Icahn's words, its current board included such "white shoe" types as Robert McNamara, former secretary of defense and president of the World Bank; Brock Adams, former secretary of transportation; and Peter Ueberroth, then commissioner of baseball and the guiding force behind the 1984 Olympics. Yet, for all its glory, Icahn wanted TWA for the same reason he had gone after every other company. "I thought TWA was undervalued," he said a year later.*

By May 1985, Icahn had acquired more than one-fifth of the company and talked about the need for making it more efficient. Management saw his moves as a bold-faced attempt to gain control of TWA and sell off its pieces. In a press release, TWA president C. E. Meyer, Jr., declared: "Mr. Icahn's presence is uninvited and undesirable." Charges and countercharges quickly filled the air. On May 21, Icahn made what Wall Street considered a rather civil bid for the airline. He offered investors $18 a share for stock that had been selling at $10 — well below the value of the company's assets.

At an almost deserted bar in the Waldorf-Astoria, Icahn later met with Meyer to discuss their differences. The conversation quickly

* Icahn wasn't the first of the New Crowd to become interested in TWA. Odyssey partners Jack Nash and Leon Levy had been attracted to TWA and the four other companies that made up Trans World Corporation (TWC) in 1983. They met with TWC management and with institutional investors and tried to persuade them that the company should be divided into five parts. Management beat back their bid but less than a year later acted on their advice and spun off TWA into a separate company, as part of the wave of corporate restructuring that was sweeping American business.

turned bitter. According to Icahn, Meyer said to him: "All you want is a fast buck. That's all you've ever done in these raids is go for the fast buck."

Icahn retorted: "If we're psychoanalyzing each other, why don't you admit what you really care about is your job, and you are afraid I am going to take it away from you?" (In this case, Icahn was wrong. Meyer had already resigned from TWA.) They glared at each other and the meeting ended.

TWA pursued its counterattack. The company fought Icahn in court, at the Department of Transportation, and in the halls of Congress. Again and again, it tried to prove that he was unfit to run an airline, but each time management lost. In the view of many merger watchers, TWA was putting itself up for sale to save itself from Icahn. Management scoured the country, searching for a white knight. Their degree of desperation showed when Frank Lorenzo, the chairman of Texas Air, surfaced as the top contender. An aggressive airline chief, Lorenzo had tried to acquire TWA in the seventies but had been rebuffed. Moreover, he was antilabor, whereas TWA had strong unions.

Unlike Icahn, though, Lorenzo was part of the little world of airline chief executives, and that was what mattered most. In the battle for TWA, Texas Air (which included Continental Airlines) also had the financial firepower to outlast Icahn.

In early June, Lorenzo hired Drexel and it put together a cash-and-bond package for the Texas Air–TWA merger that surpassed Icahn's bid. Icahn didn't fret long. If he wasn't going to get an airline, at least he would make a profit of $79 million when he sold his holdings to Lorenzo.

There was a catch. Icahn wanted an extra $16 million for so-called expenses. When Lorenzo refused to pay after a deal seemed to have been worked out with Icahn's team, Icahn exploded. And so Trans World War II began.

Icahn found an ally in the unions, whose members were prepared to accept huge pay cuts if he would save them from Lorenzo. The Texas Air chief, apparently realizing that Icahn was building support, decided that the $16 million payout to him was cheap and raised the offer to $20 million. Icahn, now bargaining from a position of greater strength, asked for $25 million. "Every time I turn over a card it gets more expensive," said the old poker player. Lorenzo rejected his $25 million demand, so Icahn turned over another card. In early August, Icahn beat Lorenzo with a higher bid only to be topped by

Lorenzo again. But now Icahn owned 45 percent of the stock and had labor on his side.

Icahn was in his office talking with the head of the pilots union when he received word that the TWA board was going to support his bid. The tense wait was over. The Icahn team applauded and whistled. He and his closest assistant, Alfred Kingsley, hugged each other. After a victory luncheon of deli sandwiches in the office, the head of the pilots union handed Icahn his pilot's jacket. Icahn smiled broadly and put it on.

"Hey, we got ourselves an airline," he exclaimed.

But he hadn't — not yet. There were new financial problems. At a New Year's Eve party at his uncle Elliot Schnall's home in Palm Beach, Florida, Icahn spent much of the time talking on the phone with his faithful aide Alfred Kingsley, a rotund lawyer-by-training dealmaker from Brooklyn, who was hammering out a new agreement with the pilots in New York. (The two worked together, as Icahn was fond of saying, like the Lone Ranger and Tonto.) New concessions were won. But they weren't enough. TWA apparently was losing money faster than Icahn could raise it. He had already sunk more than $350 million into the airline to acquire a slim majority of the stock. Now, instead of buying all the remaining shares, he simply offered to take control of TWA and run it. In addition, Drexel — which conveniently became Icahn's banker after its commitment to Lorenzo ended — provided TWA with much needed capital.

As it turned out, his victory was bittersweet. The airline he acquired was a troubled one. It had lost more than $200 million in 1985, and it still hadn't signed the contract with the flight attendants, who accused Icahn of being sexist. He charged them with not making enough of a sacrifice. His problems multiplied. One writer quipped that it was TWA who took over Carl Icahn and not the other way around.

"The Phillips deal was better," a reflective Icahn said at the time. "I never wanted to get into a fight [with Phillips], but it was important that the institutions backed me. I did it all myself. This [TWA] was anticlimactic. I still think it's good, but there is a lot more to it than I thought."

In mid-February, in another departure from his once rigid avoidance of ceremony, Icahn put up no resistance when his wife threw him a fiftieth birthday party. It was a gala black-tie affair that was held at his Westchester estate and attended by some two hundred guests. The food was bountiful, his children were frolicsome, and the musicians played on and on. After dinner, the three-piece ensemble broke into a rendition of "Happy Birthday" and Icahn blew out the candles on his four-foot-long, four-foot-wide cake — a red-and-white model of a TWA 747 Boeing jet. Two weeks later, he bought himself a birthday present: Ozark Air Lines, an eastern carrier, for which he paid $225 million. The flight of Carl Icahn into the unfriendly skies of airline ownership — and Wall Street finance — was far from over.*

---

* Icahn used TWA as an investment vehicle for his raids. He became the largest shareholder of USX (formerly U.S. Steel) and Texaco. In 1989, he sold his Texaco stake for $2 billion—a profit of more than $700 million.

# CHAPTER THIRTY

# The Big Casino

*F*elix Rohatyn wasn't present at the lavish dinner party for sixty people given in mid-September of 1985 by the powerful real estate broker and renowned hostess Alice Mason to launch the social season, but he had been drawn into the fire that generated the evening's heated exchange. The setting was Mason's art-filled dining room arranged with small dining tables spread with fine floral Porthault linen, gleaming silver, and elegant china and enhanced by arrays of red roses and candlelight.

Mason's dinners — a barometer of who was "in" socially — brought together the movers and shakers in the worlds of art, business, and politics. Among the guests that evening were Norman Mailer, Norman Lear, Gloria Steinem, real estate mogul Mort Zuckerman, and Helen Gurley Brown, but the most barbed verbal clash came from the table that included publisher Malcolm Forbes, gossip columnist Aileen ("Suzy") Mehle, *Vanity Fair* editor Tina Brown, and Carl Icahn. Mason, whose guest lists were designed to elicit the liveliest possible conversation, got more than she bargained for that night.

As they consumed the main course of saddle of veal stuffed with spinach and chicken mousse accompanied by couscous and broiled tomatoes, Icahn's tablemates listened as he held forth on two of his pet peeves: the old-boy network in business and the ineffectiveness of corporate directors. "There are a lot of people who collect their fees and don't do a damn thing," Icahn said — meaning board members.

Bristling, Aileen Mehle rallied to the support of the board on which she sat — Revlon. The cosmetics and health care giant, led by Rohatyn's friend and client Michel Bergerac, had been making headlines for weeks as a target of a hostile takeover bid.

She defended it as "a fine board, an honorable board, Mr. Icahn!"

Though Icahn denied it later, "Suzy" reported that he snapped back, "You're patronizing me!"

An interested listener at a nearby table overheard the exchange — Ronald Perelman, the raider, who in fact was the one trying to seize Revlon from Bergerac, who was being advised by Felix Rohatyn.

It was perhaps fitting that a spirited defense of Revlon that evening was made by the nation's best known chronicler of High and Nouvelle Society, "Suzy," whose weekday column appeared locally in the *New York Post*. Throughout its fifty-one-year-old history, the cosmetics company had been the very essence of glamour. Only two men had led Revlon: Charles Revson, the legendary founder, and his handpicked successor, Bergerac. The fifty-three-year-old Frenchman appropriately projected the image of sophistication, elegance, and wit.

But in the last several years, Revlon had lost some of its luster in the eyes of Wall Street. In the early 1980s, competition in the cosmetics industry intensified, demand slackened, and earnings slumped. Meanwhile, Bergerac tried to diversify, moving aggressively into the mundane, but more profitable, world of health care products. Still, like hundreds of other publicly owned companies, Revlon was a sitting duck: its stock was cheap in comparison to its earning power or what it would be worth if its holdings were broken up and sold off. With Revlon on many predators' hit lists, Bergerac had kept in close touch with his old friend Rohatyn, whom he had known since his ITT days, so that they would be prepared at a moment's notice to defend the cosmetics and health care citadel against an onslaught. When the battle for control of Revlon was over, Rohatyn's well-honed skills had been put to one of their most severe tests, his relationship with Bergerac was strained, and he had witnessed the powerful arsenal of new types of weapons at the disposal of the raiders in the mideighties.

Perelman, head of the miniconglomerate MacAndrews & Forbes Holdings, led the attack through one of its interests, Pantry Pride, a supermarket chain. To prevent outsiders from learning at which company, among a number he had researched and considered, he was taking aim, his team of lawyers and investment bankers code-named Revlon Nicole, for the seventeen-month-old daughter of one of the lawyers. Though Perelman had focused on Revlon since March, he had waited until August to make his move — which happened to be only four weeks before Alice Mason's dinner party.

The struggle for possession of Revlon was more than just another fierce takeover battle. It pitted the corporate and Wall Street mainstream against an outsider whose arriviste status was further underlined by the fact that he was financed by Mike Milken's controversial junk bonds. As Bergerac's adviser, Rohatyn, once the quintessential outsider himself, was now on the other side of the line, positioned to try to beat back a bid for a blue-chip company.

In personality and style, Bergerac and Perelman were strikingly different. The suave Frenchman, an MBA graduate of UCLA and the executive once considered the most likely to replace Harold Geneen at ITT, had been the subject of a laudatory *Time* cover story in 1978 after he had helped Revlon's sales and profits multiply. A bon vivant and brother of the French actor Jacques Bergerac, he and his wife were seen frequently on the social circuit. As Revlon chief, he had a dazzling array of corporate perks: a chauffeur-driven limousine, a private dining room, a butler, two secretaries, and a Boeing 727 lavishly outfitted with a kitchen, bedroom, living room, backgammon board, and, for big-game hunting, a gun rack. The mounted heads of wild game he had bagged on safaris hung in his office.

Perelman, an Orthodox Jew from Philadelphia, had married a wealthy woman and begun his career working for his father, but he wasn't content with doing just that and along the way acquired MacAndrews & Forbes, a maker of chocolate and licorice extracts. The marriage ended in a messy, well-publicized divorce in which his wife's detectives reportedly documented that Perelman was having an affair, and she added the charge that he was misusing money from her family. She also claimed that she owned part of her husband's interest in Mac-Andrews. The divorce was granted; her settlement included $3.8 million in cash. Perelman then married reporter Claudia Cohen, who had made a reputation as a writer, first with gossipy "Page Six" of the *New York Post,* then with her own gossip column, "I, Claudia," in the rival *Daily News,* and later with a featured spot on television. With his new wife in tow, Perelman became a regular on the New York social scene.

\* \* \*

Rohatyn hadn't been surprised when the call to arms came about Revlon, but the timing was inconvenient. It was mid-August, and he and Elizabeth were on vacation in Austria, attending the Salzburg music festival. A Lazard partner telephoned their hotel room late one night to report that Revlon was under siege and that the raider was Perelman. "After three days of missing concerts and being on the phone constantly, my wife and I decided that we might as well go home," Rohatyn recalled. His secretary chartered a jet to fly him from Salzburg to Paris so that he could catch the Concorde to New York.

Rohatyn was disturbed by the direction the takeover wave had taken over the past few years. In a speech before the American Society of Newspaper Editors months earlier, he had stressed that the nation was turning "the financial markets into a huge casino."

He laid much of the blame on his own profession:

> In the field of takeovers and mergers, the sky is the limit. Not only in size, but in the types of large corporate transactions, we have often gone beyond the norms of rational economic behavior. The tactics used in corporate takeovers, both on the offense and on defense, create massive transactions that greatly benefit lawyers, investment bankers, and arbitrageurs but often result in weaker companies and do not treat all shareholders equally and fairly. . . . In the long run, we in the investment banking business cannot benefit from something that is harmful to our economic system.

Rohatyn was sounding themes he would repeat in the ensuing years. Paradoxically, as the architect of some of the important and lucrative mergers and takeovers of the seventies and early eighties, he was also emerging as a severe critic — one who would be widely listened to and quoted — of deal mania and its consequences. It was part of his complexity: a man who in public and written utterances called for a better, more equitable society, yet a shrewd and ambitious pragmatist; a man who inveighed against the greed and unchecked speculation in his profession, yet made millions for himself and his firm from the world of takeovers; a man who condemned the increasingly bureaucratic nature of the business, yet worked smoothly within the system.

To Rohatyn, all of this was not a contradiction. He basically believed in the system but felt it had to be assessed and corrected. He valued his obligation to clients and, in fact, rarely turned down an opportunity to provide them with financial advice. As a consequence, he had been involved in three of the most infamous raids of the period. As adviser to American Express in 1979, he had been drawn into the mudslinging campaign between two pillars of the American corporate Establishment (Harold McGraw of McGraw-Hill and James Robinson III of American Express) in an abortive attempt by American Express to take over McGraw-Hill; and two years later, as adviser to Seagram, he had played a part in the hot three-way fight with Du Pont and Mobil for possession of Conoco.

In 1982, he played a brief role in the spiciest takeover of all, when he represented United Technologies — one of three companies squabbling over Bendix, maker of automotive and aircraft parts. The takeover saga could have been a subplot of *Dallas*. It entailed a tabloid-headline marriage between an ambitious corporate chieftain and his equally ambitious blonde Harvard-MBA assistant; a diabolical corporate counterattack; and more than the usual share of personal acquisitiveness and greed.

Rohatyn appeared onstage when he met with the central character of the drama, William Agee, the thirty-eight-year-old chairman of Bendix, whose assumed affair with his executive assistant, Mary Cunningham — who later became his wife — had received so much media coverage eighteen months earlier that *Time* reported that it had eclipsed national interest in "who shot J.R.?" Agee wanted to hire Lazard as Bendix's financial adviser in the company's raid on Martin Marietta, an aerospace business. What made this hostile takeover attempt so attention grabbing and different was Martin Marietta's counterattack by means of the notorious Pac-Man defense, so-named because — like the popular video-game creature — the target company had turned on its pursuer.

Rohatyn declined Agee's offer and turned the tables on him by asking if Agee would be interested in having an unnamed client of Rohatyn's acquire Bendix. As it happened, Rohatyn was then serving as adviser to Harry Gray, head of United Technologies, who was already considering Bendix as an acquisition candidate. Gray's only hesitation was his concern that such a takeover would involve an important antitrust issue. Rohatyn came up with a clever way around the problem: sell off the parts of Bendix that conflicted with United Technologies' business to Martin Marietta, whose boss was an old friend of Gray's.

The intricate, pell-mell, three-way chase between Bendix's bid for Martin Marietta, Martin Marietta's Pac-Man attack on Bendix, and United Technologies' bid for Bendix, finally drove Bendix into the arms of Allied, run by Edward Hennessy, for a $1.8 billion purchase price. The real winners were the battalions of bankers and lawyers retained by the four companies, who received fees totaling millions of dollars just for a few weeks of work.

"The Bendix deal was one of the most disgraceful displays of business enterprise that I had seen up until then," Rohatyn said in retrospect. "Harry Gray had an interest and so we tried to make a deal. I thought it was inexcusable that everybody didn't call time out and go home and leave these companies the way they were. Lazard and United Technologies were well out of it, but I think that Hennessy made a perfectly good deal."

The raiders wouldn't "go home" and leave the companies "the way they were." The assault on Revlon would not only be vicious but would prove significant for Rohatyn and for all other dealmakers as well. In this charged atmosphere, the takeover business was booming. By the end of 1985, the amount of money spent on corporate acquisitions would reach $180 billion, 50 percent more than the previous year's record high. Rohatyn's energy and talent were put into overdrive.

* * *

Rohatyn's deal crunches were softened by the relaxed, even playful, side that his marriage to Elizabeth brought to their home life. Their apartment on Park Avenue was a welcome retreat from the weekday office pressures. They often found the time either to entertain or to go out on the town to enjoy social engagements or philanthropic events. In Southampton they could work off the physical tensions of the week by playing a lot of tennis. Shortly after they were married, they had joined the exclusive Meadow Club, noted for its Waspy membership, for the purpose, they said, of getting in good games of tennis on the club's inviting grass courts and for convenience (the club was a mile from their home). Rohatyn's membership was a rare exception to the club's reportedly anti-Semitic policy,* but it wasn't unusual for him to become accepted where others had failed.

In Southampton, guests were limited to good friends, entertaining was casual, and inventive lighthearted touches were added so successfully that one in particular became a Rohatyn ritual.

Beginning in 1980 and almost every year afterward, the Rohatyns hosted an Easter-egg hunt that their close friends looked forward to with relish. All the guests were adults and many of them were Jewish, which didn't stop any of them from getting into the swing of things. For a variety of reasons they skipped 1985, but the Easter-egg hunt that had been held in 1984 was still especially cherished by the participants, who included Henry and Nancy Kissinger, Oscar de la Renta, William Paley, Victor and Betsy Gotbaum, Alan and Peggy Tishman, and Marella Agnelli, wife of the Fiat magnate. Amid a lot of giggling

---

* Rohatyn maintained that their joining the restricted Meadow Club had "no social connotations. The only exception was one time when Elizabeth and I were playing doubles with Victor and Betsy Gotbaum on a court near the road. A young couple on bikes stopped and I heard the girl say to her boyfriend, 'Isn't that Victor Gotbaum?' And the boy said, 'No, it couldn't be. This is the Meadow Club.' "

and joking, the distinguished guests darted about the property, carrying dainty wicker baskets to store any of the dyed and painted eggs they happened on. Good-natured stealing was rampant — spurred by the prospect of winning a prize: one for locating the single golden egg; one for amassing the largest number of eggs; and a booby prize for finding the fewest. The contest was rigged so that Bill Paley, the eldest player, found the golden egg.

The egg hunt was followed by a luncheon around the Rohatyns' long French oak table decorated with fresh flowers, Easter baskets, and jelly beans. Throughout the festivities, Rohatyn freshened drinks and made witty quips about the proceedings. Few were aware that he wasn't completely relaxed that afternoon; all weekend he had been preoccupied by a hotly contested takeover bid that had reached a critical stage and that obliged him to slip quietly out of the room from time to time to telephone a Lazard partner and his client's lawyer to discuss strategy. As long as a telephone was available anywhere in the world, his being out of town never put him out of reach when it came to his clients' interests.

\*    \*    \*

The phone call to his hotel room in Salzburg in the late summer of 1985 brought him up to date on the Revlon situation. When Perelman had first made overtures to Revlon in the spring, Rohatyn had counseled Bergerac not to meet with Perelman if Bergerac wasn't interested in a deal. But Bergerac had ignored Rohatyn's advice. The discussion with Perelman had only strengthened Bergerac's resolve to remain independent. Rohatyn had confidently assured the Revlon chief that Perelman would "never be able to raise the money."

At the time, it seemed inconceivable to Rohatyn — as well as to many on Wall Street — that Perelman's Pantry Pride could win. Though such formidable raiders as T. Boone Pickens and Saul Steinberg had made millions by raising the specter of junk bonds and collecting greenmail, they hadn't gone farther than that — they hadn't actually used the bonds to take over a company. Only one Drexel junk bond–backed hostile takeover had ever been successful, but it was a small deal that hadn't set off alarm bells on Wall Street.

In contrast, the signal emitted by the Revlon deal was loud and clear. By raising hundreds of millions in cash for a war chest from selling junk bonds, Milken had propelled the small-time Perelman into the big leagues. To add to the intricacy of Perelman's maneuvering, he also received help from a pair of solid Establishment institutions: Morgan Stanley, acting jointly with Drexel, provided financial advice for Perelman, and Chemical Bank — which had been outraged by the attack on it sixteen years earlier by outsider Saul Steinberg — was committed to lending Pantry Pride some $500 million. Chemical had never lent money before for a junk bond raid, and Rohatyn asserted later that he had been "amazed" at the bank's participation in a junk bond raid. "We tried to put some pressure on Chemical and some of the directors to drop out" — to no avail. Bergerac also tried, and failed, to dissuade Morgan Stanley.

Caught in what seemed like a cul-de-sac, Revlon had no choice but to mount the best defense possible. Martin Lipton, one of the top lawyers on the Revlon side, put forth a plan for a poison pill that would saddle the company with a mountain of debt if anybody acquired 20 percent or more of its stock. Revlon also fought back in court and contested whether Pantry Pride had, among other things, violated Federal Reserve rules and whether they had honestly divulged the purpose to which they would put the money. Meanwhile as another strategy to discourage Pantry Pride, Rohatyn, with the help of several Lazard partners, assisted Revlon in the repurchase of about a quarter of its shares in exchange for securities, thus saddling a potential acquirer with an added debt burden.

Bergerac and his advisers hailed the defensive efforts up to that point, and for a few weeks Perelman's bid looked dead. Even the press seemed to think so. The *New York Times* ran an article entitled "Victory by Revlon Seen Near."

But Perelman came back. Less than two weeks after Alice Mason's dinner, he made a higher bid than the original one. Pantry Pride's persistence upset Bergerac, who leveled much of the blame at Rohatyn. In a meeting in his Revlon office, Bergerac informed him: "I'm thinking of hiring another investment banker." According to Bergerac, Rohatyn responded: "If you do, it would be a great insult to Lazard."

"I don't want to do anything that would embarrass you," Bergerac assured him, and there the matter rested as the two men went back to work. (Rohatyn stated later that he didn't recall the conversation but admitted that, under the circumstances, "that's what I would have said.")

At about the time of their conversation, Bergerac, who was frustrated with the way the battle was going, began to explore other defensive tactics. He told Rohatyn that he planned to take the company private through a leveraged buyout.

"It's impossible," Rohatyn informed him. "There isn't enough time."

Time was running out, but Bergerac took steps to put a plan

into action. To finance the LBO, Revlon would sell off its fabled cosmetics business. A Manhattan leveraged buyout specialist, Adler & Shaykin, agreed to buy it. Revlon negotiated with Forstmann Little, a major LBO company, to acquire the rest of Revlon, retaining Bergerac to run these operations himself.

No one will ever know for certain if the outcome would have been different if Revlon had adhered to its original defense tactics, but once Bergerac had created his own ploy, Rohatyn and Lipton were forced to play by his rules. "Michel panicked," Lipton said later. "I thought what we were doing would work." Rohatyn remembered "a lot of sleepless nights and my having to stand up for the Forstmann deal in front of his [Bergerac's] board."

The Forstmann deal created more problems than it solved. Once the firm was committed to acquiring Revlon, Revlon virtually dismantled its poison pill defense so that Forstmann Little could make its bid, thus leaving the door wide open for Perelman. As a consequence, the heavily financed Pantry Pride rushed in with a higher bid. To get Forstmann Little to counter Perelman by topping his offer, Revlon had to grant it the exclusive rights to buy two key Revlon operations — regardless of the company's ultimate fate. Perelman quickly countered with an even higher bid. The final blow came in late October. In a court decision, Revlon's exclusive agreement to sell Forstmann Little the two divisions was deemed illegal because Revlon had violated its fiduciary responsibility to its shareholders by not trying to obtain the highest price for "the pieces of the additional Revlon empire."

Bergerac conceded defeat, and Perelman walked away with the prize for $58 a share, or $1.8 billion.

Although he and Rohatyn remained friends, the former Revlon head maintained that the investment banker's defensive strategy hadn't been particularly special or imaginative. "They were the classic moves, like in chess," Bergerac continued to claim, even years afterward. "There are these opening maneuvers and every banker knows them. This was not Felix's shining hour."

"I was sorry we weren't able to keep the company independent, which was what Bergerac wanted," was all Rohatyn would say in response.

But Lipton disagreed strongly with Bergerac's attack. "I think what Michel says is horrendous. This *was* Felix's shining hour. No one ever worked harder than we did, and we did do unique and different things."

Rohatyn's defensive strategy for Revlon embodied all his

Felix and Elizabeth Rohatyn on the grounds of their country home in Southampton. (© *Harry Benson*)

Saul and Gayfryd Steinberg at a PEN party in 1985, surrounded by writers John Irving, Gay Talese, Kurt Vonnegut, William Styron, and Norman Mailer (*left to right*). (*Photograph © 1989 by Jill Krementz*)

(*Above*) Carl Icahn and his wife, Liba (*at right*), with White House chief-of-staff Howard Baker, Elizabeth Taylor, and Malcolm Forbes (*left to right*) at *Forbes* magazine's seventieth anniversary party in 1987.     (*Right*) John Gutfreund and his wife, Susan, at the *Forbes* party.     (*Below*) Felix Rohatyn (*left*) with his wife, Elizabeth (*third from left*), and socialite Louise Grunwald, Barbara Walters, and economist Alan Greenspan (*left to right*) at the *Forbes* party.     (*All photographs this page © 1989 by Jill Krementz*)

John Gutfreund and Gianni Agnelli, Fiat automobile mogul, on Malcolm Forbes's yacht during a Fourth of July party, 1986. *(Photograph © 1989 by Jill Krementz)*

Susan Gutfreund and Brooke Astor on Malcolm Forbes's yacht, at the same party. *(Photograph © 1989 by Jill Krementz)*

Carl Icahn, chairman of TWA, at the airline's annual
stockholders meeting in 1986.  (*AP/Wide World Photos*)

Major donor Sandy Weill with his wife, Joan, attending the
Carnegie Hall reopening gala in December 1986.  (© *1986
Steve J. Sherman*)

Ivan Boesky leaving Federal Court in New York City in 1987 after pleading guilty to one charge of conspiracy. (*Marilynn K. Yee*/The New York Times)

Mike Milken with his attorney, Edward Bennett Williams, at a Congressional hearing in 1988. Milken refused to testify, invoking his Fifth Amendment right against self-incrimination. (*AP/Wide World Photos*)

Peter Cohen, head of Shearson Lehman Brothers (*center*), signing the agreement in 1987 to acquire E. F. Hutton, which created Shearson Lehman Hutton. (*AP/Wide World Photos*)

Joe Perella and Bruce Wasserstein (*right*), the odd couple of the mergers and acquisitions world. (*Vic DeLucia*/The New York Times)

Saul Steinberg and Gayfryd Steinberg in their Park Avenue
apartment.   (© *Theo Westenberger*)

Sandy Weill with his wife, Joan, on the terrace of their
penthouse apartment overlooking New York City's Central
Park.   (© *Michele Singer/Outline*)

Sandy Weill in front of his home in Greenwich, Connecticut, in 1988, at the time of his takeover of Primerica. (© *Harry Benson*)

Peter Cohen, head of Shearson Lehman Hutton, with his wife, Karen, at a Shearson reception in 1988. (*Courtesy of Shearson Lehman Hutton*)

strengths as a dealmaker — financial know-how and experience, a vast network of corporate contacts, and deft negotiating skills. It had worked many times for him in the past. But it had not worked against junk bond financing. Looking back, Rohatyn said, "The only thing we could have done differently was to embark upon a plan of liquidation and gamble that the price of the stock would go up above the tender offer price. That would have given us six to eight months to liquidate the company. I don't think there would have been enough time. The arbs had the stock and were going to tender it to whoever had the higher offer."

In accepting Perelman's bid, the shareholders — primarily the arbs and their allies — had decided the outcome. In the world of takeovers, where money is king, Perelman's money was as good as anyone else's.

Winner or loser, most of the principal players in the Revlon deal made piles of money. Drexel claimed the lion's share — more than $65 million — from Pantry Pride: Morgan Stanley received less than $25 million; the law firm of Wachtell Lipton got $10 million from Revlon, and Lazard was paid some $12 million. Bergerac lost his company but left with a $15 million golden parachute — the largest to that date. And Perelman, of course, got Revlon. It wouldn't be known for some time whether he would make a profit on the deal, but its acquisition gave him a higher footing in the business world. In keeping with his new status, he hired a well-connected social secretary, appointed Ann Getty to the Revlon board, and began hosting celebrity-filled parties at his Upper East Side town house.

*   *   *

The defeat of Revlon ushered in a new era in hostile takeovers. The junk bond predators had triumphed. If they could succeed in capturing Revlon by backing a small company like Pantry Pride, they could win almost anywhere. Rohatyn put it in perspective: "Revlon was a watershed deal for junk bonds." He acknowledged later, "It thrust me into a new world in which companies were being bought and sold and stripped apart like artichokes without taking into account the fact that a large corporation is an entity with responsibilities to employees, customers, and communities."

Rohatyn himself would remain an open critic of junk bond financing. In the next few years, as a succession of major hostile junk bond wars raged across the nation, Rohatyn neither led any of these attacks nor mounted any of these defenses. "Our [Lazard's] position may have cost us some business," he admitted. "But in terms of our standing with our clients and with the business community, I think it stood us in good stead."

Indeed, Lazard had gained and would retain a reputation as a leader in the world of takeovers, and Rohatyn's renown remained widespread as the Dean of Deals. In just two years' time, he had done a handful of friendly ones. In 1983, he had assisted Michael Dingman in merging Wheelabrator-Frye into Signal, and two years later he advised Dingman, by then head of Signal, when the company was acquired by Allied. He counseled Thornton Bradshaw of RCA in 1984, when the television and electronics company sold its CIT Financial to Manufacturers Hanover. That same year, he aided Jean Riboud of Schlumberger in the takeover of Sedco, an oil service business, and advised H. Ross Perot in the sale of Electronic Data Systems to General Motors.

Even before the Revlon takeover was completed, Rohatyn became involved in the then largest deal of them all outside the oil industry. Early in the fall of 1985, he had breakfast with John Welch, chief executive of General Electric, and got him interested in RCA. RCA had been in play for some time, and Rohatyn had already shepherded the company through two proposals: he succeeded in beating back an early-stage bid by Bill Agee of Bendix, and later kept corporate egos from being bruised when talks between RCA and MCA (on whose board Rohatyn sat) broke down. He arranged for Welch to meet Bradshaw, RCA's chief executive, in his apartment for drinks.

After GE made a friendly bid for RCA in December, all the parties involved conferred virtually around the clock seven days a week. In the middle of the negotiations, Rohatyn's mother, who lived in Paris, became ill, and he flew to France on the Concorde to see her. Twenty-four hours later, he was back in New York, exhausted, negotiating again. Ten days after the start of the talks, GE acquired RCA for $6.3 billion.

Over the next few years, Rohatyn would participate in a steady stream of takeovers. But those who knew him well sensed a subtle change in him. While his mind never strayed during his latest deal or venture, he seemed to derive more pleasure than ever before from life as a statesman-at-large — discussing international economics with President François Mitterrand of France, writing about and commenting on political and social as well as business issues that interested him, and turning his home into a veritable salon for guests who were among the brightest, most gifted, and most influential figures of our era. More than just a celebrated dealmaker, he was assuming the mantle of a modern minister of finance.

# CHAPTER THIRTY-ONE

# Ivan Who?

The land surrounding the tiny town of New Castle in upper Westchester County, New York, is known for its great estates set amid rolling hills and lush woodland. Among the most notable is one that includes a twelve-bedroom, red-brick Georgian mansion — nestled on seventy-five secluded acres off Sarles Street — alongside a cobblestone courtyard that accommodates thirty cars, two separate structures that provide living quarters for staff, and a horse barn. A former owner was John Revson, heir to one of the most glamorous fortunes in America — the Revlon cosmetics empire.

In 1978 the Revson property was purchased for $825,000 by forty-one-year-old Ivan Frederick Boesky, the son of an immigrant Russian Jew. By the end of the year, he bought another 116 acres adjacent to the property for $572,000. In the years to come he would spend far more on the estate, building a squash court, swimming pool, and garage to house his collection of classic cars. He liked display.

By 1984 Ivan Boesky was unquestionably one of the richest men on Wall Street. His wealth had just been cited on the *Forbes* list as $150 million.

It hadn't always been that way. Up until the midseventies, try as he might, everything he undertook came unstuck. But between the middle and end of the seventies, perhaps no other financier on Wall Street had made so much money so quickly from the swarm of mergers, particularly hostile takeovers, that engulfed corporate America. At the end of the decade, the private partnership he headed, Ivan F. Boesky & Co., which was largely owned by the arbitrageur himself (the other so-called partners functioned more like employees), had amassed $93 million in capital from risk arbitrage, making his one-man band the fifteenth-largest firm on Wall Street. The actual amount of money he earned was never revealed at that time because his business was private.

Still, there were more than enough hints — from the size of the huge merger deals in which he was involved to the purchase of his new, palatial home — that he was someone to be reckoned with. In a short, two-year burst of playing the high-risk, high-returns arbitrage game,* the unpromising Wall Street outsider went from being Ivan Who? to being Ivan Somebody. Not only was he redefining the arbitrage game, his name would become synonymous with criminal self-aggrandizement and greed.

Even as a youth growing up in Detroit, Ivan Boesky was driven to make money. The one money-making story he would recite with glee was how, at thirteen, with $400 he had just received as bar mitzvah gifts, he bought a used Chevrolet panel truck, painted it white, and stocked it with Eskimo ice-cream bars. The fact that he didn't have a driver's license and automobile registration didn't faze him in the least. After school, he would drive immediately to the spot where a Good Humor truck normally parked an hour later, giving him an early advantage and cutting into his competition's trade. He cleared as much as $100 a week in nickels and dimes, until the day his truck died on a hill. When a passing police car stopped to investigate, Boesky was caught as an underage driver and put out of business.

The episode was all the more revealing of his precocious interest in "the green stuff," as he called it, since he didn't have to work to earn spending money. Boesky, whose parents doted on him, lived in a comfortable suburban home with a broad lawn out front and a dark green Packard in the driveway. His father, William, indigent when he had arrived in the United States at age twelve with his family, owned three restaurants that served American fare. (Before that, the senior Boesky and his four brothers had run a neighborhood deli and had gained some celebrity as pastrami kings in the local Jewish community.)

Young Ivan fitted no predictable behavior pattern in this classical upwardly mobile middle-class family. The same year that he was

---

* Although there are several ways to play it, and many different strategies, over the years risk arbitrage has actually undergone little change. Essentially, an arbitrageur buys stock in a target company after a takeover announcement is made but before the deal is closed. The presumption is that if the deal goes through, the arb makes a spread, or profit, reflecting the difference between the price paid for the stock immediately after the announcement and the price realized when the stock is sold or exchanged for the stock of the acquiring company.

forced out of the ice-cream business, his parents sent him to the posh Cranbrook Academy, a private boarding school in the wealthy Detroit suburb of Bloomfield Hills. He proved not to be a good student and left under mysterious circumstances. He finished his high-school education at Mumford, a public school in the heart of Detroit.

During his college days, Boesky seemed to be adrift. Over the course of three years, he attended three Michigan universities without obtaining a degree. He then joined the United States Information Agency and for a year taught English to Iranians in Teheran — his interest in that city having been piqued by an Iranian friend. Once back in Detroit, he thought he knew what he wanted to do with his life — practice law. Even at the Detroit College of Law, which didn't require a college degree, Boesky was unable to stick with his studies and dropped out of law school twice in two years. By most people's standards in 1962, he was hardly the image of a young comer, certainly not to Ben Silberstein, the father of the young Michigan State coed Seema Silberstein, whom Boesky had met a year earlier and who was about to become his bride.

In marrying Seema, a smiling brunette with fine features and dark curly hair, he actually married into two prominent families — the Silbersteins and, through Seema's stepfather, the Levins.

Ben Silberstein was a self-made Detroit real estate tycoon, whose greatest jewel among his holdings was not in Michigan but in California. He owned the fabled Beverly Hills Hotel, that secluded pink palace that for decades has been the favorite gathering place of film stars, visiting royalty, and Hollywood's power elite. Boesky had never heard of the hotel, but he was not unmindful of Silberstein's wealth. For his part, Silberstein was not enamored of Seema's good-for-nothing husband and believed Boesky had wed his daughter for her money. Among family members and his cronies, he referred to his son-in-law as "Ivan the Bum," a name that hung on for years.

The Levins were an even more prestigious family than the Silbersteins. Divorced from Ben Silberstein, Seema's mother had married Dr. Samuel Levin, whose family boasted an honor gallery of successful professionals, particularly lawyers. (Two of Levin's nephews would eventually represent Michigan in Washington at the same time — Senator Carl Levin and his brother, Congressman Sander Levin.)

After his marriage, Boesky returned to law school for the third time and finally, in 1964, obtained his degree. Nonetheless, he couldn't find work as a lawyer, perhaps because, as he claimed, he applied only to Detroit's top firms.

That same year, his father died. The last few years had been hard ones for Boesky's father. The restaurants he owned had begun to fail, as middle-class residents fled their Detroit neighborhoods for the suburbs. The burden was shared by Boesky, who had worked on and off with his father when he wasn't in school. Father and son had even tried running a nightclub; it went bankrupt. For all of his family's energy — the restaurants and the nightclub — Boesky, at twenty-seven, had little to show for it. Even when his stepfather-in-law intervened on his behalf and secured for him a prestigious one-year position clerking for his brother, U.S. District Judge Theodore Levin, Boesky's prospects didn't improve. No law firm to which he applied was impressed enough to offer him a job.

He did find work in accounting at the Detroit office of Touche Ross, but the job held no greater promise for him than law. Since Seema Boesky had become restive in Detroit and since there was no reason for them to stay, in 1965 they moved to New York City. There, he contacted a former wrestling teammate from Cranbrook, who was an arb working under the legendary Cy Lewis of Bear Stearns. Although he had little understanding of Wall Street, Boesky knew that he didn't want to be a broker and that he wanted to make a lot of money quickly. Arbitrage seemed right for him.

The old familiar pattern soon repeated itself. A contact provided entrée for Boesky, but he was unable to do much with it. His interviews at various Jewish houses, including Goldman Sachs, Kuhn Loeb, Salomon, and Lazard, went badly: "All they seemed to be interested in was who my father was and what degrees I had." The snobbery of these firms grated, and he would remember the rejections. Finally, in 1966, he found a $7,200 a year job as a trainee at the small firm of L. F. Rothschild but soon switched to First Manhattan; then, after being unemployed for eight months, wound up at Kalb Voorhis, his third small brokerage firm. This time there was a difference. He was given the freedom to trade securities and enough money to make it worthwhile. Six months later he was fired. He claimed it was because he had lost $20,000 on one arbitrage play.

"That wasn't why he was let go," said Robert Gutenstein, a partner and director of institutional research at the firm. "Everybody makes and loses a little. We didn't like the way Boesky did his business. He was a professional edge skimmer and unwilling to follow instructions."

For the second time in a little more than a year, Boesky was unable to find work. Two months went by. Often he sat himself down on a Central Park bench, wondering when an opportunity would come along. Unemployment was no cause for practical concern. Silberstein, always ready to indulge his daughter, set up the Boeskys in a luxury co-op on Park Avenue at Seventy-second Street. While they lived well, Boesky hungered for work. His father-in-law's largess combined with his constant disapproval only added to the pressure.

In May 1971, Boesky moved closer to his destiny. He landed a job as head of the arbitrage department at yet another small brokerage firm, Edwards & Hanly. It gave him a platform to launch what would become the unique Boesky style. He was a plunger who was willing to risk everything on a single outcome instead of hedging his bets. He was also secretive and competitive in a field where — at least within the arb community itself — there was always a degree of camaraderie. Instead of sharing a block of stock, which was a common practice of the arbs of the day, he would buy it all for himself — even if that drove up the price for others. He soon earned a nickname among his fellow arbs, Ivan the Terrible.

Boesky's first serious brush with Wall Street regulations came in July 1974. The New York Stock Exchange found him guilty of violating its trading rules on selling short — that is, selling securities that weren't owned but borrowed, in excess of the amount his firm could cover on time. For this infraction of the rules, he was censured and fined $10,000. That hardly seemed to matter. Boesky was plotting his next move — a bold one, created by necessity.

Edwards & Hanly was failing, so he decided to start his own firm. It would be a limited partnership specializing in arbitrage, with a split of 55 percent of the profits to Boesky and 95 percent of the losses to the investors. The start-up money was provided by his family. His wife, Seema, invested $12,500; his mother-in-law, Gertrude Levin, added $400,000; her husband, Sam Levin, chipped in $150,000 and then another $100,000. Now that Edwards & Hanly had gone under, Boesky took over a few unadorned rooms at its former premises at 1 Whitehall Street. He had a seat on the New York Stock Exchange, capital to invest, and a place to play. It was April 1975. Boesky opened for business an an arb under his own umbrella. He was ready for Wall Street, even if Wall Street wasn't ready for him.

\* \* \*

The arbs were a self-contained league, suspicious of newcomers. They didn't want too many players involved in a takeover and with good reason: the more players, the narrower the spreads and the lower the potential profits for each of them. Not only were takeovers on the rise, but so were the premiums raiders were willing to pay corporate management for an acquisition. Aggressive companies were shelling out a hefty 40 percent or more over the market price in the second half of the seventies for the stock of their prey — as opposed to the measly 25 percent or so paid by the sixties raiders. (Necessity played a part in this as well. The old conglomerateurs had had their pick of unexplored territory and bought a lot of companies cheaply.) But the big and fast payoffs came at sizable risk.

While most mergers went through eventually, those that didn't could cause a bloodbath for arbs who had made a substantial investment in the target companies' shares. Among the pros, winners far outnumbered losers. As brokerage houses and professional investors began looking for investments beyond the simple buying and selling of stocks and bonds, arbitrage was enticing. The last thing the arbs needed was for outsiders to discover their specialty — which was exactly what Boesky had in mind. He was going to invite the public to join him as investors.

Boesky's showmanship smacked of P. T. Barnum's. In fact, from April through August 1975, according to his own figures, he lost $196,000. Business looked so bleak that he had to round up an emergency infusion of $750,000 from Lambert Brussels, the U.S. arm of a Belgian holding company. In the face of disaster, he was audacious. With only a handful of employees and a precarious grip on his capital, he acted like a great success. He moved his family into a handsome ten-room white colonial home on two and a quarter acres in North Greenwich, Connecticut. His children, who now numbered four, attended the prestigious Greenwich Country Day School. He hired a public relations man and spent more than $100,000 over the next year and a half promoting himself and attracting investors. He even took ads in the *Wall Street Journal,* stating that his firm was the only one devoted exclusively to the specialty of arbitrage.

Such shameless self-promotion may have doomed Boesky to criticism from his fellow arbs, but the success-haunted underdog had a clear shot at stardom. Arbitrage was relatively untapped territory, a small field that wasn't too well known or understood. And it was run by a faceless crowd. He was willing to be visible and identifiable. He was also willing to bet higher stakes than almost any other arb for the chance to win big — regardless of the risks. He was pursuing his fantasy, filling out its details as he went along, and waiting for the millions to roll in. Anyone who had $75,000 or more to invest could play along with him. It was an incredibly alluring scheme, and Boesky had groomed himself to fit the role.

He was a trim, if somewhat awkward, man, with gleaming white teeth and a mirthless smile that never masked his single-minded intensity. To save time and planning, he dressed in clothes of the same style and color every day: a dark three-piece suit tailored in New York or Hong Kong adorned by a gold watch chain fashioned after one worn by Winston Churchill. Completing the outfit was a starched white shirt with long pointed collar and gold cuff links. Only the tie varied, although it was always a dark silk.

His grandiose dream for himself belied his relative lack of success. He was an arb, yes, but he viewed the merchant bankers, especially the great Rothschilds, as the noblest of financiers. Indeed, he modeled himself after the men in that most revered Jewish family. He had worked for Jewish causes even while he had been living in Detroit, and one of his ambitions was to become a leading figure in the New York Jewish community.

Oddly enough, with his long jaw, narrow nose, and stiff, prematurely graying hair, he bore a vague resemblance to the late film star George Arliss, who had reached stardom portraying Rothschild and Disraeli. Boesky was something of an actor himself, having appeared in an off-Broadway production of *Abie's Irish Rose* in 1975. (Attracted to the stage, he had to try his wings; but, despite what some reviewers praised as an apparent talent for acting, he never pursued it.)

He made sure that everyone knew how serious he was about his ambitions. He bragged about laboring nonstop for twenty hours, living on fruit salad, cottage cheese, and quarts of coffee. He was in the office before seven and continued working into the evening. His prodigious memory for every price quote and business facet of merger negotiations was, in a sense, part of his assets. He was on the phone constantly, sometimes holding three conversations at once on three separate phones, and thought nothing of calling corporate executives at almost any hour of the day or the night, at home or at the office, in search of even the tiniest bit of news about a takeover. He spread the money around and paid well for the information he obtained.

The services he sought seemed routine enough: fees to lawyers to investigate any legal roadblocks to a merger, commissions to brokers to handle trades. Not only were the brokers eager to do business with him: they enabled him to disguise his trades by acting through third parties.

Boesky was so compulsively competitive that one could only

wonder how far he would go to get what he wanted. At work, that compulsive energy made him more than a taskmaster; he was an-overlord. Calm one moment, he would berate an employee the next. Many couldn't stand working for him and left.

Still, his methods seemed to work. He fought off his early defeats and during his first year in business managed to make a $46,000 profit. Several hundred thousand dollars more from investors trickled into his partnership funds, which he promptly invested. In early 1976, victories came easily and he wound up that year with a profit in excess of $3 million. His capital then stood at $6 million, a mere pittance compared to Goldman Sach's $90 million and Salomon Brothers' $143 million. Although those firms committed only part of that money to arbitrage, their power to buy stocks was far greater than his. But unlike the other arbs, Boesky was willing to "bet the ranch" — his capital, borrowed money, and then some — on a single play.

By typical Wall Street practices that respected the Federal Reserve Board's margin requirements, $6 million could be made to function like $12 million. Boesky apparently could stretch the limits through a variety of complex and unorthodox maneuvers so that, in his hands, the money available to him could be made to perform like perhaps ten times as much. Exactly how he managed it, under what circumstances, the amount he actually invested, or even that he did it — these were matters that Boesky never discussed. Despite his hunger for publicity, he refused to reveal his methods or his profits. As the head of a private firm, he wasn't obliged to disclose the numbers behind any deal.

Yet if he was to move into the top ranks of arbitrage, he had to make a splash to catch the eye of the big-time investing public. Giant mergers were increasingly in the news. All he needed was a championship takeover contest. And on March 29, 1977, he found one, when United Technologies went after Babcock & Wilcox, a leading maker of electric utility boilers and nuclear power reactors.

Babcock & Wilcox's stock had been trading at $34 when United Technologies chief Harry Gray made a hostile bid of $42. Boesky, who thought the stock was a good buy, jumped in as it hit $40 a share. Theoretically, he could make only $2 a share more if Gray succeeded, and to add to the risk, if Babcock & Wilcox beat back the bid, the stock was sure to fall way down on the psychological impact of that success alone. It could have cost Boesky millions. But he didn't flinch. In May, J. Ray McDermott & Co., the New Orleans builder of off-shore oil rigs, entered the fray, and Babcock & Wilcox's stock shot up to $44. Boesky bought more. He held on like a cowboy riding a rocket. Throughout the bidding war, Boesky continued to buy the stock heavily — in the neighborhood of half a million shares, averaging some $48 a share. The man who began the year with capital of $6.3 million probably risked over $20 million on his conviction that buying Babcock & Wilcox was a good bet. The bet paid off royally. McDermott won out at $65 a share. Boesky walked away with a staggering profit for the time: an estimated $7 million. The days of living off Ben Silberstein were definitely over. In less than a year he moved his family out of Greenwich to the Revson estate in Westchester, even though the Greenwich house hadn't been sold yet. The move was an assertion of his success.

He wasn't alone in making a killing on Babcock & Wilcox. Three other arbs did equally well for their brokerage firms: Richard Rosenthal of Salomon Brothers, Robert Rubin of Goldman Sachs, and Guy Wyser-Pratte of Bache. They were all under forty and they were all becoming arbitrage stars. But Boesky received the major share of attention.

In its October 1977 issue, *Fortune* ran an article entitled "A Killing in Babcock & Wilcox" that opened with a two-page spread of a triumphant, smiling Boesky talking into a pair of telephones. Suddenly Boesky was an important man on Wall Street. He relocated to roomier new offices in a modern skyscraper in the financial district. His web of contacts grew. Few introductions were needed. He seemed to love the attention, even if much of it was critical. No one in the financial world would ever wonder again who Ivan Boesky was. Well-known executives, who had not even been familiar with his name a year before, jumped to answer their phones when he called, because of the financial clout he wielded.

For the next two years his success was uninterrupted, but in the first quarter of 1980, an off-year in the merger boom, Ivan F. Boesky & Co. stumbled and slipped into the red. Boesky began to receive complaints from investors in his limited partnership. To keep the business intact, he reassured his associates that, despite the setbacks, the difficulties weren't serious.

In May, he assembled some twenty senior staff members at an unusual meeting at the Regency Hotel. He arrived late, as was his habit. Then he announced the reason for the meeting. He was leaving the firm, he informed them without warning. He wanted to assure them that no one would be hurt. The firm would continue — someone would be brought in to replace him. Fifteen minutes later, after he had turned

the meeting over to his lawyer and accountant, Boesky left. Everyone
was in shock.

Some of the worst moments between Boesky and his staff were
yet to come that fall. He planned to leave very little of his money in
the firm. The attempt to find a replacement for him failed. It was clear
that Ivan F. Boesky & Co. was to be left a mere shell of its former
self. That meant that the hard work and long hours of the senior staff
wouldn't be rewarded. To make matters even worse, Boesky called
them together for a meeting and told them that he wanted to be protected against all past and future liabilities of the firm. The others
wouldn't hear of it. He blew up and stormed out. Finally, they quit.
He told the investors in his partnership to look elsewhere for investment
opportunities after he was gone.

He was vague in explaining why the limited partnership was
no longer right for him. He spoke in general terms about wanting to
start a corporation to do certain things that were not permitted in his
former partnership agreement. He needed room to maneuver, and he
would find it.

*    *    *

Meanwhile, Boesky was plotting to start his next business,
seeking ways to amass capital to make an even bigger impact. In the
spring of 1981, the Ivan F. Boesky Corporation got under way by
selling stock worth $28 million. Boesky was reinventing himself on a
much grander scale.

Opportunity and his fascination with empire building enabled
him to enhance his image beyond the world of arbitrage, even as he
was abandoning his first great venture. Apparently he saw a chance
both to make money and to step on to a larger stage in the struggle
for control of the famed Beverly Hills Hotel, the prestigious centerpiece
in the real estate empire of Ben Silberstein, who had died in 1979. He
had left his daughters, Seema Boesky and Muriel Slatkin, equal 48
percent shares in the hotel and the remaining 4 percent swing vote to
his sister.

For his daughter Muriel and her husband, Burton, the hotel
was the fulcrum of their life. Burton Slatkin held the post of chairman
and chief executive, and Muriel Slatkin entertained VIPs at her double
cabana by the pool. They tried to buy the outstanding 4 percent left
to Silberstein's sister but balked at the asking price, a decision they
would come to regret. When the sister died the following year, Boesky
negotiated with her son to buy out the swing shares, which made him

and his wife, Seema, principal shareholders. By the following summer, he began to transform the Beverly Hills Hotel into one of his investment vehicles. Seema and her sister Muriel stopped speaking to each other.

The hotel itself was merely one asset of the Beverly Hills Hotel Corporation, which also owned a majority of the voting stock in a privately held San Diego–based chain known as Vagabond Hotels. With control of 52 percent in the corporation, Boesky had the power to do as he pleased with the Vagabond chain. In September 1983, he turned to Mike Milken and Drexel Burnham Lambert for help in taking the chain public, in large measure to generate cash to finance his growing arbitrage needs. Some $96.2 million was raised for Vagabond — more than a third of which would go into his arbitrage business.

The man who craved money and attention now also craved prestige. Through his contact with an investor in the newly formed Ivan F. Boesky Corporation, Dr. Howard Hiatt, dean of Harvard's School of Public Health, he made a generous contribution to the school and became a Visiting Committee member of its Board of Overseers, a status that permitted him membership in the Harvard Club in New York. There he held meetings and played squash daily with the assistant pro, without ever having attended a class at the premier Ivy League university.

In October, he pledged $2.5 million to the Jewish Theological Seminary of America for a library to be named after him and Seema. At the Seminary's annual dinner held at the Plaza Hotel that month, he was joyously carried around the room by, among others, Rabbi Yaacov Rosenberg, the vice chancellor.

Boesky's interest in his Jewish heritage and in Jewish education was genuine. He owned a rare collection of Judaica, which he would donate to the library. He had also been an active trustee at his children's private school and served for two years as chairman for the United Jewish Appeal-Federation of Jewish Philanthropies annual Wall Street dinner and the Wall Street division's fund-raising drive. In the coming year, 1984, he was to be the organization's national campaign chairman. The post went to large contributors who were also prepared to work hard at wooing other donors. For that fund-raising effort and for all his years of service, he would earn the honor of Man of the Year.

He could afford to be generous. In 1984, he made killings in Texaco's takeover of Getty Oil and Socal's takeover of Gulf. By most estimates, Boesky cleared $50 and $65 million, respectively, for his investments.

He moved his headquarters to the chic thirty-fifth-floor offices on Fifth Avenue that had previously belonged to the fugitive commodities trader Marc Rich. Among its special features were a $10,000 marble-topped conference table and cameras located in employees' offices that enabled Boesky, by watching a small panel of television screens near his desk, to see without being seen. Although it had been Rich who installed the cameras, they were perfectly suited to Boesky and his well-known mania for control.

His principal arb play in the waning months of 1984 provided a stern test of his dominance in the game. Oils had been good to him, and he would stick with them despite his staff's advice that virtually nothing was left to be gained in an industry that had witnessed, over the past three years, the pillaging of most of the major companies, from Conoco to Gulf. His plays in oils produced his period of greatest prosperity and he avoided hitting a dry hole — thanks in part to Carl Icahn's victory at Phillips.

*   *   *

One chilly winter afternoon early in 1985, Ivan Boesky strode into the Harvard Club, on West Forty-fourth Street off Fifth Avenue in New York City. The elegant stone-and-brick building had been the 130-year-old club's home for ninety-four years and a favorite meeting place of Boesky's for the past four. He stopped by the fireplace in the lobby, glanced around, then glided into the club's cavernous wood-paneled central room. Removing his close-fitting black cashmere overcoat and black leather gloves, he slipped into a high-backed red leather chair.

He had come to be interviewed. Often evasive or impatient in answering questions about himself or his business, on this occasion he was uncharacteristically open and friendly. In the spring, his first book was to be published and he was excited about the prospect of being an author. He said he liked the title, *Merger Mania,* because it was attention grabbing, especially for what was essentially a textbook about risk arbitrage according to Ivan Boesky. It was his last hurrah at image building before that image crumbled to dust.

"There really isn't anything about me in it," he professed. Nevertheless, the very act of writing that book was a highly revealing use of his aspirations for himself. Ivan Boesky had been re-creating himself — again. And he had done a spectacular job of assembling the props of respectability — from membership in the Harvard Club to the ownership of one of the world's greatest hotels to appearing on the avidly read *Forbes* magazine annual list of the 400 richest Americans.

Some months later, in June 1985, Boesky was sitting in a Wall Street bookstore, surrounded by mountains of *Merger Mania,* signing copies. "I think you'll be disappointed," he said jokingly to one buyer. "There's no sex. But read it anyway." Later in the year, he went on a seven-city tour across the country to promote the book. He appeared on radio and television talk shows, including "Today," and was interviewed in newspapers and magazines. But the intense media scrutiny of his book and his success at arbitrage revealed a different picture from the one Boesky tried to project. In press coverage, he left the impression that his entire high-school education had taken place at Cranbrook, the exclusive Michigan prep school he had attended as a young teen (with no mention of the public school from which he actually graduated) and that his college days had been spent only at the University of Michigan, one of several universities he had attended without ever having graduated. He also implied that he was an accountant or had a degree in accounting. In July of 1984, *Fortune* took a close look, revealing the other schools Boesky had actually attended. In May of 1985, the *American Lawyer* gave the most damning account of Boesky at work. Boesky invested heavily in Phillips when T. Boone Pickens raided the oil company and stood to lose millions when Pickens dropped his bid. But Boesky appeared to have recovered and the magazine essentially implied that he had obtained inside information from Carl Icahn during the winter of 1984–1985 and taken advantage of it — a serious violation of securities law.

Boesky and Icahn had been friends since they had both been young arbs, and for the past few years they had lived near each other in Westchester. Icahn had bought his home in Bedford after Boesky had acquired his estate in New Castle, but Boesky appeared to be the one who was pursuing the friendship. At Boesky's request, Icahn had written a strong letter of recommendation to his alma mater, Princeton, for Boesky's eldest son. In all likelihood Boesky would have been at Icahn's Christmas party, had he not been vacationing on Barbados during Pickens's Phillips raid. When Boesky found out that Pickens had settled, he hurried back like a man who, by Street estimates, had $300 million at stake, and called Icahn.

Boesky, the *American Lawyer* asserted, invited Icahn to his house to discuss the possibility of leading a raid on Phillips, following Boesky's discussions with Drexel about financing one. Several weeks later, just days before Icahn launched his raid, Boesky sold him 2.7 million Phillips shares. The block presumably helped build up Icahn's position.

After the raider had made his bid, Boesky told him he had bought 4 million shares. It wasn't known whether Boesky had purchased the stock before or after the attack, but it was abundantly clear that he had known more than any other Phillips investor about Icahn's activities. He denied ever talking to Icahn "about any stocks or deals or stocks we're involved in," but his credibility was sinking fast. *Merger Mania* provided further evidence of his questionable practices.

On the book's jacket he lied about being an adjunct professor at both New York University's and Columbia University's graduate schools of business. In truth, he had never taught at Columbia and he had not taught at NYU for two years. *Merger Mania* itself was at best a grand deception. Though Boesky was responsible for the contents, the book was ghostwritten by business writer Jeffrey Madrick, who was listed merely as the book's editor. At the very least, the book appeared to owe a great debt to a 1982 monograph entitled *Risk Arbitrage II*, published by New York University's graduate school of business and written by rival arb Guy Wyser-Pratte, who had nicknamed Boesky Piggy. Professor Arnold Sametz, who supervised the publication of NYU's monograph series, thought that Boesky was both "mad" and "dumb" to publish a book that so closely followed the monograph.

More and more, the man who would be a Rothschild — and who had actually cultivated the friendship of Baron Eli Rothschild — came to resemble Gatsby. Many found his desperate social climbing distasteful and even more so his chronic need to boast about and exaggerate his accomplishments. (For instance, when flamboyant international corporate raider Sir James Goldsmith, who also occupied offices in the same Fifth Avenue building, first met him, Boesky spent most of the time describing all the contributions he made to charity. Goldsmith reportedly refused to have any further business or social contact with Boesky.)

Somehow everything that Boesky acquired or accomplished seemed tainted. But he never stopped or even slowed down. There was the limousine with the three telephones so that he could conduct business with several parties simultaneously, even while in transit; the Gulfstream jet virtually on call; the fortieth-floor apartment near Manhattan's Sutton Place; the Rolls-Royce he tooled around in; and the estate in Westchester, with a Renoir nude in the dining room and a life-sized bronze by Maillol and other sculpture in the gardens, which were tended by several gardeners. Boesky planned to spend $375,000 on an addition to the estate that would make it look more like Thomas

Jefferson's majestic Monticello.* But his most grandiose scheme of all was to acquire more money.

On a flight back from California, Boesky confided to one of his closest associates the sum that he wanted: a billion dollars. And by the spring of 1986, with Mike Milken raising most of the capital for a new Boesky partnership, he would have it. The net around both of them would tighten as the government investigated just how legally both had become such rich and powerful men.

---

* In 1985, the Boeskys made plans to enlarge their home by building a domed structure over a new master bedroom. Four years later, it still hadn't been built, in part because the necessary zoning variance hadn't been approved.

# CHAPTER THIRTY-TWO

# The Last Great Predators' Ball

*W*hether they were admiring, skeptical, or just curious, all of them were waiting for him. Nothing else could explain why hundreds of America's top corporate financial officers, money managers, insurers, and bankers, who came from around the country, had left their offices for four days of lectures at the Beverly Hilton Hotel in Los Angeles. The businessmen in the ballroom that day were responsible for millions, hundreds of millions, even billions of dollars in assets — employee pensions, mutual funds, college endowments, philanthropic funds, corporate portfolios, individual accounts, and bank trusts. Despite this awesome array of financial power, the opening-day audience on Wednesday, April 2, 1986, was aware that Michael Milken was the polestar of the events, someone to be heard.

By 6:30 A.M. nearly every seat at every table was taken in the Hilton Hotel ballroom for the start of the seventh annual Drexel Burnham Lambert bond conference. The west-coast conference — begun in 1980 with a few corporate executives addressing fifty or so Drexel guests at the Beverly Wilshire Hotel — had grown into a major event, in which 2,000 financiers joined the top executives of more than sixty companies at the Hilton, the Beverly Wilshire, and the Century Plaza. It was a very private gathering of perhaps the greatest concentration of securities buyers and sellers in the world, a place where they met, mingled, gathered information, and made deals. Some of the most powerful names in American business would attend the conference. In this clubby atmosphere, many of the participants knew one another or were introduced to new acquaintances by old friends. A small army of security men, identifiable only by red pins on their lapels, eyed the latecomers' name tags. Despite the large number in attendance, participation was by invitation only, and those present saw their invitations to attend Milken's conference as a sign of their acceptance in the inner reaches of the financial world and as an appointment not to be missed.

Carl Icahn, Drexel's star takeover client of the past year and a principal speaker at the 1985 conference, was a reluctant no-show. A terrorist attack that left four passengers dead from a bomb explosion on a TWA plane had forced him to remain in New York.

At precisely 6:50 A.M., the scheduled time for the start of the conference, Milken climbed onto the darkened stage and into the spotlight. Two television cameras projected his image onto giant screens on either side of the stage. Now thirty-nine, he looked much younger. Perhaps he owed much of his youthfulness to a certain boyish quality in his carriage and manner. He stood back on his heels and clasped his hands behind his back, then leaned forward and gently rested his hands on the podium in front of him. He smiled pleasantly but shyly, like a well-prepared student about to recite his term paper.

Milken spoke for about ten minutes in a slow, deliberate manner, clearly not the voice of an evangelist. He offered no welcoming small talk. Instead he began with a rundown of the four-day schedule, then launched into his introduction, remarking briefly on the weak dollar, the expansion of international securities trading, the importance of good corporate management, and, of course, high-yield securities.

In making his case for junk bonds, he maintained that the American companies that were not rated "investment grade," which totaled 90 percent of all U.S. corporations with assets of more than $25 million, accounted for all the job gains in the nation within the past twenty years. By contrast, "the 500 largest corporations employed three million less people in 1985 than they employed in 1965. . . . We believe that it would be extremely detrimental to restrict the flow of capital to these companies [which issue junk bonds] that are providing the new jobs in this country and have increased the competitiveness of the United States," Milken told the audience, anticipating the Drexel Burnham television ad campaign launched in 1987 that dramatized the same point for millions of ordinary viewers.*

For his legions of followers, his introductory remarks were a comforting balm. He didn't have to rouse his audience. His junk bonds already had done that for him. He was the genial host warming up the

---

* According to the most commonly used standard — the Fortune 500 companies — this group of the largest corporations in America actually showed an increase in the number of people employed from 1965 to 1985. However, the gain was substantially less than that of total U.S. employment for the same period.

crowd for his guest speakers so that they could make the big pitch for more of the audience's billions.

First among the parade of venturesome corporate chiefs and investors who came to the podium to acclaim the riches to be reaped with the help of high-yield bonds was Ronald Perelman of Revlon, an obvious spokesman for what Drexel could do for a company. A glitzy Revlon promotional film was flashed on the screens accompanied by a driving disco beat. Top models Kim Alexis and Lauren Hutton demonstrated Revlon products, and "Dynasty" star Joan Collins made a cameo appearance to promote Scoundrel, the name of a leading Revlon perfume. Samples of Revlon products were then given out as gifts.

Afterward, Milken bounded onto the stage to express his appreciation for Perelman's talk and to remark briefly that there was plenty of money around, far more than many imagined, and a lot more waiting to be made. "The world is no longer an even world," he said. "There is a spread of two hundred fifty billion dollars between value [of corporate assets] and market value."

The smart money boys were doing their best to capture their share, and their numbers were even greater than people suspected. *Forbes* magazine, according to Milken, had gotten its facts all wrong. Instead of the few dozen people who were worth at least $500 million, there were "one thousand." Coming from Milken, such a statement couldn't be taken lightly. (Though he wasn't even mentioned by *Forbes* as among the four hundred richest men in America, many at the conference thought he belonged. That fall the magazine corrected this apparent error by listing his net worth as far exceeding $500 million. Later, it was revealed that from 1983 to 1986 alone, he was paid $600 million by Drexel and appeared to spend little of it.) And he seemed to want to make his audience believe that each of them could join the club.

At lunch, the participants were treated to a rich dessert of chocolate mousse, whipped cream, and strawberries, along with a talk on third-world debt by a panel of international economists. Later that day, they heard from Henry Kravis of Kohlberg Kravis Roberts, promoting Beatrice, KKR's $6.2 billion leverage-buyout crown jewel, followed by Lorimar chairman Merv Adelson, producer of the television series "Dallas," "Falcon Crest," and "Knots Landing," who presented the opening salvo of Adelson's financial show that would reach its climax Thursday evening with a spectacular party.

In the era of Reaganism only a personal representative of the president was missing. But at least one notable spokesman from the president's party was scheduled to appear. The pace of the conference was building. By the end of that opening Wednesday Milken had already trotted out sixteen companies, but the evening's three-ring-plus sales pitch was still to come.

Shortly after the last presentation, fleets of vans and limousines filled to capacity headed for the Beverly Wilshire, a block east of Drexel's offices. In the hotel's vast ballroom, the executives of Circus Circus Enterprises, a Nevada casino operator, overwhelmed the financiers with an avalanche of food, entertainment, and a promotional film about their gambling operations. Waitresses in gold lamé microdresses served cocktails and hors d'oeuvres, while the financiers played casino and carnival games for prizes of stuffed animals.

At seven o'clock, the lights dimmed to signal the guests to take their seats for the dinner and show. On each table the circus-theme centerpiece brimmed with lollipops, popcorn, and Cracker Jack. The guests munched, watched the promotional film, and waited to be served. During an almost incidental main course of veal and red wine, acrobats performed on the stage. By ten o'clock the show was over. Sixteen hours after it had begun, the first day of the bond conference was winding down. Milken himself was nowhere in sight. In another six hours, his day would begin again.

* * *

"Thanks," said Irwin Jacobs, chairman of the Minneapolis-based conglomerate Minstar. He was addressing Mike Milken in front of a packed audience at the opening presentation on Thursday morning in the Hilton ballroom. "It's a miracle. I'm fulfilling the American dream."

Milken, who was on Jacobs's right and out of the bright lights, accepted the shower of praise unassumingly. It could not have come from a more knowledgeable source. Jacobs, one of the most aggressive raiders on the takeover scene, had been practically born to his calling — Meshulam Riklis, still head of Rapid-American, the billion-dollar retail company that was his private fiefdom, had once been his Hebrew-school teacher. The tall, dark, broad-shouldered Jacobs, who was known as the Liquidator, had seized such firms as the Bekins moving company, the AMF bowling and sporting goods corporation, and several pleasure-boat builders.

The next speaker, Fred Carr — one of the hottest young mutual fund operators of the late 1960s and now chairman of First Executive, a $5 billion life insurance company — was among those buying lots of junk bonds. Seemingly permanently middle-aged, Carr was such a familiar figure in the financial game that he could blithely cast out the verboten words "junk bonds" and get a laugh from the knowing audience.

Increasingly, the conference took on a fraternal, though somewhat structured, atmosphere. Between sessions, in the halls and in corridors, the Wall Street financiers tended to mingle, while the institutional investors huddled in groups of three or four. Meanwhile, the corporate chieftains flanked themselves with their subordinates. Corporate stars who had made presentations, or were going to, joined the throngs in the corridors. Martin Davis, successor to Charles Bluhdorn as CEO at Gulf & Western, was surrounded by attentive associates; so was Henry Silverman, nominally the chairman of Days Inn but in reality the advance man for Saul Steinberg. Talking amicably with Meshulam Riklis was Carl Lindner, head of American Financial and one of the richest men in the country.*

Many lingered in the corridors because more was going on outside than inside the conference rooms. The corridors of power were literally here. At one point, a voice came over the hotel public address system saying: "Please clear the corridors and go to the meeting rooms." The request went unheeded. These men were used to calling their own shots and participating in a complicated web of financial activity. Their relationships went beyond the realms of mere business and friendship to a kind of reciprocal professional bond as they invested in one another's deals.

Prior to a speech given by W. Michael Blumenthal, chairman of Burroughs and a former secretary of the treasury under President Jimmy Carter, Milken performed the lead-in for an MTV-caliber show on the big screens featuring the Wall Street version of the movie *Ghostbusters*. As Dan Aykroyd, Bill Murray, and Harold Ramis shuffled through their steps, dubbed voices asked:

> *Want a better return,*
> *Who ya gonna call? Call Drexel.*
>
> *When it's money you need,*
> *And you gotta have it fast,*
> *Who ya gonna call? Call Drexel.*
> *I ain't afraid of no big deals.*

---

\* Riklis and Lindner, who had owned 40 percent of Riklis's Rapid-American, were old friends. Lindner, who followed the tenets of his Baptist Church, routinely gave away one-tenth of his annual earnings to different charities, including Jewish ones.

Those who stayed throughout the conference could shake hands with the biggest, boldest, and most notorious dealmaker in the world —J. R. Ewing a.k.a. Larry Hagman. The "Dallas" star seemed a natural adjunct to the week's proceedings. On Thursday evening, the scene shifted to the old MGM studio lot in nearby Culver City. Buses rolled onto the lot and disgorged their passengers, than headed back to the Hilton to collect more. The guests were greeted by a carnival atmosphere not unlike the one the night before. At the door a cowboy on stilts welcomed them. Inside, an organ grinder with his monkey made music, and booths were set up to serve a dizzying array of food, including roast beef, pizza, hot dogs, egg rolls, shish kabob, brownies, tacos, ice-cream sundaes, cotton candy, and strawberries with whipped cream and chocolate. It was all part of Lorimar chairman Merv Adelson's final presentation.

While the Lorimar bash went forward, some one hundred of the top money men, dealmakers, and raiders were being treated to a special separate reception, a Drexel tradition. A champagne party in Bungalow Eight at Boesky's Beverly Hills Hotel was followed by a dinner at Chasen's, a ritzy Los Angeles restaurant frequented by celebrities.

Meanwhile, back at the MGM studio, as Merv Adelson called out their names, the stars of his television series marched across the stage, while their images flashed across several TV screens. From "Falcon Crest" came Morgan Fairchild, Caesar Romero, and Jane Wyman; from "Knots Landing," Julie Harris, Donna Mills, and Ruth Roman; from "Dallas," Howard Keel, Priscilla Presley, and Deborah Shelton. Finally, Larry Hagman strode onto the stage with his television wife, Linda Gray, on his arm. Sporting a white cowboy hat and a billion-dollar smile, Hagman/Ewing tossed a fistful of nonnegotiable bills into the appreciative audience. A smiling Milken, dressed in a tuxedo, circulated among the crowd. In many ways, he outshone even the TV stars. Everyone seemed to want to shake his hand. By ten o'clock, the visitors headed to the waiting buses to return to their hotels.

* * *

At lunch the next day, U.S. senators Frank Lautenberg, Bill Bradley, and Alfonse D'Amato spoke to an audience loaded with their New Jersey and New York constituents. They covered the legislative, financial, and economic spectrum from left to right, respectively, exhorting the audience not to forget about the needs of the poor, the middle-class, and the rich.

The conference wound down late Friday afternoon (although

Armand Hammer, the head of Occidental Petroleum, would be the featured speaker during the actual finale on Saturday morning). Coastal chairman Oscar Wyatt, Jr., who with his wife, Lynn, had made every effort to be in real life what the Ewings of "Dallas" and the Carringtons of "Dynasty" were on television, spoke about his Texas energy company, fiftieth on the Fortune 500 list, and Eli Broad, the extremely wealthy California builder and insurance magnate, also spoke.

Milken himself introduced Meshulam Riklis, a longtime client, customer, and friend and the occupant of the penthouse floor of the Drexel Burnham building. (Riklis was also the husband of the well-publicized actress Pia Zadora, but in this setting, he was the undisputed star.)

"I think one of the things you learn in this business is, you learn who are the people who accept responsibility," Milken said, "and people whom you can count on through thick and thin. And those of you who have been creditors of Rapid-American and McCrory [one of R-A's subsidiaries] for the past twenty years, twenty-two years, have not had a missed interest payment or principal payment during that period of time."

Riklis smiled slyly when Milken finished and turned Milken's remarks into fodder for his impish humor. Despite the kind words from Milken about his company, Riklis wondered why he was one of the last corporate chiefs scheduled to speak.

"Can you imagine I even got up at five o'clock in the morning, one morning [this week]?" he said in his heavy Israeli accent. "It's against my religion. And I come over here and listen to all the speeches. Do you know that when I heard from Mike the first time, he called me, wanted to know about my bonds. I had a billion dollars of these high-yield bonds, unrated, in 1968. I think Mike just got out of school. He called me up one day, and he says, to talk about the bonds, 'But, Rik, these are junk.' I said, 'Mike, that's what they are.' And that's how the name junk bonds started. You see, you didn't even know. Today Mike would like to forget it. This is high yield. Even I have a tie on today. . . . What I did twenty years ago, the goyim are doing today. . . . It's certainly wonderful to see everybody making so much money."

Milken could only smile and nod his head like someone who had been hoisted unwittingly on his own petard.

\*   \*   \*

The stellar entertainment attraction came in the evening. By comparison, the extravaganzas mounted earlier in the conference by

Circus Circus and Lorimar were mere sideshows, entertaining business pitches. Friday night was Milken's event alone.

At six o'clock, it seemed as though all the money in the world was assembling in the lobby outside the ballroom at the Century Plaza Hotel. Security was tight. Cocktails were served, along with a sumptuous seafood buffet of crab, shrimp, lobster, oysters, and smoked salmon, but few of the businessmen ate much. They were too busy talking. More of them turned out for Milken's showstopper than for any other event during the four-day conference. The business at hand was business, and for a fleeting hour every visitor at the gathering had the rare opportunity to mingle with everyone else. At dinner the seating would be strictly by rank in Milken's firmament of customers.

At seven o'clock the cocktail hour ended on schedule, and the money men filed into the ballroom. One of the last to enter the room was Denver oil billionaire Marvin Davis, a towering man; Davis smiled in recognition of so many familiar faces, without seeming to notice that the crowd parted to let him pass. Like the other VIPs, Davis sat down at a table in the front of the ballroom. Each man seemed to have his own turf. Milken sat on one side of the room, while T. Boone Pickens, the raider who more than anyone else, except for Milken, had popularized junk bonds, sat on the other.

As the lights in the huge multitiered room dimmed, Senator Alan Cranston of California stepped into the spotlight onstage and introduced "my host, my friend, Mike Milken."

With practiced aplomb, Milken, attired in a tuxedo, took over the spotlight and welcomed the audience with a touch of self-deprecating humor. Television screens in the four corners of the room lit up with a slide showing a Drexel trader looking out on a rainy morning, saying: "Wow, what a day to be a workaholic." It was followed by another slide in which a Drexel infant-in-training called from his baby carriage: "Get me the Coast." Film clips of the cafeteria riot from the movie *Animal House* and the baked-bean-cum-flatulation scene from Mel Brooks's *Blazing Saddles* were shown to illustrate the exacting care Drexel took in grooming its executives. Even Drexel's much-touted packaging of third-world debt was attacked with irreverent delight. While a newscaster spoke glowingly of South America as a haven for safe, sure investments, Butch Cassidy and the Sundance Kid were shown shooting it out in Bolivia. Milken assured the guests that no expense had been spared to entertain them that evening. Knowing laughter erupted from the audience when he showed a rare film clip of Imelda Marcos singing off-key at a party.

Milken had business to conduct under the guise of humor. A

driving Randy Newman rock video — in which Los Angeles, pretty girls, and Rolls-Royces provided the backdrop — served as the transition to his theme: perception. Dustin Hoffman appeared as a woman in *Tootsie,* Julie Andrews as a man in *Victor/Victoria,* Steve Martin as Lily Tomlin in *All of Me,* and Christopher Reeve as a suddenly powerless, graying Superman. The biggest laugh of the evening came when a character from *Animal House* said: "They fucked up. They trusted us." In short, the message was that AAA-rated bonds may be in reality CCC bonds with low interest rates, so buy high-yield securities. Rock singer Madonna appeared on screen and the words to her hit song "Material Girl" ("We're living in a material world and I am a material girl. . . .") were given a Drexel twist, "We're living in a high-yield world and I am a double B girl. . . ."

If that wasn't enough to get the message across, Milken then savaged the competition. On the screens overhead, the Prudential rock was seen hurtling across the New York City skyline and Larry Hagman was shown throwing away his American Express card for a Drexel titanium one. While all of this was going on, the guests made sporadic conversation and consumed a dinner of filet mignon, asparagus, and coffee and dessert served in the dark. They knew the video was just a prelude to what was to come.

Each year, Milken had a surprise guest entertainer. In 1984, it was Frank Sinatra. The following year, it was Diana Ross, also an investor in junk bonds. Though no one knew until the last moment who the 1986 star would be, they had one clue: the two previous performers had both worked at Steve Wynn's Atlantic City Golden Nugget, another Milken client. This evening Wynn was there, and Milken now showed a Golden Nugget commercial that featured Dolly Parton as a chambermaid at the hotel.

When the stage lights came up, Dolly Parton herself, dressed in glittering pink, bounced into view. Scanning the audience, she remarked, "This looks like the original cast of the 'Lifestyles of the Rich and Famous.' " Thanking her host for inviting her, she said: "Mike Milken is a very important man. When he talks, E. F. Hutton listens." Having touched all the right bases, Parton launched into her forty-five-minute performance.

The audience was appreciative but didn't call for encores. It was close to 11:30 P.M. There were conversations to finish, morning business meetings to prepare for, and perhaps for some visitors, a weekend in Los Angeles with the family. Outside the ballroom, the guests picked up coffee mugs marked "Drexel Burnham Lambert Conference '86."

Hundreds milled in the lobby, but the crowd thinned out quickly. Milken was one of the last to leave the ballroom. Seemingly as fresh as he had been seventeen hours earlier, he accepted a few congratulatory handshakes before heading out into the night.

The bond conference had been heady, the splashiest one of them all, yet it would be remembered primarily as the last great predators' ball.

He had been in the spotlight at the conference, the acknowledged mastermind of junk bonds as the road to riches, but Milken himself remained a shadowy figure, his exact wealth still a matter of conjecture. He could not have known that shortly investigators would begin probing the shadows and that the scrutiny would result from the ripple effect of the investigation of a man he had helped enrich even as he was enriching himself — Ivan Boesky.

# CHAPTER THIRTY-THREE

# The High Cost of Excess

Not since the turn of the century and the gilded days of J. P. Morgan had Wall Street's entrepreneurs made as much money as they did in the springtime of 1986. As the great bull market was enjoying its fourth year, corporations and Wall Street seemed intoxicated with taking in more and more money faster and faster. A variety of critics voiced their apprehension about what they saw as greed that had gone out of control. Undoubtedly the shock waves from the revelations that spring about insider trading alerted the nation to how far a few were willing to go to grab secret, sure profits and to the intricacy of their illegal activities. Dubbed "the scandal" by the media, the revelations threatened to taint the entire financial community.

Beginning in May with a federal indictment against a single investment banker, the subsequent chain of events mushroomed into one of the most far-reaching financial scandals in history. Over the course of the next three years, it was revealed that more than a dozen insiders — many of them members of Wall Street's most powerful firms — as well as one of the hottest houses on the Street had amassed millions of dollars in illegal profits. In each case, the crime and the circumstances were essentially the same. The accused were charged with violating securities laws that prohibited insider trading, that is, they used material confidential information, primarily about impending merger bids, to profit from securities transactions.

As a result of the unprecedented takeover activity in the 1980s, the Securities and Exchange Commission, under the direction of former E. F. Hutton vice chairman John Shad, had vigorously pursued insider trading violations. The agency had already prosecuted dozens of cases. When corporations decided to acquire a company, typically they were prepared to pay much more for its stock than its current market price. Thus, trading on advance knowledge about a pending merger could be very lucrative.

As case after case showed, the guilty could be just about anyone with a connection or advance knowledge of a merger — from executives high up in the corporation making the bid to their friends and relatives to bankers and lawyers working on the deal to business writers. In profiting from insider information, they were draining off money that otherwise would have gone to ordinary shareholders, who certainly would have held on to their stock had they known that in a very short time, once the takeover offer was made public, they were guaranteed to be richer.* Insider trading is made even more tempting by the fact that stocks are traded in the open market and not between individuals, so that it is virtually impossible to identify the victims, thus lending an abstract quality to the crime.

Casting a long shadow over Wall Street, the scandal raised disturbing questions about the ethics and honesty of the financial community. Fear of regulation and a loss of investor confidence ran rampant. But none felt the sting of the scandal more acutely than the Jewish investment bankers and brokers. Many of those charged in the unfolding scandal were Jewish.

Dennis Levine, thirty-three, the first to be indicted in the scandal, seemed to fit the general profile of a New Crowd financier. He had grown up in middle-class surroundings in Bayside, Queens, the son of the owner of a small aluminum-siding business. Levine went to public schools straight through to an MBA at Baruch College, a branch of the City University of New York. Job hopping on Wall Street, from Smith Barney to Lehman Brothers, he landed high up in the hierarchy of the most controversial and innovative firm of the day — Drexel Burnham Lambert.

His ambition was to become as successful as the superstars of mergers and acquisitions, men like Felix Rohatyn and Bruce Wasserstein. And Levine showed every indication of succeeding. He became known as someone who was especially well informed about what was going on in M&A. For his knowledge and contacts, he was paid $1 million a year. By 1986, he seemed to be on top of the world: a wife

---

* An SEC study of 172 successful tender offers from 1981 to 1985 disclosed that in every case the price of the target company's stock rose abnormally — some 40 percent — shortly before the bid was announced. Thus, on average, a crook could nearly double his investment, even quadruple it, if bought on margin, that is, with borrowed money — and in some cases, many times that, if purchased with options — in a relatively short time.

and a child, with another child on the way, a luxury six-room co-op on Park Avenue, and an $80,000 red Jaguar.

In 1980, he had opened an account in the Bahamian subsidiary of a Swiss bank that would lead to his downfall. Through a series of secret and highly complex maneuvers, he began to trade stock illegally on the basis of inside information. Through his work at Drexel, Lehman, and Smith Barney, and his contacts elsewhere, he bought stocks in firms he knew would soon become the object of takeover bids. In five years, he made more than $12 million in illegal profits. At the time he was apprehended, he represented the government's biggest insider-trading case.

The fall of Levine rocked Wall Street to its foundations. If someone so highly regarded could be guilty, then no one, clearly, was exempt from suspicion. Before Wall Street recovered from the shock of Levine's guilty plea in May, that same month a full-blown insider trading ring of five men was exposed. The case wasn't noteworthy because of the number of men involved or the size of illegal profits. In the past, similar networks had been caught, and in this instance the sum of money was only a tiny fraction of the amount Levine had made illegally. The most disturbing aspect was the parallel between the accused and Levine. Undoubtedly, had the quintet been caught in any other year, they would have received little attention. Instead, they were viewed as part of a widening epidemic of corruption.

Four of the five were young, ambitious, educated middle-class Jews who seemed to have the best of everything. Three lived in the same East Side apartment building, where one-bedroom units rented for $2,000 a month and up. Four of the five spent their spare time exercising at the nearby Vertical Club, an "in" East Side gym, where membership cost more than $1,000 a year. (The fifth member of the group lived in Rhode Island and was a boyhood friend of one of the foursome.) What was particularly upsetting from a Jewish perspective was the fact that the network developed, in part, when one member first introduced another to a third at a United Jewish Appeal function. And the end of the scandal was nowhere in sight.

As part of his settlement with the Securities and Exchange Commission, Levine led U.S. attorneys to a number of other insiders. The most notable was Ivan Boesky, unquestionably the most aggressive, and perhaps the richest, arbitrageur on Wall Street. On Friday the fourteenth of November, just after the market had closed, the SEC announced that it had imposed on Boesky a penalty of $100 million — $50 million of which represented illegal profits from insider trading.

In an attempt to gain leniency, he agreed to cooperate fully with the ongoing SEC investigation.

It was revealed that Boesky had established a relationship with Levine in February 1985, at the time of the arb's desperate dealings with Carl Icahn, when Icahn was preparing to make his takeover bid for Phillips. Levine had provided valuable tips to Boesky on impending mergers in exchange for 5 percent of any profits Boesky collected on the basis of that information. Boesky wasn't present at the SEC's announcement. In a statement handed out after the commission's press conference, he declared: "I deeply regret my past mistakes and know that I alone must bear the consequences of those actions."

That was his last public utterance for many months. He had not been seen for some time and certainly would not be seen again on Wall Street. He was banned for life, as was Levine, from ever returning to active participation in the U.S. securities business. But his name and past activities would remain in the public eye for a long time. Many Jews worried that his trading abuses would cast a pall over the entire Jewish community. Not only was he the most important figure in the insider-trading scandal, he was deeply involved in Jewish philanthropy.

A day before the news of his crime broke, the Jewish Theological Seminary received a letter from him announcing that he was resigning as a member of the board of directors and as president of the Seminary Library Corporation, which ran the Ivan F. Boesky and Seema Boesky Family Library. Less than two weeks later, at his request, the Boesky name was dropped (it became the Library of the Jewish Theological Seminary). The bronze letters that spelled out "Boesky" lingered on the library wall a little longer but were subsequently removed.

Reports in the Jewish press, including the Long Island *Jewish World,* questioned the ability of Jewish organizations to raise money as effectively in the aftermath of the Boesky affair. Moreover, ugly suspicion was growing about the motives behind Boesky's political dealings.

Only two weeks after the Levine case surfaced, Boesky had traveled to the White House for a meeting with President Ronald Reagan to voice his support for an American arms deal with Saudi Arabia that was at odds with the view of virtually the entire Jewish community; at the time, he had been roundly condemned. Although he was a Republican loyal to President Reagan, his actions raised questions as to whether he had tried to curry favor with the White House in anticipation of the charges that the Justice Department might bring against him — but no one would ever know for sure.

As the insider-trading scandal raged on, many Jewish leaders felt obliged to speak out about Boesky and his impact on the Jews in and out of Wall Street. Just as Levine had led investigators to Boesky, it was clear that Boesky would lead them to other inside traders. Former ambassador Sol Linowitz gathered together some of the country's top Jewish leaders for a very private meeting to discuss the Boesky affair. Among those present were Felix Rohatyn, Laurence Tisch, and Rabbi David Gordis, executive vice president of the American Jewish Committee. Some expressed apprehension that there might be a backlash of anti-Semitism. The Palm Beach *Jewish World* quoted Gordis as saying that some "took an alarmist view" that Jews would be seen as fitting stereotypical negative roles as "exploiters of the economy, parasites, profiteers."

On the thirteenth of February, the furor over Boesky temporarily abated as three leading members of three preeminent investment banking and brokerage firms were arrested for insider trading. Federal agents descended on the office of Richard Wigton, head of arbitrage and over-the-counter trading at Kidder Peabody. In full view of the firm's traders, he was frisked and handcuffed before being led from the building. A block away, Robert Freeman, head of the arbitrage department at Goldman Sachs, was arrested and escorted from the building. Timothy Tabor, who until the day before his arrest was head of arbitrage at Merrill Lynch, and before that an arbitrageur at Kidder Peabody, was also taken into custody.

There was an almost audible sigh of relief among Wall Street's Jewish community. None of the three men charged was Jewish. But the relief was short-lived: another shoe had yet to drop. The reported source of the information that had led to the arrests of Wigton, Freeman, and Tabor was Martin Siegel, an M&A star who had recently moved from Kidder Peabody to Drexel as cohead of its mergers and acquisitions department. He pleaded guilty to charges stemming from his insider-trading activities and agreed to pay a penalty of $9 million.*

If anything, the shock waves on Wall Street from Siegel's admission of guilt were even greater than from Boesky's. Boesky had always seemed rather suspect. Siegel, on the other hand, had never

---

* The charges against Wigton, Freeman, and Tabor were later dropped.

been under a dark cloud. Handsome, personable, and persuasive, he was a whiz kid who had shot to the top on an abundance of brains, hard work, and talent. From modest beginnings, he had come to Kidder Peabody by way of Harvard. In many people's eyes, he had achieved the American dream writ large. He had an attractive wife (also an investment banker at Kidder Peabody), three small children, a salary of around $2 million a year, a sprawling $3.5 million home on Long Island Sound in Connecticut, and a $1.6 million co-op in Manhattan. Only thirty-eight, he had become the Yuppie role model to the point where Kidder Peabody took aspiring young bankers to visit his Connecticut retreat. In every way, he seemed the embodiment of the Wall Street professional of the future. Now his career was over.

In searching for an explanation, the *Wall Street Journal* reported that Siegel had been haunted by his father's bankruptcy, which had taken place when he was twenty, and by the fear that he too might fail just as he reached his prime. In the end, perhaps he was more like Boesky than he appeared to be on the surface. According to the *Journal,* he had been awed by Boesky's great wealth and had never forgotten his visits to the Boesky estate or the time Boesky had come to see him in Connecticut driving a pink Rolls-Royce.

The SEC charged that Siegel had begun dealing with Boesky in the summer of 1982, leaking tips about impending mergers that he was working on for Kidder Peabody — and being paid for the information.* Sometimes he received payments in a briefcase delivered by a Boesky courier. In February 1987, the *New York Times* reported on four takeovers in which Boesky allegedly profitted in excess of $33 million from information provided by Siegel. Ironically, Siegel made a reputation as one of the Street's most important merger specialists in the first of these deals, when he devised Martin Marietta's successful counterattack — known as the Pac-Man defense — against Bendix in 1982. Boesky, who had purchased Bendix shares in the four days before Siegel launched Martin Marietta's counterattack saw a profit of $120,000

---

* There may have been a pattern to Boesky's trading on insider information from Siegel and Levine. In each case, it started after Boesky had sustained his biggest arbitrage losses. Boesky's dealings with Siegel began after he lost millions on his bet that Gulf would take over Cities Service and Gulf backed out. His relationship with Levine started after T. Boone Pickens dropped his Phillips bid.

from the sale of his stock in Bendix, which was ultimately acquired by Allied. Of the four deals, Boesky's biggest profit came from the stock of Carnation in the spring of 1984. Siegel, who was Carnation's investment banker, provided Boesky with confidential information that foretold that the company was a likely takeover target. Between June and August, Boesky bought 1.7 million shares of Carnation. In September, Nestlé offered to buy Carnation and the stock price rose. (The sale ultimately went through.) Boesky sold off his Carnation stock at a profit of $28.3 million.

That was presumably the last time Siegel helped Boesky. Siegel was growing increasingly anxious about the arrangement, particularly since he had reportedly panicked when he read a *Fortune* article about Boesky in the summer: "Boesky's competitors whisper darkly about his omniscient timing, and rumors abound that he looks for deals involving Kidder Peabody and First Boston." Siegel stopped providing Boesky with information but was apparently afraid to tell Boesky outright that their relationship was over. Their meetings and talks became more and more infrequent. In fact, Siegel had not given up on insider trading; he had just switched to a safer arrangement. While continuing with his M&A work, he quietly helped to create and headed Kidder Peabody's arbitrage unit in 1984, and, according to the SEC, later swapped confidential information with Robert Freeman of Goldman Sachs. (Richard Wigton and Timothy Tabor, the two arbs who had been directly under Siegel at Kidder, allegedly were drawn into the relationship Siegel had established with Freeman.) The effort helped turn a department that was thought to have too little capital to succeed into one of Kidder's most profitable sections overnight. Meanwhile Siegel maintained a lingering connection with Boesky. At their year-end meeting, an apparently dissatisfied Boesky asked: "Don't you love me anymore?"

Shortly after that meeting, Siegel left Kidder Peabody for Drexel and at last severed his ties with both Boesky and Freeman. By then it was too late. The day in November 1986 that the Boesky settlement with the SEC was announced, Siegel was sitting in the office of lawyer Marty Lipton, a close friend, when a federal marshal walked in and handed him a subpoena concerning the investigation of Boesky; it was accompanied by a list of Siegel's own takeover deals at Kidder in the eighties. Siegel began to sob. For the information Siegel presumably passed to Boesky, he is believed to have received some $700,000 — an amount for which he threw away his career and which, in his world, was not a great sum of money.

*   *   *

With the insider-trading scandal broadening, the crimes of Levine, Boesky, and Siegel continued to generate major press and television coverage. Among Wall Street's Jewish financiers, it was an ever present topic of conversation, but concern about the matter wasn't confined to them alone. Most Jewish leaders reacted with the utmost seriousness. In April, *Present Tense* magazine sponsored a nonsectarian panel on ethics as part of its annual book awards luncheon. Pointing to "the dangers to Jews from the prominence of Jewish names in current scandals and the imagery that emerges from the visibility," Rabbi Gordis urged that "as a people we must look more deeply into the recesses of our tradition, our experience, and our values. The prophets and sages of Jewish history preached and taught a doctrine of justice, honesty, and social responsibility." Another speaker on the panel, Michael Harrington, author of *The Other America*, put the blame on a more sweeping national deficiency: "The Wall Street scandal, in which a major broker was led out of his own office in handcuffs, is part of a larger ethos of egotism and greed promoted under the Reagan presidency."

In the eighties, before and after Levine, Boesky, and Siegel were caught, the SEC processed more than a hundred cases of insider trading, and none of them indicated a pattern of Jewish lawlessness. Despite the media blitz over insider trading, these crimes accounted for only some 10 percent of all the enforcement actions taken by the SEC in 1982–1986. In the end, the Jewish element in Wall Street crime was less pervasive than it was shocking.

As time went by, the furor over insider trading — though not concern about its implications — died down, as the nation became fascinated by Oliver North and the Iran-Contra scandal. In December 1987, Boesky's sentencing on one count to three years in prison was reported in the press and on television, but without the attention-grabbing impact or sustained interest that had been aroused when Boesky was initially charged.

That didn't mean that the scandal itself had gone away. Virtually from the time Boesky confessed, the government had been investigating Drexel Burnham Lambert and Mike Milken. Milken and Boesky had done a number of deals together, and Drexel had raised a huge amount of money for the arbitrageur's last business. Moreover, Boesky had made a mysterious $5.3 million payment to Drexel for some rather unclear banking services. But that was just the beginning.

The government's case against Milken and Drexel was said to be so massive, so far-reaching, and so complex that no indictments would be seen for some time. A herculean battle was building. The government was preparing to confront one of the most powerful financiers of the century. Whatever evidence it had against Milken and his cohorts, the junk bond market kept booming. Everyone owned junk bonds — insurance companies, foreigners, individuals, savings-and-loan institutions, mutual funds, and pension funds — the total was $150 billion in 1986 — and climbing. (It would reach $200 billion by 1989.) Junk bonds were the key reason that Drexel had become the most profitable firm on Wall Street that year, with earnings of $545 million and capital of $1.8 billion. Milken, it would be revealed, had been paid $550 million in 1987 for his work the previous year.

While the Securities and Exchange Commission and the U.S. attorney in New York City were gathering information, Drexel and Milken prepared for their defense. They hired a battery of top-notch lawyers, and the firm reportedly stocked a huge war chest. It also launched a massive advertising campaign — believed to have cost some $140 million — revolving around the theme that its efforts to help businesses raise money benefited every American. Milken scored a public relations coup when he met with Soviet leader Mikhail Gorbachev during his visit to the U.S. in December 1987 to discuss the possibility of pursuing joint Soviet-Drexel business ventures.

Though throughout 1987 and much of 1988 they were under the shadow of the government investigations, Milken and Drexel continued to dominate the junk bond market. An ascetic, who didn't drink alcohol, caffeine, or carbonated beverages, Milken made one small change in his habits — but a major one for him. He began talking to the press, though only about finance. But he repeatedly invoked his Fifth Amendment rights against self-incrimination during an appearance in the spring of 1988 before a Congressional subcommittee looking into Drexel's financial practices. The SEC and Justice Department investigations dragged on so long that during that time, Boesky began his sentence at a minimum-security prison in California and Dennis Levine completed his prison term and was released. Meanwhile Wall Street waited for the government to present its case.

At last, in September of 1988, the Securities and Exchange Commission brought a civil suit against Drexel, Milken, and others, charging them with violations ranging from illegal insider trading to defrauding clients to stock manipulation. (In addition to Milken, the SEC brought charges against his brother, Lowell Milken; two other

Drexel employees; Drexel client and Miami financier Victor Posner; and Posner's son, Steven Posner.) The SEC alleged a close, secret alliance between the defendants, who were said to have used Boesky's organization as a "front" — for which Boesky paid Drexel $5.3 million in March of 1986 as its share of the illegal insider-trading profits they had made together. The government agency also charged that from 1984 until late 1986 Boesky was a virtual agent of Drexel, repeatedly acting at Drexel's direction, buying stocks in takeover situations with Drexel clients and manipulating securities prices in ways favorable to Drexel. The 184-page civil complaint, filed in the federal court in Manhattan, listed eighteen deals — sixteen with Boesky — in which Milken and others allegedly violated securities regulations. In no two deals was the way he was charged with violating securities regulations the same.

It was the most sweeping government action since the passage of the nation's securities laws in the 1930s. Revealing charges that were potentially even more serious, the United States attorney's office sent Drexel a letter the same day, announcing that a federal grand jury was looking into a broad range of criminal charges involving securities fraud, mail and wire fraud, and criminal racketeering.

Drexel and Milken pulled their resources together. The firm now had capital of $2.3 billion and reportedly $650 million was earmarked for a long, tough fight. Milken even joined Drexel's public relations effort and hired a PR firm early in 1988 to help repair his tarnished image.

A few days after the SEC charges were filed, he fulfilled a longstanding commitment of his own to take 1,700 underprivileged children to see a New York Mets game with tickets donated by Drexel and the Milken Family Foundation.* Surrounded by grateful youngsters, "Michael," as they called him, passed out pretzels.

In December 1988, Drexel agreed to plead guilty to six felony counts, including securities, mail, and wire fraud, to pay $650 million

---

* The trip was organized by Variety International, a charitable organization to which both Drexel and the Milken Family Foundation had contributed for several years. In 1987, Milken and his wife donated $92 million to the Milken Family Foundation and to three other foundations — a sum that was 50 percent larger than their total contributions for the past five years. According to a Milken spokesman, the increase in their donations had nothing to do with the continuing investigations into Milken's business operations.

in fines, and to set up a trust fund to compensate investors who had lost money as the result of Drexel's crimes*. Meanwhile, the Justice Department continued its investigation of Milken. At Drexel's Beverly Hills office, traders and salesmen who had remained loyal to him were doing a brisk business selling T-shirts with the words "Mike Milken — We believe in you." Nevertheless, in late March, the government brought the full force of its might down on Milken. In a ninety-eight-count indictment, the Justice department charged the Junk Bond King with violating the federal racketeering law (RICO) and committing mail and securities fraud and laid claim to $1.2 billion of his assets, an unprecedented figure. (These assets included his income from Drexel from 1983 through 1987, which totalled more than $1.1 billion; the $550 million he had earned in 1987 alone was more than all except the top forty-one Fortune 500 companies earned that year.)

Unlike Ivan Boesky, Dennis Levine, Martin Siegel, and Drexel itself, Milken refused to reach a settlement with the government. In a prepared statement released at the time, he declared, "In America, an indictment marks the beginning of the legal process. . . . I am confident that in the end I will be vindicated."

One immediate effect of his indictment was his automatic suspension by Drexel. When the annual Drexel bond conference was in full swing a week later, Milken, the former king of the ball, was in New York, entering his not-guilty plea.†

Throughout the financial community and the nation, the scandal raised concerns about unchecked financial dealing. Those concerns reached far beyond the insider-trading issue. When the stock market had come crashing down on October 19, 1987, it had sent tremors of fear all over America. That day, the stock market suffered the worst percentage plunge in its history, worse than on the day of the Great Crash, October 29, 1929. The Dow dropped 508 points — from 2,347 to 1,739, or 22 percent — as investors, large and small, were caught

---

* Two months out of the decade it had helped to define, Drexel Burnham Lambert, unable to meet several hundred million dollars' worth of financial obligations, declared bankruptcy and went out of business. The junk bond market that had provided the financing for so many hostile takeovers was rocked, but the firm's collapse had a minimal impact on the economy.

† Faced with the threat of even more far-reaching indictments, Milken eventually pleaded guilty to six felony counts related to securities transactions and to pay a $600-million fine in a plea agreement with the prosecutors. He will be sentenced in October 1990.

in a trading spiral that totaled a record 604 million shares for the day. Climaxing a two-month descent after peaking at 2,722 on August 25, the Dow's drop reflected total market losses of some $1 trillion in equity value. The shock waves of October 19 caused markets to plummet from London to Tokyo.

"There was a pre-Monday world, and now there is this world," John Gutfreund told the *New York Times*. The excesses of the last five years had finally caught up with the investment community. Despite ups and downs, cycles of growth and pause, a zigzagging pattern of dislocations and adaptations, and despite the sounding of alarms in recent years, there had been a sense in America of uninterrupted expansiveness and boom, of more and more money to be made by investing money, of unprecedented starting salaries for bright young people holding newly minted MBAs, of the possibility of flying higher and higher in the money balloon. Now the balloon was punctured and before it would be patched up again, some 40,000 jobs would be lost on Wall Street alone.

But the tremors of the crash didn't produce the predicted immediate cataclysm. The last two years of the decade saw mergers and leveraged buyouts go forward at prices that hadn't been forecast at the time of the crash and that didn't seem to be hampered by it. Nevertheless, the business world continued to be haunted by the high cost of excess and its potential consequences.

# CHAPTER THIRTY-FOUR

# The Once and Future King?

As soon as plans were disclosed in the summer of 1985 for a 925-foot-high twin-towered skyscraper that was to be built at Columbus Circle, diagonally across the street from the southwest corner of Central Park, civic groups joined together in a clamor of opposition that could be heard all the way down to Wall Street. Salomon Brothers was slated to be the first and foremost tenant of the imposing building. The mighty Wall Street firm intended to leave the offices that had housed it for fifteen years and head uptown, to a setting that would appropriately proclaim its standing as the nation's largest and most powerful investment bank. Salomon had expanded so rapidly that its employees — whose numbers had more than doubled in the last five years — were jammed together without adequate working space. Extra desks and hundreds of new computer terminals had been added to the Room — Salomon's much vaunted trading floor — which, despite its vast size, was now painfully overcrowded.

John Gutfreund had teamed up with multimillionaire realtor Morton Zuckerman of Boston Properties to build the skyscraper, at an estimated cost of $455 million, on a three-acre site where the Coliseum stood. It would dominate the skyline, and its towers would provide Salomon's growing work force with a three-story trading room and an adequate number of offices — a fitting symbol of Salomon's power. Salomon was willing to pay far more than the going market rate to lease the space. It was making so much money — it would earn a record $557 million by year's end — that the executive committee approved the move despite the cost. Susan Gutfreund was said to be so taken with the architect's renderings that she had sketches of the building engraved on a set of crystal vases.

The move never took place. Although hundreds of people had demonstrated against the proposed building — claiming that it was far too huge, that it would overburden the neighborhood resources, and that it would cast a large shadow over Central Park in the afternoon — Salomon had been unresponsive and announced that it would pull out if the building were reduced or redesigned. When Salomon did pull out, in December 1987, before the old Coliseum could be razed or one batch of concrete could be mixed and poured for the new foundation, it had nothing to do with civic conscience.

If ever a firm had grown, like Topsy, in an imbalanced way, it was Salomon in the 1980s. It was notable for its excesses and the price of those excesses. Thus, well ahead of the stock market crash of October 19, 1987, Salomon Brothers had begun to experience the first consequences of its lack of moderation and its dizzyingly rapid growth. The fallout would shake it up profoundly, cost the firm millions of dollars, and raise serious questions about John Gutfreund's leadership.

Some executives, including a few of the most influential on Wall Street, had been alarmed by heated expansion without adequate discipline and planning. In their eyes, Gutfreund was still the best at motivating his team to gain an advantage in the market, using the firm's huge capital to dominate the game, but he had the short horizon of a trader.

"John always had a tendency to go with the group that was making money at that moment in time, even if they displayed poor judgment," recalled a former member of the executive committee. "That was one of his shortcomings as a manager."

A former Salomon executive believed that the firm's plan to build "a monument to itself" was influenced in part by something else: Susan Gutfreund's extravagant tastes. "Corporations inevitably take on the identity of their leaders," he explained. "For thirty years Gutfreund had made business his priority. Now he had other priorities as well. The impact Susan had on John was tremendous, and it undoubtedly has had its effect on the firm."

\* \* \*

During much of the difficult period at Salomon in 1987, Susan Gutfreund seemed to have virtually dropped out of the New York social scene. Items about her stopped appearing regularly in the gossip columns and fashion tabloids. Her disappearance from view didn't represent prudent modesty in the face of Salomon's troubles. In fact, she was in France, preparing for her version of the siege of Paris. She had always set her sights high. Now she was aiming to gain entry to the old-world grand society that was the legacy of the French from the time of the Sun King and the court of Versailles and that had always accommodated people with money and talent. John Gutfreund would have to provide the money. She had the talent and had practiced all the right moves.

New York had been a superb training ground for the former airline stewardess. The Gutfreunds had become prominent enough so that, in 1985, when she presented her husband with his fourth son, John Peter, the child was dubbed "the baby of the year" in the fashion tabloid *W*. The sight of the couple and their son in his regulation English pram, accompanied by his nanny, was a familiar one on the Upper East Side, the chic neighborhood that housed their new apartment purchased when they had outgrown the duplex at River House along with such scandals as the Christmas tree episodes.

In keeping with their new more refined image, the Gutfreunds' Fifth Avenue co-op had been converted into a model of Establishment good taste and grandeur.* Susan Gutfreund chose as their decorator the legendary eighty-year-old Frenchman Henri Samuel, who had decorated homes for the Hearsts, Rothschilds, Vanderbilts, and the Aga Khan, among others. He was also famed for the rooms he had designed for the Metropolitan Museum of Art that displayed prized French furniture.

A hint of Susan's future aspirations was evident in the renovated twenty-five-room apartment. The Gutfreunds commissioned Samuel to create the equivalent of a luxe French mansion, evoking for at least one visitor the Ritz of Paris. The walls of the double-height entrance hall were stone paneled. A Monet painting of water lilies was displayed. Everything was designed to maintain the first impression of great luxury. A magnificent central staircase led to a grand salon furnished with signed eighteenth-century French and Russian antiques. Columns and Roman antiquities flanked the salon's entryway. A "jardin d'hiver" (winter garden) offered a breathtaking view of Central Park. There were two dining rooms (one for large formal parties) and a smoking room with tooled leather walls for Gutfreund. Nesting within the apartment was a separate small one for the baby and his nanny. By one estimate, the cost of decorating the duplex was more than $20 million. At that rate, even Gutfreund — one of the highest paid executives in

---

* The one unpleasant reminder of their early forays into New York Society was the unsold apartment in River House with its opulent use of marble and cavernous circular tub beneath overhead mirrors. The co-op was finally sold in 1988.

the nation, with a salary of $3.2 million in 1986 — was out of his spending league.

That didn't curtail Susan Gutfreund's interest in entertaining lavishly and in accumulating possessions for the apartment. Under the tutelage of New York socialite Jayne Wrightsman, widow of the oil magnate Charles Wrightsman, who had become fond of her, she was learning about French antiques — enamel boxes, marquetry, and other French adornments — so that she could navigate buying from dealers and bidding at auction. Her hobby was expensive.

Surely Gutfreund the Tweaker would have had something to say about the new apartment — had he not reincarnated himself. It was as if the man who had spat out profanities at the slightest provocation, played cruel practical jokes, and who had thrown a trash can at a subordinate had been sanitized and reissued. In part as the result of adopting the refinements of old money, he had toned down his previous public persona as the rough-hewn pit boss.

*  *  *

The Gutfreunds' style of conspicuous consumption paralleled the seemingly uninhibited growth at Salomon and other major Wall Street firms fueled by the bull market of the mideighties. "If you didn't have an increasing number of people, it would look like your firm wasn't an aggressive enough manager," Harold Tanner, former head of Salomon's corporate finance department, explained, looking backward. But Salomon's growth was both conspicuous and haphazard. It added 1,000 people to its work force in 1986 alone; expenses skyrocketed. Its coffers were further strained by the expense of its international reach. At a time when major American Wall Street firms were moving aggressively abroad, Salomon was moving faster, proclaiming the "globalization of finance." The most extreme example was its immensely enlarged London operation. To accommodate the London staff, Salomon acquired a huge space in Victoria Plaza, right above Victoria Station and just a few blocks away from Buckingham Palace, and spent an estimated 25 million pounds building a trading floor even larger than the one in New York.

Henry Kaufman, Salomon's influential economic guru, whose views were widely respected, was one of the most critical of such rapid expansion. "Salomon hired employees expecting revenues to follow," he said later. "I had deep concerns about the speed with which we hired people. Apart from the cost factor, you cannot teach people what Salomon is all about if they've only been there for a couple of years."

Salomon's spending spree hurt earnings. Making matters worse, the firm faced stiff competition in several of its traditional businesses, including commercial paper and municipal bonds. In April 1986, Salomon's stock, which had reached a high of 59, began to decline and traded in the midthirties by fall.

Internally, these problems sparked a heated controversy that divided Salomon into two camps over its immediate and future direction. Corporate clients had increasingly demanded that their investment banks provide junk-bond financing and merchant banking, services Salomon had felt it prudent to shun. A group of younger executives, including executive committee member Thomas Strauss, urged going into these new, potentially profitable areas. A few of the older, more seasoned, executives, including Henry Kaufman, resisted, believing such moves would one day create a heavy burden of debt. Kaufman wanted the firm to stick with its principal business of helping to provide capital for America's largest corporations. Gutfreund sided with the Strauss group.

In the fall of 1986, he promoted three younger executives to the newly created Office of the Chairman to share with him important responsibilities. Thomas Strauss became his second in command as president; William Vouté, a trader, was named vice chairman; and Lewis Ranieri, head of the mortgage-backed securities department, was also named a vice chairman. Since Strauss had been the architect of Salomon's international expansion, his elevation was seen as an affirmation of Salomon's global ambitions.

Kaufman and Richard Schmeelk, the firm's top investment banker, were passed over. In response, Kaufman resigned from the board of Salomon Inc, though he remained head of the research department and on the executive committee. Schmeelk resigned from the executive committee, maintaining that he wanted to lighten his work load, but in truth he was a traditionalist, like Kaufman.

The shakeup didn't change the underlying problems. Consequently, early in 1987 Gutfreund began attacking costs by instituting company-wide budgeting, a common corporate practice previously unheard of at Salomon. That summer he surprised Wall Street by ousting Lew Ranieri, who less than a year before had been promoted to vice chairman. Inside Salomon, that action was applauded by many who felt Ranieri was a divisive force in a firm that could ill afford dissension now.

Ranieri, one of the newcomers of Italian descent who had begun to be visible on Wall Street, seemed to personify the classic Salomon success story. He had started out in the mail room as a clerk on the night shift. Less than twenty years later, he had risen to number-three man at the firm and second in line, after Tom Strauss, as Gutfreund's successor. More than any other individual, Ranieri was responsible for developing mortgage financing — virtually nonexistent before the eighties — into one of the most profitable businesses at Salomon. Despite his success, by many accounts he was a poor manager, an intimidating heavyset man with a hot temper and a prankster's sense of humor. He would sometimes sneak up on a colleague and cut his tie or suspenders. Once he mutilated a trader's tuxedo and on another occasion glued the drawers of a trader's desk closed and his phone to its cradle. Before his sudden departure, he had been a vocal opponent of Salomon's wide-scale international expansion and its move into merchant banking.

"There are separatist movements at the firm," Gutfreund told a reporter after the firing. "I guess this restructuring came about because we decided that if we didn't force the firm together, it would grow further and further apart."

More than ever, Gutfreund needed to maintain unity.

*     *     *

While John Gutfreund sought unity in his business arena, his home life became fractionized. Susan Gutfreund was enjoying her time in Paris — accompanied by John Peter and his nanny — where the Gutfreunds had bought quarters on the Rue de Grenelle in an elegant eighteenth-century mansion that surrounded a courtyard. The mansion was also home to couturier Hubert Givenchy and industrialist Jacques Bemberg. As their decorator, the Gutfreunds had again selected the esteemed Henri Samuel, who was helping Susan to assemble another collection of fine French antiques. To the astonishment of French acquaintances, the Gutfreunds also installed a huge eat-in kitchen. They pooled resources with Givenchy and Bemberg to build a $1 million underground parking garage so that their cars wouldn't have to be left in the courtyard overnight.

Susan Gutfreund found Paris social life even more to her taste than that of New York. To be properly coiffed for all the events she was attending, she turned to Laurent Gaudefroy, known as the King of the Chignon. She recognized a great hairdresser when she met one. "He's one of the most talented coiffeurs I've ever known," she said later. "When you see beautiful hair at a gala or a grand dinner here, you can almost be sure that it was Laurent who did it." Among Gaudefroy's famed clients were Queen Margrethe of Denmark and the fabulously wealthy party giver Beatriz Patino, who jetted him all over the world for her grand soirees.

Even as Gutfreund struggled to reverse Salomon's sagging profits during the week, he often flew over on the Concorde to join his family on weekends. Some members of the firm viewed his schedule with dismay. As one top Salomon executive at that time commented, "You can't commute on weekends to Paris, stay out at dinners or parties until one or two in the morning, fly back to New York, and show up in the trading room at seven-thirty in the morning well briefed and alert about the business of the firm."

Meantime, Susan was having a lot of fun in Paris, shopping for furnishings with the help of Henri Samuel and spending lavishly on clothes. She reportedly bought apparel from Givenchy, St. Laurent, Ungaro, and the hot new designer Christian Lacroix, who was becoming known as much for his extraordinary prices (in the range of $10,000 to $40,000 for his couture) as for the flamboyance of his frocks. Best of all, she was making her way in French Society, having become particularly friendly with Jacqueline and Victoire de Ribes and the Rothschilds.

Like his wife, John Gutfreund seemed to enjoy the glamour and sophistication of international society, though at times his usual self-confidence (some would say arrogance) seemed to recede in such company. "When you sit next to him at a dinner party, he's at a loss over what to say to a woman, unless you ask him what he thinks about the stock market or politics," said an international socialite. "If you ask his opinion about a major art show, he stammers and appears quite unhappy."

If Gutfreund wasn't lionized socially in Europe, he made up for it by the recognition he received for his philanthropic activities back home. In May of 1986, as a vice chairman of the New York Public Library, he had attended the first grand landmark gala of that year in celebration of its seventy-fifth anniversary, along with Mayor Koch, Donald Trump, Barbara Walters, Norman Mailer, Kurt Vonnegut, Oscar de la Renta, and Brooke Astor, a member of the board of trustees and honorary chairman of the library.

It had soon become commonplace for Gutfreund to be seen at these affairs and in such company. By association, he had become linked with them. In the few interviews he has granted, he has gone to great lengths to present himself as a modest, genteel banker, someone who was simply doing his job. Referring to his 1984 coup in wresting control of Phibro-Salomon away from David Tendler, he offered a low-key recollection: "I didn't set out to be number one. It somehow became my responsibility." Aside from business, he has been portrayed by the press as a man who likes listening to Mozart, reading the works of modern authors such as William Kennedy, and donating large sums of money, his own and his firm's, to worthwhile causes. Salomon Brothers was in the $500,000-to-$1-million category of donors to the New York Public Library in 1987.

Gutfreund had reached the point where an Establishment fundraising evening could be built around him alone — in no small measure because his name had become a drawing card for big money. In April of that year, he was the guest of honor at the thirty-second annual Senator Robert F. Wagner Memorial Dinner-Dance, a $350-a-ticket black-tie affair, to raise money for college scholarships for qualified New York high school graduates. The high and mighty paid tribute to Gutfreund with their contributions. The roll call of patrons ranged throughout the investment and commercial banking firmament, as well as encompassing the legal and political spheres. Sitting at John and Susan Gutfreund's table were Robert F. Wagner, Jr., the late senator's son and former three-term mayor of New York City, and Gutfreund's library-patron friend Brooke Astor.

\* \* \*

John Gutfreund's social position seemed secure. His position at Salomon was another matter, and outside of Salomon there was speculation about his future. It hadn't helped that in the spring of 1987, after a year of dwindling profits, Salomon's largest shareholder — Minorco, an investment company controlled by South African diamond baron Harry Oppenheimer — had wanted to sell its Salomon shares.\* His investment banker, Felix Rohatyn, conveyed the news to Gutfreund, but Gutfreund was unwilling to meet his client's price. Oppenheimer's dissatisfaction grew, and soon he began casting about for another buyer. In September, Rohatyn lunched with Bruce Wasserstein, cohead of mergers and acquisitions at First Boston, and told him that Oppenheimer wanted to sell his Salomon block. Wasserstein, in turn passed the information on to Ronald Perelman. It was an odd role for Rohatyn, a forceful critic of the raider's Revlon takeover, who had now helped put his friend John Gutfreund's company in play. Perelman was definitely interested in the Oppenheimer block and said that he might acquire as much as 25 percent of Salomon stock.

---

\* When Phibro acquired Salomon Brothers, Minorco, an investment company controlled by Harry Oppenheimer, was Phibro's largest shareholder. In 1987, Minorco owned 14 percent of Salomon Inc.

Gutfreund had had no faith in Perelman's assurance that he would be supportive of management. "Believing Mr. Perelman has no hostile intentions is like believing the tooth fairy exists," he said. Though it wasn't disclosed at the time, Gutfreund apparently was so affronted by the prospect of working for what he considered a hostile interloper that he informed Salomon's board of directors he was prepared to resign and expected most of Salomon's senior management to depart with him. "I never stated it as a threat," Gutfreund revealed later. "I was stating a fact."

Under pressure from the aggressive corporate raider, an angry Gutfreund finally took decisive action to block Perelman's raid. It would be costly, but Gutfreund seemed to feel it was worth it. While Perelman, a devout Jew, was celebrating Yom Kippur, the Salomon chief arranged for Salomon to buy the Oppenheimer block at well above its market price: $38 a share, or $809 million. He then sold a 12 percent stake in Salomon for $32 a share, or $700 million, to a white knight — Berkshire Hathaway, run by his old friend Nebraska investor Warren Buffett.

Many of the Salomon executives were outraged by the deal. They felt it was executed in haste and secrecy, and, worst of all, they believed that the stock had been sold too cheaply. Salomon's shareholders were furious as well. (Investors filed nineteen lawsuits against the company's board of directors.) Gutfreund had rebuffed Perelman but at a considerable price to his own good will and search for unity.

He was still on the defensive. In mid-October, he shocked Wall Street by jettisoning Salomon's municipal bond business, in which it had been dominant since the midsixties (and where he himself had started). The commercial paper department was shut down at the same time. To justify the retrenchment, Gutfreund cited increasing competition in those fields. The ax fell on hundreds of employees. The bloated London office was hard hit. In all, some 800 of Salomon's 6,500-member work force would be out fast. News of the heavy slashing at Salomon leaked to the press before the employees were notified — a clear sign of turmoil within the firm. Gutfreund and his lieutenants had always excelled at keeping business secrets, as anyone familiar with the earlier Phibro merger knew well. Two Salomon employees learned of the massive layoffs on their honeymoon and, like everyone else, wondered if they were next on the hit list. They hurried home to await the news; they were among those let go.

One event followed another — all of them negative. Caught on the front line and already weakened, Salomon was badly hurt by the crash of October 19, 1987. When the figures were totaled at the end of December, Salomon had endured the worst financial quarter in its history, posting losses of some $89 million. Much of the deficit came from the $51 million cancellation payment following the decision to abandon the costly and controversial plan to move to Columbus Circle.

"The world changed in some fundamental ways, and most of us were not on top of it," Gutfreund admitted, oddly echoing the charge the New Crowd had leveled at Our Crowd, but with a difference: "We were dragged into the modern world." Having been "dragged," he hoped to regain his and Salomon's position as lead sprinters.

Salomon's problems and the Gutfreunds' profligate scale of living were easy targets as symbols of unrestrained excess, and once again they drew fire.

In the same week in January 1988, two cover stories appeared — one in the *New York Times Magazine* and the other in *New York* — both critical of Salomon's chaotic expansion, Gutfreund's leadership in recent years, and the Gutfreunds' personal life.

Responding to those articles, some friends quickly came to their defense, including those who remembered John Gutfreund washing dishes at Montefiore Medical Center (to which he contributed generously) during the workers' strike and those who knew Susan Gutfreund's work on the Citizens Committee — among them, the impeccable Marietta Tree.

Nonetheless, the buzz about them continued on the social circuit. And Susan Gutfreund still managed to attract unwanted attention, even when she did her best to suppress it. For instance, there was the flap over the Susan Gutfreund song. A young British performer named Christopher Mason had written a humorous ditty about her that he had performed at several New York Society parties. One stanza and chorus went as follows:

> Now Susan is living in Paris
> And she flies back and forth all the time
> Tho' to say it's not fair
> She is now in the air
> More than when she first met Valentine,
> But her stewardess days are behind her
> She's a lady, intelligent too,
> When she flies through the skies,
> It should be no surprise
> She has much better things now to do.
>
> And though Salomon Brothers is waning
> And Susan is getting too grand

> *The Gutfreunds are darling young people*
> *Oh, why can't the world understand?*

An item in *Women's Wear Daily* may have left readers with the impression that Mason was planning to sing the song at a forthcoming New York Public Library fund-raiser. Susan Gutfreund was said to have complained to the gala's chairwomen — Annette Reed, Brooke Astor, and Susan Newhouse — insisting that the song be withdrawn. It turned out to be an embarrassing mistake. Susan Gutfreund apparently had got it all wrong. Mason had never considered performing the song.

After that, when Mason performed at private functions — where hosts, some of whom considered him a budding Noel Coward, paid $3,000 to hear his humorous light barbs at Nouvelle Society — guests often requested the Susan Gutfreund song. Mason refused; he didn't want to offend her.

Around the same time, hints of trouble between John and Susan Gutfreund surfaced in a gossip column item, which claimed that they might be renegotiating their marriage. The talk didn't die down. While John Gutfreund spent most of his time in New York devoting himself to rebuilding the firm, she was at their apartment in Paris or flying off to Portugal. Several socialites, who claimed to have heard it from reputable sources, spread the news that the Gutfreunds were planning to separate. Wags speculated that John wasn't rich enough for Susan anymore.

Certainly he wasn't making nearly as much money as he had before. At the end of 1987, Gutfreund had announced that he was voluntarily taking a $2 million pay cut. The bonuses of all top executives were slashed, and, at his own suggestion, he took no bonus at all. In lieu of it, he accepted 300,000 options on Salomon's stock. Most likely these options wouldn't be worth much unless Gutfreund turned the company's earnings around. He received his $300,000 annual salary, plus $800,000 of cash deferred from 1984. All this was a far cry from the millions he had brought home in the past.

Yet John and Susan continued to show up together in high style at some of the most opulent international events of the summer season. They were among the couples attending the ball in Paris to benefit the Franco-American foundation for the Château Blérancourt. In September 1988 they attended what many considered the grandest social extravaganza of the year — the ball given by Lily Safra in honor of her husband Edmond's birthday at their new vacation home: La Leopolda, an immense palace in Villefranche on the Côte d'Azur, France, which had formerly been the property of Belgium's King Leopold. No expense was spared. There were flowers from Holland, an entire orchestra flown in from California, and a seated dinner for three hundred people in an oversized tent whose sides were painted to resemble Pompeiian mosaics; a feast was prepared by star chef Roger Vergé of the Moulin de Mougins. As a memento, each female guest was presented with an enamel box depicting the palace. The guests included Prince Rainier, Princess Caroline, and the Niarchos clan.

For the occasion, Susan Gutfreund wore a simple white mousseline Chanel dress: "With the opening of a palace like this, the home and the hostess should be the stars," she said later. "I wanted to dress to disappear like a rat in the woodwork."

That same month the Gutfreunds attended the opening of an exhibition by world-renowed British sculptor Henry Moore at the Royal Academy in London, which had been underwritten by Salomon Inc. Susan appeared at the reception wearing a black lace dress, her hair done up in a plait. There was one hint of discord between them. When the time came for John Gutfreund to deliver his brief remarks as Salomon's representative, she had already left the reception.

In September she was also in New York for a number of glittering events she attended with her husband, including the fortieth birthday party of Pat Kluge, wife of billionaire John Kluge. It was held in the ballroom of the Waldorf Astoria, which had been transformed into the interior of a Viennese Belle Epoque palace.

Among the society women who lunched at fashionable restaurants like Le Cirque the talk was that the Gutfreunds were not getting divorced after all.

Despite reports of restraint in Nouvelle Society — in response to the crash and the continuing Wall Street scandal — the galas and lavish private parties continued at a frantic pace. The prediction in Christopher Mason's clever song, written for *W* on the nouvelle restraint, that women showing up in ostentatious gowns "will be ostracized quickly with fashionable frowns" by the fashionable themselves, didn't prove to be entirely true. Apparently Susan Gutfreund wasn't alone in believing that the gilded eighties were far from waning. "All the experts tell you that there is a lot of money around," she said in October. "I think people who buy haute couture are going to buy no matter what. They may buy one or two fewer things because conscience tells them it is more prudent." According to a Parisian woman who knew the couture houses, Susan herself had begun to buy far less recently, out of consideration for Salomon's troubles and her husband's reduced earning power.

* * *

The fall of 1988 finally brought John Gutfreund some measure of relief. The financial turmoil appeared to be over — at least for a while. He seemed to be turning Salomon around. Earnings for the third quarter were double what they had been for the same period of the previous year. Senior management was now virtually composed of Gutfreund loyalists. The tenth anniversary of his leadership of the firm came and went and was hardly noticed by the business press. In November Salomon announced plans to move its headquarters, along with 3,000 of its 4,500 New York employees, to rented space in a new building in lower Manhattan — Seven World Trade Center — that cost considerably less than the midtown Coliseum site.

Yet there were those who felt that Salomon was still in a weakened state. During the past two years, many of the key executives (besides Ranieri, who was fired), had departed. Henry Kaufman, who rejected the new direction the company was taking and his reduced role in it, resigned to start his own consulting firm. Richard Schmeelk, the firm's top investment banker, quit as well. Ira Harris, the Chicago-based dealmaker who had opened up the mergers field for Salomon in the late sixties and who in recent years had been increasingly at odds with Gutfreund, defected to rival firm Lazard Frères. Raymond Golden, Salomon's first chief financial officer, resigned, as did his successor, Gerald Rosenfeld. Both men said they were looking for new challenges, though neither had been at his post at Salomon for very long. Harold Tanner and Peter Gottsegen, two of the firm's highest ranking and most respected investment bankers, quit, partly because they had been passed over for promotions. E. Craig Coats, a close lieutenant of Tom Strauss's, left, saying he was tired of corporate life and missed the more freewheeling partnership days at Salomon. Vice chairman William Vouté, a veteran trader, departed over Gutfreund's decision to emphasize merchant banking.

Throughout the wave of resignations, Wall Street wondered whether Salomon had enough experienced people left to shepherd the firm into the future. By background, many of the remaining senior executives were still traders. Gutfreund himself had come to power as a trader and had been one of the best in an area that required daring and quick reflexes. But to rebuild Salomon, strong financial management and long-term strategy were needed. With the inroads made in

Wall Street by commercial banks and in the wake of the crash, competition in the securities industry had never been fiercer. For the first time since the early eighties, Salomon had fallen from the top position in its prime business of underwriting. That was to be expected after the firm had dropped out of the municipal bond business, but it made the climb back all the more difficult.

Following the unsuccessful approach by Perelman, Salomon had taken steps to protect itself against raiders, such as developing a poison-pill plan. More importantly, as long as major Salomon stockholder Warren Buffett remained Gutfreund's strongest supporter, the company appeared safe from a takeover.

But it wouldn't be easy to win back Solomon's former power and glory. Gutfreund would have to do better than ever before. Competition had always made him try harder, and he had always expected the same from his employees. Those who couldn't handle the heat and rivalry ultimately left or were forced out. "Salomon Brothers has never been a place for the timid," said Kaufman. "You had to stand there and defend yourself or express your views, and if at times you didn't hit hard, you had problems surviving in a business sense. That was part of the image and the style of Salomon Brothers for a long time and to some extent it still is."

Gutfreund seemed to have withstood the assaults from within and from without the firm. Salomon had survived the worst of the crash, as had most of Wall Street. "It's still a very strong firm with a lot of wonderful, capable people," Harold Tanner commented. "And I don't know anybody who could run Salomon better than John Gutfreund." But the winds that had blown through the Salomon fortress had shown cracks in its structure. Within the company, support for Gutfreund still held. Many employees who stayed there primarily because of him put their own money on the line. In the first year of the aftermath of the crash of October 1987, Salomon employees bought 1.5 million of the company's shares. They were betting on the future and on Gutfreund's leadership.

The results for 1988 were better than the previous year. The firm's earnings rebounded and the board of directors rewarded him with $4 million in salary and bonus. Gutfreund himself remained bullish: "We're on the right track," he declared in February of 1989. But Wall Street was less sanguine about the prognosis for the firm. During this period Salomon's stock languished. The journey back to the top for Gutfreund would be tough and uncertain.

# CHAPTER THIRTY-FIVE

# Primerica Time

J oan Weill had always wanted to ride with her husband in one of the horse-drawn carriages that tour Central Park and the surrounding area, but somehow they had never managed it. Finally, on the evening of December 15, 1986, after thirty-one years of marriage, her wish was granted. It would be a ride she could not even have imagined in their early days together. As they stepped out of the carriage that had brought them to Carnegie Hall on West Fifty-seventh Street, she asked mischievously, "Do you know how much this ride is costing you?"

Weill smiled. He knew only too well: $2.5 million, the amount they had donated to the Carnegie Hall restoration campaign.

They descended onto a sidewalk crowded with elegantly dressed men and women chatting and greeting one another on their way into the auditorium. In a city accustomed to gala events, this one had a special aura. Carnegie Hall was the place to be that night.

The illustrious concert hall, which had been shut down for a total renovation after ninety-five years, was reopening seven months later. Sandy Weill, as cochairman of the restoration fund, had helped to raise the $50 million that the renovation cost. He had used all of the persuasive skills that had served him so well in business. He took friends, colleagues, and acquaintances to lunch at the Four Seasons, where he made his fund-raising pitch. "Word got around that if Sandy Weill invited you to lunch, the tab would be at least $100,000," Joan Weill recalled. The Weills' gift of $2.5 million was the largest personal contribution to the landmark since Andrew Carnegie had donated $3 million back in 1891.

For some New Crowd members, admission to the social order dubbed Nouvelle Society in the popular press was among the most coveted fruits of their success. It meant being noticed outside of the financial community and taking one's place alongside Felix and Elizabeth Rohatyn, John and Susan Gutfreund, and Saul and Gayfryd Steinberg in the upper reaches of the social whirl. Not all of the New Crowd had a desire to belong, but more and more of them seemed to want to enjoy the glamour of this grand world — at least occasionally. That was part of the allure of the Carnegie Hall reopening.

Among the 2,800 ticketholders, who paid anywhere from $50 to $2,500 for their seats, were the high and the mighty of the old monied Establishment, people such as David and Laurance Rockefeller, Brooke Astor, Lee Radziwill, Alice Tully, Arthur Ochs Sulzberger, John Loeb, and Margaret Ryan (the daughter of Our Crowd's Otto Kahn). The television cameras covering the event could focus on celebrities from the worlds of entertainment, politics, and the media, including Gregory Peck, Maureen Reagan, Henry Kissinger, Larry Hagman, and Tom Brokaw. The first-generation superrich were also present, from publishing magnate Rupert Murdoch to oil baron Armand Hammer to the superstars of the New Crowd.

An impressive contingent of past and present Salomonites made their way into the auditorium: James Wolfensohn, John Gutfreund, Richard Rosenthal, and Gedale Horowitz. The Bear Stearns group was represented by Ace Greenberg — who squired Gloria Vanderbilt — and two of his closest lieutenants, John Rosenwald and Alvin Einbender. Saul and Gayfryd Steinberg were there, with his brother Robert and his wife. Leveraged buyout champion Jerome Kohlberg was there, as was raider Carl Icahn, whose donation of $500,000 had won him the honor of having a balcony named after him. Felix Rohatyn, who had recently become a member of the Carnegie board, and his wife, Elizabeth, joined the audience.

Weill's involvement and the size of his donation to the esteemed hall accorded him a special standing in New York City that his former string of brokerage acquisitions for Shearson, his penthouse overlooking Central Park, his estate in Connecticut, and even his American Express card had not. Virtually overnight, he had become a presence in New York Society. The Weills were seated in one of the choicest locations in the house — a first-tier box, dead center — alongside James Robinson III, Weill's former boss at American Express, and the latter's new wife, Linda Gosden (a public relations powerhouse whom he had married soon after he and Bettye Robinson were divorced).

Weill claimed he harbored no ill feelings toward Robinson, and the two had maintained a cordial relationship throughout the long period of inactivity and uncertainty Weill faced after he resigned from American Express. During the next year top-executive jobs had slipped out of Weill's grasp. He wanted a niche that suited him, but he was finding it difficult. As she had done so often in the past, Joan Weill served as her husband's sounding board: "I tried to keep him from jumping into something just because he didn't have anything to do. I wanted to be sure his motives were the right ones." Finally, he focused on Commercial Credit, a Baltimore-based financial services company, and with $10 million of his own money, he helped finance its acquisition in October of 1986. That was good timing. It happened just weeks before the Carnegie Hall reopening.

That night, his place in the business world wasn't uppermost in his mind. He could sit back and enjoy the moment. The select audience was treated to a spectacular concert that lived up to its expectations of the evening. Under the direction of Zubin Mehta, the New York Philharmonic performed music by Wagner and Haydn, as well as a composition by Leonard Bernstein written expressly for the occasion. Mezzo-soprano Marilyn Horne and violinist Isaac Stern were accompanied by the Philharmonic in a selection from Bach's *St. Matthew Passion*. Then, in a wide swing of musical style, Frank Sinatra sang to the sound of Peter Duchin's orchestra. World-renowned pianist Vladimir Horowitz stunned the audience in a surprise appearance.

Weill, whose only prior musical experience was playing the bass drum with the Peekskill Military Academy band and who had been an infrequent concertgoer, had joined the restoration fund at the suggestion of an American Express director. "I had a tour of Carnegie Hall and met a lot of interesting people. I found myself getting more and more involved." But he had been hesitant when James Wolfensohn, the former Salomon partner who was chairman of Carnegie Hall, tried to enlist Weill as chairman of the restoration campaign. "That was in 1984, and I knew what was going on at American Express. I didn't know how much free time I would have. And I had never run a major fund-raising drive before."

That changed as soon as he and Joan attended a fund-raising concert and heard violinist Isaac Stern and cellist Mstislav Rostropovich, a Russian exile, speak about how much Carnegie Hall meant to the residents of New York City. Joan Weill observed the expression on her husband's face. He was visibly moved. She whispered, "I know what you're about to do. You're going to agree to be chairman." He did agree, but only if he and Wolfensohn could be partners and co-chairmen. After he left American Express he offered to resign as co-chairman of the drive because he no longer had the power of his firm behind him, but Isaac Stern urged him to stay on. "Fortunately my good friends remained my good friends, and I was able to be a very effective fund-raiser," Weill commented.

When the last "bravos" and "encores" had finally quieted down and the audience filed out of Carnegie Hall, Sandy and Joan Weill joined the Wolfensohns and the performers — among them, Stern, Sinatra, Mehta, Bernstein, and Horne — at the exclusive Petrossian restaurant for a postconcert supper of caviar, smoked salmon, medallions of veal, pastries, and champagne. For Weill, the night had a magical, fantasy-land quality that lasted long after the festivities wound down at 3 A.M.

* * *

In acquiring Commercial Credit, Sandy Weill was taking the long road back. He hadn't exactly been down and out — the Weills had accumulated enough money to live in a style they could easily maintain. They had never been ostentatious, but they continued to add a few ornamental things to their penthouse, including several important early twentieth-century American paintings. They counted Gerald Ford among their friends, along with other luminaries such as Henry Kissinger, actress Glenn Close, advertising mogul Jerry Della Femina, and demi-billionaire Lewis Rudin. Weill's time had been occupied with his work for Carnegie Hall.

But all that wasn't enough for a man used to running a business empire. Rejection was hard to take; inactivity was frustrating. That period of his life became a test of character as well as of will. Sandy Weill had found a way to maintain his equilibrium. Success had moderated his earlier fears of failure, and he felt he had learned how to succeed. He developed a way of looking at the bright side — whatever happened had happened "for the best" — and he was on the alert for opportunities.

After resigning from American Express at the age of fifty-two (when the board rejected his proposal to acquire Fireman's Fund), he hadn't meant to take early retirement, but for a while he felt as if he had. When Fireman's Fund went public in 1985, it came as no surprise that Weill wasn't at the helm — one of his former lieutenants was — since Amexco's board had refused to let him buy out Fireman's Fund. Then E. F. Hutton, which was crippled by criminal charges of fraud at the time when Weill was rapidly becoming Wall Street's most eligible executive, looked to Merrill Lynch to fill its number-two slot. Weill seemed to take that in stride and maintained that the job hadn't really interested him: "It would have been like trying to do the same thing all over again."

BankAmerica did interest him. At one time the San Francisco-based bank had been the largest bank in America, but when Sandy Weill mounted a major campaign to take it over in early 1986, it was losing money and could have used the infusion of $1 billion Weill was prepared to raise in exchange for becoming its chief executive. Despite the wariness between Weill and Peter Cohen and his cordial but once-problematic relationship with James Robinson, Shearson had agreed to put up the money to participate in what promised to be one of the most spectacular deals in history. Cohen and Robinson flew to Pebble Beach, California, where Weill was scheduled to play in a golf tournament, to help him devise a strategy for presenting a proposal to the bank's board. When the two men left after a few hours of discussion, Weill had a signed commitment from Shearson for the $1 billion he needed.

But Weill hadn't counted on the strong opposition from BankAmerica's head and board of directors, a highly conservative group who were suspicious of Wall Street. In an effort to stop him, the head of the bank rounded up allies. One of the most vocal was John Gutfreund, whose Salomon Brothers served as the bank's chief financial adviser. (It wasn't the first time Gutfreund and Weill had clashed. Gutfreund had attempted, unsuccessfully, to persuade his friend Edmond Safra not to sell Trade Development Bank to Shearson.)

This time Gutfreund threatened to quit as BankAmerica's adviser if the Weill proposal was approved. "If you want to do this, go ahead, but you can do it without us," he told the board. BankAmerica didn't need Weill or his help, Gutfreund insisted, to raise a billion dollars. There were other sources.

The bank's board soundly rejected Weill's offer. He announced afterward that he wouldn't pursue a hostile takeover; that wasn't his style: "There was no way that I would think about doing this at all without the complete blessing of the board and the community."

He licked his wounds in an office provided by his former firm, Shearson, that was in some ways like an executive graveyard, as John Loeb, who was Weill's next-door neighbor in an office also provided by Shearson, no doubt knew. Weill spent much of his time there researching companies and industries, trying to decide what he wanted to do next. "He missed the action and the phone calls," said an associate. "The phone didn't ring much."

When the phone did ring, it was often his wife calling, suggesting they take in a movie. He refused. He didn't want to leave the office in the middle of a work day, even if there wasn't much to do.

He preferred a set routine to none at all; he hadn't given up on himself and felt he had no reason to. When he returned home at the end of the day, Joan was often out at a benefit meeting. Many of the calls that came to the apartment were for her about the benefit she was working on. Weill found himself answering the telephone and saying, "Joan Weill's office."

Joan understood that the hardest part for him was to be relatively idle when so much of his life had been spent working toward specific goals. In suggesting going to the movies she was trying to get him to "lighten up" a bit. She tried to think of other ways to distract him. Sometimes they met for lunch at the Four Seasons. They had long talks. They could use a vacation, she felt. The Weills took a two-week trip to Paris and London with their children, Marc and Jessica, and Jessica's husband, Nathan Bibliowicz. It was the first time the family had been to Europe together, one bonus of his unemployment. "With me not working, and them doing well, they could see me as a little bit vulnerable and that made us even closer. It was a good trip," Weill reflected.

Whatever vulnerability he might have felt, he never acknowledged it publicly and insisted, in retrospect, that he had no regrets about the decisions he made, including his decision to yield his position as chief executive officer at Shearson while he was at American Express.

"I'm one of the world's great rationalizers," he said in a moment of self-assessment years later, "and I feel things have a way of working out for the best. Everyone told me, including Joan, that I should keep my power base at Shearson to force my way into a stronger position at American Express. My decision was not to do that. If I had wanted to run Shearson still, I wouldn't have sold the company. I wanted Shearson to grow in the American Express environment. If I had to do it all over again, I would have done the same thing." He also recalled that "I was ready to try something else," but that didn't prevent him from feeling "very frustrated" and "down." He still felt he was ready for "something else." His ambitions at American Express had been part of that, a desire to move from Wall Street into the corporate heartland. His acquisition of Commercial Credit was a step in that direction.

A month after the grand reopening of Carnegie Hall, Weill was back on West Fifty-seventh Street for further festivities. This time the ceremony was in his honor. The 268-seat Carnegie Recital Hall — now renamed the Weill Recital Hall in recognition of his contribution — reopened. It had always served as a place where less-known, usually younger, musicians could try out. He and Joan were thrilled to see their name above the door. In addition to improved acoustics, the renovations combined elegance with comfort — teal blue chairs and carpets, off-white walls trimmed in gold, and three Austrian crystal chandeliers. "It's a little jewel," he commented. Joan felt they had reason to be "very proud of the legacy we're leaving our family and grandchildren."

Again, the New Crowd turned out in force. Among the 150 guests who attended the black-tie reception that followed a concert celebrating the opening of the refurbished Weill Recital Hall were James Wolfensohn, Ace Greenberg, Ira Harris, Bruce Wasserstein, and Weill's old partners Arthur Carter and Marshall Cogan. It felt good to be surrounded by friends and associates as well as family, including Joan's mother, who had come from Sherman Oaks, California, for the event. A poised and beaming Sandy Weill welcomed the assembled guests, remarking, "I consider it an honor to work in such a great and fun place that does so much for young artists." Joan, fashionably dressed in a long red silk Pierre Cardin gown with a pleated top and artfully placed fabric roses on both shoulders, listened attentively. From then on, they would have a permanent niche in the New York cultural world.

\*    \*    \*

Sandy Weill was always willing to concede that sheer good luck had contributed to his success on Wall Street, but his associates attributed it to a lot more than luck. His apprentice years sitting glued to his stock quotation computer terminal hadn't given him tunnel vision. They felt that, in fact, it had given him a good eye for reading Wall Street and for assessing the right time for the right move. His old gang at Shearson also felt he had another, less definable quality: he knew how to motivate them and appreciate them, which gave them confidence in their own convictions and moves. They had made a lot of money under him. Now that he was off the Street, so to speak, and needed them, they came through for him.

When he acquired Commercial Credit in October 1986, he staged a full-time "road-show" around the United States and abroad for several weeks, promoting the stock. The $780 million issue — one of the largest initial public offerings ever — was snapped up quickly. Its biggest boost came from the Shearson brokers, who sold a large chunk to institutional and retail investors.

He ran Commercial Credit from its headquarters in Baltimore, returning home on weekends. (It was a temporary base for him. He planned, if the company became profitable, to find office space in New York.) He and his half dozen top executives stayed in leased hotel rooms at the Harbor Court, overlooking the seaport. Most of them were former American Express finance veterans who were attracted by the opportunity to rebuild a company and by an attractive stock options package that Amexco couldn't match.

Working at Commercial Credit did involve some downward mobility in terms of corporate perks and privileges. Instead of a corporate jet, Weill and his financial veterans flew on commercial airlines; and instead of chauffeur-driven limousines, they had two blue station wagons at their disposal — a Chevrolet and an Oldsmobile — and a garage attendant.

Turning Commercial Credit around would take all of Weill's entrepreneurial savvy. Glad to be back at the helm, he got an early start on the workday. His chief financial officer, who occupied the room next to Weill's, could smell Weill's cigar smoke around 6:30 A.M., about fifteen minutes after breakfast arrived.

"In a way it was like going back to camp again and participating in color wars," Weill recalled. "We shared common activities and goals. We became a very close team as well as very good friends." Weill was in his element. Once again — as had been true for him at Shearson — he could draw energy from and energize a "close team," and they were all involved in the venturesomeness of starting anew. "It was a wonderful, intense experience," Weill said, "and it made the older members of the group feel younger." On one occasion, he was photographed for a business magazine having dinner with a group of young trainees. "These are the people who made this country," Weill announced proudly, "not the investment bankers."

The Weill team sold insurance, made loans, and issued credit cards to middle-class and blue-collar customers across America. The company's stock was rising, and his reputation was rising again accordingly. Within a year, Commercial Credit was making money. Ironically, Fireman's Fund lost money in 1987 and BankAmerica fired the man Weill had tried to replace.

Still, pleased as he was by the success of Commercial Credit, it kept him away from New York and his family. That left a void. Talking to Joan every day was not the same as being with her. "We had never been apart that much before," Joan Weill said ruefully, looking back. "When he came home for weekends, we had to cram everything into two days, and he was often tired and cranky. I kept busy with my own projects and I saw friends, but we missed each other."

Her comings and goings were noted occasionally in the gossip columns and the "people-watching" media, as were his — the parties they attended, the restaurants they ate in, and the charities they benefited. Joan Weill took this type of attention in stride and she understood its meaning. "It's always amused me to see how the photographers' attitude toward you changes when your husband gets to be somebody," she recalled. "Some years ago when we attended Betty and Jerry Ford's thirty-fifth wedding anniversary party, Sandy wasn't well known outside the business community. He went up to the *Women's Wear Daily* photographer, who was covering the event, and said, 'I think my wife looks very nice. How about taking her picture?' The photographer said, 'Why? Who is she?' Now that same photographer takes my photo at social functions."

Joan derived great satisfaction from her active support of Citymeals-on-Wheels, a voluntary group that cooperates with the New York City Department for the Aging to bring decent meals to homebound elderly New Yorkers. For three years she had served as chairperson of Citymeals' annual Restaurant Week, during which elaborate fund-raising dinners, luncheons, and parties took place at some of the top New York restaurants such as Lutece, Le Cirque, and Gotham Bar and Grill. She herself had raised more than $1 million from the business community.

Much as she enjoyed "giving something back" for all life had given her, the core of her life had always been her husband, their children, and the corporate family. By the end of a year of having her husband based in Baltimore, she wanted him home again, though she accepted the situation.

Her hopes were soon fulfilled. In September of 1987, Weill moved into an office complex in a new skyscraper in mid-Manhattan. Construction was still under way, but when it was finished, the complex would cover two floors. (Baltimore remained Commercial Credit's headquarters in name only.) The Weills had little time to enjoy his return. A few weeks later the stock market crash sent Commercial Credit's stock tumbling way down to the level it had been when Weill took over. It was a blow.

The crash brought with it opportunities, too. Almost immediately, Weill had a shot at acquiring E. F. Hutton, already weakened by a securities scandal that led in 1986 to criminal charges that it had defrauded its commercial banks of deposits worth millions of dollars. It couldn't survive on its own after the crash. Weill was approached by Bob Fomon, Hutton's former chief executive, who had the ear of the board but no real authority. However, another suitor for Hutton quickly surfaced, one with more muscle, Shearson. Peter Cohen acquired Hutton that December, for about half of what his firm would have paid the previous year, an apparent coup. Almost at once, Shearson rivaled Merrill Lynch as the largest retail brokerage in America and enhanced its position as an elite banking house. Now when Peter Cohen spoke, Wall Street listened.

Sandy Weill never missed a beat. He had no time — and, according to him, no inclination — to dwell on the irony of his former lieutenant's taking the glittering prize away from him. "I wish him [Cohen] well. Shearson was a better match," Weill acknowledged.*

He was still in the market for a major acquisition. He turned his attention to the brokerage house of Smith Barney, the beleaguered Club 17 alumnus, which had also suffered in the crash. It was now owned by a conglomerate named Primerica — once the container-and-packaging company known as American Can but now an insurance-and-mutual-fund giant based in Greenwich, Connecticut — headed by Gerald Tsai, the Shanghai-born wunderkind money manager of the Go-Go Years.

Weill knew Tsai reasonably well; they had lived near each other in Greenwich until Tsai's recent divorce and remarriage. Preliminary talks about a Weill takeover of Primerica went nowhere. The price Tsai set in January 1988 was too high.

But Tsai was still concerned about Primerica's earnings, which had been hurt by the acquisition of Smith Barney just four months before the crash. He talked it over with his old friend Ira Harris, who had just recently switched from Salomon Brothers to Lazard, and Felix Rohatyn. After studying the company, both Lazard men strongly recommended a merger with another financial company with complementary strengths. It was time to reopen discussions with Weill. Ira Harris called him.

He met with Harris, Rohatyn, and another Lazard partner in June. "From the start, we were talking about something larger than Smith Barney — the whole company or pieces of it," Weill told Joan with genuine excitement. His Commercial Credit had plenty of cash to spend — its earnings had rebounded sharply.

---

* As it turned out, both men were wrong—Cohen for making the match with Hutton, and Weill for publicly endorsing it. Hutton proved far too much for Shearson to swallow. The problems of the firm, now known as Shearson Lehman Hutton, escalated month by month and ultimately cost Cohen his job early in 1990.

Sandy Weill was on his way to making his comeback. His completed Commercial Credit offices in New York reflected his corporate style. The complex — which was designed by the architecture firm Skidmore Owings & Merrill and supervised by Nathan Bibliowicz, Weill's son-in-law — had the Weill stamp all over it. A corridor was constructed between the glass-walled exterior of the building and the outer windows of the offices that housed the Weill team. That corridor gave everyone in the offices easy access to the others, providing for the same kind of atmosphere and boyish camaraderie that had existed at Shearson. A boardroom resembling a two-story modern glass cathedral was situated at one end of the corridor and a library of smaller, but similar, proportions — with red walls, black leather tufted sofas, a round salt-and-pepper rug, and the latest Weill working fireplace — was located at the other. The photo of his old childhood home in Brooklyn — which had first hung in his office at American Express — moved with him to his new plush office. It had become for him a kind of talisman. From unexceptional origins, he had built a financial empire. Now he was trying to build another. He was in a position to expand.

During the Primerica negotiations, he met only twice with Tsai but held extended meetings with his investment banker from Morgan Stanley and with his lawyers. The Commercial Credit number crunching team was led by Jamie Dimon, Weill's bright young chief financial officer, who was to him now what Peter Cohen had been a decade before.

In August, while Weill was in the midst of negotiations, Jessica Weill Bibliowicz gave birth to a baby boy. Weill raced downtown to see his grandson Tommy and congratulate his daughter, then returned to the meeting. Later that month, when Jessica took the baby to the Weills' Greenwich home for a visit, the proud grandfather cradled his grandson in one arm while conducting a lengthy discussion on the phone with his investment banker about the terms of the Primerica deal. Between one Thursday evening late that month, when Weill and Tsai met to resolve the remaining monetary terms (Commercial Credit would acquire Primerica for $1.7 billion in stock), and the following Monday, when the legal ramifications had been worked out over the weekend and the boards of both companies had given their approval, Sandy Weill had achieved another major coup of his career. Though, as is usual in mergers of this magnitude, many technical steps remained before the deal would be final, late Monday afternoon an exhausted but exhilarated Weill phoned his wife at home to tell her that Primerica was his.

The combined companies would keep the Primerica name, but the former messenger from Brooklyn would be in charge of a giant diversified financial services empire — with assets of over $17 billion and sales of nearly $5 billion — offering insurance, brokerage, banking, and credit card services. It had more than 195,000 full- and part-time agents selling life insurance and mutual funds, 2,200 stockbrokers, and over 500 consumer-lending and home-mortgage offices. It also had many billions of dollars under management. In short, a true financial supermarket.

Joan Weill knew how many different strands of her husband's aspirations were intertwined in the Primerica network — the financial tycoon and the old retail broker whose initial steps toward success on Wall Street had been through selling stocks to average people. She relished Weill's telephone call, and her response ran true to form for the concerned wife who enjoyed nurturing her family and who knew her husband was spent with fatigue.

"Sandy," she said into the telephone, "we'll have an early evening. I'll make a chicken."

"No, let's go to Le Cirque tonight to celebrate."

When Joan arrived at the expensive East Side French restaurant, which had become a favorite gathering place for the "in" crowd, she found her husband having a drink with a party of people already seated. Coincidentally, Jerry and Cynthia Tsai had also chosen Le Cirque for dinner with friends.

When they were seated at their own table, the Weills received a bottle of champagne, compliments of the Tsais. Sandy and Joan graciously acknowledged the gift. Champagne was the perfect drink for the occasion. They toasted each other. "You know, we're starting out all over again," he told her. She laughed and responded, "It will be like building another family. We'll have less time to do it, but we'll certainly have more experience."

In the *New York Times,* Felix Rohatyn called the Primerica/Commercial Credit deal "an old-fashioned merger done by old-fashioned people." It had been executed in a friendly manner by Weill and Tsai —old Wall Street hands — with the help of Harris and Rohatyn —among the first investment bankers to put their stamp on the mergers scene in the modern era. It was a classic takeover involving two companies in the same industry.

Weill, whose modest means had once led him to struggle to meet grocery bills and to dream of doing well enough to own a deep-fryer and a Kodak Carousel projector, now saw the biggest challenge of his career from the vantage point of experience: "I wouldn't say it scares me as much as when I was beginning. If I made a mistake then, it would have been the end of my career."

Some Wall Street observers did feel that Weill had made a mistake, that troubled Smith Barney was the weak link in the Primerica chain, and that if Gerald Tsai couldn't make a great success of running Primerica, perhaps Weill was overly confident about his own chances.*

Weill had his defenders, who believed his approach as a business player was cautious and balanced — "he doesn't overpay for anything" — and that "he keeps an eye on the big picture in the industry."

Weill himself looked forward to the challenge: "I think I'm going to have a lot of fun."

He was back on center stage in the corporate world after a three-year absence. He had enough personal money to weather any storms and had developed enough resilience to cope with defeat and to rebound. But center stage was his arena. He was back in the big time.

---

* Immediately after acquiring Primerica, Weill took steps — one harsh and the other speculative — to turn the company's brokerage house, Smith Barney, around. Less than two weeks before Christmas (1988), the firm fired more than 150 employees. In April (1989), Smith Barney acquired nearly half of the troubled Drexel's retail brokerage operation, thus effectively increasing its sales force by 25 percent in an effort to bring in much-needed new accounts.

# CHAPTER THIRTY-SIX

# Minister of Finance

*F*elix Rohatyn was learning how to waltz. It was a weekday night at the Rohatyns' Park Avenue apartment. Although the hour was late, he and Elizabeth were gliding across the floor of the foyer as he attempted to master the rhythmic steps. One-two-three, one-two-three. The reason was simple. This year — 1986 — instead of their usual ski holiday, Elizabeth had arranged a European trip with a stop in Vienna (his birthplace and the waltz capital of the world) to attend a black-tie New Year's Eve ball. As they danced in wide, sweeping circles, they engaged in a steady stream of droll commentary on his progress. Such moments of unguarded sheer fun had become an integral part of his life.

Rohatyn had learned at an early age never to take anything for granted, but he acknowledged that he was gradually coming to terms with what he referred to as his "refugee mentality," which had prevented him from living as luxuriously as his considerable wealth would allow and which had taught him that what was secure today could be put at risk tomorrow. Though he wasn't content to rest on his laurels, he had perhaps never found life more gratifying. His stature as Lazard's top investment banker were recognized internationally. He provided economic advice to numerous government officials and corporate leaders. As chairman of the Municipal Assistance Corporation of New York City, he had the power of the New York purse — billions of dollars — and the authority to spend it. His opinions on economic and social issues were sought out by the press. His network of friends and movers and shakers reached across the United States and abroad.

In addition, his marriage to Elizabeth Vagliano in 1979 had made a major difference in his life. The marriage, which had followed many difficult years of unrelenting challenges and stress, infused his personal life with a greater degree of lightness and balance. He seemed to take more pleasure in being himself. Practicing the waltz at home after attending a social function was part of that difference.

In Vienna on the night of the New Year's Eve ball, Felix Rohatyn, attired in a tuxedo, and his wife, wearing a ballgown and long white gloves, appeared on the crowded dance floor with 3,500 other waltzers. An orchestra composed entirely of women played loudly. To the Rohatyns' disapppointment, the jammed, noisy affair was far from elegant. Resolutely, Rohatyn grabbed his wife around the waist and moved in one direction while she moved in the other.

His demeanor was serious, his brow furrowed. They started again. And again.

"Darling, let's bag it," she suggested. "It's the music that's throwing us off."

With the same determination and intense concentration that he applied to negotiating a complicated deal, he insisted: "Let's have one more try."

And try they did until they were finally spinning around the congested ballroom. Exploding with laughter, they came to a sudden stop and left. They had had their waltz. They savored such times of uninhibited jollity. He had reached the point where he could feel more fulfilled in all phases of his life.

"For about fifteen years, beginning in the midsixties, I was involved with one crisis after another, both personal and professional," he recalled. "There was the pressure of the New York Stock Exchange, the ITT crisis, my first marriage ending, and of course the New York City crisis. The entire decade of the seventies was for me a very difficult period. The hearings [the 1972 Senate hearings at which Rohatyn testified about the ITT acquisition of Hartford] were the worst period of my life. I was publicly involved in something I felt utterly no responsibility for and caught in the cross fire of political warfare.

"At the end of the seventies, it was really a coincidence that my personal life took a turn for the better and became sunnier and more stable about the same time that the professional crises that I had to deal with came to some kind of resolution. You can use yourself up living on the edges of cliffs. If you do it too much, the law of averages is going to catch up with you. I feel very fortunate that that didn't happen."

*   *   *

The resolution of the "cliffhangers" — particularly the one involving the New York City crisis — brought Rohatyn international-celebrity status. At the same time he formed two very important international relationships: his "French connection" with President

François Mitterrand of France and his "Israeli connection" with Mayor Teddy Kolleck of Jerusalem. He was profiled in the *New Yorker* and was the subject of cover stories in the *New York Times Magazine,* the *New Republic,* and *Newsweek,* where the hated nickname of Felix the Fixer had been turned on its head. Shown towering over an urban skyline, Rohatyn was proclaimed "The City's Mr. Fixit." In the lead of the *Times Magazine* article, he was named "the most eminent investment banker in the world, the man who saved Wall Street and later New York City from financial catastrophe."

"Mitterrand was always fascinated by the New York City experience," Rohatyn said. "How did we get the unions together with the banks, how did we deal with the issues here?" Following the election of Mitterrand as president of France in 1981, Rohatyn had become an adviser to the Gallic leader. They had been introduced by a mutual friend, Jean Riboud, chairman of Schlumberger, and had quickly formed a special bond.

In France, on several occasions, the Rohatyns dined with the Mitterrands and close family members at their little house on the Left Bank. "There was no waitress and Mrs. Mitterrand would serve," Rohatyn noted.

When the Rohatyns had the opportunity to reciprocate at a dinner party in their Park Avenue apartment duplex, there was nothing *intime* about the occasion. Being entertained by a head of state at his home was one thing. Entertaining a head of state on his travels was another. On the day of the event, the Rohatyn apartment was searched thoroughly by French security, but that was just the beginning.

The Rohatyns had invited a select group of friends with a special interest in France: W. Michael Blumenthal, well-known columnist Joseph Kraft, *New York Times* executive Sydney Gruson, and their wives. "Someone from Mitterrand's staff called to say that a close friend of the president's also would be coming," Elizabeth Rohatyn recalled. "We set a place for him."

Then, "Quite late in the day I was informed that four members of Mitterrand's staff had to be included — apparently Mitterrand must be in telephone contact with the Elysée Palace in Paris at all times. I was told I should have dinner for these gentlemen. I put an elegant round table in our upstairs bedroom and called the caterer and ordered four more dinners. Then the American security team made an unscheduled appearance, because we didn't know we were supposed to notify them. Our French housekeeper, who was somewhat naive and spoke very little English, escorted them through the apartment. When they came to the bedroom, they asked, 'What is this table for?' The maid said, 'The Mitterrands and the Rohatyns are going to eat there.' Once we got through all the security and protocol, the evening was a great success."

Rohatyn also became a regular visitor to Israel, where his advice as an expert on cities was valued by the mayor of Jerusalem. Teddy Kollek asked Rohatyn to become chairman of the Israel Museum. "It will give you a positive reason to come to Jerusalem once a year for the annual meeting," Kollek told him. "It's not political and it doesn't mean that you have to be supportive of any government or order. It will be a way for you to identify yourself with Jerusalem. And I won't leave your office until you say yes."

Rohatyn agreed to take on the post. "I knew he meant it and I knew he was right. It was irresistible. I did it for four years."

It was the first time in his adult life that he had worked steadily for a Jewish cause. "I'm not religious," he said. "But I'm a Jew and I love Jerusalem. It's a magic city."

*    *    *

He had gone "national," as his friend Victor Gotbaum had pointed out, when he became a prominent and respected critic of Reaganomics, and he had gone "international" when he made political contacts abroad. But Rohatyn's critical analysis wasn't confined to municipalities or to the vagaries of the city street he knew best — Wall Street. He also had some things to say about the role played by the American economy at home and globally. He filled up columns of newspapers and magazines with his writing on the subject and had published enough articles in the *New York Review of Books* and elsewhere to put together a collection of his views: *The Twenty-Year Century: Essays on Economics and Public Finance,* which appeared in 1983.

In the introduction, Rohatyn explained the book's title: "In 1941 Henry Luce stated that the twentieth century would be known as the 'American Century.' The 'American Century' lasted only twenty years. From 1945 to 1965 the United States dominated the world: we were the foremost military power, the industrial leader, the dominant financial power. . . . From 1965 to date, the American economy has oscillated between growth and inflation, and recession combined with unemployment. . . ."

His tone was pessimistic — he saw serious trouble ahead for the economy unless the government played a far more significant role in stimulating business growth — but he had hopeful suggestions that called for bipartisan political participation: he advocated an industrial policy to make America more competitive through restructuring of basic industries with government credit assistance; the stabilization of the international monetary system; and the reallocation of resources from the military-industrial complex to the nation's inner cities and rural areas and from one region of the country to another so that "all geographical areas (and thereby all classes and races) share the burden as well as the benefits this country has to offer. . . ."

He offered a broad blueprint for the nation's future: "America cannot survive half rich, half poor, half suburb, half slum. If the country soon wakes up, it will not do so by way of the old liberalism, which has proven itself incapable of coping with our present problems. It will do so only by building a mixed economy, geared mostly to business enterprise, in which an active partnership between business, labor and government strikes the kind of bargains . . . that an advanced Western democracy requires to function, and that, in one form or another, have been made in Europe and Japan."

The attention paid — both favorable and unfavorable — to *The Twenty-Year Century* helped to circulate Rohatyn's views. He established credentials as a business leader who was critical of the way the economy was conducted and as a Wall Street guru who was critical (in his 1984 address to the American Society of Newspaper Editors) of Wall Street's conduct in hostile takeovers. Rohatyn saw no paradox in his role as critical insider of the Wall Street community, and he was about to play the part once again — this time as a member of New York's social and philanthropic world.

* * *

By the mideighties, the Rohatyns appeared regularly in the society and fashion pages, attending one society benefit after another during the social season. Rohatyn, whose philanthropic interests in past years had included Independence House, a residential and rehabilitation center for youthful ex-felons, and Alvin Ailey, the black dance company, now was also on the boards of the Astor Foundation, led by Brooke Astor, and the New York Philharmonic — two gilt-edged institutions. He was expanding his awesome array of contacts to the only arena he had not yet explored fully: High Society. But, even so, he would risk speaking his mind.

The social world was shocked by the speech he delivered at the City Club of New York in November of 1985, which was quoted by gossip columnist Liz Smith in the *Daily News*. He began diplomatically enough, acclaiming New Yorkers as unmatched in their generosity and involvement with nonprofit institutions, but "while dazzling benefit dinners are attended by our richest and most elegant New Yorkers, and millions of dollars are raised for our golden institutions, it is increasingly difficult to find money for less glamorous needs. If our wealthiest institutions were to exercise more restraint over the proportion of charitable funds they try to absorb; if our most energetic, glamorous, and wealthy citizens were to become involved with community houses, the 'Y,' shelters for the homeless and programs for unwed mothers; then New York would be a much better place for her citizens."

Elizabeth Rohatyn made much the same points at about the same time to Liz Smith; her remarks were also printed in the *Daily News*. Unquestionably, the Rohatyns didn't make their criticism casually. He admitted later that he and his wife had spent months mulling over their fund-raising position. The timing of their comments coincided with the up-coming gala scheduled to be hosted by Elizabeth Rohatyn for the Lenox Hill Neighborhood Association, of which she was chairwoman. The association always felt an acute money shortage in taking care of all the needs of the 15,000 poor people the settlement house serviced on Manhattan's Upper East Side. The Rohatyns wanted the wealthy to provide more assistance.

The ensuing controversy was actually no more than a tempest in a delicate porcelain tea cup. Still, their remarks weren't appreciated by the old-monied rich of New York, he conceded later. What created even more of a flap was that many of these people were the new friends Rohatyn had met in Wasp upper-crust society. Retribution of a subtle nature followed. The Rohatyns were not socially chastised, but he noted "eloquent silences" at parties when the topic of charities came up. Despite all the right steps that made him one of the wealthiest men on Wall Street, Rohatyn, according to his friend Victor Gotbaum, "has never been completely comfortable being linked with the very rich."

Rohatyn himself claimed that he had taken issue with charity excesses simply because he sought to correct something he felt was wrong, just as he had lashed out the year before against the mergers and acquisitions world in which he made his living. Since then, more than once he had told a reporter, "It's getting more and more difficult for me to do the things we do in dealmaking because in the last analysis I don't think that's what I want on my tombstone."

* * *

His life was too complex and his interests too diverse to be circumscribed by the single word "dealmaker." No one stepping into his office at Lazard Frères would have doubted that it belonged to someone who was terribly busy. His wooden desk — still a working one — was piled high with papers and reports.

The furniture was seviceable: a small sofa covered in a plain navy fabric, a rust-colored upholstered chair, a coffee table, a simple side table between the two windows, a small television set, nondescript beige carpeting, and beige-and-claret-printed draperies. On one wall were a grouping of family photographs, including a picture of his Southampton house and a montage of snapshots of his sons taken when they were young. The only art was a watercolor of Venice done by his wife and a lineup of small, inexpensive Holbein prints behind his desk — placed there by a former secretary.

In most respects, it resembled the workplace of a middle-management executive, except for some telling details: the more than two dozen awards, honorary degrees, presidential and gubernatorial citations, photographs with high-ranking people (including one of Rohatyn taken with Jimmy Carter, Ed Koch, Hugh Carey, Jacob Javits, and others on the steps of City Hall), cartoons, and other such touches.

The office suite was in keeping with Lazard's policy of low overhead, but it was also in keeping with the "messy functionalism" that had always characterized Rohatyn's work space. If it lacked the trappings of his position, nonetheless it was almost always a hub of activity and sometimes it was very tense.

The takeover frenzy was enough to keep everyone hopping. Beginning with General Electric's acquisition of RCA at the end of 1985, Rohatyn had been involved in an incredible string of deals — both friendly and hostile. Even when his clients were making hostile bids, he tried to keep matters from becoming overheated. Throughout the decade "Felix was," W. Michael Blumenthal said of him, "very good at calling the shots under fire."

Most of Rohatyn's clients tended to agree with Blumenthal's assessment of him and valued his advice.* ITT chief Rand Araskog

---

* There was one notable exception — Michel Bergerac had used sharp-edged words to describe Rohatyn's unsuccessful defense of Revlon against raider Ronald Perelman.

called Rohatyn "a very good listener. I would lay something out and he would give me his reaction. When it gets down to dealing with another chief executive, he's terrific at setting the ambience and then leaving the two of us alone to talk." Lew Wasserman of MCA considered Rohatyn a good friend and "one of our brightest directors. He had something you don't find much of: common sense." And Blumenthal was also quick to point out: "I know this is going to sound self-serving, but smart people like to be surrounded by smart people."

In fact, in the spring of 1986, Blumenthal was pleased to have Rohatyn at his side when, as head of Burroughs, a computer company, he mounted an attack against Sperry, a rival computer company. The two corporations had had friendly discussions in 1985, but the talks hadn't produced an agreement. Blumenthal vowed to come back with a hostile bid. A year later, he was ready to launch a raid. Sperry rejected the first offer but agreed to pursue discussions. When the talks broke down, Rohatyn and his counterpart for the Sperry forces — Bruce Wasserstein —were able to patch them up.

Blumenthal relied heavily on Rohatyn. "From the beginning, I didn't make a move without talking to Felix. He knows my thinking. Whom you choose is a matter of style. I'm a manager. I'm inexperienced in these things [hostile takeovers]. That's the way it is with most CEOs. . . . He was very good at explaining what was going on with the board [of Sperry] since he knew it. He has such a wide network."

Part of the network was Sperry director Richard Shinn, an original member of the MAC brain trust, which helped to move matters forward smoothly. (The Sperry board ultimately approved a deal with Burroughs for $4.4 billion. The new company was called Unisys.)

Rohatyn barely had time to catch his breath before he became immersed in another deal unlike any he had worked on before. He would serve as the intermediary for the latest Japanese invasion of Wall Street and, in the process, would contribute to the effort to take the mergers and acquisitions business into the future and to break down the barriers between investment banking and commercial banking.

*    *    *

Since the passage of the Glass-Steagall Act in 1933, investment banks and commercial banks had been separated by law. By the mideighties, the lines between the two had blurred considerably. Foreign banks were becoming a major new source of capital for the Street's leading investment banking houses. By 1986, the Japanese had become among the heaviest investors in U.S. securities.

It was not so surprising that Rohatyn, on everyone's list as one of the leading dealmakers on this side of the Pacific, would be called in on a matter involving Japanese investors. In January 1986, after being contacted by McKinsey & Company, a management consulting firm, Rohatyn met with their client, the commercial bank Sumitomo, the third-largest bank in the world, with assets of $136 billion. He was told in confidence that Sumitomo was interested in acquiring a position in the investment house of Goldman Sachs. It was rare for Rohatyn to find himself dealing in a language he didn't understand, but he agreed to take on the assignment and made plans to meet Sumitomo's top executives in Japan.

Soon afterward, hundreds of the glittering rich turned out at Sotheby's for Elizabeth Rohatyn's annual fund-raiser to benefit the Lenox Hill Neighborhood Association. In all, $400,000 was raised. The men — among them, Oscar de la Renta, Bill Blass, John Pierrepont — wore either black tie or dark business suits. The women — who included Brooke Astor and socialite Annette Reed — appeared in designer originals. Some of the women, particularly the younger ones, donned metallic shoes and sparkling jewels in keeping with the night's space-age theme. *W* described the event as "one of New York's most celestial evenings — star-printed tablecloths, columns transformed into smoking rockets and a walking, talking robot named Robutler." Ironically, the event featured many of the elements the Rohatyns had attacked.

A few weeks later, the Rohatyns headed for Tokyo.

The purpose of the trip remained a closely guarded secret. They couldn't even tell Rohatyn's son Nicky, who happened to be working for an American bank there, that his father had actually come to see a client. Rohatyn met with the top Sumitomo executives and their interpreters at a secluded guest house owned by the bank, and he and Elizabeth were entertained at both Japanese- and Western-style restaurants. Two days later, they returned to New York, and Rohatyn set the wheels in motion. A meeting, the first of several, was scheduled for March between the Sumitomo executives and John Weinberg, head of Goldman Sachs.

Throughout July and into early August, all the interested parties — Rohatyn, his partners, the Goldman Sachs team, the Sumitomo representatives, and the ever present interpreters — worked patiently. Whatever deal they structured had to satisfy not only both sides but also the United States government, whose approval was required for all ventures between commercial and investment banks. The agreement that was reached involved Sumitomo's paying $500 million to Goldman

Sachs — giving the investment banking firm a much needed boost to its capital. In return, the Japanese bank would eventually be entitled to a 12.5 percent stake in Goldman Sachs but without any say in how the partnership was run.

It was an especially complicated deal. "You had regulatory problems. You had geographical distance. You had cultural differences. You had language problems," Rohatyn explained. But he seemed to enjoy matching wits with skilled lawyers and dealmakers.

* * *

If Rohatyn had one unfulfilled longing, apparently it was to serve as secretary of the treasury. He had been reluctant to discuss it publicly, but his friends were less reticent about his ambitions: "He's dying to become secretary of the treasury, and by 1980 he was on everybody's shortlist [of candidates]," said W. Michael Blumenthal, a former secretary of the treasury under President Jimmy Carter. "He's my choice."

Rohatyn had met with Jimmy Carter in 1980 during the president's bid for reelection. When Carter's chances turned bleak, Rohatyn confided to Rand Araskog of ITT how disappointed he was to see Carter's shot at a second term slip away.

Eight years later, when Michael Dukakis won the Democratic nomination and appeared at first to have a solid chance of being elected, Rohatyn seemed to be better poised than ever. "He was really positioning himself, writing a lot of articles and speaking," Blumenthal observed. "He's not publicity-shy. . . . He asked me what he should do or not do; how he should conduct himself. I said, 'Don't go running after it. Don't have a high profile. Lighten up.' "

Rohatyn didn't remember even "posing the question" and maintained that he didn't know whether he would have "felt comfortable with Dukakis."

It didn't matter.

Dukakis lost by a wide margin.

A few months later, Rohatyn still denied that he had "gone after a cabinet post," but admitted, "If some president I'm comfortable with asked me, I would serve in his cabinet. After all," he added, "anyone who is an athlete wants to play in the Olympics."

For the present he could continue to enjoy his established role in public service on a familiar stage. He remained committed to his agenda for New York City that boosted MAC bonds as a vehicle for positive change. In 1988, thirteen years after its creation, MAC had raised a total of $9.5 billion and refinanced $10 billion at lower rates. "I have a platform, and I have enormous financial influence in this city," he declared that year, in a candid rare admission of his clout, "and I intend to use it — whether it's applying the MAC surpluses in trying to develop a new school construction program — $600 million has already been pledged [for another project]. Two years ago we put almost a billion into mass transit, conditional on certain changes."

Over the years, he had also served on a number of policy-making boards and organizations: the Council on Foreign Relations, the [New York Governor's] Council on Fiscal and Economic Priorities, the National Economic Commission; he was cochairman, along with Lane Kirkland (president of the AFL-CIO) and Irving Shapiro (former chairman of Du Pont) of the Industry Policy Study Group, an ad hoc panel whose members included Senators Edward Kennedy and Bill Bradley.

His aspirations for a cabinet post had to remain on a back burner. Meantime, there were always deals that required his attention. He became involved in one that roused national debate, both for its sheer size and for its implications: the bidding war for RJR Nabisco, the tobacco and food company, the nineteenth-largest industrial corporation in America.

In mid-October 1988, when RJR's management proposed taking the company private in a leveraged buyout, Lazard and Dillon Read teams were hired by a special committee of outside directors to evaluate the proposal. Eventually two other suitors entered the scene with bids to take over the company — First Boston and Kohlberg Kravis Roberts.

As the senior member of the Lazard team hired by the special committee, Rohatyn worked closely with the other bankers and lawyers evaluating numerous highly complicated bids and counter-bids during the six-week contest. "It was a very difficult deal," he said simply. "I think the committee handled itself well and we handled ourselves well." By the end of November a winner emerged: Henry Kravis's firm walked away with the prize for a staggering $25 billion.

Gulf & Western head Martin Davis, one of RJR Nabisco's directors, who had hired Rohatyn to advise management about the sale of the company, lauded his efforts: "Everyone thinks we know everything about everything. This was an enormously complicated deal and we needed Felix."

At the height of a crucial negotiation or takeover battle, the telephone might ring at all hours at home, and in Rohatyn's office his four phone lines were often lighted at once. Though he now relied heavily on others to do the actual numbers work, he still became totally absorbed when involved in a deal. "He's in another realm," his wife commented. "He's thinking about the options, the various outcomes — all the components are floating around in his head. One of his most innovative qualities is his problem-solving ability, and he still finds that area of his work very exciting."

During peak work periods, Rohatyn suffered from occasional migraine headaches. "I've had migraines since I was a child," he revealed, "but being in the investment banking business hasn't helped." At the end of a pressured day, he usually had a drink or two to help him relax. The alcoholic beverage he preferred — outside of wine or beer — was vodka on the rocks.

But before the workday was over, his administrative assistant and his executive secretary screened a huge volume of mail and about one hundred telephone calls a day. In addition to deal-negotiation conversations, he was also on the phone with people like Governor Mario Cuomo and his top aides, senators and representatives, leaders of business, government, labor, and law, and associates in philanthropic works.

Right after the first furor they had caused, the Rohatyns had spoken out again on charity issues. "There is so much concentration on the gala and on catching a glimpse of the gala-goers, we are losing sight of the purpose of the exercise," he told the *New York Times* in January of 1986. "The opulence of some of these affairs becomes an embarrassment when one remembers the misery the charity is trying to alleviate."

He had no easy solutions, he said, but he had been considering a number of ideas, including persuading some prosperous, prestigious institutions to adopt smaller agencies that were struggling to survive financially but were clearly fulfilling community needs. He and his wife explained their proposed remedies to *Manhattan, inc.,* in a cover story that had photos of the couple. Shortly afterward, the controversy heated up.

*W* published an article in May of 1986 entitled "Felix the Cat and Snow White vs. the Social Sisters." The author took Elizabeth Rohatyn to task for her "holier-than-thou attitude" and ascribed the Rohatyns' position to his personal political ambitions, without having checked their side of the story (Rohatyn labeled that charge "ludicrous"). The article quoted his questioning the constructive contribution to charity when the women involved "are flying to Paris for a fitting of their clothes, and flying back on the next Concorde," and then pointedly commented: "Let's forget for the moment that Snow White [Elizabeth Rohatyn] had Bill Blass whip up a special number for her appearance at the Carnegie Hall benefit last year."

The article also claimed that because Brooke Astor, honorary chairman of the board of trustees of the New York Public Library, was displeased with Elizabeth Rohatyn's criticism, Rohatyn had pledged $200,000 to the landmark on Forty-second Street, allegedly as a peace offering to Mrs. Astor. Mrs. Astor herself had referred only elliptically to her attitude toward controversy: "Enough has been said." Later she defended the big institutions such as the library, which was founded by her husband's family: "Big institutions don't have all that much money because of inflation and union contracts going up. But," she also conceded, "in some cases, there have been too many flowers and too much food."

In the wake of the contretemps, Elizabeth Rohatyn resigned from the Women's Council of the Memorial Sloan-Kettering Cancer Center, because she had become too controversial. "I would take the same stance on charities if I had to do it again," she commented at a later date, "but I would have wanted less fuss made over it. The *Manhattan, inc.* cover story which triggered the whole thing should have been just a column."

Rohatyn acknowledged increasing the couple's long-standing contribution to the library but claimed it had "absolutely nothing to do with the debate about charity balls." He remained on the board of the Astor Foundation, and his wife remained a trustee of the library. They would be true to their stated belief in the need to help smaller charities, particularly those that directly benefited the poor. They committed their own money to the program begun by millionaire Eugene Lang, "I Have A Dream," the educational project in which wealthy sponsors "adopt" a school class and pledge to provide for the college education of those who don't drop out. In 1986, the Rohatyns adopted a junior high school class of some sixty youngsters from the Lower East Side —kids who apparently might otherwise not even dream of being able to afford college tuition.

At the start of each academic year, Elizabeth Rohatyn organized a party for the class. In 1988, when the students were approximately thirteen years old and more interested in their social life, she planned a rather formal dinner at the community house near the school. All the boys wore ties and the girls their best outfits. Each table had a different color scheme — blue, green, yellow, pink — with matching paper tablecloths, plates, and place cards. After a series of noncompetitive games, the students devoured a lunch of lasagna, salad, and chocolate cake covered with flowers. One boy took photos with the Rohatyns' Polaroid camera and each student left with a memento of the party.

Elizabeth visited with the students at school every week, and Rohatyn invited small groups to his office on a regular basis. "In the two years since we've been involved with the program, we've only lost two of our students because of grades or emotional problems," he noted with pride in their achievement.

The appointments with the students remained a constant on his calendar, which was always crowded with meetings, visitors, speaking engagements, civic responsibilities, and social and philanthropic engagements. The Rohatyns needed to call "time out" to relax from their hectic schedule.

Routinely, they tried to save Sunday nights for a casual dinner, after their return to New York from Southampton. It was often at an East Side Italian restaurant, where they were joined by such friends as ABC executive Roone Arledge; Barbara Walters and her husband, Merv Adelson, head of Lorimar Pictures; Clay Felker, publisher of *Manhattan, inc.*, and his wife, best-selling author Gail Sheehy; or by two of Felix's three sons: Nicky, an investment banker formerly with Morgan Guaranty Trust in Tokyo and now working in its New York office; and Michael, a composer of popular music. (His other son, Pierre, a designer of glassware for the Japanese-owned Mikasa, lived in Slovenija, Yugoslavia, where he worked for Mikasa.) Rohatyn had a much closer relationship with his sons now that they were grown. "He was always devoted to them when they were young," recalled a friend, "but somehow he was always slightly distant."

Elizabeth Rohatyn exerted a positive influence in family matters and helped arrange many get-togethers and festivities. In the spring of 1988, she planned a family birthday party in Southampton on the date of Rohatyn's sixtieth birthday and Pierre's thirtieth. "All the boys are Geminis and have birthdays within a few days of one another," she said. They ate a simple but favorite family dinner of grilled swordfish, fresh vegetables, and potatoes, followed by a yellow cake with chocolate icing that had Felix's and Pierre's names in different sections. "We had a wonderful evening together and made toasts and laughed and exchanged stories," Elizabeth recalled.

As a birthday present she gave her husband an Egyptian statue because of his growing interest in collecting art and antiquities. Elizabeth's daughter, Nina Griscom, who was there with her constant escort, plastic surgeon Dr. Daniel Baker, presented Rohatyn with a little booklet she had put together filled with humorous cartoons. His sons gave him books. Such casual, fun-filled evenings with the people he cared about the most were very special to him. He had never believed that it took elaborate settings or rituals to make important occasions special.

That didn't mean that he didn't enjoy the fruits of his considerable wealth. Though he maintained he had never felt deprived of anything he really wanted in the past, he now allowed himself more personal luxury.

Nowhere was this more apparent than in the Rohatyns' recently acquired Fifth Avenue co-operative apartment overlooking Central Park. The two-bedroom apartment had been purchased in 1987 and furnished in restrained but elegantly expensive taste by Boston decorator William Hodgins. It was a permanent and substantial home filled with Impressionist paintings, eighteenth-century drawings and pastels, books on many subjects, and family photographs. Light spilled into the painted off-white living room highlighted by a soft palette of dusty pink, pale coral, bluish green, and tobacco. There were two comfortable furniture groupings — each with a sofa and chairs that encouraged one to linger. A striking Regency writing table piled high with art books divided the room. At one end was a working fireplace adorned with a domed eighteenth-century Venetian mirror. The floor was covered with an eighteenth-century Aubusson rug.

The room reflected the personal taste of its owners, who had selected many of the eclectic antique pieces themselves — a Russian bench, a Regency console, several antique French chairs, a panel from a Chinese screen made into a coffee table, and needlepoint cushions. Tall glass doors — covered with shirred curtains — led to the library, a restful, virtually all-beige room with contemporary painted paneling, three book-lined walls, a big sofa and chairs covered in a natural beige raw silk fabric, a fireplace graced by an important nineteenth-century French painting, photos and other family memorabilia, and a breakfast table in the window. In the dining room, set off by a needlepoint rug, the long, lacquered-mahogany Louis Quinze table with oval-backed reproduction French chairs seated up to fourteen. Bookcases and a banquette stood against one wall. A crystal Regency chandelier provided lighting. The feeling was very European, a deliberate choice on Elizabeth Rohatyn's part. ("It's an ambience that Felix is comfortable with," she said.)

"In my eyes, our apartment is fairly spectacular," Rohatyn commented. "I didn't realize how dark our old apartment was until we bought this one. We have a wonderful view and so much light. I'm past sixty, and I think one has to enter into middlescence, or whatever it is, going gently into the good night."

The apartment provided a splendid setting for entertaining. As they had done in the early years of their marriage, they still gave dinner parties for no more than fourteen people to encourage conversation. Society caterer Glorious Food still provided the repast. The only difference was that now their circle of friends and acquaintances had grown even more diversified and global.

"Felix and Liz have the only genuine salon in New York," said Kati Marton, author of a biography of Raoul Wallenberg and wife of Peter Jennings, the anchorman for the ABC evening news. "The mix of people is so staggering. You never quite know whom you'll get, but you're always assured of a stimulating evening. Part of their genius is spotting interesting people. You are expected to talk. It's not for the shy. Whatever the topic is, it will be tossed around the table — not in a didactic or pedagogic way. Elizabeth is the most natural hostess I've ever met. She's very much in control, but she manages to make it look very easy and to make first-comers feel very relaxed. Both Felix and Elizabeth are so down to earth. There are no airs about them. What you see is what you get. There are no hidden agendas."

Kati Marton and Peter Jennings attended one Rohatyn dinner party, along with Nobel Peace Prize laureate Elie Wiesel and his wife and translator, Marion; Soviet specialists Marshall and Colette Shulman; executive editor of the *New York Times* Max Frankel and his wife, a member of the *New York Times* editorial board, Joyce Purnick; president of Memorial Sloan-Kettering Cancer Center Dr. Paul Marks, and his wife, Joan Marks, director of the human genetics program at Sarah Lawrence College; Lorimar head Merv Adelson, who came without his wife, Barbara Walters, because she was away interviewing Libyan leader Muammar el-Qaddafi; and Pat Bradshaw, a writer and the widow of onetime head of RCA Thornton Bradshaw.

After an abbreviated cocktail hour, the guests moved to the dining room table set with place cards and decorated with low arrangements of short-stemmed mixed flowers for an exquisite meal of curried crabmeat soufflé, rare filet of lamb, string beans, mashed potatoes, and an elegant form of baked apple for dessert. Rohatyn began the conversation at the table by asking Wiesel, who had recently returned from a visit to the Middle East, to discuss his views on the Palestinian uprising in the West Bank. Eventually everybody was drawn into the discussion.

Max Frankel and Joyce Purnick had also recently returned from a trip to the Middle East, and Peter Jennings, who had spent a few years living in Beirut, had considerable knowledge of and interest in the area. The conversation was informative, lively, occasionally argumentative, but always interesting and rewarding. Before the dinner was over, the talk had ranged from the AIDS crisis in New York City and the problems with a clean-needle program for drug addicts to the arms reduction agreement with Gorbachev. Both the Rohatyns and their guests declined to discuss what had been said.

"What we say in this apartment is really private," explained Elizabeth Rohatyn. "People come and they talk freely and it's stimulating and fun and sometimes combative. Part of the pleasure is knowing it's not going to be repeated."

By mogul's standards and considering the complexity of their life-style, the Rohatyns kept a relatively small staff. In New York, they employed a housekeeper and a cook; in Southampton, a maid who came to clean several times a week. The Rohatyns drove an Audi station wagon on weekends. During the week, he used a car service or walked to the office carrying his old brown satchel briefcase. On the street Rohatyn got the kind of recognition granted a celebrity, even though he was no longer making daily headlines.

He claimed he didn't miss the excitement of being in the limelight. "The good press is heady," he admitted. "But when you get bad press and when you're being attacked, you don't want to wake up because you know something terrible is going to happen. You want to pull the covers over your head and say, leave me alone.

"In the New York City crisis there was a lot of exposure. You always worried about whether they [the journalists] had it right, whether the coverage itself created problems if you hadn't touched all the bases.

"After a while you yearn for a bit of shade — though when that happens you have kind of withdrawal symptoms for a while. I still have what I call a maintenance dose of publicity. I'm sufficiently in the news but not so much and not so controversial — except when it comes to charity — that I have to worry about it. You're out of the fray every day, out of the passions and controversy. I can live without the front page, as long as I occasionally get on the editorial page. I have a very nice life and there's no reason not to enjoy it. I've paid my dues."

# *Epilogue*

$A$s a stage for acting out personal ambitions on the themes of wealth, power, and social status, Wall Street has few parallels. The New Crowd who made their way on that stage in the last forty years did not leave Wall Street or corporate America exactly as they found it. They and their counterparts in other businesses — modern media barons, computer whizzes setting up shops in basements and in garages, electronic geniuses, pioneers of leisure-time services, and mass marketing entrepreneurs — challenged the dominance of the old corporate culture, overturned the traditional rigid management hierarchy, and introduced a freewheeling style that was responsive to market forces. As in the period after the Civil War, when the financiers of that era underwrote a massive change in the nature of the American economy from an agricultural to an industrial base, the New Crowd, a hundred years later, helped to finance the transformation of America from an industrial phase to the present postindustrial one.

In the process, the New Crowd broke the stranglehold of the Establishment Wasp bankers and their Our Crowd competitors, set a standard for achievement on Wall Street that swept past the restrictive barriers of class and family connections, and extended profit centers to newer financial activities such as block trading, risk arbitrage, a wide range of retail securities products, financial futures, listed trading of options, junk bond financing that helped companies expand and made almost every company vulnerable to a takeover, and leveraged buyouts that restructured corporate entities and raised critical debt levels. They provided vast amounts of liquidity that fueled the stock market and enabled it to take off to new heights that hadn't been projected previously and whose full impact has yet to be assessed. As the last pages of the decade of the eighties were being written, there were signs of strain: firms were retrenching all over the Street and the grand vision of the Superbroker providing a full spectrum of financial services seemed clouded; Wall Street and corporate financial practices were coming under scrutiny in magazine articles and books. In the 1990s some high-flying houses and individual shakers and makers will undoubtedly be shaken up and shaken out. Tougher times and less stability have been predicted for the financial world. But volatility was the force that had ushered in the New Crowd to begin with, and they had spent their Wall Street lives dealing with the ups and downs of the market.

The New Crowd benefited from the changing of the guard in America that had, by the end of the 1980s, culminated in a major shift in the ruling alignment of wealth, influence, status, and power throughout the country. Their visibility in the economy and on Wall Street was matched by their emergence as major figures in the New York social hierarchy. Like the nouveaux riches who preceded them — the Astors, Vanderbilts, and Rockefellers — the New Crowd turned their money to advantage and acquired the privileges and obligations of the very rich.

In the long run — again, like their predecessors throughout American history — by their dazzling displays of wealth spent on homes, balls and parties, weddings, clothes, collections of art and antiques, and other trappings of luxury, and through their support of museums, libraries, colleges, hospitals, and other philanthropic institutions, a number of them may be remembered more for how they spent their money than for how they made it.

\* \* \*

They will also be remembered for the fundamental change they forged in the Who's Who of Wall Street. Unlike previous generations of the newly rich on the Street who rose to wealth and power — a process as old as the story of America itself — they did not form exclusionary enclaves. The hierarchies and affiliations within the New Crowd are fluid, and even as some members have aged and acquired the patina of established wealth and position, newcomers rather than family members have rushed in to fill the ranks below them. In that way they differ profoundly from Our Crowd and their Wasp Establishment counterparts. They opened a door that would be difficult to close again on anyone of the "wrong" class, background, and religion — and even the "wrong" color or sex. They made careers on Wall Street accessible and they made the game more competitive and colorful. For the mix of people on Wall Street in the future, that may be the enduring imprint of the New Crowd.

# A Partial List of People Interviewed

George Ames, Rand Araskog, Herman Badillo, George Ball, Michel Bergerac, Roger Berlind, Robert Bernhard, Kenneth Bialkin, W. Michael Blumenthal, Ivan Boesky, Ludwig Bravmann, I. W. Burnham, Hugh Carey, Arthur Carter, Maurice Cerier, Alger Chapman, Howard Clark, Jr., Steven Clifford, Marshall Cogan, Karen Cohen, Peter Cohen, Martin Davis, Disque Deane, Richard Dicker, Tim Dunleavy, John Ehrlichman, Alvin Einbender, Donald Engel, Dwight Faulkner, Richard Fay, Clay Felker, Joseph Flom, Vicki Frankovitch, Merrill Freeman, Stephen Friedman, Hélène Gaillet de Barcza, Harold Geneen, James Glanville, Lewis Glucksman, J. Harrison Goldin, Jack Golsen, David Gordis, Sheldon Gordon, Victor Gotbaum, Harry Gray, Mark Green, Alan Greenberg, Sydney Gruson, Robert Haack, Ira Harris, Larry Hartzog, Samuel Hayes, Edward Hennessy, George Heyman, Irving Howe, Carl Icahn, Nicholas Ihasz, Harry Jacobs, Ludwig Jesselson, Frederick Joseph, Herman Kahn, Mark Kaplan, Henry Kaufman, Daniel Kelly, Nan Kempner, Thomas Kempner, Alfred Kingsley, Richard Kleindienst, Edward Koch, Jerome Kohlberg, Robert Lakachman, Bernard Lasker, Arthur Levitt, Jr., Janet Levy, Leon Levy, Peter Levy, Sherman Lewis, James Ling, Robert Linton, Kenneth Lipper, Martin Lipton, Frances Loeb, John Loeb, Hugh Lowenstein, Peter Maas, Jeffrey Madrick, Mark Mallard, Paul Manheim, David Margolis, Alice Mason, William May, Mary McDermott, George McGovern, Andrew McLaughlin, Aileen Mehle, Vincent Murphy, Edmund Muskie, Jack Nash, Stephen Peck, Joseph Perella, H. Ross Perot, Jay Perry, James Robinson, Elizabeth Rohatyn, Felix Rohatyn, John Rosenwald, Steven Ross, Jon Rotenstreich, Robert E. Rubin, Robert S. Rubin, Morris Saffron, Andrew Sage, John Salomon, William Salomon, Arnold Sametz, David Schiff, Elliot Schnall, William Simon, John Slade, Howard Stein, Barbara Steinberg, Gayfryd Steinberg, Robert Steinberg, Saul Steinberg, Donald Stone, Thomas Strauss, Donald Stroben, Harold Tanner, Robert Townsend, Raymond Troubh, Lewis Wasserman, Bruce Wasserstein, Joan Weill, Sanford Weill, John Weinberg, John Welch, Frederick Whittemore, James Wolfensohn, Louis Wolfson, Walter Wriston, and Frank Zarb.

# Notes

## Chapter 1: The End of an Era

3 History of Harmonie: Morris Saffron (ed.), *One Hundred and Twenty-Five Years 1852–1977 The Harmonie Club.*

4–5 "Our Crowd": S. Birmingham, *"Our Crowd,"* pp. 7–8

5–6 Details of John Loeb's youth and education: Margaret Loeb Kempner, "Recollections: A Personal Memoir" (unpublished, 1980).

5–6 Description of Frances and John Loeb's wedding and life-style: Frances Loeb, "For My Family: A Memoir" (unpublished, 1982); also interview with Frances Loeb.

7–8 The Weills' wedding and their life together: Interview with Joan Weill.

8–9 The first Shearson Loeb Rhoades board meeting: Interviews with John Loeb, Sandy Weill, Jack Nusbaum, Sherman Lewis, Peter Cohen, George Sheinberg.

## Chapter 2: The New Crowd

12 Commercial banking and Jews: Robert A. Bennett, "No Longer a WASP Preserve," *New York Times,* June 29, 1986.

12 The absence of Jews in banking, insurance and oil: S. L. Slavin and M. A. Pradt, *The Einstein Syndrome,* pp. 26–40.

16 "Money becomes a way": Myron Magnet, "The Money Society," *Fortune,* July 6, 1987.

## Chapter 3: First Stirrings

22 "My father": Interview with Sandy White.

22–23 National Dairy anecdote: Robert Sheehan, "Let's Ask Sidney Weinberg," *Fortune,* October 1953.

28–29 Charges in the 1947 antitrust suit against the securities industry: Harold R. Medina, *Corrected Opinion of Harold R. Medina in United States of America v. Henry S. Morgan, Harold Stanley, doing business as Morgan Stanley & Co., et al.,* filed, Washington, D.C., February 4, 1954.

29 Underwriting standings (through 1949): Ibid.

30–31 Details of Gus Levy's early years and marriage: Interview with Janet Levy.

31–32 Levy at Goldman Sachs: Interview with Robert Mnuchin and L. Jay Tenenbaum.

31 History of arbitrage: Guy P. Wyser-Pratte, *Risk Arbitrage II*, p. 1.

33 Levy at Apple Hill Farm: Interview with Peter Levy.

36 Anti-Semitic attack on Louis Wolfson: Interview with Louis Wolfson.

## Chapter 4: Deal Architect

40 Rohatyn distributing anti-Nazi pamphlets and wearing the star of David armband: Interview with Felix Rohatyn.

42 Brothel anecdote: Interview with Rohatyn.

48 ITT attack on the *New York Times* reporter: R. J. Schoenberg, *Geneen*, pp. 214–216; also interview with Eileen Shanahan (the *New York Times* reporter who was harassed by ITT).

## Chapter 5: A House Divided

49 Capital ranking of CBW: *Finance*, annual capital position, March 1969.

53 "He had such terrible clothes": Interview with Daniel Cowin.

53–61 History of CBW: Interviews with Weill, Arthur Carter, Marshall Cogan, Arthur Levitt, Jr., Roger Berlind, Joan Weill, Kenneth Bialkin, and others.

54 Peter Potoma's troubles: "Big Board Suspends Partner of New York Broker Firm for 1 Year," *Wall Street Journal*, July 20, 1962; also interviews with Carter, Berlind, and Weill.

57 CBW partners' ridicule of one another: Interviews with Cogan, Carter, Weill, Levitt.

58 Reliance deal: Charles N. Stabler, "How a Securities Firm and a Few Institutions Can Influence a Merger," *Wall Street Journal*, January 26, 1970; also interviews with Saul Steinberg, Carter, Cogan.

59–60 Ouster of Carter: Interviews with Weill, Cogan, Levitt, and Carter. (Carter claims that he left of his own accord.)

## Chapter 6: The House of Salomon

63 Ferdinand Salomon's life: R. Sobel, *Salomon Brothers*, pp. 2–3; also, interviews with John Salomon and William Salomon.

63–64 Arthur Salomon's dominance: Interviews with Merrill Freeman, Irving Kaufman, Daniel Kelly.

64 Percy Salomon's health: Interviews with Kelly, William Salomon, John Salomon.

65 Herbert Salomon's humor: Interviews with Kelly, John Salomon.

67 William Salomon as "floorwalker": Interviews with Kelly, Kaufman.

67 Smutny's purchase of Haloid: Interview with former Salomon partner.

68–69 Palace revolt: Carol J. Loomis, "Living It Up in a Salomon-Sized World," *Fortune*, April 1970; also R. Sobel, *Salomon Brothers* and interviews with Kelly, John Salomon, William Salomon.

70 Harold Stuart's reaction to Billy Salomon: Interview with Halsey Stuart banker who was present.

## Chapter 7: Moving Up

71 "I wanted us to be the best": Gutfreund to journalist in unpublished interview.

71 "Hager, you're full": Interview with Halsey Stuart banker who was present.

72–74 John Gutfreund's early years: Interviews with William Salomon, Robert Bernhard, and others.

72 Century loses some of its exclusivity: Interviews with several members.

73 "My parents": Gutfreund to journalist in unpublished interview.

73 "A typical ambivalent, young Jewish man": Ibid.

74–75 Underwriting ranking for Salomon: Leading Syndicate Managers (table), *Investment Dealers' Digest*, February 1967.

75 "You've got it": Interview with a Salomon partner.

76 "Get off your ass": Interview with Merrill Freeman.

76 "I've tried to use": James P. Roscow, "William R. Salomon, Investment Banker of the Year," *Finance*, December 1970.

77 "I stayed awake all last night": Interview with Jay Perry.

78 "Let's get our name": Interview with Perry.

79 "You clean it up": Interview with Jonathan Bigel.

79–80 Gutfreund's and Simon's prank involving Robert Dall: Interview with Robert Dall.

## Chapter 8: Enormous Changes

85 "Fails to Deliver" details: Robert W. Haack, *Statement of Robert W. Haack, President, New York Stock Exchange. Before the Committee on Interstate and Foreign Commerce, Subcommittee on Commerce and Finance of the House of Representatives,* Washington, D.C., February 26, 1969.

86–87 Chemical Bank bid by Saul Steinberg: "Leasco Chairman Says Banking Interests Firm, But Target Isn't Decided," *Wall Street Journal*, February 10, 1969; also H. Erich Heinemann, "Leasco Affirms Interest in Chemical Bank," *New York Times*, February 12, 1969.

86 Anti-Semitic remarks made to Steinberg during Chemical Bank bid: Interview with Saul Steinberg.

86 "A pretty good gutter fighter": J. Brooks, *Go-go Years*, p. 248.

87 "I always knew": Ibid, p. 259.

## Chapter 9: Crisis

89 Felix Rohatyn called "possibly the best in the business": Everett Mattlin, "Felix Rohatyn: The M&A Man's M&A Man," *Corporate Financing*, February 1970.

91–92 Donald Stroben talks with Roger Berlind: Interview with Donald Stroben.

92 The Stock Exchange's $7.6 million offer: J. Brooks, *Go-Go Years*, p. 326.

92–95 Winning over Hayden Stone's subordinated lenders: Interviews with Rohatyn and Robert Haack.

94 Meeting in Golsen's office: Interviews with Jack Golsen, Marshall Cogan, and Larry Hartzog.

94 Cogan's remarks about Jews and the Hayden Stone affair: Interview with Cogan.

95–96 How CBWL benefited from the actions taken by the New York Stock Exchange: C. Welles, *The Last Days of the Club*, pp. 244–245.

96 The rescue of du Pont: J. Brooks, *Go-Go Years*. pp. 336–345; also interviews with H. Ross Perot and Rohatyn.

96 "The sacking of Rome by the vandals": C. Welles, *The Last Days of the Club*, p. 252.

## Chapter 10: On the Firing Line

98 The Italian bank affair: C. Reich, *Financier*, pp. 297–307.

99 Phone conversation between Richard Nixon and Richard Kleindienst: R. Schoenberg, *Geneen*, pp. 266–267. Also interviews with Richard Kleindienst and John Ehrlichman.

98–101 Charting of Rohatyn, ITT, and government's movement during the Hartford settlement talks: United States Senate, *Hearings Before the Committee on the Judiciary (nomination of Richard Kleindienst, of Arizona, to be Attorney General)*, Washington, D.C., 1972.

100 "I want out!": J. Brooks, *Go-Go Years*, p. 344.

101–102 Rohatyn's role in the Muskie campaign: Interviews with Rohatyn and Edmund Muskie.

104 Unidentified source naming Felix Rohatyn as central to the ITT plan: A. Sampson, *The Sovereign State of ITT*, p. 212.

106–107 Kleindienst hearings: U.S. Senate, March 1972.

107 Press reaction to Rohatyn's ITT work: "The Fallout from the I.T.T. Affair" (editorial), *Fortune*, May 1972.

108 Rohatyn's separation from his wife: Interview with de Barcza.

108 Rohatyn's move to the Alrae: Interviews with de Barcza and Rohatyn.

109 "The Man Most Responsible": The Remarkable Felix Rohatyn," *Business Week*, March 10, 1973.

## Chapter 11: Unbridled Ambition

111 Lewis Glucksman called "crude": K. Auletta, *Greed and Glory on Wall Street*, p. 48.

113–114 Glucksman's rise: Interview with Lewis Glucksman and Andrew Sage.

116 "I'm sick and tired": Interview with Glucksman.

## Chapter 12: To Build an Empire

119–120 CBWL-Hayden Stone goes public: CBWL-Hayden Stone, Prospectus, October 1, 1971.

120–122 The case against Topper: Securities and Exchange Commission Docket, *SEC v. Topper Corporation, et al.*, Litigation Release No. 6145/ November 12, 1973.

123 Picking a new CEO: Interviews with Weill, Arthur Levitt, Marshall Cogan, Roger Berlind.

123 The case against Seaboard: Securities and Exchange Commission Docket, *The Seaboard Corporation, et al. (C.D.C.A.)*, Litigation Release No. 6269/ March 5, 1974.

125–126 Roger Berlind's departure: Interviews with Weill, Levitt, Berlind, and Peter Cohen.

## Chapter 13: Rohatyn City

127 Rohatyn's and Hélène Gaillet de Barcza's life together: Interviews with de Barcza.

127 Rohatyn spending time with friends: Interviews with Rohatyn, de Barcza, Jim Lipton, Clay Felker.

128 "I had no involvement in politics": Jeremy Bernstein, "Allocating Sacrifice," *New Yorker*, January 24, 1983.

129 "I've just reviewed": Interview with Lipton.

129 "We're trying to keep the patient alive": F. Ferretti, *The Year the Big Apple Went Bust*, p. 214.

130 "Everybody would be lining up": Interview with Rohatyn.

131 "The possibility of revenue increases": F. Ferretti, *The Year the Big Apple Went Bust*, p. 246.

132 "He said that?" Interview with Peter Maas.

133 "Like someone stepping into a tepid bath": F. Ferretti, *The Year the Big Apple Went Bust*, p. 196.

## Chapter 14: Hardball Politics

136 Breakfast at the Regency: Peter Andrews, "The Art of the Business Breakfast," *Institutional Investor*, August 1979.

136 "You see the politicians": Marylin Bender, "If Financial Coups Are Percolating, It's Breakfast Time at the Regency," *New York Times*, July 7, 1976.

138 Argument between Perry and Rosenthal: Interview with Perry.

138 John Gutfreund's view of Simon's possible return: Interviews with William Salomon, William Simon, Frederick Whittemore, Vincent Murphy.

139 "I'm not normally known as a political person": Michael C. Jensen, "Young Millionaires Are Big Contributors to McGovern," *New York Times*, August 23, 1972.

139 John Gutfreund's contribution to George McGovern's 1972 campaign for president: The Office of Federal Elections of 1972. Itemized contributions and itemized sales for collections, November 15, 1973.

139 Gutfreund in South Dakota: Interview with Henry Kimelman.

139 "Some day you'll understand": Interview with Simon.

140 "Shakeup in the 'bulge group' ": Phyllis Feinberg, "Investment Banking's Battle of the Bulge," *Institutional Investor*, January 1980.

141 Billy Salomon's talks with William Simon: Interviews with Salomon and Simon.

142 Goldman Sachs conviction: M. C. Jensen, *The Financiers*, pp. 190–209.

## Chapter 15: At the Top of the Crowd

143–149: History of Bear Stearns: Interviews with Alan Greenberg, John Rosenwald, John Slade, Richard Fay, and others; also *The History of Bear Stearns: A Partnership of Individuals* (Incomplete draft to 1984), Bear, Stearns & Co. Inc.

150 Bear Stearns capital ranking: *Finance*, 1980.

150 Greenberg's memo to partners: Leslie Wayne, "A Daring Dealmaker Piles up Profits," *New York Times*, June 12, 1983.

## Chapter 16: Epitaph for Loeb Rhoades

151 Topper settlement: "Shearson Settles 3 Suits Over Topper Collapse for $1.7 Million Total," *Wall Street Journal*, February 25, 1976.

155–156 Carl Loeb's youth and career: M. L. Kempner, *Recollections, A Personal Memoir*.

156–157 Early history of Loeb Rhoades: T. A. Wise, "Wherever You Look, There's Loeb, Rhoades," *Fortune*, April 1963.

158–163 Shearson's acquisition of Loeb Rhoades: Interviews with Weill, Peter Cohen, Thomas Kempner, Andrew McLaughlin, Joan Weill, and others.

161–163 Background of Shearson and Loeb Rhoades merger: Securities and Exchange Commission, Form 10-K, *Shearson Hayden Stone Inc.*, for year ending June 30, 1979.

161–163 Details of Loeb Rhoades office transfers to Shearson: *Shearson Loeb Rhoades Inc.* Joint Proxy Statement (with American Express), June 1, 1981.

162 Revised terms of Shearson and Loeb Rhoades merger: *Shearson Loeb Rhoades Inc.*, Proxy Statement, October 14, 1980.

163 Capital ranking of Shearson Loeb Rhoades: *Institutional Investor*, "Ranking America's Biggest Brokers," April 1980.

163 Shearson's earnings and Weill's compensation: Ibid.

## Chapter 17: Starting Over

164–165 Vagliano's background: Interview with Elizabeth Rohatyn.

165 "Of all the people I've seen": C. Reich, *Financier*, pp. 352–353.

167 "He has to have his place in the sun": "Notes on People," *New York Times*, January 4, 1979.

167 "Moral conflict of interest": Lee Dembart, "Koch and Rohatyn in New Clash Over Hiring of Lazard by M.A.C.," *New York Times*, March 7, 1979.

167 Koch regrets feud: Lee Dembart, "Koch Regrets His Feud That Forced Out Lazard," *New York Times*, March 26, 1979.

167 "I'm delighted the governor": "Mayor and Rohatyn End Their Rift," *New York Times*, May 19, 1979.

167 "He told me he had no desire": Ibid.

168 "Going national": William Serrin, "Rohatyn 'Going National,' Doubts Free-Market Future," *New York Times*, April 21, 1981.

168 "Sometimes we went to two hockey games": Interview with Elizabeth Rohatyn.

169–170 "Behind the stern, forbidding": C. Reich, *Financier*, p. 356.

171–171 Geneen and ITT: R. Schoenberg, *Geneen*, pp. 283–324.

170 "He can run": R. Schoenberg, *Geneen*, p. 300.

171 "I've always said": Interview with Rohatyn.

172 "There was always a great mixture": Interview with Barbara Walters.

172 Description of the Rohatyns' Southampton home and art: Interview with Elizabeth Rohatyn.

172–173 Details of merger wave: W. T. Grimm & Co., *Twenty-Two-Year Statistical Review*, Chicago, 1985; also Federal Trade Commission, *Statistical Report on Mergers and Acquisitions 1979*, Washington, D.C., 1981, and Malcolm S. Salter and Wolf A. Weinhold, *Merger Trends and Prospects for the 1980s*, U.S. Department of Commerce, Washington, D.C., 1980.

## Chapter 18: Superbroker

182–189 Negotiations between American Express and Shearson: Interviews with James Robinson, Howard Clark, Jr., Weill, and Peter Cohen; also Tim Carrington, *The Year They Sold Wall Street*. pp. 182–199.

185–188 Meeting in Connecticut: Interviews with Alger Chapman, Sherman Lewis, Dwight Faulkner, George Sheinberg, Cohen, and Weill.

187 Bernard as only Jewish partner at Morgan Stanley: Wyndham Robertson, "Future Shock at Morgan Stanley," *Fortune*, February 27, 1978.

187 Women on Wall Street: Beth McGoldrick and Gregory Miller, "Wall Street Women: You've Come a Short Way, Baby," *Institutional Investor*, June 1985.

191 Luncheon for Amexco and Shearson wives: Interviews with Karen Cohen and Joan Weill.

191–192 "We survived": Speech by Weill, June 29, 1981.

## Chapter 19: New Alliances

195 Salomon gets the IBM deal: Walter Guzzardi, Jr., "The Bomb IBM Dropped on Wall Street," *Fortune*, November 19, 1979; also interview with Henry Kaufman.

195 Underwriting ranking for Salomon: *Institutional Investor*, "Financing Sweepstakes I," April 1981.

196–198 History of Philipp Brothers: A. C. Copetas, *Metal Men*, pp. 52–62.

197 Engelhard's eating habits: Interview with Robert Zeller.

198 Phibro's interest in Salomon Brothers: Interviews with William Salomon, Zeller, Mark Kaplan, and others; also, R. Sobel, *Salomon Brothers*, pp. 171–177.

198–199 Susan Penn apparently eager to meet rich men, not forthcoming about her past: Interview with former friend.

199 Susan Penn pampering herself: Susan Gutfreund to author.

200 Vanderbilt controversy: Michael Goodwin, "Vanderbilt Suit Upsets Placid River House," *New York Times,* May 31, 1980.

201 MAC II hired to decorate after August: Carol Vogel, "Susan Gutfreund: High Finances, High Living," *New York Times,* January 10, 1988.

201 Details of Gutfreunds' wedding: Interview with former friend.

202 "He was shocked": Susan Gutfreund to author.

## Chapter 20: The Road to Tarrytown

203 "I don't understand": Interview with Mark Kaplan.

203–208 Tarrytown meeting to announce sale of Salomon Brothers: Interviews with Craig Stearns, Stanley Arkin, Robert Bernhard, Robert Dall, Jon Rotenstreich, Thomas Strauss, Kenneth Lipper, James Wolfensohn, Harold Tanner, Peter Gottsegen, and others.

206 Gutfreund's remark about William Salomon: Interview with a former partner.

209–210 Gutfreund's meeting with William Salomon: Interview with Salomon and Henry Kaufman.

210 Salomon's criticism of Gutfreund: Interview with Salomon.

211 Gutfreund's phone conversation with Daniel Kelly: Interview with Kelly.

211 Salomon as fourth-largest firm on Wall Street: "Ranking America's Biggest Brokers," *Institutional Investor,* April 1981.

## Chapter 21: "Do You Know Me?"

214–216 Weill's bid for the presidency of American Express: Barry Rehfeld, "Deal Maker," *Esquire,* November 1983, and unpublished material.

217–220 TDB deal: Interview with Peter Cohen and T. Carrington, *The Year They Sold Wall Street.* pp. 219–224.

220 Gutfreund on board jet: Interview with Cohen.

## Chapter 22: Billions Up for Grabs

223–224 First Boston's M&A department: Interviews with Bruce Wasserstein, Joseph Perella, and William Lampert.

228 "Jewish dentist" defense: K. M. Davidson, *Megamergers: Corporate America's Billion-Dollar Takeovers,* p. 24.

228 Flom's counterattack: Ibid., pp. 70–71.

230 Rohatyn's earnings in 1982 and 1983: Partnership proposals. *Pearson: The Three Lazard Houses,* May 18, 1984 and Lazard (New York) partnership papers.

## Chapter 23: The Junk Bond King

232–233 Mike Milken's early years: Interview with Louis Ramirez (a teacher at Milken's high school) and others; also C. Bruck, *The Predators' Ball*, p. 24.

236 Milken as Mr. Junk Bond: Vartanig G. Vartan, "Hidden Treasures In Junk Bonds," *New York Times*, September 26, 1976.

236–237 Growth of junk bond sales and trading: Allan Sloan and Howard Rudnitsky, "Taking In Each Other's Laundry," *Forbes*, November 14, 1984; also Drexel Burnham Lambert, *The Case for High Yield Securities*, April 1986.

## Chapter 24: Greenmail

239 "I'm no takeover artist": E. W. Allison, *The Raiders of Wall Street*, p. 24.

239–240 Saul Steinberg's involvement with Pergamon: John M. Lee, "Share Vote Gives A Victory To 30-Year-Old New Yorker," *New York Times*, October 11, 1969. Also J. Russell Boner, "Pergamon Holders' Meeting Slated Today Seen As Showdown in Battle for Control," *Wall Street Journal*, October 10, 1969.

241 Most of their friends were older: Interview with Barbara Steinberg.

241 Steinberg's donation to Jewish charities: Interview with Brian Martin (Steinberg representative).

241–242 Woodmere donation: R. Slater, *The Titans of Takeover*, p. 97.

242 Pulte charges: "SEC Accuses Actor, 2 Others of Violations in Sale of Pulte Stock," *Wall Street Journal*, August 30, 1978.

242 Pulte settlement: Peter W. Bernstein, "Fear and Loathing in the Boardroom," *Fortune*, December 15, 1980.

242 Bus stop scandal: Ibid.; also, Howard Blum with Leslie Maitland, "New York Bus Shelter Case: Business, Law and Politics," *New York Times*, May 19, 1980.

244 Meetings between Saul Steinberg and Richard Dicker: Interviews with Dicker and Steinberg; also Robert J. Cole, "Penn Central Accuses Reliance Chief of 'Unlawful Scheme' to Gain Control," *New York Times*, November 8, 1979.

244–245 Charges by Laura Steinberg: Mark J. Evans, Decision by Judge Mark J. Evans in the Supreme Court of the State of New York, County of New York: Special Term Part I (in the suit brought by Laura Steinberg against Saul Steinberg), December 29, 1980.

245 "She's a liar": Leslie Maitland, "Illegal Gift Alleged in Bus Shelter Case," *New York Times*, May 23, 1980.

245 Quotes on Steinberg in *Fortune:* P. Bernstein, *Fortune*, December 15, 1980.

245 Bronston jail term: Arnold H. Lubasch, "Bronston Gets 4 Months in Bus-Stop Fraud Case," *New York Times,* January 3, 1981.

245 Steinberg's letter saying he hadn't "the faintest inclination": *New York Times,* August 10, 1981.

246 By his own estimates, he had given away millions: Interview with Martin.

246 Steinberg's art sale: Rita Reif, "At Auction, Wallets Were Close to the Vest," *New York Times,* May 21, 1981.

246 "I buy a lot of hard art": Wendy Lyon Moonan, "Barony on Park Avenue," *Town & Country,* November 1985.

247 Meeting and marriage of Gayfryd and Saul Steinberg: Interview with Gayfryd Steinberg; also Tina Brown, "Gayfryd Takes Over," *Vanity Fair,* November 1986.

247–248 Description of Steinberg apartment: W. L. Moonan, "Barony on Park Avenue," *Town & Country,* November 1985; also interview with Gayfryd Steinberg.

248 Steinberg's personal life: Interview with Gayfryd Steinberg.

249 "It's the largest gambling casino": Saul Steinberg, "Maximizing Investment Decisions," Speech given at the Wharton Entrepreneurial Center, Executive Dinner Forum, The Wharton School, Philadelphia, Pennsylvania, March 28, 1984.

249 Saul Steinberg's view of Disney management: Interview with Steinberg.

250 Steinberg and Drexel relationship: Securities and Exchange Commission, Form 10-K, *Reliance Group Holdings, Inc.,* 1984.

251 Settlement of Disney deal: J. Taylor, *Storming the Magic Kingdom,* pp. 115–134; also interview with Steinberg.

252 Gayfryd Steinberg as Scaasi patroness: "The New American Establishment," *U.S. News & World Report,* February 8, 1988.

253 Gayfryd Steinberg as "queen of Nouvelle Society": Ibid.

253 Gayfryd Steinberg as successor to Astor: Ibid.

253–255 Description of Steinberg and Tisch wedding: George Dullea, "Candlelight Wedding Joins 2 Billionaire Families," *New York Times,* April 19, 1988; also "Wedding Royale: Let 'Em Eat Cakes," *Women's Wear Daily,* April 20, 1988 and interview with Gayfryd Steinberg.

## Chapter 25: Squeeze at the Top

257–258 Lewis Glucksman's views on Pete Peterson: Interview with Glucksman.

259–260 Equitable luncheon: K. Auletta, *Greed and Glory on Wall Street,* pp. 5–9.

260 Peterson's reaction the following day: Ibid., pp. 25–27.

262 Peter Cohen's meeting with Stephen Schwarzman: Interview with Cohen. Also K. Auletta, *Greed and Glory on Wall Street*, pp. 193–194.

262–263 Lewis Glucksman on selling Lehman and dealing with American Express: Interview with Glucksman.

## Chapter 26: Solemn John

266 Gutfreund's remarks in *Fortune:* Carol J. Loomis, "The Morning After," *Fortune*, January 10, 1983.

266 "Marble minimalist": Marie Brenner, "The Class Menagerie," *New York*, September 19, 1983.

266 Description of River House: Interview with two guests.

266 "A Proustian evening": Carol Vogel, "Susan Gutfreund: High Finances, High Living," *New York Times Magazine*, January 10, 1988.

266 Elaborate gilt candelabra adorned each table: Ibid.

266 Size of Susan Gutfreund's staff: "Susan Gutfreund," *On the Avenue*, April 1983.

266 The Gutfreunds' nonstop partying: Interview with former friend.

266 "When I come home": Interview with former friend.

267 Susan Gutfreund luncheon for the Citizens Committee: *On the Avenue*, April 1983.

268 "She collects things": Colin Leinster, "The Man Who Seized the Throne at Phibro-Salomon," *Fortune*, December 24, 1984.

268 "From the wrong side of the tracks": David Michaelis, "The Nutcracker Suite," *Manhattan, inc.*, December 1984; also, author interview.

268–269 The first Christmas tree: D. Michaelis, "The Nutcracker Suite"; also author interviews.

270 Details of Blenheim reception: *On the Avenue*, April 1983, D. Michaelis, "The Nutcracker Suite," and L. Lapham, *Money and Class in America*, p. 70.

270 Susan Gutfreund entertained by Lord Weidenfeld: M. Brenner, "The Class Menagerie."

271–272 Second Christmas tree: D. Michaelis, "The Nutcracker Suite," and author interviews.

272 "Two-headed monster": C. Leinster, "The Man Who Seized the Throne at Phibro-Salomon."

272 Gutfreund's takeover of top spot at Phibro: Interviews with William May and others.

273 Susan Gutfreund's party in Paris for her husband: D. Michaelis, "The Nutcracker Suite."

273 Cost and address of new Gutfreund apartment: Ibid. Also John Taylor, "Hard to Be Rich," *New York*, January 11, 1988.

273 Tenant list at 834 Fifth Avenue: Jesse Kornbluth, "The Working Rich," *New York*, November 24, 1986.

273 "The not-so-benevolent King of the Street": Anthony Bianco, "The King of Wall Street," *Business Week*, December 9, 1985.

274 "I am addicted to this business": Beth McGoldrick, "Salomon's Power Culture," *Institutional Investor*, March 1986.

## Chapter 27: Endstopped

281 Arthur Levitt's view of party honoring Weill: Interview with Levitt.

283 Weill's decision to leave American Express: Interviews with Weill, Peter Cohen, James Robinson, and George Sheinberg. Also Chris Welles, "American Express Thrives on Diversity," *Los Angeles Times*, June 30, 1985.

## Chapter 28: The Calling of the Cards

287–288 History of UJA-Federation: Interviews with Maurice Cerier, Sanford Solender, Jerry Rosemarin, Carl Glick, and Stephen Peck; also C. Silberman, *A Certain People*, pp. 185–198 and A. J. Karp, *Haven and Home*, pp. 287–291.

## Chapter 29: Eye of the Storm

289 History of "21": John Homans, "Making Old '21' Young," *New York Times Magazine*, February 15, 1987.

290 Favorable *Wall Street Journal* story: Lawrence Rout, "A Risk Arbitrageur Plays Dangerous Game of Betting on Mergers," *Wall Street Journal*, February 22, 1979.

291 "Afraid to venture out in the world": Interview with Carl Icahn.

292 "I can't get married": Interview with Icahn.

293 "Short-term, fast-buck, turnover approach": "Stockholder Meeting Briefs," *Wall Street Journal*, April 24, 1979.

293 Tappan charges: "Tappan Asserts Holder Seeking a Board Seat Ran Afoul of Big Board," *Wall Street Journal*, April 10, 1979.

293 Icahn violation: "Icahn and Company Fined by Big Board," *Wall Street Journal*, November 12, 1974.

294 Saxon fraud: Michael Siconolfi, "Saxon Chief Pleads Guilty in Fraud Case," *Wall Street Journal*, September 4, 1985.

295 "In our business, if you want a friend": Interview with Icahn.

295 "If the price is right": Interview with Icahn.

295 "Maybe I'm just another Jew": Interview with acquaintance of Icahn.

297 "I'm happy the shareholders benefitted": John S. DeMott, "The High Price of Freedom," *Time*, March 18, 1985.

298 "Mr. Icahn's presence is uninvited": R. Slater, *Titans of Takeover*, p. 86.

299 "All you want is a fast buck": M. Johnston, *Takeover*. p. 280.

299 "If we're psychoanalyzing each other": Ibid.

299 "Every time I turn over a card": Interview with Icahn.

300 "Hey, we got ourselves an airline": Interview with Icahn.

## Chapter 30: The Big Casino

302–303 Alice Mason's dinner party: Interviews with Alice Mason, Aileen Mehle, and Carl Icahn.

304 Ron Perelman's publicized divorce: C. Bruck, *The Predators' Ball*, pp. 198–201; also David Blum, "The Shy Stripper," *New York*, November 18, 1985.

305–306 Rohatyn's Bendix strategy: P. F. Hartz, *Merger*, p. 109.

307–308 Easter egg hunt: David McClintick, "Life at the Top, The Power and Pleasures of Financier Felix Rohatyn," *New York Times Magazine*, August 5, 1984. Also interview with Elizabeth Rohatyn.

309 Trying to persuade Morgan Stanley and Chemical: C. Bruck, *The Predators' Ball*, pp. 210–211.

309 *New York Times* predicts Revlon victory: Robert J. Cole, "A Victory by Revlon Seen Near," *New York Times*, August 28, 1985.

309 Bergerac considering firing Lazard: Interviews with Michel Bergerac and Rohatyn.

310 "Michel panicked" and "I think what Michel says": Interview with Martin Lipton.

311 Perelman hired social secretary: C. Bruck, *The Predators' Ball*, p. 236.

## Chapter 31: Ivan Who?

314–322 Boesky's academic and employment record (through 1981): Securities and Exchange Commission, Schedule D of Form BD, *TheoJon Corporation*, March 13, 1981 (date received by SEC).

316 "That wasn't why": Interview with Robert Gutenstein.

317 Actions taken against Ivan Boesky by the New York Stock Exchange: New York Stock Exchange Actions, Ivan F. Boesky, July 25, 1974.

317 The organization of Boesky's first arbitrage business: Certificate of Limited Partnership, *Ivan F. Boesky and Co.*, New York County, October 31, 1974 (and various amendments).

318 Boesky's financial record: Hudson Funding Corporation (A Wholly Owned Subsidiary of Ivan F. Boesky & Company, L.P.), Confidential Private Placement Memorandum, February 18, 1986.

321 Boesky's big splash in *Fortune:* Eleanor Johnson Tracy, "A Killing in Babcock & Wilcox," *Fortune,* October 1977.

321 He was leaving the firm: Interviews with Boesky and staff member who attended meeting.

325 "I think you'll be disappointed": "People," *Institutional Investor,* June 1985.

326 Boesky's denial of talking to Icahn "about any stock": Quoted in Steven Brill, "The Roaring Eighties," *American Lawyer,* May 1985.

326 Comparison of *Merger Mania* and *Risk Arbitrage II:* Interviews with Jeffrey Madrick, Stephen Wasserman (Boesky's editor) and Arnold Sametz. Also I. Boesky, *Merger Mania,* 1985 and G. P. Wyser-Pratte, *Risk Arbitrage II,* 1982.

## Chapter 32: The Last Great Predators' Ball

329 Percentage of companies that are investment grade: Drexel Burnham Lambert, "The Case for High Yield Securities," April 1986.

## Chapter 33: The High Cost of Excess

341 "I deeply regret": Peter T. Kilborn, "Big Trader to Pay U.S. $100 Million for Insider Abuses," *New York Times,* November 15, 1986.

341 Ivan Boesky at the White House: Walter Ruby, "Ivan Who? UJA Leader Leaves Dais for Court Date," *Long Island Jewish World,* November 28, December 4, 1986.

342 "An alarmist" view: Michael Schwartz, "Irangate and Boesky Affair Worrisome to Jews," *Palm Beach Jewish World,* January 30, 1987; also, interview with David Gordis.

343–344 SEC charges against Siegel: William Glaberson, "Wall St. Informer Admits His Guilt in Insider Trading," *New York Times,* February 14, 1987.

344 "Don't you love me anymore?" James B. Stewart and Daniel Hertzberg, "The Wall Street Career of Martin Siegel Was a Dream Gone Wrong," *Wall Street Journal,* February 17, 1987.

345 American Jewish Committee discussion: Ben Levitman, "AJ Committee Probes Mystery of Vanishing Ethical Values," *Long Island Jewish World,* April 24–30, 1987; also, interview with Gordis.

347 Milken public relations effort and charitable contributions: Interview with Ken Lerer (Milken's public relations representative).

347 Milken at the Mets game: Interview with Jimmy Sunshine (Variety Club administrator).

348 Milken T-shirts: David A. Vise and Steven Coll, "Coworkers Rise to Milken's Support," *Washington Post*, January 12, 1989.

## Chapter 34: The Once and Future King?

350 Columbus Circle project: Joyce Purnick, "Site of Coliseum to be Purchased for $455 Million," *New York Times*, July 12, 1985.

350 Paying more than the going market rate for new offices: John Taylor, "Hard to Be Rich," *New York*, January 11, 1988; also interview with former Salomon executive.

350 Engraved crystal vases story: J. Taylor, "Hard to Be Rich,". Also Beth McGoldrick, "Salomon's Power Culture," *Institutional Investor*, March 1986.

351 Susan Gutfreund keeping a low social profile: Interview with former friend.

352 "Baby of the year": B. McGoldrick, "Salomon's Power Culture," *Institutional Investor*, March 1986.

352 Estimate of the cost of decorating at $20 million: J. Taylor, "Hard to Be Rich."

353 Location and cost of London offices: Ibid.; also interviews with former Salomon partner.

355 Ranieri's pranks: Ida Picker, "Can Lew Ranieri Make It on His Own?" *Institutional Investor*, June 1988.

355 "There are separatist movements": James Sterngold, "A Sweeping Shift at Salomon," *New York Times*, July 24, 1987.

355 Details of Gutfreund's Paris home: C. Vogel, "Susan Gutfreund: High Finances, High Living," *New York Times Magazine*, January 10, 1988.

355 "He's one of the most talented coiffeurs": Elizabeth Allen, "Beauty Scoop," *W*, May 2, 1988.

356 Gaudefroy's clients: Ibid.

356 Cost of Lacroix clothing: Interview with Lacroix saleswoman at Bergdorf Goodman.

356 "I didn't set out to be No. 1": C. Leinster, "The Man Who Seized the Throne at Phibro-Salomon," *Fortune*, December 24, 1984.

357 Gutfreund at Wagner affair: Interview with Caroline McMullen.

358 "Believing Mr. Perelman": J. Taylor, "Hard to Be Rich."

358 "I never stated it": James Sterngold, "Too Far, Too Fast," *New York Times Magazine*, January 10, 1988.

359 "The world changed": Ibid.

359 Tree defense of the Gutfreunds: Marietta Tree, Letter to the editor, *New York*, February 1, 1988.

359 "Now she is living in Paris": Interview with Christopher Mason.

360 The Gutfreunds attend benefit: "The Follies Parisiennes," *W*, July 11, 1988.

360 The Gutfreunds attend the Safra ball: Dennis Thim, "Eye" column, *W*, September 5, 1988.

361 Details of Safra ball: Ibid., and interview with guest.

361 Gutfreunds attend Henry Moore exhibition: Interview with guest.

361 "All the experts tell you": Richard Buckley and Jennifer Ash, "Stormy Weather," *W*, October 3, 1988.

## Chapter 35: Primerica Time

364–365 Carnegie Hall celebration: Donal Henahan, "Carnegie, at 95, Reopens with Several Surprises," *New York Times*, December 16, 1986.

368 "If you want to do this": Gary Hector, *Breaking the Bank: The Decline of BankAmerica*, Boston: Little, Brown, 1988. p. 284.

375 "An old-fashioned merger": Felix Rohatyn quoted in Robert J. Cole, "2 Leading Financiers Will Merge Companies in $1.65 Billion Deal," *New York Times*, August 30, 1988.

376 "He doesn't overpay" and "keeps an eye": Anthony Pearce-Batten (securities analyst) quoted in Linda Stowell, "Working Weill Builds a Financial Giant," *Daily News*, November 27, 1988.

## Chapter 36: Minister of Finance

379 "The most eminent investment banker": David McClintick, "Life at the Top," *New York Times Magazine*, August 5, 1984.

380 "In 1941 Henry Luce stated": F. G. Rohatyn, *The Twenty-Year Century*, p. 3.

381 "America cannot survive": Ibid., p. 137.

382 Liz Smith column, *Daily News*, December 1, 1985.

382 *W*'s description of Lenox Hill fund-raiser: "Eye" column, *W*, February 10, 1986.

382 Rohatyn "has never been completely comfortable": Interview with Victor Gotbaum.

382 "It's getting more and more difficult": Interview with Rohatyn.

388 "There is so much concentration on the gala": Kathleen Teltsch, "Rohatyns Question Charities' Focus on Glitter to Get Funds," *New York Times*, January 5, 1986.

388–389 *W*'s criticism of the Rohatyns: "Felix the Cat and Snow White vs. the Social Sisters," *W*, May 19, 1986.

389 "Enough has been said": Bowen Northrup, "How Felix Rohatyn Spoke His Mind, Started Media Event," *Wall Street Journal*, June 24, 1986.

# Selected Bibliography

## Books

Adler, Cyrus. *Jacob H. Schiff: His Life and Letters,* Vols. I and II. New York: Doubleday, Doran, 1928.

Allison, Eric W. *The Raiders of Wall Street.* New York: Stein and Day, 1986.

Auletta, Ken. *The Streets Were Paved with Gold.* New York: Random House, 1979.

————. *Greed and Glory on Wall Street: The Fall of the House of Lehman.* New York: Random House, 1986.

Birmingham, Stephen. *"Our Crowd."* New York, Evanston, and London: Harper & Row, 1967.

Boesky, Ivan F. *Merger Mania.* New York: Holt, Rinehart, and Winston, 1985.

Brooks, John. *The Go-Go Years.* New York: Weybright and Talley, 1973.

Brown, Stanley H. *Ling: The Rise, Fall, and Return of a Texas Titan.* New York: Atheneum, 1972.

Bruck, Connie. *The Predators' Ball: The Junk Bond Raiders and the Man Who Staked Them.* New York: Simon & Schuster, 1988.

Copetas, A. Craig. *Metal Men.* New York: G. P. Putnam's Sons, 1985.

Carrington, Tim. *The Year They Sold Wall Street: The Inside Story of the Shearson/American Express Merger, and How It Changed Wall Street Forever.* Boston: Houghton Mifflin, 1985.

Carosso, Vincent P., *Investment Banking in America.* Cambridge: Harvard University Press, 1970.

Davidson, Kenneth M. *Megamergers: Corporate America's Billion-Dollar Takeovers.* Cambridge: Ballinger, 1985.

Ferretti, Fred. *The Year the Big Apple Went Bust.* New York: G. P. Putnam's Sons, 1976.

Halberstam, David. *The Reckoning.* New York: William Morrow, 1986.

Jensen, Michael C. *The Financiers.* New York: Weybright and Talley, 1976.

Johnston, Moira. *Takeover: The New Wall Street Warriors: The Men, The Money, The Impact.* New York: Arbor House, 1986.

Hartz, Peter F. *Merger*. New York: William Morrow, 1985.

Hoffman, Paul. *Lions of the Eighties*. New York: Doubleday, 1982.

Karp, Abraham J. *Haven and Home: A History of the Jews*. New York: Shocken, 1985.

Kalcich, Joyce (ed.). *Fact Book 1985*. New York: New York Stock Exchange, 1985.

Kleindienst, Richard G. *Justice: The Memoirs of Attorney General Richard Kleindienst*. Ottawa, Illinois: Jameson, 1985.

Krefetz, Gerald. *Jews and Money: The Myths and the Reality*. New Haven and New York: Ticknor & Fields, 1982.

Lacy, Robert. *Ford: The Men and the Machine*. Boston: Little, Brown, 1986.

Lampert, Hope. *Till Death Do Us Part*. New York: Harcourt Brace Jovanovich, 1983.

Lapham, Lewis H. *Money and Class in America: Notes and Observations On Our Civil Religion*. New York: Weidenfeld & Nicolson, 1988.

Little, Royal. *How to Lose $100,000 and Other Valuable Advice*. Boston: Little, Brown, 1979.

Madrick, Jeff. *Taking America*. New York: Bantam, 1987.

Reich, Cary. *Financier*. New York: William Morrow, 1983.

Rohatyn, Felix G. *The Twenty-Year Century: Essays On Economics and Public Finance*. New York: Random House, New York, 1983.

Saffron, Morris (ed.). *One Hundred and Twenty-Five Years 1852–1977 The Harmonie Club*. New York: privately published, 1977.

Sampson, Anthony. *The Sovereign State of ITT*. New York: Stein & Day, 1973.

Schoenberg, Robert J. *Geneen*. New York: W. W. Norton, 1985.

Silberman, Charles. *A Certain People: American Jews and Their Lives Today*. New York: Summit, 1985.

Slater, Robert. *The Titans of Takeover*. Englewood Cliffs, New Jersey: Prentice-Hall, 1987.

Slavin, Stephen L., and Mary A. Pradt. *The Einstein Syndrome: Corporate Anti-Semitism in America Today*. Washington, D.C.: University Press of America, 1982.

Sobel, Robert. *N.Y.S.E.: A History of the New York Stock Exchange, 1935–1975*. New York: Weybright and Talley, 1973.

——. *Salomon Brothers, 1910–1985: Advancing to Leadership*, New York: Salomon Brothers, 1986.

Taylor, John. *Storming the Magic Kingdom: Wall Street, the Raiders, and the Battle for Disney*. New York: Alfred A. Knopf, 1987.

W. T. Grimm & Co., *Twenty-Two-Year Statistical Review*. Chicago: W. T. Grimm, 1985.

Wechsberg, Joseph. *The Merchant Bankers*. Boston: Little, Brown, 1966.

Welles, Chris. *The Last Days of the Club*. New York: E. P. Dutton, 1975.

Wilson, John W. *The New Venturers*. Reading, Massachusetts: Addison-Wesley, 1985.

Zweigenhaft, Richard L., and G. William Domhoff. *Jews in the Protestant Establishment*. New York: Praeger, 1981.

## Magazines, Newspapers and Other Material

Adler, Stephen. "First Boston's M & A Prodigy." *The American Lawyer*, January 1983.

Ascher, Carol. "Greed and Ambition on Wall Street." *Present Tense*, January/February 1987.

Andrews, Peter. "The Art of the Business Breakfast." *Institutional Investor*, August 1979.

Arenson, Karen W. "First Boston's Merger Makers." *New York Times*, April 21, 1981.

Bartlett, Sarah. "Sandy Weill Is Doing Just Fine on Main Street, Thank You." *Business Week*, September 21, 1987.

Bear, Stearns & Co. "The History of Bear, Stearns: A Partnership of Individuals." New York: Bear, Stearns, 1984. Draft..

Bender, Marylin. "If Financial Coups are Percolating, It's Breakfast Time at the Regency." *New York Times*, July 7, 1976.

Bennett, Robert A. "Salomon Bros. Investment House to be Sold to Commodity Trader." *New York Times*, August 4, 1981.

Berg, Eric N. "Accused Executive Study in Contrast." *New York Times*, May 14, 1986.

Bernstein, Jeremy. "Allocating Sacrifice." *New Yorker*, January 24, 1983.

Bernstein, Peter W. "Profit Pressures on the Big Law Firms." *Fortune*, April 19, 1982.

———. "Fear and Loathing in the Board Room." *Fortune*, December 15, 1980.

Bianco, Anthony. "The Growing Respectability of the Junk Heap." *Business Week*, April 22, 1985.

———. "The King of Wall Street." *Business Week*. December 9, 1985.

———. "Power on Wall Street." *Business Week*, July 7, 1986.

Blair, William G. "Charles Bluhdorn, 56, Is Dead; Led Gulf and Western Industries." *New York Times*, February 26, 1983.

Bleakley, Fred R. "Big Phillips Arbitration Loss Seen." *New York Times,* December 27, 1984.

———. "Diverse Icahn Investor Group." *New York Times,* February 21, 1985.

Blumstein, Michael. "After the Coup at Phibro-Salomon." *New York Times,* August 12, 1984.

Boesky & Company, Ivan F. *Hudson Funding Corporation (A Wholly Owned Subsidiary of Ivan F. Boesky & Company, L.P.), Confidential Private Placement Memorandum.* February 18, 1986.

Boesky & Company, Ivan F. Certificate of Limited Partnership (and various amendments). New York County. October 31, 1974.

Boner, J. Russell. "Pergamon Holders' Meeting Slated Today Seen as Showdown in Battle for Control." *Wall Street Journal,* October 10, 1969.

Brean, Herbert. "It's Easier to Make a Million than a Hundred Thousand." *Life,* November 22, 1954.

Brenner, Marie. "The Class Menagerie." *New York,* September 19, 1983.

Brill, Steven. "Conoco: Great Plays and Errors in the Bar's World Series." *American Lawyer,* November 1981.

———. "The Roaring Eighties." *American Lawyer,* May 1985.

Brown, Tina. "Gayfryd Takes Over." *Vanity Fair.* November 1986.

Bruck, Connie. "My Master Is My Purse." *The Atlantic,* December 1984.

———. "Kamikaze." *American Lawyer,* December 1985.

*Business Week.* "Fast and Canny Traders." June 27, 1964.

———. "The Toughest Kid in Block Trading." October 4, 1969.

———. "The Remarkable Felix Rohatyn." March 10, 1973.

———. "A Maverick Pushes into Wall Street's Club." April 3, 1978.

———. "Inside Philipp Bros., A $9 Billion Trader." September 3, 1979.

———. "A Trading Superstar Is Born." August 17, 1981.

Carley, William M. "Carl Icahn's Strategies in His Quest for TWA Are a Model for Raiders." *Wall Street Journal,* June 20, 1985.

Carrington, Tim. "Phibro Will Buy Salomon Brothers for $550 Million in Cash and Debt." *Wall Street Journal,* August 4, 1981.

———. "Shearson Names Peter A. Cohen Chief, President." *Wall Street Journal,* January 7, 1983.

CBWL-Hayden Stone. Prospectus. October 1, 1971.

Cole, Robert J. "Penn Central Accuses Reliance Chief of 'Unlawful Scheme' to Gain Control." *New York Times,* November 8, 1979.

———. "The Secret Life of an 'Arb.'" *New York Times,* June 24, 1984.

———. "High Stakes Drama at Revlon." *New York Times*, November 11, 1984.

———. "Icahn Ends Offer for Phillips: All Shareholders Get More." *New York Times*, March 5, 1985.

Coll, Steve. "The Puzzling Wall Street Saga of Dennis Levine." *Washington Post*, May 22, 1986.

Cowan, Paul. "The Merger Maestro." *Esquire*, May 1984.

*Current Biography*. "James Ling." April 1970.

———. "Charles Thornton." February 1970.

DeMott, John S. "The High Price of Freedom." *Time*, March 18, 1985.

Dodosh, Mark N. "Tappan in Middle of Proxy Fight, Ends Bid for Holder Approval of New Preferred." *Wall Street Journal*, April 5, 1979.

Donnelly, Barbara. "The Battle for the Junk-Bond Dollar." *Institutional Investor*, June 1985.

Dorfman, Dan. "Heard on the Street." *Wall Street Journal*, February 16, 1972.

Drexel Burnham Lambert. The Case for High-Yield Securities. Corporate report, April 1986.

———. Annual Review: Fiftieth Anniversary, 1984.

Dreyfus, Joel. "The Firm That Fed on Wall Street's Scraps." *Fortune*, September 3, 1984.

Dryansky, G. Y. "Henri Samuel Lends a Regal Touch to the Very Rich." *On the Avenue*, April 1985.

Dunkin, Amy, and Cynthia Green. "Bergerac Lost Revlon — But No Tears Please." *Business Week*, November 4, 1985.

Ehrbar, A. F. "Upheaval in Investment Banking." *Fortune*, August 23, 1985.

Epstein, Edward Jay. "Raider's Nadir?" *Manhattan, inc.*, September 1985.

———. "Inside the Secret World of Mike Milken." *Manhattan, inc.*, September 1987.

Fabrikant, Geraldine. "The G.E.–RCA Merger: Crafting a Megadeal." *New York Times*, December 13, 1985.

Federal Election Commission. Individual Contributions, May 12, 1985.

Federal Trade Commission. Bureau of Economics. Statistical Report on Mergers and Acquisitions, 1979. Washington, D.C.: U.S. Government Printing Office, 1981.

Feinberg, Phyllis. "What Makes Sandy Run?" *Institutional Investor*, May 1980.

———. "Dreaming Up Creative Merger Ideas," *Institutional Investor*, June 1980.

First Boston. Annual Review. 1975, 1976.

*Forbes.* "Forbes Four Hundred." October 27, 1986.

Foreman, Craig. "Old World Traditions Include Insider Trading." *Wall Street Journal.* February 8, 1989.

*Fortune.* Editorial. "The Fallout from the ITT Affair." May 1972.

Garcia, Beatrice E. "Commercial Credit to Buy Primerica Corp." *Wall Street Journal,* August 30, 1988.

Gill, Mark. "Milken Takes the Stands." *7 Days,* September 28, 1988.

Glynn, Lenny. "Inside the Safra-American Express Divorce." *Institutional Investor,* April 1985.

Glenn, Lenny, and Elizabeth Peer. "Felix: The Making of a Celebrity." *Institutional Investor,* December 1984.

Goldman Sachs. Annual Review. 1983, 1984.

Grant, Linda. "Drexel Burnham Finds Self in Heady Company." *Los Angeles Times,* March 11, 1984.

Gurwin, Larry. "The Scorched Earth Policy." *Institutional Investor,* June 1979.

Hawkins, Chuck. "Raider or Manager?" *Business Week,* October 27, 1986.

Heinemann, H. Erich. "Leasco Affirms Interest in Chemical Bank." *New York Times,* February 12, 1969.

*Institutional Investor.* "Corporate Sweepstakes." March 1979, and annual issues through March 1988.

Kahn, E. J., Jr. "Director's Director." Parts 1 and 2, *The New Yorker,* September 9, and September 16, 1956.

Kaiser, Charles. "U.S. Is Studying Bus-Shelter Deal for Any Conflict." *New York Times,* March 16, 1979.

King, Michael L. "Carl C. Icahn, Dissident Tappan Holder, Wins Proxy Battle, Emerging as Director." *Wall Street Journal,* May 1, 1979.

Kinkead, Gwen. "Behind the Salomon Brothers Buyout." *Fortune,* September 7, 1981.

———. "Ivan Boesky, Money Machine." *Fortune,* August 6, 1984.

Koshetz, Herbert. "Amex Censures Hayden Conduct." *New York Times,* November 13, 1973.

Labaton, Stephen. "Drexel Concedes Guilt on Trading; to Pay $650 Million." *New York Times,* December 22, 1988.

———. U.S. Files Charges Against Drexel; A Guilty Plea By Firm Is Expected." *New York Times,* January 25, 1989.

Laing, Jonathan. "New Face, Old Look?" *Barron's,* September 28, 1988.

Lampert, Hope. "Saul Steps Out." *Manhattan, inc.,* October 1985.

———. "John Gutfreund's Last Stand?" *Manhattan, inc.,* February 1989.

Lee, John M. "Share Vote Gives a Victory to 30-Year-Old New Yorker." *New York Times*, October 11, 1969.

Leinster, Colin. "The Man Who Seized the Throne at Phibro-Salomon." *Fortune*, December 24, 1984.

———. "Carl Icahn's Calculated Bets." *Fortune*, March 18, 1985.

Loomis, Carol J. "Living It Up in a Salomon-Sized World." *Fortune*, April 1970.

———. "Harold Geneen's Moneymaking Machine Is Still Humming." *Fortune*, September 1972.

———. "The Further Misadventures of Harold Geneen." *Fortune*, June 1975.

———. "The Shakeout on Wall Street Isn't Over Yet." *Fortune*, May 22, 1978.

———. "The Morning After at Phibro-Salomon." *Fortune*, January 10, 1983.

Lubasch, Arnold H. "Bronston Gets 4 Months in Bus-Stop Fraud Case." *New York Times*, January 3, 1981.

McClintick, David. "Life At the Top, The Power and Pleasures of Financier Felix Rohatyn." *New York Times Magazine*, August 5, 1984.

McGoldrick, Beth. "Salomon's Power Culture." *Institutional Investor*, March 1986.

McMurray, Scott. "Salomon's Innovative, Risky Style Creates Profits and Some Problems." *Wall Street Journal*, September 17, 1984.

Magnet, Myron. "The Money Society." *Fortune*, July 6, 1987.

Medina, Harold R. United States Circuit Court. *Corrected Opinion of Harold R. Medina in United States of America v. Henry S. Morgan, Harold Stanley, doing business as Morgan Stanley & Co., et al.* February 4, 1954.

Metz, Tim. "The Conoco Chase." *Wall Street Journal*, August 6, 1981.

———. "Artful Advisor: How First Boston Corp. Turned Itself Around Amid a Merger Mania." *Wall Street Journal*, April 21, 1982.

Metz, Tim, and Maria Shad, "Seagram Ends $2.3 Billion Bid for St. Joe." *Wall Street Journal*, April 8, 1981.

Meyer, Priscilla S. "Posner's Firm Wins Its Fight to Purchase All of UV's Assets." *Wall Street Journal*, November 29, 1979.

Michaelis, David. "The Nutcracker Suite." *Manhattan, inc.*, December 1984.

Moonan, Wendy Lyon. "Barony on Park Avenue." *Town & Country*, November 1985.

Morgan Stanley & Co. *Morgan Stanley & Co., Inc.: A Brief History* (unpublished). New York: Morgan Stanley, 1977.

New York Stock Exchange Actions. Ivan F. Boesky, July 25, 1974.

*New York Times*. "Arbitrageurs Battling Tappan Management." April 5, 1979.

Noble, Kenneth B. "How the Sale of Salomon Enriched Former Partners." *New York Times,* September 23, 1982.

Nussbaum, Bruce. "Amex Rex." *Manhattan, inc.,* June 1985.

Rehfeld, Barry. "Deal Maker." *Esquire,* November 1983.

Reich, Cary. "Salomon: The Spectacular Debut of an International Upstart." *Institutional Investor,* January 1978.

———. "The Man CEO's Love to Hate." *Institutional Investor,* October 1982.

———. "Fundraising: The Sultans of Solicitation." *Institutional Investor,* July 1985.

———. "Milken the Magnificent." *Institutional Investor,* August 1986.

Ricks, Thomas E. "SEC's Failed Probes of Milken in Past Show Difficulty of Its Mission." *Wall Street Journal,* January 25, 1989.

Robards, Terry. "Wall Street Survives New Crisis, Unknown to Public." *New York Times,* March 26, 1971.

Rohatyn, Felix G. "On a Buyout Binge and Takeover Tear." *Wall Street Journal,* May 18, 1984.

———. "Ethics in America's Money Culture." *New York Times,* June 3, 1987.

Rosenbaum, Ron. "Meet Felix and Liz Rohatyn, Society Dissidents." *Manhattan, inc.,* April 1986.

———. "The Great Gatsby of Wall Street." *Manhattan, inc.,* August 1986.

Rosenberg, Hilary. "Saul Steinberg's Insurance Blues." *Institutional Investor,* April 1987.

Rosenstiel, Thomas B. "Drexel's Bond Traders Like Their Daily Grind." *Los Angeles Times,* March 11, 1984.

Rottenberg, Dan. "The Most Generous Living Americans." *Town & Country,* December 1986.

Rout, Lawrence. "High Roller: A Risk Arbitrageur Plays Dangerous Game of Betting on Mergers." *Wall Street Journal,* February 22, 1979.

Ruby, Walter. "Ivan Who? UJA Leader Leaves Dais for Court Date." *Long Island Jewish World,* November 28, December 4, 1986.

Rudnitsky, Howard, Allan Sloan, and Richard L. Stern with Matthew Heller. "A One-Man Revolution." *Forbes,* August 25, 1986.

Rustin, Richard E. "Hayden Stone, Shearson Discuss Possible Merger." *Wall Street Journal,* May 29, 1974.

———. "Brash Broker: Sanford Weill Runs Shearson with Rigor but an Informal Style." *Wall Street Journal,* August 14, 1979.

———. "Topper Corp. Being Investigated by SEC on Whether It Disclosed Its Ills Properly." *Wall Street Journal,* July 13, 1972.

Salter, Malcolm S., and Wolf A. Weinhold. *Merger Trends and Prospects for the 1980's*. Washington, D.C.: U.S. Department of Commerce, 1981.

Sandler, Linda. "Drexel Burnham Lambert Finds a Niche." *Institutional Investor*, October 1981.

Securities and Exchange Commission. *SEC v. Topper Corporation, et al.* Docket. Litigation Release No. 6145: November 12, 1973.

———. *The Seaboard Corporation, et al. (C.D.C.A.)*. Docket. Litigation Release No. 6269: March 5, 1974.

———. Form 10-K. Hayden Stone, June 30, 1974.

———. Shearson Hayden Stone, June 30, 1975.

———. Shearson Hayden Stone, June 30, 1979.

———. Shearson Loeb Rhoades, June 30, 1980.

Selby, Beth. "The Twilight of the Syndicate." *Institutional Investor*, August 1985.

Shnayerson, Michael. "The King of Carnegie Hall." *Vanity Fair*. December 1986.

Shearson Loeb Rhoades and American Express Company. Joint Proxy Statement. June 1, 1981.

Sheehan, Robert. "Let's Ask Sidney Weinberg." *Fortune*, October 1953.

Sloan, Allan. "A Chat with Michael Milken." *Forbes*, July 13, 1987.

Sloan, Allan, and Howard Rudnitsky. "Taking in Each Other's Laundry." *Forbes*, November 14, 1984.

Sloane, Leonard. "Gustave Levy, Investment Banker Who Led Goldman, Sachs, Is Dead." *New York Times*, November 4, 1976.

Sterngold, James. "The Pawns Differ: Icahn Still Winning." *New York Times*, February 6, 1985.

———. "The Tense, Secret Talks Behind Goldman Move." *New York Times*, August 8, 1986.

———. "Too Far, Two Fast." *New York Times Magazine*, January 10, 1988.

Stewart, James B., and Daniel Hertzberg. "The Wall Street Career of Martin Siegel Was a Dream Gone Wrong." *Wall Street Journal*, February 17, 1987.

———. "SEC Accuses Drexel of a Sweeping Array of Securities Violations." *Wall Street Journal*, September 8, 1988.

Stowell, Linda. "Working Weill Builds Finance Giant." *Daily News*, November 27, 1988.

Swartz, Steve, and Bryan Burrough. "Drexel Faces Difficulty Whether It Settles Case or Gambles on a Trial." *Wall Street Journal*, September 9, 1988.

Swartz, Steve, and Matthew Winkler. "Salomon Claims Its Turnaround Strategy Is Paying Off." *Wall Street Journal,* February 8, 1989.

Taylor, John. "Hard to Be Rich: The Rise and Wobble of the Gutfreunds." *New York,* January 11, 1988.

Teltsch, Kathleen. "Rohatyns Question Charities' Focus on Glitter to Get Funds." *New York Times,* January 5, 1986.

*Time.* "Those Hired Guns." January 29, 1979.

————. "The Conglomerate War to Reshape Industry." March 7, 1969.

Tracy, Eleanor Johnson. "A Killing in Babcock & Wilcox." *Fortune,* October 1977.

U.S. Senate. Committee on the Judiciary. Hearings on the Nomination of Richard Kleindienst, of Arizona, to be Attorney General. Washington, D.C., 1972.

Vartan, Vartanig G. "Hidden Treasures in Junk Bonds." *New York Times,* September 26, 1976.

————. "Shearson and Loeb to Merge." *New York Times,* May 15, 1979.

Vermeulen, Michael. "Yes, It's True What They Say About Bruce Wasserstein." *Institutional Investor,* April 1984.

————. "How Peter Cohen Became the Top Banana." *Institutional Investor,* August 1984.

*W.* "Felix the Cat and Snow White vs. The Social Sisters." May 19, 1986.

*Wall Street Journal.* "Highland Capital Says Icahn & Co. Is Bidding for Many of Its Shares." December 4, 1975.

————. "Highland Capital Corp. Takeover Is Averted; Chairman Buys Stock." August 3, 1976.

————. "Tappan Asserts Holder Seeking a Board Seat Ran Afoul of Big Board." April 10, 1979.

————. "Shearson Settles 3 Suits Over Topper Collapse for $1.7 Million Total." February 25, 1976.

Weberman, Ben. "The King of the BB's." *Forbes,* December 5, 1983.

Welles, Chris. "The Colossus of Phibro." *Institutional Investor,* December 1981.

————. "American Express Thrives on Diversity." *Los Angeles Times,* June 30, 1985.

White, Shelby. "Ace Greenberg's Tricks." *Institutional Investor,* March 1981.

Wise, T. A. "The Bustling House of Lehman." *Fortune,* December 1957.

————. "Wherever You Look, There's Loeb, Rhoades." *Fortune,* April 1963.

Wyser-Pratte, Guy P. *Risk Arbitrage II.* Monograph. New York: New York University Graduate School of Business, 1982.

Zagorin, Adam. "Lone Wolf of Wall Street." *Manhattan, inc.,* October 1984.

# Index